A HISTORY OF CANADA

**FROM THE TREATY OF UTRECHT
TO THE TREATY OF PARIS
1713-1763**

A
HISTORY OF CANADA

Volume Three: From the Treaty of Utrecht to the
Treaty of Paris, 1713-1763

BY GUSTAVE LANCTÔT
of the Royal Society
TRANSLATED BY MARGARET M. CAMERON

HARVARD UNIVERSITY PRESS
CAMBRIDGE, MASSACHUSETTS
1965

Printed in Canada

A
MARIE
MA CHERE FEMME

ACKNOWLEDGEMENTS

Once more the author has pleasure in expressing his thanks to the Canada Council, whose financial assistance has enabled him to complete the research for this work.

It is also a pleasant duty to acknowledge his debt to many individual helpers. Mr. Robert de Roquebrune read the manuscript. The Assistant Deputy Minister, Pierre Brunet, facilitated the work of research in the National Archives by lending the services of Mr. Paul Dumas, Miss Corinne Richard and Miss Juliette Bourque. In the Parliamentary Library, under the direction of Mr. Guy Silvestre, Mr. Lucien Lusignan and Mrs. Foster helped in the consultation of printed material. Miss Marguerite Mercier and Miss Jacqueline Trépanier, at the Bibliothèque Saint-Sulpice, and the staff of the University of Montreal were most generous in providing information of every kind. To all these persons the author wishes to express his thanks.

Finally, he must acknowledge a special debt to the Humanities Research Council, which, by means of a grant from Canada Council funds, helped to defray the cost of publication.

CONTENTS

		PAGE
Foreword		vii
1.	Financial Situation and Indian Policy	3
2.	Fluctuations in the Fur Trade	11
3.	Dupuy's Innovations. Quarrels Among the Clergy	21
4.	The Beauharnois-Hocquart Régime and the Search for the Western Sea	30
5.	Acadia Under English Rule	41
6.	Ile Royale, Hudson Bay and Newfoundland	49
7.	Capture of Louisbourg	61
8.	War of the Austrian Succession	70
9.	Anglo-French Rivalry in the Ohio Valley	79
10.	Founding of Halifax and Expulsion of the Acadians	90
11.	Colonization: Renewed Efforts	101
12.	Economic Expansion	110
13.	Administration and Social Institutions	122
14.	Bigot's Régime. Hostilities Before the Declaration of War	131
15.	First Hostilities in the Seven Years' War	142
16.	The Surrender of Louisbourg and the Victory of Carillon	153
17.	The English Offensive and the Battle of the Plains of Abraham	163
18.	Victory of Ste. Foy and the Capitulation of Montreal	174
19.	1763	188
20.	Review and Retrospect	195
21.	Canada at the Time of the Cession	201
Documents		215
Bibliography		255
Notes		265
Index		299

ILLUSTRATIONS

Between pages

Marquis de Montcalm   146-7
General Jeffery Amherst
Mme. Elisabeth Bégon
Mme. Angélique Péan
Habitants Dancing a Minuet
Habitants Playing Cards

English and French Warships in Louisbourg Harbour   162-3
Quebec City at the Time of Cession
The Bishop's Palace, Quebec City
Battle of the Plains of Abraham

MAPS

Page

Explorers' Routes   55
Ohio Region   82
Eastern Seaboard and Inland   124-5

FOREWORD

The first volume of this work described the early part of the brief history of New France, from its origins to the inception of royal administration in 1663. The second volume covered the period of colonization, from the beginning of the royal régime to 1713 and the Treaty of Utrecht. The third volume, completing the story of French rule in Canada, presents a study of the expansion which continued without interruption from the Treaty of Utrecht to the English conquest, completed in 1760 and confirmed three years later by the Treaty of Paris.

Thus the third volume opens with the Treaty of Utrecht by which France lost to England the Acadian bastion, the colony of Placentia and the Hudson Bay territory. In spite of these peripheral losses, however, Canada still possessed an immense domain extending from Labrador to the Great Lakes, the Mississippi and Louisiana.

Moreover, in compensation for territorial losses, Utrecht gave the country thirty years of peace, the longest peaceful period in its history. Freed from the servitudes and difficulties of war, the people could now devote their energies to exploiting the natural wealth of field, river and forest.

The economic activity which began with the establishment of peace was soon fostered by a concourse of circumstances. To make up for the loss of Acadia, the French colonized Ile Royale and fortified its capital, Louisbourg. Overnight the new colony created a market for Canada's grain, vegetables and cattle, as well as for boats, sailing ships and lumber. Moreover, within a few years Louisbourg became the focal point of a growing triangular trade between Canada, the West Indies and France, and the base of an active and open contraband trade with the prosperous English colonies.

Now that she had achieved her ambition to reduce the power of Louis XV in Europe and acquired Acadia and the Hudson Bay territory, England was in a peaceful mood, and France seized the opportunity to try to restore her finances. In pursuance of this policy her ministers of Marine doled out niggardly subsidies for the administration and development of her Laurentian colony whose economic growth was thus almost entirely dependent on the initiative of the colonists themselves. But almost without help from the mother country, and with limited resources of its own, the colony continued to expand. More land was brought under cultivation, new crops were introduced, naval construction and small industries were built and foundries established, while at the same time the population increased four-fold.

In the course of these years an evolutionary process was growing in scope with each succeeding generation. Under the influence of physical environment, economic conditions and social concepts, a new human species, the French Canadian people, was evolving and taking shape.

It was Canada's misfortune that at the very moment when her territorial structure was being fixed and her national character being formed, she became involved in two wars. The first, the War of the Spanish Succession, had little effect on the territorial integrity of the country. But the second one, the Seven Years' War, enkindled further by the greed of the American colonies, ended, despite Montcalm's victories, in the capitulation of Montreal (1760). With the Treaty of Paris (1763), Louis XV and Choiseul, their own "house being on fire," abandoned the Canadian "stables" to the naval superiority of England. The curtain fell on a glorious past during which dauntless explorers and steadfast colonists—men and women—had prepared the ground, laid the foundation and built a new France on American soil.

A HISTORY OF CANADA

FROM THE TREATY OF UTRECHT
TO THE TREATY OF PARIS
1713-1763

Chapter One

FINANCIAL SITUATION AND INDIAN POLICY

Vaudreuil in France. The problem of finance: the issue and depreciation of card money; its suppression in 1719. The King's profit. Death of Louis XIV. A new system of royal administration. Policy of independence for the Iroquois. Revolt of the Fox tribe; their defeat and submission. Military situation of the colony. Protest riots at Longueuil against defence corvées.

During the summer of 1714, the Governor, the Intendant and the members of the Sovereign Council assembled in the cathedral in Quebec where Mgr. de Saint-Vallier chanted a *Te Deum* to celebrate the peace of Utrecht. In the evening candles were lighted in all the windows, and a salute was fired by the cannon on the ramparts. These signs of "sincere joy" were described with some complacency by Vaudreuil in a letter to the Minister, but joy was mingled with bitter regret for the loss of Newfoundland, Acadia and especially the Hudson Bay territory with its profitable fur trade. In the "sad Treaty of Utrecht" a far-sighted contemporary already detected the threat of a future conquest of Canada. The only persons who could find in it any real cause for rejoicing were the militiamen for whom it marked the end of twenty years of forced military service and campaigning.[1]

In the autumn, Vaudreuil was granted leave by the King to rejoin his wife who had been in France since 1708. Madame de Vaudreuil had become the protégée of Pontchartrain at court. She was not only charming and intelligent but also persistent, and she used the Minister's protection to the advantage of her husband and his family. Thanks to the interest of Madame de Maintenon, she was appointed assistant governess to the chil-

3

dren of Louis XIV's grandson, the Duc de Berry. Vaudreuil
did not return to Canada until October 1716, and during the
interval his powers were delegated to the Governor of Montreal, Claude de Ramezay. Ramezay was an energetic and ambitious man, interested in a number of business enterprises. He
was also difficult to get along with, and he had more than once
opposed the Governor's policies.[2]

At this time Canada's financial situation, which had been
deteriorating for years, became really critical. The problem was
created on the one hand by the excessive quantity of card
money in circulation, and on the other by the condition of the
Royal Treasury depleted by the War of the Spanish Succession.
Each autumn the Intendant prepared and sent to France his
forecast of expenses for the ensuing year. Pontchartrain examined this budget and, under the impression that he was giving
proof of competence, slashed ten, twenty, or sometimes thirty
per cent from the proposed figure.[3] In the course of the following summer the amended budget came back to Quebec with
funds for the current year, either in specie or in the form of
merchandise which, when sold in Quebec, Montreal or Three
Rivers, brought a profit to the King.[4]

But it sometimes happened that in the interval the Canadian treasury was without funds for one reason or another:
delay in the arrival of funds, unexpected expenses, or a slow
turnover of royal merchandise. It was in such circumstances that
in 1685 the Intendant, de Meulles, issued the first card money.
The administration again had recourse to the expedient the
following year, and the cards were redeemed when funds arrived
from France. Louis XIV immediately expressed his disapproval,
not of the principle, but of the method which had been followed. He considered it "extremely dangerous" to use cards
which could easily be counterfeited.[5]

In spite of royal disapproval, de Meulles' successor, Champigny, had recourse to this easy method of procuring new
money in 1690, and again in 1691. Receiving no criticism
from the Minister, Champigny authorized additional issues. As
the cards provided a convenient substitute for cash in a country
that lacked metal currency, many of them were not presented
for redemption and they "were current in business." In 1699,
when Pontchartrain discovered that they were still in use, he

ordered that all cards be withdrawn from circulation and prohibited further use of the system.[6]

On receipt of this order, Champigny immediately redeemed
and burned the cards in circulation, a total of 33,000 *livres*.
However, in spite of his assurances to the Minister, he made a
fresh issue. Then his successor, Beauharnois, abused the system
to the point where so much paper money was in circulation that
cards representing a face value of more than 100,000 *livres* were
repudiated by the clerk of the Marine Treasury. As a result, the
value of the card money fell and the price of goods rose. On the
one hand there was depreciation, on the other, inflation. By
1705 the cards had fallen into such disrepute that the new intendant, Raudot, was forced to issue an order requiring their
acceptance in business.[7]

In 1707 Raudot in his turn was faced with empty coffers. He
obeyed the letter of the law, but forced the clerk of the treasurer
of the Ministry of Marine to issue "notes on the treasury."
"You are just issuing more cards under another name," wrote
Pontchartrain, furious at the Intendant's "lack of attention" in
carrying out orders. But, as the Minister had to admit, "times
were so difficult" that the King could do nothing to help "a
country which gave him no returns and which relied so heavily
on him." For at that time France was herself involved in a very
serious financial crisis. Thus, the treasurer of the Ministry of
Marine could not redeem the bills which had been issued in
Canada, and his clerk in Quebec could advance only a quarter
of the funds required for carrying on the country's business in
1709 and 1710. In 1710 and 1711 Vaudreuil and Raudot had to
"create more cards," and the practice continued until the value
of cards in circulation reached the figure of 1,600,000 *livres*.
The ensuing depreciation "made the price of goods increase
four-fold," and the Minister feared that "the cards might be a
total loss."[8]

At the end of the war Canadian holders of card money were
faced with ruin. When peace was restored, the Marine Council,
while recognizing that the creation of card money had been "an
absolute necessity" for Quebec, immediately sought means to
withdraw the cards from circulation. Bégon's project to buy
them in at half their face value was adopted, and in May 1714
Pontchartrain dispatched orders to the Intendant to put it into

effect. Beginning in 1715 the clerk of the Marine treasurer in Quebec was to call in 320,000 *livres* worth of cards each year. They were to be redeemed in cash at half their value, and the operation was to continue until all cards had been withdrawn from circulation.[9]

Louis XIV had at first been "reluctant" to accept this measure because of "the loss" it imposed on his Canadian subjects; but he was persuaded to adopt it when he was convinced that it would not fall heavily on card-holders since prices had risen and they had made considerable profits on their sales. The colonists in general were only too glad to receive half value for the money which had threatened to become completely worthless.[10] The only persons who were not compensated in any way for their losses were those who lived on salaries or wages: officers, civil servants, employees and those "who did not engage in trade."[11]

As might have been foreseen, the withdrawal of card money proved a difficult operation for an exhausted Royal Treasury. The redemption of cards withdrawn in 1714 and 1715 was suspended, and in 1717 Versailles authorized Bégon "to create new card money for the last time." Finally a royal declaration issued by the Regency Council on July 5, 1718 stipulated that card money was to be abolished in the autumn of that same year.[12] The final date for withdrawal was later set at 1719, at which time any cards which had not been presented for redemption ceased to be legal currency.[13] Thus, in the autumn of 1719, Canada's curious card money ceased to exist. An official account establishes the fact that, besides the first issues which were immediately redeemed, between 1702 and 1717 Quebec created 3,355,115 *livres* worth of card money. On the cards issued between 1709 and 1717 and redeemed at half value the Royal Treasury made a profit of 1,181,315 *livres*. At the same time Versailles abolished the premium of one third of its value which had been attributed to French money circulating in Canada.[14]

Louis XIV had died four years before Canada was finally freed from the burden of her depreciated currency. Before he was overtaken by death on September 15, 1715, the Sun King had already been severely buffeted by adverse fortune. History must record that he was the true creator of New France, since it was during the period of royal rule, from 1663 to 1672, and under the direction of Colbert's genius, that Talon laid the economic foundations of the country and Laval organized its church. Then, unfortunately for Canada, Louis XIV conceived an ambition, skilfully fostered by Louvois, to dominate Europe, and refused to put into execution Talon's grand plan for a French kingdom in America. He reached the peak of his power in 1678 with the Treaty of Nymwegen. Then his haughty temper and aggressive policies, and the impolitic revocation of the Edict of Nantes, united his enemies in a series of coalitions which finally imposed upon him the disastrous Treaty of Utrecht. He had, nevertheless, founded a great colonial empire and made Versailles the centre of a civilization so advanced in literature, arts and ideas that the whole continent adopted it and became a "French Europe." The King's son and grandson had pre-deceased him, and the great-grandson who succeeded him as Louis XV was only five years old. Philippe d'Orléans would act as regent, and Louis XIV, who had little faith in the discretion of his nephew, left a will in which he tried to limit his powers. The Parlement, however, nullified the will and confirmed the Regent in all the powers he had claimed. Philippe d'Orléans was forty years old. He was handsome, intelligent and likeable, but he was also a notoriously irreverent free-thinker and a shameless rake. Reacting against the absolutism of Louis XIV, he introduced a new system of administration. In conjunction with the Regency Council, he set up six councils, or ministries, each of which dealt with one branch of public affairs. The ministers, who during the previous reign had been directed by the King, were now replaced by councils acting under the authority of the Regent. The councils were purely deliberative bodies whose decisions acquired force of law only after they had been approved by the Regency Council which was presided over by the Duc d'Orléans himself. The chairman of the Marine Council, in whose province the colonies fell, was the Comte de Toulouse, a legitimized son of Louis XIV and Madame de Montespan, who proved to be a conscientious but undistinguished administrator.[15] The Regent occupied the summit of the political pyramid, but in order to safeguard his own freedom and his life of pleasure, he appointed his former tutor as principal minister. The Abbé (later Cardinal) Dubois was the son of an apothecary, intelligent, well-educated and extremely ambitions, but his administration was unimaginative, prudent, parsimonious and generally unimpressive. His chief aim was to preserve the peace, and England, whose temper at the time was also peaceful, fostered his spirit of pacificism by paying him a pension. From such an administration in Versailles, Canada could hope for no more than routine direction and a minimum of financial help. If the country was to make any progress it would have to draw on its own resources.

The Treaty of Utrecht had not solved the chronic problem of Quebec's relations with the natives. During the war, thanks to the influence of French interpreters with the Senecas and the Onondagas, and in spite of English intrigues, the Iroquois had kept the peace which they had concluded with Callières and which had been maintained by Vaudreuil. England had long claimed that the Five Nations fell within her sphere, while France asserted that by their treaty with Tracy they had recognized her sovereignty. The Iroquois themselves, faithful to their wise and far-sighted policy, rejected every suggestion of allegiance and proclaimed themselves to be completely independent. They took care not to destroy any useful contacts, but at the same time they acted "in such a way as to be dependent neither on the English nor on us [the French]." With unconscious naïveté, they even offered "their mediation" in case of a rupture between the two great European powers. Meanwhile they preached peace; after the losses they had suffered in twenty-five years of war, a period of peace would allow them "to strengthen their numbers by annexing the Andastes," and also to increase their fur trade with the western tribes. They had always favoured the interests of the English, who were their immediate neighbours, and they needed western furs to trade for English munitions and blankets.[15a]

The aim of the Anglo-Iroquois alliance was still to divert the trade of the Indians who were attached to the French. From the Illinois country in the south to Michilimackinac in the north, the English "had emissaries everywhere, while the Five Nations sent belts by underground routes." These belts bore secret messages urging the nations of the upper country to buy English goods which were represented as cheaper and better than the corresponding French articles. As a preliminary to the execution of their grand plan, the immediate object of the Iroquois was to form an alliance with the Outagamis, the Fox tribe which occupied the country west of Lake Michigan, and in order to achieve this end they tried to induce Canada's Indian allies in the West to make peace with the Foxes. Vaudreuil countered these intrigues with generous gifts of arms and other articles. He made such good use of the chiefs' influence that he succeeded in maintaining peace among the tribes friendly to the French while at the same time keeping them hostile to the Foxes.[16]

The campaign of 1712 had only partly broken the arrogant spirit of this latter tribe, which was still obsessed with a desire to avenge itself on the French and their allies. Its warriors attacked the Illinois, the Ottawas and the Hurons, and at Green Bay they killed one Frenchman and captured five others. Vaudreuil met their bold challenge by launching the punitive expedition which he had been considering for two years.[17] A detachment of Indians from Sault St. Louis and Hurons from Detroit opened the campaign by routing a strong band of Kikapoos and Mascoutins, allies of the Foxes. This action took place on September 20, 1715, and eleven days later a force of 400 Foxes was cut to pieces.[18]

In the spring of 1716, Louvigny reached Michilimackinac with a force of 400 Frenchmen and 275 Indian allies. He laid siege to the main village of the Fox tribe behind whose triple stockade a force of 500 warriors and 3,000 squaws was massed. Louvigny opened fire on the fort with cannon and musketry, and the Foxes, terrified at the prospect of an assault, agreed to surrender. The terms imposed upon them—that they should give up all their prisoners, pay the expenses of the expedition and hand over six chiefs as hostages—were duly executed, after which Louvigny completed his mission by establishing peace among the other tribes who were still warring among themselves.[19]

Vaudreuil was also perturbed by the threat of a rupture between England and France, for the English colonies were already protesting that the Treaty of Utrecht should have given Canada and Cape Breton to England. Vaudreuil pointed out to the authorities in Versailles that the English colonies had 60,000 men capable of bearing arms, whereas, for the defence of a vast country, he could muster only 628 regular soldiers and 4,488 militiamen. As a result of his plea, he was authorized to complete the fortifications of Quebec and to build a wall around Montreal. The latter would cost 6,000 *livres* a year of which the Seminary of Saint-Sulpice would pay one third and the citizens of Montreal two thirds. The farmers of the "neighbouring villages" would be required to contribute the necessary labour.[20]

These corvées were the cause of the most serious sedition in the history of New France. When, in August 1717, Vaudreuil announced the King's decisions, the people of Montreal, realizing that their town was completely defenceless, accepted without question those which affected them. Only the people of Longueuil, opposite Montreal on the south shore of the river, declared themselves opposed to the imposition of corvées. Vaudreuil went immediately to Longueuil, where he found the militiamen assembled and armed. At the manor house a delegation of their leaders protested in such disrespectful fashion that they were roughly handled by the Governor's guards. They then went out and rejoined their companions who stood with rifle in hand in an attitude of defiance. Vaudreuil went back to Montreal, but returned the next day to Longueuil at the head of a troop of regulars. He was about to give the orders to open fire on the mutineers when a delegation made up of the parish priest, the seigneur and the principal habitants from the neighbouring seigniory of Boucherville, intervened to plead for them. The Governor agreed to pardon the mutinous parish on condition that ten ringleaders give themselves up as prisoners. These leaders were taken to Montreal where they were kept in prison for three months. Then, in November, as they professed repentance, and as their cells were quite unfit for occupation in winter, Vaudreuil granted them their freedom. He could do so all the more readily since their punishment had had a magical effect, and all the parishes had agreed to carry out the order requiring them to contribute corvées.[21]

Chapter Two

FLUCTUATIONS IN THE FUR TRADE
AND RELIGIOUS ORGANIZATION
1714-1725

Economic recovery. Bégon monopolizes profits. Situation of the fur trade: reduced territory, voyageurs, *contraband trade. Revival of* congés. *Monopoly of the West India Company. English competition on the Mississippi and at Niagara. The French post at Niagara and the English post at Oswego. Military marriages. Organization of parishes. Number of priests. Recall of Bégon. Wreck of the* Chameau. *Death of Vaudreuil.*

As Vaudreuil was suppressing the hostile activities of the Foxes and Bégon was carrying out the programme to eliminate card money, the colony began to profit by the security of her trade and the reorganization of her finances, and Canada thus entered a new phase of economic activity. The farmers' interests were served by the high price of wheat, and those of the merchants by the creation of a market in the new colony of Ile Royale. Bégon, who had succeeded the Raudots as Intendant in October 1712, had shown himself to be an intelligent and practical administrator and had achieved his aim of stimulating production and export trade.[1]

But soon Canadian merchants were complaining to Versailles that the Intendant was creating a monopoly for his own profit. A decree of January 14, 1714 forbade the private sale of wheat and ordered that it be turned over to the Intendant at a fixed price of thirty *sous*. The order was duly carried out, but when the wheat was resold at sixty *sous* there was a "riot" in Quebec. Bégon made use of the royal bakery to make bread, which he sold at a very high price; and, after prohibiting the export of

11

grain, he built three ships to carry his flour to the West Indies. When these facts were reported to Versailles, the Intendant was severely reprimanded. He stood convicted, in the eyes of the Minister, of greed, injustice and a desire to create his own trade monopoly, and he was warned that if his conduct gave rise to any further complaints he would be recalled. Bégon admitted that he was engaged in trade, but, as no further action was taken, he continued on the same course as before.[2]

No new industries could be introduced since the Marine Council maintained the principle already established by Pontchartrain: the colony must be the servant, and never the rival, of the mother country. To a suggestion made in 1716 that the iron mine in Three Rivers might be exploited, he gave a short answer: there was enough iron in France to supply all Canada's needs. The following year, when a Parisian hatter, La Lande, asked permission to establish a hat factory, his request was rejected with the same finality: the West India Company held the beaver monopoly.[3]

In spite of renewed activity in agriculture and export trade after the Treaty of Utrecht, the fur trade remained the chief factor in the economic life of the country, although its pattern had been altered by a fresh complication. D'Iberville had first attracted Canadian furs to Louisiana by establishing a warehouse there. This policy was continued under La Mothe-Cadillac and the financier Antoine Crozat, to whom Louisiana was farmed out. Canadians, tempted by facilities for trade in the new colony, began to settle in the Mississippi valley and to trade with the Louisiana posts, thereby reducing Canada's profits.[3a]

In 1706, after the failure of the Canada Company, which cost the Royal Treasury 154,716 *livres*, the beaver monopoly was transferred to the firm of Aubert, Néret and Gayot, whose lease was to run to December 31, 1717. The King reserved to himself the Tadoussac fur trade and all trade through Fort Frontenac. He left Tonty in possession of the Detroit post, which was also excluded from Aubert's monopoly. With the cession of the Hudson Bay territory to England, Canada was cut off not only from the finest fur country but from the northern sea route to Europe. Henceforth, furs had to be gathered from the country surrounding the Great Lakes and brought down to the St. Lawrence by the inland waterways. Beaver still made up the great bulk of the fur harvest. Other skins, listed here in diminishing order of their importance in the trade, were: wildcat, marten, bear, otter, deer or moose and mink.[3b] The value of the beaver harvest ranged from 330,000 *livres* between 1705 and 1715 to an annual average of 200,000 *livres* in the twelve years following. About two thirds of these skins were used by the French hat industry. The other third went to Holland, where a large part of it was sold for export to Russia.[3c]

A contemporary declared with some exaggeration that "all Canadians, without a single exception, are traders." "Each according to his means" supplied trading goods to the *coureurs de bois* or *voyageurs* who were drawn from every social class. Some came from influential families, but most of them were humble city or country folk. All were young, for only young men could stand the hardships of such a life. Their journeys lasted for months, they paddled heavily-laden canoes, and at the portages they carried canoes and heavy bales of fur or merchandise over rough, wild country. Every *voyageur* traded in brandy which, thanks to the Indian's irresistible passion for alcohol, brought in "immense profits." For, in spite of protests from the clergy and orders from Versailles, Vaudreuil allowed the transport and sale of brandy under the specious pretext that if he did not do so the Indians would take their beaver to the English. Pontchartrain accepted this excuse and tolerated the trade, although at the same time he recommended naïvely that it should be carried on "in moderation."[4] Naturally, traders and *voyageurs* who wanted to put themselves in the best possible position for extorting furs from the Indians, sold as much brandy as they could. In consequence, drunken Indians were guilty of "the wickedest acts"; some even went so far as to "ill treat" missionaries.[4a]

Such were the the conditions in which more than two hundred *voyageurs* with trading packs and stocks of brandy "roved the back country in search of profit and a libertine's life." According to Vaudreuil, who was himself interested in the fur trade, their occupation had its good points: the *voyageurs* made excellent fighters in time of war, they kept Quebec informed of Anglo-Indian intrigues and they stimulated the sale of French merchandise.[5] On the other hand, contraband trade was encouraged by the high prices they got when they exchanged their skins for *écarlatines,* the red English blankets on which the Indians set a very high value. In 1709 the King forbade the sale of beaver to the English, but the greed for gain was more powerful than any royal orders and the contraband trade continued, by way of the Ottawa and Lake Ontario, and on the Richelieu River. Even the Indians from Sault St. Louis, Sault-au-Récollet and the Lake of Two Mountains continued to trade in Orange, thus making it possible for Montreal merchants to offer English blankets for sale. How could the tide of fraud be stemmed when it was rumoured that Vaudreuil and Ramezay were involved in the illicit traffic and that Bégon allowed it certain "facilities"?[6] The Récollet Father Michel was accused of trading beaver with the English, twenty bales of furs were seized in a presbytery, and Judge Bouat of Montreal was condemned to a year in prison for dealing in contraband.[7]

Fur trading was gradually becoming a more complicated business. Faced with competition from English goods, Néret and Gayot could point out that their powder was of superior quality, and that their brandy was better than rum. But these arguments had little weight in comparison with the attraction of the blankets which were the chief article of trade, and which were highly prized since the Indian who had an English blanket to replace his fur mantle could sell the latter. In 1714, in order to satisfy the demands of native clients, Versailles abrogated its own laws to the extent of allowing the importation into Canada of "three hundred English blankets."[8]

Confronted with a very special problem in Canadian trade, Versailles made an attempt to stamp out the contraband plague by granting an amnesty to all *coureurs de bois* who returned to the colony. This first amnesty of 1714 had little effect, but a second, declared in 1716, induced many *voyageurs* to make their peace with the law.[9] In order to employ these men, the King's order of April 1716 re-established the system of twenty-five *congés* a year. The *congés* were to be distributed each year to poor families who would resell them to traders. However, when the administration in Quebec, acting on its own authority, also issued a number of private permits, the Marine Council prohibited any such action and decreed that no *congés* would be granted after 1718. Since the monopoly of Néret and Gayot was to expire in 1717, and the Canadians were opposed to its renewal, Versailles was considering the removal of all trade restrictions.[10]

It was at this point that John Law, the famous and rashly ingenious Scots financier, proposed to restore France's finances. His great "system" first embraced all the revenues of the kingdom, and then colonial commerce as well. In 1717 he formed the *Compagnie d'Occident* to which the Regent granted a monopoly of the resources of Louisiana. At the same time the Company was given the exclusive right, for a period of twenty-five years counting from January 1, 1718, to sell beaver in France. Canadians might "trade within the colony" either among themselves or with Indians, but they were required to deliver all their furs to the Company's warehouses. In May 1719 the West India Company absorbed the *Compagnie d'Occident* and thus acquired the monopoly of Canadian trade. In June, in order to help the Company enforce its monopoly, Versailles prohibited the sale of foreign merchandise in the colony and authorized the search for such merchandise in all houses including "ecclesiastical" residences. If any contraband was found, it was to be burned in public and its owner was to be fined.[11] With a few slight modifications in its manner of operation, and with the condition that the price of beaver was to be increased, the monopoly of the West India Company was confirmed in 1722. It remained in force until the end of the régime.[12] In 1726, constantly struggling against fraudulent importation by *voyageurs* and Indians, the Company managed to obtain from Versailles a renewal of the old interdictions and a new order authorizing the confiscation of clothes made of foreign cloth. All these measures, interdictions, fines and confiscations, together with the rise in fur prices, seem to have produced the desired effect. In 1726, 135,000 beaver skins were delivered in Quebec, whereas previously the number had remained more or less fixed at some 60,000 a year.[13]

Meanwhile the English were becoming more aggressive in their encroachment upon French territory and their efforts to divert the flow of Indian trade. As early as 1714 Carolina merchants, profiting from the peace of Utrecht, had been trading in the Mississippi valley, where soon after they established three depots.

In order to protect its trade against the intruders, Louisiana

built a post on the Wabash and appointed Bienville to command it. Shortly after this, merchants from Albany were ex-
changing merchandise and rum for beaver with the tribes in the
region of Niagara where New York refused to recognize the
prior rights of New France. "The French," wrote Governor
William Hunter in 1718, "have posts and establishments at several points on the Mississippi and the Lakes. They maintain
that these countries, and the right to trade there, belong to
them. If these possessions should be extended and colonized,
they would threaten the very existence of the English settlements. I do not know what basis they offer for their claim." In
1720, in order to restrain the encroachment of the American
colonies, Vaudreuil ordered a post to be built at Niagara. The
Senecas refused to comply with English demands that they demolish the palisade, and in the autumn of 1720 Joncaire established himself in the post and stocked it with trading supplies.[14]

In July 1721 William Burnett, the new governor of New
York, sent a protest to Vaudreuil. The French action, he
claimed, constituted a violation of the Treaty of Utrecht, since
the Niagara region was Iroquois territory, and the Iroquois
were English subjects. To this Vaudreuil replied that Niagara
had always belonged to the French, and that La Salle had had a
post there more than fifty years earlier. In 1722 Burnett established a trading depot on the Oswego River, four leagues from
Lake Ontario, and the post became a regular centre for English
trade.[15] In 1725 Vaudreuil replaced the stockade at Niagara
with a stone fort, and in 1727 Burnett built a fort and installed
a garrison at Oswego. In July 1727 the Governor of Quebec
protested in vain that this last action of the English was an
infraction of the Treaty of Utrecht.[16]

Thus the two adversaries maintained their positions. Under
Cardinal Fleury, who became Prime Minister in 1726, France's
chief concern was to establish the situation at home. In America
she limited herself to asserting her rights in Niagara and closing
the door to English intrusions on her trade there, while the
English remained as determined as ever to get possession of the
native trade and the Ohio valley. The two opposing forces were
separated by ill-defined frontiers, and their rivalry was to result
in the next Anglo-French war on American soil.

Canada's domestic peace was ruffled by a few minor disputes. In the religious sphere, Versailles continued to regulate the number of members in each religious community, as well as the character of the vows taken by members and the habit which they wore. Vaudreuil protested against the celebration of military marriages without his permission. On the other hand, Mgr. de Saint-Vallier, while denouncing the licentious conduct of certain officers, was also indignant at the Governor who, by withholding, sometimes for years, the permission required for the marriage of an officer or a soldier, encouraged misconduct and illegitimate births. The Bishop also deplored the limit set on the number of nuns when the country had more unmarried girls than bachelors.[16a]

On instructions from the King, Vaudreuil ordered the Attorney-General, Mathieu Collet, to establish the boundaries of the colony's parishes. On September 20, 1721 the Governor, the Bishop and the Intendant jointly recognized the boundaries as they were defined in Collet's memorandum, and on March 3, 1722 this action was confirmed by the King. The forty-one parishes which fell under the jurisdiction of Quebec extended on the north shore from Ste. Anne-de-la-Pérade to Baie St.-Paul, and on the south shore from the Eschaillons seigniory to Kamouraska. Three Rivers had only thirteen parishes, from Batiscan to Maskinongé on the north, and from St. Pierre to St. François on the south. Montreal's domain extended on the north from Ile-au-Pas and Berthier to Ste.-Anne-du-Bout-de-l'Ile, and on the south from Sorel to Châteauguay. It included thirty parishes. Thus, from Kamouraska to Châteauguay the country counted eighty-four parishes. But to serve these parishes there were only sixty priests, of whom fifty-one lived in presbyteries while the others boarded. Some parishes had to be satisfied with the services of the nearest priest; others, including a number of seigniories, were mission parishes served by a neighbouring curé or an itinerant priest. In both cases a regular incumbent was appointed only after a parish had acquired "a sufficient number of inhabitants to provide for the maintenance and support of a curé."[17] This first division of the country into parishes evoked protests from priests and parishioners alike: two royal orders of 1724, referring complaints to the Governor, the Bishop and the

Intendant, were followed by a third, dated January 23, 1727, which sanctioned a review of the earlier delimitation.[18]

The clergy, who supplied the spiritual needs of a population of eighteen thousand souls, were an honourable and devoted body of men. There were, in all, one hundred and forty priests: sixty curés in rural parishes, ninety priests attached to the Quebec Seminary, twelve Sulpicians in Montreal, twenty-four Jesuits and thirty-two Récollets.[19]

Canada had been directly affected, during these years, by a change in administration in the mother country. Having attained the age of twelve years and his royal majority, Louis XV was crowned at Rheims on October 20, 1722, and formally assumed direction of his kingdom in a *lit de justice* held on February 22, 1723. He kept as his chief adviser Cardinal Dubois, the first man in France ever to hold the title of Prime Minister. Cardinal Dubois died in the course of the summer, and the Duc d'Orléans, who replaced him, also died three months later. His successor, the vain and incompetent Duc de Bourbon, was completely under the influence of his mistress, the Marquise de Prie, and when he revealed his incompetence in international politics, the sixteen-year-old King dismissed him. Louis then called to the ministry his former tutor, André Hercule Fleury, who within a few weeks was created Cardinal. In 1726 when he became the King's chief adviser, Cardinal Fleury was seventy-two years old. The aim of his administration was not to bring glory either to France or to her colonies. Instead, this wise, modest and intelligent man gave his country sound, economical, prudent government, long years of peace, and growing prosperity.

After the King's effective accession, the councils, which had been modified during the Regency, resumed their earlier status. The Marine Council, which had jurisdiction over Canadian affairs, again came under the direction of the Minister of Marine. In the latter office, the Comte de Morville was replaced in August 1723 by the Comte de Maurepas.[20] The new minister was a man of keen wit and sarcastic humour, quick to seize ideas but disinclined to explore them very deeply. However, he at once became interested in Canada and its economic expansion.

In spite of Bégon's manipulation of Canadian commerce in his own interest, Pontchartrain had maintained him in his function in Quebec, but complaints of his malpractice were so specific that Maurepas ordered him to return to France to answer the charges. A successor, Edmé-Nicolas Robert, was appointed on February 22, 1724, and embarked in July at La Rochelle with his wife and his young son. But he died on board the first evening out, when the ship was still in sight of the French coast. Guillaume Chazelles, whom the King had chosen to replace Robert, set sail on the *Chameau* in July 1725, but, by some unexplained accident, on the night of August 27-28, the ship ran aground and was wrecked on a reef two leagues from Louisbourg. In this disaster the three hundred and sixteen passengers perished and the cargo was a total loss. Among the bodies washed ashore were those of M. de Chazelles, La Porte de Louvigny, the Governor-elect of Three Rivers, several officers and a number of priests.[21] As a result of the death of his two successors, Bégon was allowed to remain in office until 1726, and the inquiry into his conduct was suspended. When he returned to France in the autumn of 1726, he was well received and given the post of Marine Intendant in Le Havre.[22]

Vaudreuil had died on October 10, 1725, after twenty-two years in the Canadian administration. In spite of the criticism of his enemies, La Mothe-Cadillac, d'Auteuil and Ramezay, with whose schemes he had interfered, the people of the colony admired him and mourned their loss sincerely.[23] It was true that soon after he arrived as a poor official, Vaudreuil began to draw clandestine profits from the fur trade.[24] It was true too that he had received the pay of a garrison for the Château Saint-Louis and a personal guard, a garrison and a guard which existed only on paper. It was said that he was ruled by his wife and that he favoured the interests of his family and relations, and Raudot even alleged that in the discharge of his duties as governor he was not always guided by a spirit of integrity and justice.[25] However, in spite of his weaknesses, which were those of the age, in spite of his disagreements with Mgr. de Saint-Vallier and quarrels with successive intendants, it is nonetheless true, and the point is an essential one, that under Vaudreuil the country enjoyed a period of domestic peace and prosperity. A brave soldier and a sound tactician, he did not allow the enemy to violate the country's frontiers. He used his skill in diplomacy to keep the western tribes at peace with one another and to keep

the Iroquois neutral. Finally, he put an end to the incursions of
English traders into the country beyond Lake Ontario. Within
the limits of his jurisdiction, town and country people alike
were well governed. They could count on a sympathetic hearing
of their case, even when they were guilty of insubordination.
Vaudreuil's best memorial is to be found in such achievements,
in the useful tasks accomplished, sometimes in the face of great
difficulties and in the turmoil of personal dissension, throughout a long career.

Chapter Three

DUPUY'S INNOVATIONS
QUARRELS AMONG THE CLERGY
1725-1734

Canadians excluded from the office of Governor. Appointment of Beauharnois. Dupuy's new schemes; his efforts to extend the prerogatives of the Intendant. Disagreement between the Chapter and the Council on the occasion of Mgr. de Saint-Vallier's funeral. Royal sanctions imposed on the various parties in the quarrel. Dupuy recalled. Dissension among the clergy. The episcopal succession. The Foxes again on the warpath; dispersal of the tribe.

On the death of Vaudreuil, Charles Le Moyne, Baron de Longueuil, took over temporary administration by virtue of his position as Governor of Montreal. His father, the first Charles Le Moyne, who had rendered invaluable service under Maisonneuve, had received a patent of nobility from Louis XIV, and he himself had been attached to the royal armies in France between 1672 and 1679. After his return to Canada he served with distinction in the Anglo-Indian wars, and as envoy to the Iroquois. Since two governors of Montreal before him, Callières and Vaudreuil, had sought and obtained the post of Governor-General, Le Moyne in turn solicited promotion to the same office. He based his request on his long career in the service of the colony, and Pontchartrain answered that he would have been "glad" to be able to grant it.[1]

However, the honour which Le Moyne had earned was denied him for the somewhat curious reason that the late governor had been guilty of nepotism. In the colony, within his own sphere of action, Vaudreuil had always given preference to his own and his wife's relations, while both he and Madame de

21

Vaudreuil plied the King and the Minister with a relentless succession of requests for favours. In Vaudreuil's case the Court had hesitated to appoint a governor with a Canadian wife, and now that these fears of favouritism had been realized, it became a matter of policy that no Canadian should hold the office of Governor-General.[2]

The Vaudreuils' excessive family loyalty resulted in the following astonishing rule which was sent as a directive to Pontchartrain: "The Governor-General must not be a Canadian, nor have any relations in Canada; but must be sent from France. He must be a man of quality, and a general officer. He must have neither children nor a young wife fond of society. . . . His whole attention must be devoted to the honour of the King, and the interests of the kingdom and the colony." It was small wonder that in an atmosphere such as this, the candidature of Longueuil, a member of the large Le Moyne family, did not receive the support it deserved.[3]

The new governor, Charles de la Boische, Marquis de Beauharnois, was appointed on January 11, 1726. A captain in the Royal Navy, he also enjoyed the advantage of being related to the Minister of Marine, Pontchartrain. He was the younger brother of the intendant François de Beauharnois, who had been recalled from his post because of commercial involvements. He was fifty-six years old and had married a mature, childless widow. Thus he met all the conditions required by the Minister. He enjoyed the reputation of a wise, just and honest man, in whom foresight was married to a spirit of initiative.

A few months earlier, on November 23, 1725, the King had promoted Charles Thomas Dupuy to the office of Intendant. Dupuy belonged to an ancient seigniorial family. His mind, which had been disciplined by the study of Descartes and the law, and later in the higher tribunals of France, was essentially legalistic and logical. He was at the same time a man of vision and a tireless worker.[4] After the long reign of Vaudreuil and the commercial manœuvres of Bégon, the arrival of Beauharnois and Dupuy in August 1726 aroused much interest and great expectations.[5] Instructions from Versailles to the new officials insisted more urgently than ever on the importance of the fur trade. The first requisite for its expansion, so read these instructions, was the maintenance of peace among the tribes around the Great Lakes. It was equally important to put a halt to the intrusions of the English, who were already seeking to infiltrate the west country, and thus to make themselves masters of the rest of America. The Iroquois should be persuaded to dislodge them from Oswego and to incite the allied Indians to plunder any English traders who ventured into French territory. Since the English used brandy as an article of barter, it would be necessary, to the King's great regret, to offset this advantage by allowing licence holders to trade a limited quantity of alcohol. Finally, it was of the utmost importance that no English merchandise be allowed to enter Montreal and that business profits be reserved for the inhabitants of the colony.[6]

Immediately on his arrival, Dupuy acquainted himself with existing conditions and drew up a programme of reorganization embracing every phase of his functions: justice, finance, agriculture, business, seigniorial and municipal administration. In his desire to organize everything, he even invaded the domains of the Church and the army. Moreover, as he became conscious of the extent and importance of his functions, he succumbed to the temptation to add to his own personal prestige. He wrote to Versailles to solicit for himself the additional title of Intendant of Marine, which the Minister refused forthwith. In Canada, he sought permission to be escorted, at official ceremonies, and even in the church, by two marines. This honour was refused, diplomatically, by the Governor.[7]

Dupuy must be admired for the resolution with which he faced the rather chaotic state of his departments and created an orderly administration. He made an excellent start in this task by clarifying and regularizing Canada's tangled system of finance.[8] At the same time, since almost every phase of daily life came within the Intendant's sphere of influence, he issued directives dealing with every conceivable subject, directives which, in many cases, were useful and beneficial. For example, an order published in June 1727 proposed that Quebec should be "beautified" by a "fountain with a pool" and "a promenade for public recreation." It also contained excellent regulations for the building of houses and for fire protection. But other innovations irked the colonists and were the cause of complaints. An injunction which ran counter to the royal edict of April 12, 1667 encouraging early marriages, forbade men to marry before the age of thirty, and girls before the age of twenty-five.

It was this wide-ranging programme of reforms which caused Beauharnois to say of Dupuy: "In this country he is general, bishop and intendant."[9] It was a fact that Dupuy, in his pride at exercising such sweeping powers, came to consider himself the Governor's equal in the hierarchy of administration. When summoned by the Governor to meetings in which they were to synchronize their programmes and compose their joint dispatches for Versailles, he did not appear.[10] Maurepas intervened after receiving complaints not only from the Governor but from colonists. He censured Dupuy for wishing a personal guard, and rebuked him for issuing vexatious regulations. He also intimated to him very clearly that he was second in importance to the Governor, whose invitations he was not free to refuse. Soon after this, d'Aigremont accused the Intendant of sending false reports of Beauharnois' conduct to Versailles.[11]

In Quebec, perhaps because they were both authoritarians and reformers, Dupuy and Mgr. de Saint-Vallier soon became fast friends. The Bishop's confidence in the Intendant was such that, when he became seriously ill, he appointed him as his executor. The Bishop died during the night of December 25-26, 1728 at the Hôpital Général where he had taken up residence, and his body was transferred to the chapel of the Hôpital to lie in state. The day after his death the Cathedral Chapter appointed the curé of Quebec, Canon Etienne Boullard, as Capitular Vicar of the diocese. Canon Boullard informed the archdeacon, Canon de Lotbinière, that the Chapter was arranging for a funeral at the Cathedral, and that after the service the body would be brought back to the Hôpital Général where Mgr. de Saint-Vallier had chosen to be buried.[12]

It was the privilege of the archdeacon, by virtue of his office, to officiate at the burial of the Bishop, and Canon de Lotbinière refused to give way to the capitular vicar. When the archdeacon's refusal became known, it was rumoured that the Chapter meant to have the body removed and to have it lie in state in the Cathedral before the funeral. Whereupon, on January 2, Dupuy directed the archdeacon to proceed with the funeral at once. On that very day, towards nightfall, Canon de Lotbinière celebrated the requiem mass in secret in the chapel of the Hôpital, and the burial took place immediately afterwards.[13]

On learning that the ceremony was taking place, the Abbé Boullard and the members of the Chapter immediately went into action. Announcing that the Hôpital was on fire, they sounded the tocsin, after which the canons and a few priests hurried to the Hôpital about a mile away, and rushed into the empty chapel, followed by a crowd of townspeople. When it was revealed that the interment, as well as the funeral service, was already an accomplished fact, Canon Boullard summoned the Mother Superior to his presence, and, on her refusal to comply, announced that she was deposed and the church interdicted. He then drew up a formal statement which he read and deposited in the chapel.[14]

These interdicts were at once reported to the Intendant, who, by an order of January 4, summoned the Chapter to appear before the Council in order to justify its assumption of authority. Boullard obeyed the summons, but refused to recognize the competence of the Council in a purely ecclesiastical matter. The councillors nonetheless confirmed the rights of the archdeacon in the administration of the diocese. On Sunday, January 11, Canon Boullard had his interdiction of the chapel read from the pulpit, and on the following day the Council answered by declaring the interdict null and void.[15]

The situation gave Dupuy the chance he desired to play the leading rôle. Calling into play all his legal science and all his powers of oratory, he persuaded the councillors to adopt his ideas and demand that the clergy recognize the authority of the Council. A succession of orders, issued throughout January and February, rebuked Boullard and the Chapter, required the canons to retract their decisions and condemned the capitular vicar to a fine of one thousand *livres*. The immediate result of the Intendant's autocratic decisions was dissension throughout the religious life of Quebec.[16]

The situation became so grave that the Governor felt he must intervene. Accordingly, he sent an official communication to be read at the Council meeting of March 18. In this letter the Governor expressed regret that, without first consulting him, the Council had made decisions in matters concerning the clergy. Moreover, by virtue of his authority and for the public good, he ordered that further action in the questions under dispute should await a royal decision on the matter. After hearing the Governor's message, the councillors at once replied that such a document violated the rights of the Council, that they would disregard the orders which it contained and that they would bring a complaint before the King's Council.[17] The Governor then called on the troops and militia officers to publish his order in the town and in the country districts, while soldiers of the garrison slashed copies of orders from the Intendant and the Council which had been posted at church doors.[18]

Dupuy's next move was to dismiss the officers of justice who obeyed the Governor's orders. Beauharnois realized that two councillors, d'Artigny and Gaillard, who never failed to support the Intendant, were accomplices in this manœuvre. Accordingly, he issued an order, dated May 13, requiring them to withdraw, one to Beaumont and the other to Beauport. The two councillors took refuge in the Intendant's house, and on May 29 Dupuy ordered them to remain in Quebec pending a royal decision. The whole country was aroused and united in support of the Governor and the clergy against the vexatious Intendant and the obsequious councillors.[19]

In Versailles reports of these clerico-political quarrels provoked displeasure and stern measures from which the Intendant was the first to suffer. The King had already had some reason to be "displeased with his conduct." He was now declared to be guilty of acting with "passion" and of following very "irregular" procedure, and was recalled forthwith. Maurepas made this decision known to Dupuy on June 2 (1728); he was "very sorry" to have to perform this painful duty, and he assured the Intendant that he would "do his best to reduce the penalty" once he was back in France. The Chapter was also reprimanded; the Minister expressed the King's pained surprise that the Chapter should have denied the archdeacon's prerogative, and thus been the cause of the "disorder" which had ensued. The King also expected that in future the canons would act in a "greater spirit of harmony" and with "more charity." Boullard's action in raising the interdict against the Hôpital chapel was approved, but the Council was required to quash its own decisions against the Chapter. Beauharnois' turn came the following year (1729) when Maurepas censured him for having exceeded "his powers by suspending the Council's proceedings." Moreover, by exiling d'Artigny and Gaillard, he had attributed to himself "a power which belonged only to the King." However, in order to safeguard the Governor's authority in the colony, "the matter would be kept secret and the two councillors would even be reprimanded." The reprimand was to be administered by the Intendant.[20]

Even in death, Mgr. de Saint-Vallier was the cause of discord in the colony, and his qualities had never been those of a peacemaker. His conviction that all his decisions and actions were inspired from on high made him self-willed and difficult, unable to accept advice from any quarter. In his anxiety to achieve perfection through regimentation, he disrupted the imperfect order already in existence. Mgr. de Laval and the other ecclesiastical dignitaries even alleged that his indiscreet zeal had made of him an involuntary "instrument of Satan." Against such passionate outbursts, we must place the facts. The second bishop of Quebec was a man whose life was informed with burning zeal and Christian charity. His *Ritual* and *Catechism* provided firm doctrinal bases for his diocese, and he founded three hospitals and spent close to 1,000,000 *livres* of his own private fortune for the benefit of the sick and the needy.[21]

As successor to Mgr. de Saint-Vallier the King appointed Mgr. de Mornay, who had been coadjutor for thirteen years and who did not come to Canada either as coadjutor or as bishop. In 1729 Mgr. Dosquet was appointed coadjutor to act for Mgr. de Mornay and, when the latter resigned in 1733, Mgr. Dosquet became the titular bishop of Quebec. The new prelate first undertook the task of re-establishing discipline in the religious communities, and even in priests' households. For some curés, unhappy with their lot, were demanding that tithes be raised to the rate which prevailed in France, while the conduct of others was not far from scandalous. The Bishop tried also to restore harmony in the Chapter, where Canadian canons complained of being excluded from high offices, while the French priests who occupied these offices alleged that their Canadian confrères were unsubmissive and ambitious to extend their own authority. After Laval and Saint-Vallier, Mgr. Dosquet attacked the liquor problem. Reviving a long-dormant order of Mgr. de Laval, he prohibited the sale of brandy to the Indians, and declared that,

in cases involving infraction of this order, absolution was reserved for the Bishop's decision. This last effort on the part of
the bishops to destroy the double curse of Indian drunkenness
and Indian exploitation was defeated by the opposition of the
Governor and the Minister, who maintained the established
custom and continued to authorize a limited traffic in intoxicating liquors.[22]

After a period of four years in France (1735-1739), Mgr.
Dosquet resigned without returning to Canada. His successor,
Mgr. de Lauberivière, a young man of twenty-eight, died in
August 1740 within a month of his arrival in Quebec, and in
December of the same year the King appointed the Abbé Du-
breuil de Pontbriand to the vacant see. Mgr. de Pontbriand, who
was consecrated in Paris in March 1741, and who arrived in
Canada on August 23, was the last bishop appointed during the
French régime.[23]

While Quebec was beset with religious dissensions, the
Foxes were up to their old tactics in the West. They attacked
the Illinois, who were allied with the French, and they killed a
lieutenant and seven soldiers on their way from Louisiana to
the Missouri. This fresh outburst of hostilities convinced Beauharnois that the Foxes must be exterminated. Accordingly, in
August 1728 a force of four hundred French and twelve hundred Indians under M. de Ligneris set out for the Wisconsin
and burned the Fox villages, which they found deserted.[24] The
Foxes had fled towards the East and the Illinois country, where
they succeeded in arousing the Mascoutins and the Kikapoos. In
October these latter tribes captured sixteen Frenchmen, but
one of the prisoners, Father Guignas, used his influence to gain
freedom for himself and his fellow captives and to re-establish
peace between these nations and the French.[25]

In August 1730 the largest Fox village was besieged by a
force composed of three French and Indian detachments, one
from Louisiana, under M. de Saint-Ange, and the others commanded by M. de Villiers and M. de Noyelles, commanders of
Fort St. Joseph and Fort Miami. During the night of September
8 the Foxes slipped through the forces surrounding their fort,
and escaped with their families; but the allies caught up with
them the following day, and killed three hundred warriors, as
well as a number of women and children.[26]

In 1731 the allied Indians tracked down the scattered remnants of the tribe and inflicted further losses upon them. The following year, a band of Fox Indians, brought to bay, declared their submission to M. de Villiers.[27] M. de Villiers' triumph was, however, short-lived; the following year he and eight of his men were killed in a surprise attack by a band of Sakis, allies of the Foxes. These new enemies were attacked in their turn and put to flight by the French; whereupon Foxes and Sakis together retreated to the right bank of the Mississippi and built a fort on the Des Moines River.[28] When, in August 1734, a Franco-Indian force under de Noyelles attacked the fort and killed twenty warriors, the Sakis promised to end their alliance with the Foxes and to respect the French. However, it was only after suffering further defeat at the hands of the Missouri and the Kansas Indians that they went to Green Bay and declared their submission to M. de Lusignan, the commander of the fort. Abandoned by their allies, the last Foxes sought refuge with the Sioux north-west of the Mississippi and disappeared from the Canadian scene.[29]

Chapter Four

THE BEAUHARNOIS-HOCQUART RÉGIME AND THE SEARCH FOR THE WESTERN SEA
1729-1751

Intendant Hocquart. Scarcity of currency and creation of card money. Proposal for a general tax. Smallpox and fire in Montreal. Montreal-Quebec highway. English encroachment on French territory. La Vérendrye's search for the Western Sea. Lake of the Woods massacre. La Vérendrye's sons approach the Rockies. La Vérendrye in difficulties; he resigns his commission. La Vérendrye's commission renewed; his death. The French in Alberta.

Dupuy's successor, Gilles Hocquart, appointed in March 1729, crossed the ocean on the *Eléphant* in company with Mgr. Dosquet. They reached Quebec in August, after their ship had run aground at Cap Brûlé, ten leagues below the city. Having taken a lesson from the exaggerated pretentions of Dupuy, the councils in Versailles were determined to restrain any ambition on the part of the new official to compete with the Governor. Hence, Hocquart was given the modest title of *Commissaire-ordonnateur*. He soon showed, however, that he possessed the gifts of a great administrator: vision, lucid intelligence, energy, ability to organize and direct. He was therefore commissioned as Intendant in February 1731, and the services which he rendered during the next seventeen years mark him as Canada's greatest intendant after Talon. Although he was personally interested in the St. Maurice ironworks, he was perhaps the only one of Canada's intendants to derive no personal profit from his official position. His conduct in this respect was, as Montcalm later remarked, "unlike the habit of colonial intendants."[1]

Beauharnois and Hocquart were wise enough and generous

enough to avoid the animosities and quarrels which had marred
the former administration, and under them the country pros-
pered. They had, however, inherited the currency problem with
its long history. The peace of Utrecht had made it possible for
companies to increase production, and the founding of Louisbourg had opened a new market for their products. But commercial activity was seriously hampered by the scarcity of coin
in the colony. Each year the King's ship brought a large quantity of specie from the Royal Treasury, chiefly for payment of
the troops, but much of it went back in the autumn to pay for
imports, and part of what remained was hoarded. The dearth of
small change had become so acute since 1719, the year card
money was abolished, that in 1722, in an effort to silence complaints, the West India Company fabricated and sent to Canada
20,000 *livres* of copper money. The people, however, refused to
accept it because it was heavy and awkward to handle, and its
circulation was limited to the colony. It had, therefore, to be sent
back to France.[2]

As the monetary situation became constantly more difficult
with the passage of years, merchants and clients were united in
their demand for the revival of card money, and it finally became apparent that such action could not be avoided. Accordingly, on March 2, 1729 the King signed an order for the fabri-
cation of 400,000 *livres* in card money. Cards in denominations
of twenty-four, twelve, six and three *livres* were to be signed by
the Governor and the Intendant, while for those representing
one *livre*, or still smaller values, fifteen *sous*, ten *sous*, or
seven *sous* six *deniers*, the signature of the Marine Controller
was sufficient. Seventy-five thousand cards from the two thousand packs sent out from Versailles in 1729 were signed by the
Governor and the Intendant in that same year. The people of
Quebec, having apparently forgotten completely the sad fate of
the earlier issue of card money, greeted the latest one joyfully.
Such was their confidence in the new money that they began to
hoard it, with the result that it too became scarce. In 1733 a new
issue of 200,000 *livres* was authorized, and the cards, which were
redeemed promptly on presentation, continued to command
credit.[3]

A decree of August 5, 1732 brought about a change in the
financial administration of Canada by removing the Canadian

taxes of the *Domaine d'Occident* from the "General Farms" and handing them over to be collected and administered by the Department of Marine. These revenues, including import and export duties, domanial and seigniorial fees, and profits from the Tadoussac fur trade, were quite modest; in 1733, after expenses were met, they yielded a profit of 37,772 *livres.*[4]

Canadians were not concerned as to who collected existing duties and fees, but in 1733 a proposal was made which, if it had been adopted, would have touched them much more closely. As the Minister was laying financial plans for the year, he made the observation that, whereas Canada's fiscal contribution was almost negligible, the colony cost the Royal Treasury 600,000 *livres* a year. From this premise, he drew the curious conclusion that freedom from taxes bred laziness in the habitant, who, since he had no financial obligation to the state, lacked the incentive to harder work which such an obligation would provide. Maurepas concluded that a direct tax would serve the colonists' own interests: the more they had to pay, the harder they would work and the more loyal and submissive subjects they would be.[5] But Beauharnois and Hocquart, who had more experience than the Minister with the unsubmissive spirit of the Canadians, pointed out that, in order to collect a headtax from the townspeople and an income tax of two and one half per cent from farmers, they would require 600 more soldiers. As these reinforcements would cost 140,000 *livres* a year and the tax would bring in 40,000, Maurepas abandoned the idea of taxing the recalcitrant Canadians.[6]

Although the plague of taxation did not descend on Canada, the country was smitten by several others in the course of this period. In 1732 Montreal was shaken by an earthquake; tremors continued for several days, rocking houses and bringing down walls at the Hôtel-Dieu and the Récollet monastery.[7] The following year smallpox, introduced into the city by an Indian from the Lake of Two Mountains, spread throughout the country and reached epidemic proportions. In spite of the heroic devotion of the hospital sisters in the three towns and of the three doctors, Sarrazin, Berthier and Benoist, nine hundred persons died.[8] On April 10, 1734 Montreal was once more struck by ill fortune when the Hôtel-Dieu, its chapel and forty-six houses were destroyed in a fire which had been set by a

Negress with a grudge against her mistress, Madame de Francheville. The culprit was brought to trial, condemned and hanged,
and her body was burned, but her accomplice, Claude Thibault, escaped. The whole town and the whole country helped
generously in the rebuilding of the hospital; some gave money,
some bags of wheat, others free labour. Versailles contributed
a subsidy of 10,000 *livres*, and a temporary grant of 1,500 *livres*.[9]

These catastrophes did not prevent the authorities from
continuing their efforts to improve certain public services. As
the population of the country grew, the people began to suffer
from the inadequacy of their means of communication. Between Quebec and Montreal there was no continuous carriage
road, but only comparatively long stretches in the more populous seigniories. Passengers and goods were transported on the
river in canoes or small boats. In winter, a road was marked out
on the ice with spruce trees. The mails followed the river route
while official dispatches were sent overland by special messenger. Bégon inaugurated a system of public transport in January 1721 when he granted a monopoly in this field to Nicolas
Lanouillier, agent general for the *Compagnie des Indes.*
Branches were established in Quebec, Three Rivers and Montreal, and the monopoly was to run for twenty years. Transport
of letters, parcels and travellers would be provided by cabriolets
and ferries.[10]

It was not until ten years later that construction was begun
on the highway between Quebec and Montreal. Canada had
had an official road-surveyor since 1667, although the Bécan-
cours, father and son, who held the office between 1667 and
1730, regarded it as a pure sinecure and remained completely
inactive. On the death of the younger Bécancour, the King, on
March 26, 1730, appointed Jean Eustache Lanouillier de Boisclerc to succeed him," and, with the encouragement of Hocquart,
construction of a road on the north shore was begun. It
progressed rapidly, thanks to the energy and practical knowledge of Boisclerc, and to the fact that he could count on corvées
to supply the labour. Over long distances, where roads through
seigniories already existed, it was only necessary to establish
links from one seigniory to the next, but along Lake St. Peter,
where there was no road of any kind, they had to break ground
for a long stretch of highway. In no way discouraged by such

difficulties, Boisclerc went steadily on with the task of surveying and building roads and bridges, and providing ferries over the wider rivers. In 1737 it was possible to travel from Quebec to Montreal in four days in a one-horse carriage, and in 1739 Hocquart made this journey "very comfortably." An added advantage was that the road made fresh land available for settlement along Lake St. Peter. In 1736 fifty tenants had already taken up holdings there. In 1739 Boisclerc also opened a road linking La Prairie, on the south shore opposite Montreal, with Fort Chambly and the Richelieu, the river highway to Lake Champlain and the English colony of New York.[12]

As early as 1732, Hocquart had thought of resuming work on the Lachine canal. The canal had been begun in 1680 by Dollier de Casson at the expense of the Sulpicians, and in 1706 another Sulpician, the Abbé Breslay, had recommended to the Minister that it be completed. Canoes could not go upstream against the fierce St. Louis rapids; so that along this stretch of the river goods had to be transported by cart at considerable expense, while the perilous journey downstream by way of the rapids often entailed loss of property and sometimes loss of life. The canal would have provided a safe and more economical alternative route, and in 1738 Beauharnois and the Intendant recommended to the Minister that it be built; but Maurepas rejected the proposal. The reason alleged for the refusal was that the project presented insurmountable difficulties. In reality Maurepas did not dare to risk an expense of 250,000 *livres*.[13]

All through this period, the English colonies made steady progress in population and in wealth. Their agriculture, their fisheries, their shipbuilding and their West Indian trade were all in flourishing condition. Many of their merchants specialized in the fur trade, and settlers on the outskirts of the colonies kept pressing onward, always eager to appropriate land beyond their ill-defined frontiers. With the advent of peace, they resumed and intensified their ambitious infiltration into territory which had been in French hands from the time of the earliest European colonization. The colonists from Massachusetts kept moving eastwards towards the St. John River, while traders from New York sent expeditions up to Lake Ontario. In the south, English settlers from Virginia and Carolina reached the Ohio and the Wabash. Traders from the different provinces went up to the country around the Great Lakes, where, with the Iroquois as their intermediaries, they sought to monopolize the trade with the western tribes.[14]

Reacting to commercial and territorial invasion as Vaudreuil had done before him, Beauharnois began to prepare the country for the eventual possibility of war. Since the western defences were assured by the new stone fort at Niagara, he set about barring the invasion route by Lake Champlain. In 1731 he built a palisaded fort at Pointe-à-la-Chevelure, where the strong frontier post of St. Frédéric was to be erected in 1737.[15] At the same time he pressed on with the construction of a stone wall around Montreal,[16] and remembering earlier raids, he ordered farmers to build picket fences in the country.[17] As Quebec was the key post for the defence of the country, he requested that its fortifications be strengthened, but the King replied that such an undertaking would involve quite unnecessary expense. Both Fleury and Walpole were pursuing a policy of peace, relations were excellent between the courts of Versailles and St. James's and war was a very distant and improbable eventuality.[18]

Still another problem was disturbing the colony. With the cession of Hudson Bay to the English, Quebec could see a large part of the rich fur harvest from beyond Lake Superior passing into the hands of the English. It was this situation which gave rise to a revival of La Salle's scheme to discover the way to the Western Sea, the Pacific gateway to China and India. On their way across the continent, explorers could establish posts which would divert towards French traders furs on their way to Hudson Bay. In 1716 Vaudreuil presented a plan, which was approved by Versailles on condition that private citizens, to whom trading rights would be granted, should assume the expenses of any explorations which might be undertaken. In July 1717 Vaudreuil entrusted the mission to La Noue, who established a post at Kaministiquia (near Fort William), but who was prevented from going any farther by a war between the Sioux and the Cristinaux.[19] Versailles did not, however, give up the idea. The only known routes to China, India and Japan involved circumnavigation either of Africa or of South America. The westerly voyage would be shortened considerably if a way could be found to the Western Sea. Since the Jesuits had, in the course of their missionary journeys, acquired an extensive knowledge of western geography, Louis XV commissioned Father Charlevoix, who had spent four years in Canada, to cross the continent to the Pacific. Charlevoix's commission was granted in 1720, and in June 1721 he was already in Michili-mackinac questioning commanders of posts, traders and Indians, whose unreliable information led him to conclude that the famous sea was not far west of Lake Superior.[20]

The different expeditions against the Fox tribe made it impossible to undertake any further expedition, and, in spite of several abortive attempts, it was not until 1727 that Quebec again took effective action. Since it was generally considered that the search should be directed towards the source of the Missouri, Beauharnois granted trading rights in that region to a Canadian company, the *Compagnie des Sioux*. Boucher de Montbrun built a palisaded fort on Lake Pépin and christened it Fort Beauharnois, but the company was more interested in trade than in exploration. A second company, which succeeded the first in 1731, pursued a similiar policy until the post was abandoned in 1737.[21]

It was at this point, when the idea of western exploration seemed completely dead, that Pierre Gaultier de La Vérendrye entered upon the scene. La Vérendrye was the son of a governor of Three Rivers. After serving, at the age of nineteen, in three expeditions against the English, he had gone to France and had fought at Malplaquet where he had been wounded five times. Back in Canada, he established himself as a trader at La Gabelle, near Three Rivers. In 1728 he was appointed commander of the post of Kaministiquia, and there he conceived the desire to discover the Western Sea. Indians had assured him that "it was only ten days' journey" from Lake Winnipeg. Two years later he was granted permission by Beauharnois to establish a post on Lake Winnipeg. He was to meet all expenses and to pay a fee of 3,000 *livres* a year for trading rights.[22]

After forming a company with some merchants from Montreal, La Vérendrye set out with his three sons and his nephew La Jemmeraye. They arrived at the Grand Portage, or Kaministiquia, in August, and La Jemmeraye was sent to build Fort St. Pierre on Rainy Lake. The following year, La Vérendrye was on the Lake of the Woods, where he built Fort St. Charles, with living quarters, chapel, store and powder magazine. It was excellent hunting country with an abundance of wild oats, and the Crees, who occupied the region, allied themselves with the French.[23]

During 1733 and 1734 La Vérendrye continued to gather geographical information from the Crees and the Assiniboines, to whom he distributed presents from the King, and whom he urged to trade with the *bourgeois* at the French post rather than with the English. In the spring of 1734 he entrusted to a companion, Cartier, the task of building Fort Maurepas at the mouth of the Red River, while he himself took the year's harvest of furs down to Montreal. When the furs were sold and it became apparent that "expenses had greatly exceeded profits,"[24] La Vérendrye's partners withdrew their support and he had to seek help elsewhere. Although Beauharnois bore witness that he "could not be suspected of any motive other than the good of the colony," Versailles refused to incur "any expense in connection with this enterprise," and even insinuated that those interested "were losing nothing in it."[25] Obviously neither Louis XV nor Maurepas had any idea of the cost of exploring vast expanses of unknown country. Nor could they conceive the difficulties which had to be surmounted; to them "portage" was only a word.

In 1735, since no help could be expected from France, Beauharnois authorized La Vérendrye to lease his trading rights to merchants for a period of three years, this on condition that he pursue his explorations and that he do no trading himself. After disposing of his lease, La Vérendrye was able to renew his stores and equipment and return to Fort St. Charles. It was not long, however, before the expedition was overtaken by disaster.[26] In 1736 the Monsonis opened hostilities against the Sioux; then, in order to forestall reprisals, they claimed shamelessly to have been mere tools of the French. The ruse succeeded in its object of diverting the hostility of the Sioux towards the French, upon whom they swore to be avenged. Early in June a band of Sioux, which had invaded the Lake of the Woods region, was informed of the presence of Frenchmen in the vicinity.[27] These were a party of twenty-four men led by Jean-Baptiste de La Vérendrye and Father Aulneau, who had left Fort St. Charles the day before for Michilimackinac. On June 6 they camped for the night on an island in the Lake of the Woods. The next day, at dawn, the Sioux warriors fell on the sleeping men, whom they killed and scalped, and whose heads they "placed on beaver robes."[28]

The sad news reached La Vérendrye on June 22, but he refused the offers of the Crees and the Assiniboines to march against the Sioux. Deciding instead to seek orders from the Governor, he returned in September 1737 to Montreal, where he arrived "almost destitute."[29] Although heavily burdened with debt, he managed to procure fresh equipment, and in June 1738 he set out again for the West.[30]

From Fort Maurepas, La Vérendrye advanced into unknown country, and when, on September 25, 1738, he reached the fork of the Red River and the Assiniboine, he became the first white man to set foot on the present site of Winnipeg. On October 3 he began the construction of Fort La Reine, where Portage La Prairie now stands. From there, he set out on October 18 with twenty-six Frenchmen and as many Indians for the country of the Mandans on the upper Missouri. He hoped to obtain information from this tribe about the Western Sea, and when he reached their first village on December 3 he was well received, although his visit was not without its misfortunes. His bag of presents was stolen, and he suffered an even more serious loss when his interpreter, a young Cree, "decamped to go after an Assiniboine woman with whom he had become infatuated." In January 1739, before leaving the Mandan country, La Vérendrye gave the Indians a lead plate marking the fact that he had taken possession of the land in the name of the King of France, and in February he was back at Fort La Reine.[31]

In April La Vérendrye's son Louis-Joseph went up the Saskatchewan as far as the junction of the two branches. In the spring of 1740 La Vérendrye himself, having learned that his effects had been seized by his creditors, went down to Montreal, where, "at great loss," he managed once more to put his affairs in order. The Governor opened his house to him, and such powerful protection helped him to refute the insinuations of those who reported to Versailles "that he thought only of piling up a fortune." In fact all he had got out of the venture was "a debt of 40,000 *livres*."[32]

With his equipment again renewed, the explorer left Montreal in June 1741 and reached Fort La Reine in October. In order to create bases for trading and exploration in the west, he sent his son Pierre to build Fort Dauphin on Lake Dauphin, and established Fort Bourbon on the Moose River, thirty leagues from the Saskatchewan. In the spring, still hoping to find the way to the Western Sea by the South, he sent his two sons, Pierre and Louis-Joseph, to the Mandan country, while he stayed at Fort La Reine in order to protect his associates' furs against possible Indian raids.[33]

In May 1742 the La Vérendrye brothers, with two other Frenchmen, reached a Mandan village on the Missouri, on the site of Bismarck. In November they were in the village of the people of the Bow, whose chief declared his "perfect friendship" towards them. The explorers accompanied the chief in a visit to the South, and on January 1, 1743 they were "within sight of the mountains." These mountains were the Black Hills of Dakota announcing the first rise towards the Rockies. The explorers' hopes ran high; doubtless the top of the hills would afford a glimpse of the long-sought-for sea. But, to their intense disappointment, the party turned east again without climbing the mountains. Back at the village of the Little Cherry tribe on the Missouri (on the site of Pierre, South Dakota), they buried a lead plate bearing the arms of France, and thereby signified that they were taking possession of the country in the name of the King. In July they returned to Fort La Reine[34] where they found La Vérendrye beset with still further difficulties. Intertribal wars had reduced the beaver crop, but his creditors refused to accept this as a reason for deferring until the following year the payment of 50,500 *livres* which he owed for equipment.[35] This time the forces arrayed against him, war, debts, lack of interest and lack of faith on the part of Versailles, were too much even for his stubborn courage, and in 1743 he asked to be relieved of his post.[36]

Noyelles, who was chosen by Beauharnois to replace La Vérendrye, added nothing to his predecessor's discoveries, and in 1747 he too resigned. Meanwhile Beauharnois had succeeded in his efforts to have La Vérendrye promoted to the rank of Captain, but Maurepas added unjust imputations even to the notice of promotion. The new governor, La Galissonnière, supporting La Vérendrye as staunchly as had Beauharnois, declared that

"everything that has been alleged against the explorer is false."
In 1749, after further representations from the Governor, Louis
XV granted the Cross of Saint Louis to the father, and ensigns'
commissions to the two sons.[37] Finally convinced by the facts
which Beauharnois and La Galissonnière had set before him,
Maurepas recognized his error and invited La Vérendrye to resume his exploration. With great magnanimity and fine courage
the explorer, who was now sixty-four years old, accepted the
mission, but he was not destined to accomplish it. He died three
months later, on December 5, 1749.[38]

Thus, before his death, this greatest figure in Canadian exploration was accorded "reparation, justice and honour."
Greater than Jolliet, and even than La Salle, who had only to
follow the course of the Mississippi, La Vérendrye covered half
a continent and ventured into pathless regions occupied by
hostile Indians. And he accomplished these feats in spite of
slanderous rivals and the pettiness and stupidity of Versailles.
His intelligence and tireless energy surmounted every difficulty
and gave France a vast domain stretching from Lake Superior to
the Saskatchewan and the Dakota Rockies, the most extensive
territory ever brought to the Crown by a single man.[39] He
secured for France the alliance of many Indian tribes and he
won for her the opportunity, which she allowed to slip, to capture the rich fur trade of the Great West and to cut it off from
the English on Hudson Bay.

La Vérendrye's sons applied to the Governor, La Jonquière,
for a commission to continue the work begun by their father.[40]
But the Governor chose instead to appoint one of his own men,
Charles Le Gardeur de Saint-Pierre, who also became a partner
in the company. With his centre of operations established at
Fort La Reine, Saint-Pierre spent the year 1750 maintaining
peace among the tribes and looking after his trading interests.
In 1751 he sent the Chevalier de Niverville from Fort Poskoyac
to build a post three hundred miles farther up the North Saskatchewan. This post, in territory which is now within the
province of Alberta, was completed in May 1751 and named
Fort La Jonquière. It marked the farthest point reached by the
French in their search for the Western Sea. They did not reach
their goal, but their failure may be considered a success for the
time, since Mackenzie and his French-Canadian *voyageurs* did
not reach the Pacific until 1793, more than forty years later.[41]

Chapter Five

ACADIA UNDER ENGLISH RULE
1713-1749

~~~~~~

*Terms of the Treaty of Utrecht. Situation of the Eng-
lish in Acadia. Hostility of the Abenakis. Rôle of the
clergy. Concession granted by Queen Anne. English
opposition to the departure of the Acadians. Reasons
for their opposition. The oath of allegiance. Armstrong and Wroth grant right of military neutrality.
Philipps exempts the Acadians from serving against
France. English sophistry.*

~~~~~~

By the Treaty of Utrecht, the greatest disaster in her short
history, Acadia was lost to France and became the English colony of Nova Scotia. Article XII of the treaty stipulated that
France ceded Acadia "with its ancient boundaries." According
to the French interpretation, this meant only the southern half
of the Acadian peninsula, following a line drawn from Ile
Longue in the Bay of Fundy to the Strait of Canso. England, on
the other hand, claimed the whole peninsula, the north shore of
the Bay of Fundy, and the territory beyond, as far north as the
St. Lawrence. The treaty accorded to the Acadians the right
either to migrate within a year to any other country, or to
remain and become British subjects. In the latter case, they
were to enjoy "the exercise of the Roman Catholic religion, in
so far as this is permitted by the laws of Great Britain."[1]

After the capture of Port Royal in 1710, Nicholson had left
a garrison of four hundred men under Samuel Vetch who, as
Governor of Port Royal, became Nova Scotia's first English
governor. When the Treaty of Utrecht confirmed English possession of Acadia, various proposals for colonization were ad-

vanced. These all remained abortive, as did the project, conceived in New England in 1715, of adding the new colony to the existing confederation.[2] Thus Nova Scotia continued to be a territory inhabited by Acadians and occupied by two garrisons, one in Annapolis, the seat of administration, and the other in Canso, the centre of fishing activities. A few English families and a few merchants from New England settled in the vicinity of these two posts. All civil and military authority resided in the person of the Governor. In 1714 Governor Nicholson appointed a council of captains, but this council ceased to exist before the year was out. On April 25, 1720 Philipps created a purely advisory council of ten members, all officers or civil administrators, since the anti-Catholic oath of office excluded any possible Acadian representation. However, in order that the French inhabitants might have some part, no matter how slight, in the administration of the country, Philipps invited them to choose a certain number of "deputies," who would act in their name, submit petitions to the authorities, and make known the Governor's decisions. The Acadians accordingly elected twenty-four representatives, and elections continued to be held each year on October 10. The deputies had no political function, but they acted as arbiters in cases of minor importance. Appeals from their decisions could be made to the Governor and his council. In 1730 an administrative decision required Acadians to pay their seigniorial rents, not to the former landlords, but to the English authorities.[3]

The native population showed itself considerably more refractory than the Acadians to the presence of the English. Small Indian settlements at Antigonish, Beaubassin, Minas, La Hève and Cape Sable counted in all some 759 inhabitants, of whom 253 were warriors. Using as intermediaries missionaries and governors of Canada and Ile Royale, Versailles continued to send presents each year to these Indians, and to urge upon them the need to resist the English occupation. So successful was this policy that the Indians did not hesitate to demonstrate their hatred in overt acts of hostility. Indeed, one reason alleged by the Acadians for refusing to swear allegiance was that, by taking the oath, they would expose themselves to the risk of being attacked and slain in their houses. Threats to this effect were, they asserted, daily occurrences, and it was true that in 1734

Indians swore vengeance against any Acadian who did any building for the English.[4]

The missionaries and the priests who served the French population were in Acadia by virtue of the guarantee given in the treaty and renewed by Philipps in 1727.[5] They were paid by France, and, while they were advised to act discreetly and not to arouse English suspicions, they were also directed to keep their flock faithful to the mother country. Failure to achieve this latter object would evoke royal "displeasure." It was not until later, when all hope of attracting the Acadians to French territory had been abandoned, that priests were instructed not to interfere in any way in matters concerning government or temporal affairs.[6]

In the early years, the presence of French priests undoubtedly created political complications and serious problems for the English authorities. While the conduct of certain missionaries, such as Father Félix Pain and Father Justinien Durand, was above reproach, the "excessive zeal" of others was censured by governors well aware of their subversive activities. In 1718 Caulfield complained that missionaries were fomenting trouble among the Indians, and in 1720 Philipps expressed the opinion that the Acadians would continue to be intractable as long as the priests then in the country remained in office. The authorities had, then, some reason to be anxious and suspicious, and it is hardly surprising that they kept an annoyingly close watch on the clergy, nor that, in spite of an increasing population, they refused to admit a correspondingly larger number of priests.[7] Another article of the treaty had, however, been modified in the Acadians' favour when, on June 23, 1713, Queen Anne again declared that they could choose freely either to become British subjects and enjoy the rights pertaining to such status, or to leave the country. The letter differed from the treaty in setting no time limit for their departure.[8] The colony had about three or four thousand inhabitants grouped, for the most part, at Port Royal, Beaubassin, Minas and Chepody.[9] The farmers, who made up almost the entire population, were deeply attached to the land. They had some five thousand head of cattle, sheep and pigs, and these, with the products of the land, the orchard and the poultry run, supplied most of their needs. They had river and sea fish in abundance, while the forests provided wood for building. Like most of their contemporaries they were generally illiterate, and they observed and maintained the legal customs, the religious prescriptions, and even some of the superstitions, which had been brought from France. Guided by the counsel and judgement of their priests and of a few leaders who had the advantage of a little learning, they remained unshaken in loyalty to their faith and to the mother country.[10]

With the change in sovereignty, the people of Acadia were faced with the difficult choice between going into exile in order to remain French subjects, and accepting British allegiance in order to remain in their own country and to preserve their heritage. In September 1713 they declared that they would not swear an oath which contravened their duty to the King of France and their religion. Rather would they abandon their possessions and emigrate to Ile Royale. Some of their number went to the island to look over the land which was offered to them, Versailles promised them free provisions for a year, and the colonists began to build boats[11] and asked the mother country to send them rigging and larger vessels.[12]

The exodus appeared imminent. On August 13, 1714 three hundred heads of families appeared before an officer from Louisbourg, Denys de la Ronde, and agreed to go to Ile Royale. But Nicholson, who was now Governor, issued orders that they were not to leave,[13] and Vetch declared to the Lords of Trade that Nova Scotia would be ruined if the Acadians emigrated, since the country needed their labour and the produce which they supplied. Nicholson's deputy, Lieutenant-Governor Caulfield, added a further argument: the Acadians provided protection against Indian raids.[14] The concurrent opinions of such competent observers led the English to adopt a policy of opposition to emigration, but, for the time being, they did not press the matter of the oath of allegiance.[15] In January 1715, after the accession of George I, Caulfield once more called upon the colonists to fulfil this obligation. They objected that they could not take the oath since they were pledged to emigrate; whereupon the Lieutenant-Governor asked for further instructions from London. Meanwhile, at the request of the Acadians, a frigate was dispatched from Louisbourg with orders to proceed to Annapolis, and to take on board "those who presented themselves." But it encountered such bad weather that it put back into harbour.[16]

For two years the situation remained stationary. Then, in August 1717, Richard Philipps was appointed Governor, and John Doucette Lieutenant-Governor, of Nova Scotia, whose English population was still limited to the two garrisons and a few families in the vicinity of the garrison posts. In November Doucette ordered the Acadians to take the oath of allegiance. They replied that they were "ready" to swear that they would take up arms "neither against His Britannic Majesty nor against France." This was their first proposal of an oath which would leave them free to maintain a strict military neutrality. Their stubborn attitude was duly reported in London, but, since the English population in the colony was still very small, the Governor was instructed not to attempt to punish the Acadians for their disloyal conduct.[17]

The Acadians themselves still saw no clear solution to their problem. In order to be able to live once more in a French and Catholic country, they were ready to give up their farms and their homeland, but they were not convinced that Ile Royale had enough good farming country to support their families and their stock, and they did not want to "expose themselves to the risk of dying of hunger." Some people from Minas had come back from the island after refusing an offer of two paltry *arpents* of land, and stories were told of settlers at Port Toulouse who were living in conditions of dire poverty.[18] In France the lack of enthusiasm for emigration was interpreted, quite unjustly, as apathy. The clergy was threatened with royal "displeasure" if this state of affairs was allowed to continue. Then an alternative was offered: it was suggested that colonists migrate to Ile St. Jean, which was nearer than Ile Royale and had an abundance of fertile soil. Unfortuately, this solution also proved unworkable. The local authorities, in the person of the Governor, vetoed the Acadians' requests for permission to leave the country. At the same time Fleury, stubbornly faithful to his peace policy, refused to ruffle the Anglo-French entente by intervening in their favour in London.[19]

Finally the English authorities, having concluded apparently that this period of indecision had lasted long enough, decided to take action. Accordingly, they appointed as Governor a man of influence and authority who was at the same time capable of understanding and diplomacy. On April 19, 1720 Richard Philipps issued a proclamation announcing to the Acadians that the King required them to take the oath of allegiance within four months. Those taking the oath would enjoy all the rights of British subjects and the free exercise of their religion. By an order which violated the promise given by Queen Anne, those who chose to leave the country were forbidden either to sell their property or to take any of it with them.[20]

In May the Acadians replied that they could not subscribe to any oath except an oath of neutrality exempting them "from bearing arms against anyone." They also demanded a longer period in which to effect their removal to "the territory of the King of France," and the right to dispose of their property, "as had been done at the evacuation of Placentia." At the same time they reported their position to the Governor of Ile Royale, M. de Saint-Ovide, who pointed out to Philipps that the terms of his proclamation violated both the terms of the Treaty of Utrecht and those of Queen Anne's warrant. A report was also sent to Versailles. It elicited a doubly unsatisfactory answer: on the one hand the English habitually managed to evade their obligations; and on the other the Acadians could not be exempted from taking the oath of allegiance, always providing, however, that they remained free to practise their religion.[21] In spite of Versailles' failure to support their cause, the stubborn Acadians succeeded in maintaining their resistance. They refused to take the unqualified oath, and the Governor, knowing that their departure would strengthen Ile Royale and make it very difficult to provision the English garrisons, did not dare to force them to withdraw from their position. Not only did he agree to postpone the time limit for their departure, but, faced with their categorical refusal to "take up arms against the King of France," he proposed that they be allowed to take an oath binding them "to give no help of any kind to the enemies of His Majesty," that is, in effect, an oath recognizing their right to remain neutral. To this the Lords of Trade in London replied that there was no hope of making the Acadians "good subjects of His Majesty whilst the French Governors and their Priests retain so great an influence over them; for which reason we are of the opinion that they ought to be removed so soon as the forces which we have proposed to be sent to you shall arrive in Nova Scotia for the protection and better settlement of your province; but as you are not to attempt their removal without His Majesty's positive orders for that purpose, you will do well in the meanwhile to continue the same prudent and cautious conduct towards them. . . ."

This letter shows that England had first conceived the idea of deportation thirty-five years before the event actually took place. For the moment, maintaining a policy of skilful and soothing palliatives, Philipps exacted nothing from the Acadians and gave them no promises.[22]

Philipps' term of office ended in 1722, and the question of the oath was again brought up by his successor, Lawrence Armstrong, a man of uncertain temper, harsh or brutal according to his mood. Knowing that the Acadians, encouraged by their priests, proposed to migrate to Ile St. Jean rather than take the oath, he summoned the inhabitants of Annapolis to a meeting on September 26, 1726 and once more offered them the rights of British subjects, with freedom of religion, if they would swear allegiance. When, once again, they refused to accept the text of any oath which did not contain a clause exempting them from "bearing arms," he had the clause added in the margin of the French text. He did not, however, insert it in the original which he sent to London.[23]

Having achieved his object by these unscrupulous means, Armstrong sent Ensign Robert Wroth to Minas in October 1727 to administer the oath of allegiance to the inhabitants. When they refused to accept any formula which did not specifically exempt them from military service, Wroth, acting "in the name of the King," granted to those who signed the oath freedom from the obligation to bear arms, as well as the right to sell their property if they chose to leave the country.[24]

When these concessions were reported in London, the Lords of Trade expressed deep displeasure. In September 1728 Philipps, who had been appointed Governor for a second time, was instructed to require all Acadians to take the oath in its unmodified form. At the same time France recognized England's right to exact obedience in this matter.[25] In November 1729 Philipps arrived in Annapolis; in January 1730 he reported that he had administered the unqualified oath to all the inhabitants of the town, and in September he made the same report for the whole population of the country along the Bay of Fundy. In making these statements Philipps was telling the truth, but not the whole truth. He omitted to say that if the Acadians, for the first time, accepted the unqualified formula, it was because, in his official capacity as the King's representative, he had declared to the inhabitants of Minas and the neighbouring valleys that he exempted them from bearing arms and from making war against either the French or the Indians.[26]

Thus, on three different occasions, by Armstrong, Wroth and Philipps respectively, the Acadians were granted the right to remain neutral in case of armed conflict between France and England. These engagements had not always been obtained by strictly honourable or honest means, but they were official. The question of the oath, disposed of for the time being, remained dormant for a period of twenty years. It did not arise again until 1749, when the English began to colonize the country.

Chapter Six

ILE ROYALE, HUDSON BAY AND NEWFOUNDLAND
1713-1763

~~~~~~

Ile Royale: resources; the capital, Louisbourg; eco-
nomic development; administration; industry, fishing
and commerce. English intrusion. Social life in Louis-
bourg. Mutiny. The English on Hudson Bay. Com-
merce and exploration. The English in Newfound-
land; settlement, fisheries, commerce. French attacks.
Treaty of Paris.

~~~~~~

Even before the conclusion of the Treaty of Utrecht, France
foresaw that she would be obliged to cede the two outposts,
Acadia and Newfoundland, which protected Canada's flank.
Since she did not want to "abandon the rest of North America"
to England, she made plans to colonize and fortify Cape Breton
Island.[1]

The younger Raudot's reports had pointed out the advantages offered by this island, eighty leagues in circumference and
separated from the continent by the narrow Strait of Canso. Advancing like a bastion into the North Atlantic, it could threaten
communication between England and her colonies, while at the
same time it guarded the gates of Canada against English fleets.
With its rocky soil and foggy climate, it was of little agricultural
value, but, on the other hand, it had fine forests of spruce and
birch and an abundance of soft coal. Moreover, it would be an
excellent base for the fishing industry, since its coastal waters
teemed with cod of a very high quality. An establishment on
Cape Breton Island would be a guardian outpost for Canada; it
would also make France mistress of the North Atlantic fisheries,

provide her with shelter for her ships and serve as a base for trade between Quebec, the mother country and the West Indies.[2]

As soon as the Treaty of Utrecht was signed, a start was made on the execution of the project. Priests in Acadia were instructed to urge their parishioners to migrate to the new colony. On September 2, 1713 Saint-Ovide de Brouillan took possession in the King's name of the island which was to be known henceforth as Ile Royale. He found one Frenchman and thirty Indian families on the island, and he brought with him one hundred men: officers, soldiers, administrators and servants, as well as ten women and twenty-three children. Two thirds of these colonists had been evacuated from Placentia. After establishing them at le Havre-à-l'Anglais, Saint-Ovide sailed away to make his report to the Minister in Versailles.[3]

The choice of le Havre-à-l'Anglais as the colony's principal establishment received royal approval, and the new town was christened Louisbourg. The site was approved, however, only after some hesitation. The harbour was "fine, safe and big," but, surrounded as it was with low, marshy or stony ground with little forest cover, it would be difficult to fortify and to defend. On the other hand, and this point was essential, its situation was excellent for fishing and commerce. It was for this reason that it was finally chosen, rather than the fine harbour of Saint Anne's Bay, now renamed Port Dauphin, farther north on the east coast. The shores of Saint Anne's Bay offered fertile soil and thick forest, but the bay itself was considered to be too far from the fishing banks.[4]

On January 1, 1714 M. de Costebelle, the former governor of Placentia, was appointed Governor of Ile Royale, and in April a *commissaire-ordonnateur* was chosen to assist him. This civil administrator, M. de Soubras, was subordinate to the Intendant of Canada.[5] An English force under Colonel Moody was to take possession of Placentia in 1714, and Costebelle, who had received orders to transport the inhabitants to Cape Breton, spent the summer of 1714 organizing their migration. According to the census of 1711, Placentia had a population of 225. Most of this number went to Cape Breton, although not all went to Louisbourg. The excellent quality of the land about Port Dauphin and the ease with which the harbour could be defended had led Versailles to select this site, for the time being at least, as the Governor's residence. Orders were also given for the establishment of a post at Port Toulouse on the south coast, near the Strait of Canso.[6]

By 1715 the colony of Ile Royale was beginning to take shape. The majority of its civilian population of some 700 had come from France or from Placentia; with the garrison of 250 or 300 soldiers, they made a total of about 1,000. Most of the men were fishermen, from Newfoundland or France or from the Basque country. The native Micmacs, of whom there were about one hundred, lived by hunting and fishing. The diet of the French fishermen consisted almost entirely of cod and mackerel. The officers of the garrison fared better, since cattle, sheep and chickens were imported from France, and there was enough fertile soil to provide wheat and a few vegetables: beans, cabbage, celery and lettuce. Strawberries, raspberries and blueberries grew wild, and partridge and deer were native to the island. Wine was imported from France, although the colonists more often drank a sort of local beer made with yeast, spruce cones and molasses. It was a healthy and refreshing drink, although not particularly pleasant to the taste.[7]

In spite of early difficulties, the colony soon took root and began to grow. It was true that French apathy, English opposition and reports of the infertility of the soil all combined to discourage the hoped-for Acadian immigration. But the rich cod banks attracted fishermen, and fishing soon became the mainstay of the island's economy, while the woods of the interior provided small quantities of beaver, marten and fox for the fur trade. As early as 1714, the irrepressible New England merchants were sending ships to Cape Breton, where they were soon joined by trading vessels from Breton, Basque and Mediterranean ports.

In 1716 Versailles initiated a vigorous programme of settlement. Workmen were recruited, shipyards were established and the Governor and the Intendant granted holdings to tenants.[8] The following year, reversing an earlier decision, the King agreed to grant seigniories on condition that the seigneurs bring in settlers. The Sieur de la Boularderie became seigneur of the island which still bears his name, while Ile Madame was granted to Ruette d'Auteuil and Ile St. Jean to the Comte de Saint-Pierre.[9]

As the population increased, the King provided the island with the colonial administration typical of the period. He created bailiff's courts at Louisbourg, Port Dauphin and Port Toulouse. He instituted a Superior or Sovereign Council composed of the Governor and the Intendant of New France, neither of whom was ever present at meetings, the Governor and the *Commissaire-ordonnateur* of Ile Royale, the King's Lieutenant, three councillors, an attorney-general and a clerk. This Council was to dispense free justice, giving final judgment in all Crown cases, and in appeals from judgments handed down by any of the bailiff's courts. Officially the colony was under the jurisdiction of the Canadian authorities. In fact, it was quite independent of the senior colony; the Governor and the *Commissaire-ordonnateur* received their orders directly from Versailles.[10]

In the autumn of 1717 Costebelle died, and the appointment of Saint-Ovide as Governor, in July 1718, was a very popular one. After much hesitation, Versailles finally confirmed the decision to make Louisbourg the capital, and in 1719 a medal was struck to mark the event.[11] The year 1719 also saw the beginning of a period of expansion for the colony. Versailles provided sums amounting to 124,071 *livres* in provisions, merchandise and munitions, without counting expenditures for fortifications. Most of the grand total, which may be estimated at 150,000 *livres* benefited the workmen and the merchants, since foreign trade was prohibited and officers of the Crown could not engage in commerce. Three occupations were open to the people of the colony; fur-trading, coal-mining and fishing. However, the number of fur-bearing animals was small and the people of France did not like Cape Breton's soft coal. Hence, fishing was by far the most important of these three industries. In 1719 the fisheries produced 156,526 quintals of fish and 2,236 barrels of oil, representing a total value of three million *livres*. The quantities of fish and oil varied from year to year, but without any noticeable decrease in their monetary value.[12]

News of the rich fisheries spread fast, and French fishermen flocked to the island once the foundation of Louisbourg had assured them of a safe haven and provided facilities for curing and disposing of their catch. Trading vessels brought essential manufactured goods from France such as clothes, blankets, shoes, hardware, salt, woven materials, nets, groceries and wine. Canada provided meat, cereals, vegetables and wood. From the French West Indies came sugar, molasses, rum, coffee, cotton and tobacco. Even Acadia sent grain, poultry and cattle. Such an affluence and variety of products resulted in a constantly increasing volume of sales and exchange. Louisbourg became an active and prosperous pivot of a trade triangle involving the West Indies, France and Canada. The volume of trade increased so rapidly that the number of ships docking in Louisbourg rose from 31 in 1717 to 97 in 1723, of which 77 came from France and 20 from Canada and the West Indies. Among 118 vessels entering the harbour in 1726 were some from New England; these brought cargoes of grain, fruit and other foodstuffs and axes. In 1723, in order to stimulate commerce, the King abolished the licence fees for fishing boats and duties on cod imported into France. In 1727 the duty on coal was also abrogated.[13] The increase in population resulting from prosperous trade was stimulated in other ways. Seigneurs were pledged to settle their holdings. The King recruited workmen for the colony and released soldiers so that they might establish themselves on the land. He reserved shore leases for immigrants with families or for men about to be married and he provided thirty brides for artisans. From 1700 to 1715 the population rose to 2,870 in 1723, exclusive of six companies of soldiers numbering about 360 men.[14]

One natural consequence of the growth of Louisbourg was that it presented an obstacle to the activities of the New England poachers on French fishing grounds. On September 18, 1717 Captain Smart, under orders from Massachusetts, seized two French boats at Canso, and declared that they had been captured in English waters. George II ordered that the boats be restored, but the order was not carried out.[15] In reprisal, a Franco-Indian band attacked the English post on August 8, 1720, and killed two men. The attackers also seized 18,000 *livres* worth of personal effects and merchandise, for which France later promised compensation.[16] At this point the matter was referred to the commission which had been provided for in the Treaty of Utrecht to negotiate disputed frontiers, and which was in session in Paris. However, when the British envoys discovered that their own maps placed Canso Island on the French side of the line, they withdrew and did not reapppear.[17]

During the years that followed, the colony continued to prosper. In 1740 the value of her fisheries was 3,061,465 *livres,* while the overall figure for her trade was 2,536,868 *livres,* of which 1,277,881 represented imports and 1,258,987 exports. Thus the excess of the value of imports over that of exports was only 18,894 *livres.*[18]

The trade volume of Ile Royale, with a population of 4,000, was two-thirds that of Canada, with a population ten times as large.[19] To complete the picture, it should be noted that army officers and state officials, as well as ordinary civilians, engaged in the contraband trade which flourished along the coasts of the island.[20] In 1737 Versailles' budget for the colony was increased to 216,012 *livres* of which 128,900 *livres* would be required for Louisbourg's fortifications. This sum gives some indication of the military strength of the forts, which between 1714 and 1742 absorbed the enormous total of 3,000,000 *livres.*[21]

In 1740 two new administrators assumed direction of the colony. The *Commissaire-ordonnateur,* François Bigot, who had been appointed in April of the previous year, belonged to a recently ennobled family with some influence in Versailles. Ambitious for wealth, he was soon to use his office, as well as his intelligence and his native energy, for the benefit of his private commercial enterprises. Du Quesnel, appointed Governor in September 1740, was a naval officer. Lacking both in diplomatic flexibility of mind and in firmness, he was considered "capricious, changeable" and surly.[22]

The population of Louisbourg increased from 1,400 in 1737 to 2,900 in 1750. It was a surprisingly large capital for a small colony set in primitive country, and it enjoyed a surprisingly lively and pleasant social life. An imposing wall, with bastions and carved gates, enclosed the stone and wooden houses. The towers of the Governor's residence and the hospital stood out prominently, as did the Récollet monastery and the convent of the Sisters of the Congregation. Army officers and government officials often married daughters of rich business men, and their little society had an animation all its own. The town boasted a dancing master, as well as dressmakers; and the ladies gave balls, card parties and outings on the ramparts, while the men could

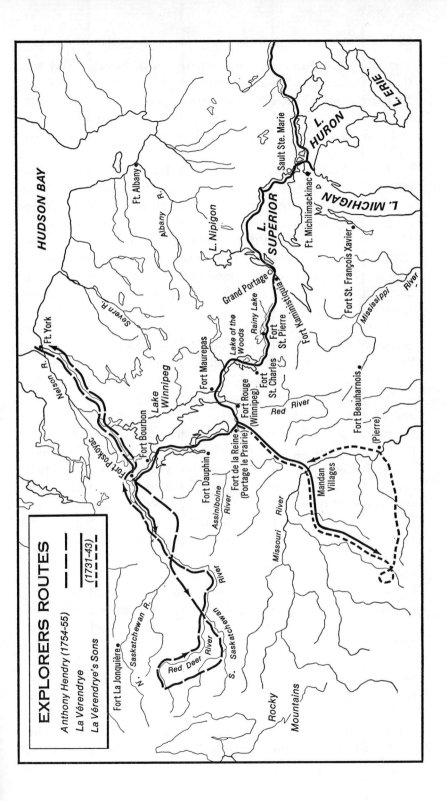

EXPLORERS ROUTES

Anthony Hendry (1754-55) — · — · —
La Vérendrye ——————
La Vérendrye's Sons (1731-43) - - - - -

HUDSON BAY

Ft. York
Nelson R.
Severn R.
Ft. Albany
Albany R.
L. Nipigon
Sault Ste. Marie
L. HURON
L. ERIE
L. MICHIGAN
Ft. Michilimackinac
L. SUPERIOR
Grand Portage
Rainy Lake
Lake of the Woods
Fort St. Pierre
Fort Kaministiquia
Ft. St. François Xavier
Mississippi River
Fort Maurepas
Lake Winnipeg
Fort Bourbon
Fort Poskoyac
Fort Rouge (Winnipeg)
Fort St. Charles
Red River
Fort Beauharnois
(Pierre)
Fort Dauphin
Fort de la Reine (Portage le Prairie)
Assiniboine River
Missouri River
Mandan Villages
Fort La Jonquière
N. Saskatchewan R.
Saskatchewan R.
Red Deer River
River
S. Saskatchewan R.
Rocky Mountains

also enjoy the purely masculine pastimes of hunting and billiards. There were, besides, public festivities from time to time. Each royal birth, each French victory, was celebrated with a solemn *Te Deum*, and after the religious ceremony the Governor and the officers were hosts at dinners which were followed by balls.[23]

Life in Louisbourg had, however, its less happy aspects. Army officers, disobeying standing instructions, engaged in business and even in contraband trade. How could they be expected to do otherwise when the example was set by Governor Saint-Ovide and Captain Du Vivier, and when Bigot, whose function should have precluded him from any such activity, was associated in every variety of business enterprise? With officers whose first concern was their own private interest, and who were sometimes even guilty of diverting a part of their troopers' pay into their own pockets, discipline could not fail to deteriorate. The garrison had on its roster some dubious characters and some real "scoundrels," and the Swiss Protestants of the Karrer regiment constituted another potential source of trouble. Moreover, the soldiers lived in conditions which were not conducive to order and discipline. The officers, who made a profit from the regimental canteens, did not make any serious effort to discourage drunkenness among their men. The Governor's capricious outbursts further undermined the officers' authority. The men complained of the verminous condition of the barracks. The seething ferment of discontent and insubordination finally resulted in an explosion. On December 27, 1744, at the instigation of the Swiss companies, the troops mutinied, presented themselves before the Governor "with bayonets fixed" and demanded better conditions of service. They then looted stores in the town. Order was restored after Du Quesnel had promised redress for the most flagrant abuses, but the officers were left wondering how such troops would conduct themselves in the presence of the enemy.[24]

Although the Treaty of Utrecht had established England's ownership of Hudson Bay and Strait, the task of fixing the limits of English territory surrounding the Bay was left to be settled by a commission made up of representatives of the two countries concerned. Basing their claim on the clause in the Treaty which ceded the Bay with the streams, shores, rivers and

"Places situate in the said Bay and straits and which belong there unto," the English claimed that the frontier should follow the height of land, and that the sources of all rivers draining into the Bay should lie within it. The French, on the other hand, claimed that the line should run from Cape Chidley to a point one league north of Lake Mistassini, and thence in a westerly direction to a point eight leagues north of Lake Superior and the sources of the Mississippi.[25] When, in the autumn of 1714, Nicolas Jérémie withdrew from Fort Bourbon (York) on the Nelson River, this post, the most important fur centre on the Bay proper, passed into the hands of the Hudson's Bay Company, which already had posts, Albany and Moose River, on James Bay. Thus the Company enjoyed a monopoly of the fur trade in the Hudson Bay country, a monopoly which it exploited by very simple means and at great profit to itself. Its ships left England in the spring, laden with merchandise which was exchanged at the various posts for furs. The ships sailed back to England in the autumn with cargoes of furs which were later sold in England, Holland and Russia.[26]

Since this competition threatened to cut off the fur supply from the far West, the Canadian policy was to try to divert the Indians of the region from the English posts on the Bay. About 1715 Canadian agents began to work on the rivers running towards Albany and Moose River, while others established themselves on Lake Nipigon. After 1731 La Vérendrye built a chain of posts designed to intercept Indian traffic on its way to York. In 1745 and 1747, during the War of the Austrian Succession, France and Canada conceived, but did not execute, the much more ambitious design of attacking the English establishments on the Bay. In this struggle for the western fur trade, the French were handicapped by the cost of transport between Montreal and Lake Winnipeg, but they had the advantage of friendly relations between their *voyageurs* and the Indians. On the other hand, the English company's costs were much lower and they had a much bigger European market.[27]

Anxious to exploit its advantages to the full, the Hudson's Bay Company again turned its attention to exploration, a field in which it had been inactive for more than twenty years. In 1689 Henry Kelsey, a young agent in the Company's employ, had explored the country south-west of Churchill in search of

unknown tribes and new fur sources. In six weeks he had travelled two hundred miles. He was the first white man to describe
the musk-ox, and he was also the first white man to penetrate
west of Lake Winnipeg. During his second journey, which
lasted two years, from 1690 to 1692, he entered into relations
with the Crees and the Assiniboines. However, the Company
now had abundant sources of furs, and after Kelsey's return to
Fort York it did not encourage further exploration.[28]

In July 1717 the Company sent out its second explorer.
Setting out from Churchill in a south-westerly direction, Richard Norton encountered the Plains Chipewas, some of whom
returned with him to trade at York. In 1721 he travelled north-
west and brought back Indians of the Northern and Copper
tribes.[29] Thirty-three years later, Anthony Hendry undertook a
much more extensive and daring journey. In June 1754 he set
out from Fort York, accompanied only by his Indian canoemen.
He paddled up the Hayes River to Lake Knee, and from there,
setting his course due west, continued to the Minago River
which he followed to Moose Lake. Twenty-five miles farther on,
he visited the French fort of Poskoyac (Le Pas), on the Poskoyac River. He paddled six miles up the Saskatchewan to the
Carrot River; then, travelling overland, he reached the South
Saskatchewan which he crossed north of Saskatoon. Three days
later he discovered the North Saskatchewan, probably near
Elbow between Prince Albert and North Battleford. After following the shore of the river for some time, he struck off to the
south-west. A journey of many days brought him to the Red
Deer River and the Blackfoot country, where he spent the
winter. In the spring he explored north to Lacombe, whence he
followed the Red Deer south to its confluence with the South
Saskatchewan. He then journeyed down the South branch as far
as the forks, a little east of Prince Albert, and into the main
river. A few days later he was back in familiar country. Retrac-
ing his steps over the route which he had followed on the outward journey, he arrived at Fort York on June 20, 1755. This
remarkable journey of twelve months had taken him farther
west than any previous explorer had ventured, to a point between Red Deer and Lacombe.[30]

In 1737 the Company, convinced by the arguments of Arthur Dobbs, sent two ships, the *Churchill* and the *Musquash,* to

search for the North-West Passage, and in 1742 a second expedition, under Captain Christopher Middleton, who left the service of the Company to direct it, was sent out by the Admiralty. The expeditions reached the sixty-sixth degree, north latitude, but achieved no useful results. After these ventures the Company made little effort to explore new country. Instead, it devoted its resources to developing still further the activities of its prosperous trading posts.[31]

The Treaty of Utrecht had also ceded to Britain the whole island of Newfoundland, thereby wiping out the French colony of Placentia, whose population was transported to Ile Royale. At that date, the English population of Newfoundland was less than two thousand. Justice was administered by the "admiral of the fishing fleet," but appeals could be made to the captain of the official convoy for the year, who received the title of Governor in 1728. The number of settlers on the island increased very slowly, chiefly with the arrival of Irish immigrants driven out of their country by a series of famines. In 1741 the colony had about six thousand inhabitants, of whom eight hundred lived in St. John's. Its only resources were cod fishing and whale and seal hunting. St. John's also became an active commercial port, where New England vessels discharged food supplies, wines and liquors and took on cargoes of merchandise which had come from England in the fishing boats.[32]

During the War of the Austrian Succession, a French ship under Captain Du Vivier appeared outside Placentia, but it was driven away by a storm, and the projected invasion did not take place. During the Seven Years' War, however, the colony did not fare so well. On June 24, 1762 a fleet of four vessels commanded by the Chevalier de Ternay landed 700 soldiers at Bay Bulls. After seizing the town without striking a blow, the force, under the Comte d'Aussonville, marched on St. John's whose garrison of 45 soldiers and 125 sailors also surrendered. This rapid conquest delighted Louis XV, but his joy was shortlived. As soon as news of the fall of St. John's reached Halifax Lord Colville sent five ships with 6,000 men under Colonel Amherst to recapture the town. The French ships, whose commanders realized that this force was much too strong to be resisted, seized the opportunity to slip out of the harbour through the fog, abandoning the garrison which surrendered on September 18.[33]

Five months later (February 10, 1763) France and England signed the Treaty of Paris, which confirmed English possession of the whole island and ended a territorial rivalry which had lasted more than a century. French subjects retained their fishing rights, as well as drying rights on the shores of the island, from Bonavista on the east coast northward and down to Cape Riche on the west. The islands of St. Pierre and Miquelon were ceded to France, but with the condition that they should not be fortified.[34]

Chapter Seven

CAPTURE OF LOUISBOURG
D'ANVILLE'S EXPEDITION
1744-1746

War of the Austrian Succession. Du Vivier captures Canso. Siege of Port Royal. Vulnerable situation of Louisbourg. Expedition of Warren and Pepperell; siege of Louisbourg. Capture of the Vigilant. *Surrender of Louisbourg. Capture of Ile St. Jean. Counter-offensive commanded by d'Anville. Storms, scurvy, death of d'Anville. Failure of expedition. English offensive; Noble defeated at Grand-Pré.*

By a curious whim of history, the question of the Austrian succession brought to America the war which Beauharnois had been expecting for so many years. When the Emperor Charles VI died in 1740 leaving no male heir, the Kings of Prussia and Poland and the Elector of Bavaria contested the right of Maria Theresa to inherit her father's dominions. The following year, France formed a coalition with Spain and the three candidates for the succession, and in 1742 a French army, under the Comte de Belle-Isle, captured Prague. Thereupon, George II, in violation of Hanover's convention of neutrality, furnished subsidies to Maria Theresa. Although there had been no formal declaration of war between England and France, an English army joined the Austrian troops and defeated Noailles at Dettingen in March 1743. At the same time British squadrons were stopping and plundering French ships on the high seas. Cardinal Fleury maintained his obstinate opposition to any rupture of the peace right up to his death in January 1744, but when his influence had been removed Louis XV felt that he could no longer ignore Britain's provocative acts. Accordingly, France declared war on Great Britain on March 15, 1744.[1]

A letter from Versailles brought the news to Louisbourg on May 3, two months before it reached Boston. The dispatch recommended that privateers should be sent out to molest English commerce and to capture the English post at Canso. With all speed, Du Quesnel sent a fleet with a force of 374 men under the command of Du Vivier to Canso. News of the declaration of war had not yet reached the post and its commander, Patrick Heron, surrendered with his 120 men on May 24 (1744). The dilapidated wooden fort was burned and the prisoners were taken to Louisbourg, whence they were repatriated to Boston in September.[2]

In August Du Quesnel sent Du Vivier on a second mission, to invest Port Royal. His force of fifty men was duly disembarked and was joined by some two or three hundred Micmacs who had been recruited by the Abbé Le Loutre. As Du Vivier was preparing the ground for the assault which was to be launched after the arrival of promised reinforcements, Captain de Gannes appeared with a commission from the Governor and ordered him to return with his detachment to Louisbourg. On October 25, not long after these orders had been executed, three French ships, armed with sixty-five guns, arrived to carry out the part of the plan assigned to them, but, finding no land force to support them, they were obliged to return to Ile Royale.[3]

Du Quesnel had died suddenly on October 9, and as his successor, Le Moyne de Châteauguay, was detained in France by illness, Du Chambon assumed temporary authority. From the beginning of hostilities, French and British corsairs had been active on the American sea routes. Bigot had placed some of his capital in privateers, and English colonial commerce suffered severe losses at the hands of French ships based on Louisbourg. But the English had an even larger number of privateers sailing from Boston and Rhode Island ports, and these took a still heavier toll from Franco-Canadian trade and from French fisheries.[4]

In June, when the news of war reached Quebec by way of Louisbourg, Beauharnois set about the task of strengthening city walls and forts, and even building defence towers in the rural districts. He drew up the roster of the militia and alerted the Indian allies. Joncaire brought assurance from the Seneca village that, provided the French did not attack Oswego, the

Iroquois would remain neutral. Quebec sent flour, cattle and other food supplies to Louisbourg and in return asked for arms, since one third of the Canadian militia had no rifles.[5]

Early in the autumn, Beauharnois received a request from Du Quesnel for a detachment to take part in an offensive in Acadia. The force, which included one hundred Canadian volunteers, with eighty Abenakis, Algonquins and Hurons, left Quebec, under the command of Lieutenant Paul Marin, on January 26, 1745. In June, as it was camped before Annapolis, Marin received orders from Du Chambon to proceed to Louisbourg "in all haste."[6] For Louisbourg, the so-called "Gibraltar of America," had become the principal stake in the war; France meant to hold it, England was determined to capture it. The town, which was built on a tongue of land about half a league in circumference, was encircled by a wall with bastions armed with cannon, and protected by the crenellated fort of La Grave and the Royal Battery. A battery on the Ile de l'Entrée cut off access to the harbour. But the situation of Louisbourg, however excellent it might look on paper, was, in fact, quite precarious. Its fortifications were unfinished, and the provision of powder was insufficient for its 116 cannon. The capital's defence force consisted of eight companies of marines, some 560 men in all, and 800 militiamen. And it must not be forgotten that the marines were the men who had mutinied the previous December. What confidence could be placed in such troops?[7]

On the British side, the project of conquering Louisbourg had been germinating for several years. With the outbreak of war, it became the prime objective of the New England expansionists, and, more especially, the people of Boston. Their aim was two-fold: first they wanted to prevent the constant losses which corsairs from Louisbourg inflicted on Anglo-colonial shipping, and, in the second place, they were eager to seize the fortress which would make it possible for them to monopolize the fishing on the rich Acadian banks.[8]

The Governor of Massachusetts, William Shirley, a former lawyer and a man of boundless energy, immediately became the soul of the movement. In January (1745) he won the support of New Hampshire, Rhode Island and Connecticut for his scheme. Warren, who commanded the fleet guarding the coast, promised the powerful support of his warships. Galais, a renegade in the service of Boston, reported that the defences of Louisbourg were in bad shape, and that the soldiers were ripe for mutiny. Accordingly, as Shirley wanted to exploit the element of surprise, the expedition was organized with the greatest dispatch. It set sail from Boston on March 24, 1745 and three weeks later entered Gabarus Bay, two leagues west of Louisbourg. The fleet, commanded by Warren, numbered more than one hundred ships. A rich merchant, William Pepperell, commanded the land force of 4,400, whose well-paid volunteers had been promised freedom to pillage the town. There were also 4,000 marines and sailors on the warships and transports. Some 8,500 men, therefore, were assembled to lay siege to a town defended by 1,600 soldiers, militiamen and fishermen.[9]

On May 11 the first glimmer of daylight revealed enemy ships, with sails half-furled, off Flat Point, two miles from the walls of Louisbourg. On the orders of Governor Du Chambon, a detachment of 110 men was sent out under Captain Morpain to prevent the enemy's troops from landing, but the French soldiers were beaten back by a superior force. The next day, the besiegers took possession of the Royal Battery outside the walls and opened fire on the town. The guns of Louisbourg replied with a heavy cannonade.[10] On May 18 Du Chambon, called upon by Warren and Pepperell to surrender, replied that he would answer "through the mouths of his cannon."[11]

During the next few days the English militiamen occupied the surrounding country,[12] while Pepperell set up new batteries which pounded the town and destroyed a number of houses.[13] On May 28 a French ship was sighted. It was the *Vigilant,* a ship of war mounting sixty-four guns and carrying five hundred men, as well as much-needed ammunition and supplies. Unfortunately, her commander, M. de la Maisonfort, instead of entering the harbour immediately, went in pursuit of an English frigate.[14] Thereupon, three other enemy ships came into action, and after a hard-fought battle, the *Vigilant* was forced to surrender. For Louisbourg, it was a catastrophe.[15]

Elated by this success, Pepperell redoubled his cannonade. On June 15 a squadron of six warships arrived from England, and for two days, June 18 and 19, the land batteries poured red-hot balls into the town.[16] As roofs fell in and walls crumbled, women were evacuated from the ruined houses and sheltered in the casemates. The French guns were powerless against the heavy English artillery, and the demoralized inhabitants petitioned the Governor to capitulate. A council of war, held on June 26, agreed that the fortress could not withstand the assault which appeared imminent. Du Chambon immediately opened negotiations with Warren and Pepperell, and on the following day terms of surrender were agreed upon: the garrison would be granted the honours of war, the religion of the inhabitants would be respected, and they would be repatriated to France with their effects.[17]

Thus fell France's bastion in America. Its fortifications, which had cost 3,605,535 *livres,* had held out for forty-eight days. The New Englanders, whose casualties amounted to only 105 dead and 119 prisoners, had been called upon to display skill as tacticians rather than courage as fighters. Their victory was, nonetheless, a remarkable feat of arms for inexperienced militiamen, and full credit for it must be given to their prudent and skilful general, Pepperell.

The English left the French flag flying over the fort in Louisbourg. By means of this ruse they captured three French vessels whose cargoes, worth 600,000 pounds sterling, were handed over as prizes to Warren and his officers and men. In New England news of the capture of Louisbourg was hailed with pride and joy. The church bells of Boston rang out, and the "providential" victory was celebrated by journalists and clergy alike. In London, press and Parliament rejoiced, and the victory was announced to all the people by cannon salvos, illuminations and bonfires. Shirley received congratulations from the Prime Minister, Pepperell was created Baron, and Warren was appointed Governor of Ile Royale, with the rank of vice-admiral.[18]

In July the New England fleet seized Ile St. Jean, whose tiny garrison succeeded in escaping from its post at Port La Joie. As no transport was available for the six hundred Acadians living on the island, they were allowed to stay on their land on condition that they remain "neutral" and furnish any provisions which might be required of them.[19]

On the French side, Du Chambon and his troops had fought with more courage than skill, against a force four times greater than their own. Fifty men had died and 95 had been wounded, and their store of powder had been reduced to 47 barrels. Sold-

iers and inhabitants, to the number of 4,460, were transported
to France, but the terms of capitulation were violated in that
they were not permitted to take their effects with them.[20] When
news of the blockade of Louisbourg had reached Versailles,
Maurepas had dispatched a relief squadron under Périer de
Salvert. However, Salvert had learned in mid-ocean of the surrender and had returned to his home port without striking a
blow. Marin and his detachment had abandoned their Acadian
offensive in order to go to the help of Louisbourg, but they too
heard of the disaster while they were still on the way, and they
returned to Quebec.[21]

Soon after the capture of Louisbourg, Shirley began to dis-
cuss with the English authorities a project for the conquest of
Canada. According to the plan, an army from the mother country, under the command of General Saint-Clair, would be joined
by a colonial force of five thousand men. It would also have some
support from the Iroquois nations. But the expedition had to be
postponed for lack of available warships. Moreover, English
forces were needed at home to deal with the invading armies of
the Pretender Charles Edward. After the defeat of the Scottish
forces at Culloden (1746), the project was revived, but the
rumour of a French expedition to reconquer Louisbourg caused
a further postponement of the plan to invade Canada by the St.
Lawrence.[22]

To France, still rejoicing over the great victory of Fontenoy
(May 11, 1745), news of the fall of Louisbourg came as a great
blow. Although the disaster was the direct result of Maurepas'
temporizations and his blind optimism, he took no effective action to repair it, hoping, no doubt, that the captured fortress
would be restored at the end of the war. Meanwhile he ordered
that the leaders of the Louisbourg mutiny be brought to trial.
The net result of his zeal was that one sergeant was beheaded,
two soldiers were hanged and penalties were meted out to a few
others, a full year after the crimes had been committed.[23]

But public opinion, especially in military and commercial
circles, refused to accept passively the blow to France's trade
and prestige which the loss of Ile Royale represented, and Versailles, aware of this current of thought, decided to reconquer
the American bastion upon which the future existence of Canada
depended. The minister assembled a truly formidable armada;

eighteen ships of the Royal Navy and two fireships escorted thirty-four transports carrying three thousand men. The force, including troops and seamen, counted seven thousand men, and the ships were armed with eight hundred guns. The commander of the expedition, the Duc d'Anville, was an admiral of thirty-five years of age without experience in naval warfare. To him was entrusted the three-fold mission of reconquering Louisbourg, Acadia and Placentia.[24]

In the royal instructions to the admiral a clause directed that if, after capturing former Port Royal, there were any inhabitants "on whose fidelity he considered he could not count, he was to make them leave the colony and send them either to old England or to some one of the colonies of that nation."[25] This instruction should not be interpreted, as for some curious reason it sometimes has been, as a French project of deportation. It was merely a question of an essential police precaution, the expulsion from the country of a few harmful individuals, traitors who had gone over to the service of the enemy.

One of the senior naval officers accompanying d'Anville, the Marquis de La Jonquière, had been appointed Governor of Canada (March 15, 1746). Beauharnois, who was beginning to feel the weight of years, and who was also seeking promotion in the navy, had received permission to return to France on the arrival of his successor, but La Jonquière was not to rejoin his post until after the naval campaign.[26]

After a long delay in the harbour of the island of Aix, d'Anville's fleet finally got under way in June. On its long voyage across the ocean, it was beset and further delayed by misfortunes of every sort: head winds, flat calm, gales. Food ran short, and the water ration was cut to one glass per day. Dysentery and scurvy were rampant. Some of the ships turned back, two were disabled, one was destroyed by fire and one transport sank with all on board. Finally, on September 20 d'Anville's ship reached Chebucto Harbour (Halifax) where it was joined by the rest of the fleet before the end of the month. The voyage had lasted between eighty and one hundred days.[27]

Still further disasters were to follow. On September 27 the admiral died, broken by failure and adverse fortune. The troops, which had landed, were decimated by illness. The vice-admiral, d'Estournelles, assumed command, but, his mind unhinged by the hopelessness of the situation, he attempted suicide. That same day (October 1) La Jonquière took command of the expedition, and with resolute courage tried to restore the morale of his men and to implement the Minister's directive. After being reprovisioned with stores provided by loyal Acadians and Indians, the fleet set sail on October 24 for Port Royal. But, still dogged by misfortune, it encountered fog and gales. Fighting ships and transports became scattered, and La Jonquière, discouraged and finally convinced that "it was impossible to undertake any action," issued a general order to set a course for France. After a painful voyage, during which they were harried by enemy raiders, the ships straggled into their home ports in the course of November and December. The expedition had cost France 2 fighting ships, 21 transports, and 587 men.[28]

Previously, acting on instructions dispatched by the Minister in January, Beauharnois had sent a detachment of 700 men under Captain Roch de Ramezay to invest Annapolis in anticipation of the sea attack by the squadron from France. This force, which left Quebec on June 5, arrived on July 10 at Baie Verte where it disembarked to await the arrival of d'Anville. In September, on learning that the French fleet had arrived in Chebucto, Ramezay and his army proceeded to Annapolis. They held the town under siege until November 3 when a letter from La Jonquière brought the news that the expedition had been abandoned. The next day Ramezay raised the siege and on December 1 he established his troops in winter quarters at Beaubassin.[29]

As soon as the Canadian force withdrew from Annapolis, the English commander, Major Mascarene, made plans to drive it out of Acadia with the help of reinforcements sent by Shirley from Boston. Accordingly, in November, Colonel Arthur Noble assembled 500 men at Grand-Pré. In January when the news of this manœuvre reached Beaubassin, Ramezay organized a preventive expedition. Two hundred and thirty-six Canadians and 30 Micmacs under Antoine Coulon de Villiers left Beaubassin on January 18 and travelled 60 miles on snowshoes to reach Grand-Pré on February 11. At three o'clock in the morning "the chaplain gave the general absolution," and the troops rushed on the ten houses occupied by the enemy. Nine houses were captured forthwith, and Colonel Noble fell in the struggle. Only one house, built of stone, put up a brief resistance, after which its commander also agreed to surrender, on condition that his troops be granted the honours of war and that they be evacuated to Annapolis. The English casualties were 130 dead and 15 wounded, while only 7 French soldiers were killed and some 15 wounded. Villier's detachment then returned to Beaubassin, "the most convenient point" for keeping watch on the enemy's movements. They stayed there until June when, as provisions were running short, they were obliged to return to Quebec.

Chapter Eight

WAR OF THE AUSTRIAN SUCCESSION
1744-1752

Beauharnois on the defensive. Raids against English posts. Mohawk attacks. French expeditions. Indian plots in the West. Defeat of La Jonquière's relief fleet. La Galissonnière appointed Governor. Political importance of Canada. Defensive strategy. Treaty of Aix-la-Chapelle; restoration of Louisbourg. Céloron de Blainville in the West. Revival of Ile Royale: fishing, trade, fortifications.

While hostilities were concentrated at the strategic points of Louisbourg and Annapolis, Beauharnois turned his attention to Canada's defences and, after fortifying Quebec, strengthened the Lake Champlain frontier by building up Fort St. Frédéric. Then, since the Acadian expedition had reduced his stock of supplies, he was obliged to remain on the defensive. He succeeded, however, in keeping the Iroquois neutral and in winning the support of the western tribes.[1]

After the fall of Louisbourg, realizing that Canada was threatened with invasion, Beauharnois decided to adopt the policy of his predecessors, Frontenac and Vaudreuil, and to forestall English attacks with raids against their frontier settlements. On November 29 (1745) Lieutenant Paul Marin led a force of four hundred French and two hundred Micmacs and Abenakis against the village of Sarastau, fifteen leagues from Fort St. Frédéric. They burned all the houses and returned in December to Montreal with one hundred prisoners, men, women and children. A certain number of prisoners were bought from their Indian captors by civilians from Three Rivers.[2]

Throughout 1746, from March to December, raiding parties brought in prisoners from whom information could be obtained.

The parties, which were generally made up of Abenakis or of Ottawas and Mission Indians, and which sometimes included Canadians, made forays in the regions of Albany and Boston.[3] Other raids were organized by the French themselves. Thus in August (1746) Rigaud de Vaudreuil, at the head of four hundred militiamen and three hundred western Indians, advanced as far as the Connecticut River where he captured Fort Massachusetts and its garrison of twenty-two men. Then he ravaged and burned everything for fifteen leagues around: "granaries, mills, churches, tanneries, etc."[4] Fired with indignation at the scalpings and burnings, the colonists immediately wrote to Shirley denouncing this return to the old savage methods of Indian warfare and, more especially, the custom of paying a bounty on scalps.[5]

With the double purpose of defence and retaliation, they initiated preparations for an expedition against Fort St. Frédéric by offering a premium of thirty pounds to each recruit. They assembled three thousand men at Sarastau and established a camp thirty leagues from the fort.[6] But the Governor of New York refused to allow them to proceed with their plan of attack, since he feared that it might irritate the Lake Ontario Indians by exposing them to raids from the western allies of the French. In March (1746) the Iroquois reaffirmed their policy of neutrality, despite English efforts to enlist them as allies. In September the English colonists invited all five nations to a great council at Albany, but they won support only from their immediate neighbours the Mohawks, who were dependent on them for all their supplies, and who were, moreover, traditionally hostile to the French. In November a party of Mohawk warriors killed two carpenters in the Lake Champlain country and three farmers at Soulanges.[7] At the same time they burned two houses with their barns. After these overt acts of aggression, Beauharnois summoned the Indians from the Great Lakes to meet in council on March 17 in Montreal. There, to the customary accompaniment of pomp and ceremony, he declared war on the Mohawks and offered the hatchet to his allies from the West, who made lengthy speeches of acceptance. The Indians then formed a number of war parties to carry hostilities into New York and Connecticut.[8] Thus, after forty-five years of peace, Indian warfare had been resumed. At the Albany conference, deputies from all the Iroquois nations except the Mohawks had hurled insults at the envoys who proposed that they should renounce their neutrality and ally themselves with the English. But, although theirs was the only tribe which had declared itself hostile to the French, the Mohawks persuaded the Indians of Sault St. Louis not to fight, but to "let the whites clash with each other." Hence, when they marched against the Mohawks with French detachments, the Sault Indians gave three warning shots as they approached the enemy. When reprimanded by their French officers for such trickery, they promised "to do better" in future.[9] The Mohawks continued their forays in the regions of Fort St. Frédéric, Châteauguay, Soulanges, Chambly and Les Cèdres. For greater safety against such raids, a number of families along the Chambly River abandoned their farms and moved to the north bank of the river.[10]

Counter-measures were taken against the danger of raids; guard posts were established on the rivers, and war and scouting parties were organized in Montreal to be sent out as the need arose. In June bands of Mohawks were defeated on Ile Perrot and at Châteauguay, while Indians from the West and from the colony harried English frontier settlements with repeated forays from which they returned with numerous scalps and prisoners.[11]

In 1747 the French undertook several expeditions of greater military importance. In March a detachment under the Chevalier de Niverville burned 5 forts and 100 houses near Haverhill. The inhabitants had fled before the attack. In June Rigaud de Vaudreuil, with 780 Canadians and Indians, invaded English territory in the region of Fort St. Frédéric. Two hundred members of this force, under M. de Saint-Luc made a surprise attack on Fort Sarastau, inflicting on the enemy a loss of twenty-eight killed and forty-one prisoners. On July 9 Vaudreuil brought up all his troops, but, opposed as he was by a strong garrison and artillery, he abandoned the idea of capturing the fort and returned to Montreal.[12]

These repeated incursions into their territory roused the English colonists to fury. In August five thousand volunteers were encamped in Boston ready to invade Canada, and awaiting only the arrival of a fleet with regular troops from the mother country. New York was preparing to march against Fort St. Frédéric, the rallying point for French and Indian parties, and the bridgehead from which they spread death and ruin in the frontier settlements. But none of these projects of invasion was realized. After Fontenoy (1745) the Duke of Cumberland had suffered another defeat at Lawfeld in July 1747; England had to turn her attention to other matters and the invasion of Canada had to wait.[12a]

Meanwhile, although for the moment Canada was safe from English aggression, a threat to French prestige was posed in the West where two Englishmen succeeded in winning over Nicolas, the chief of the Hurons of Sandoské. With the Iroquois acting as couriers, belts were sent to various tribes who formed a plot to wipe out the French at Detroit. The plan was to have been carried out at Whitsuntide, but the commander, Longueuil, forewarned by a Huron woman, was able to gather most of the inhabitants into the fort. Several Frenchmen had already been attacked, however, when the *voyageurs* on their way down from the western explorers' posts reached Michilimakinac. Their presence and the arrival of 150 men in Detroit relieved the situation, paralysing the movements of the disaffected tribes and reassuring those whose allegiance was wavering. Soon envoys from the Miamis came to seek peace from Longueuil. On April 28, 1748 a great council was held at which Ottawas, Potawatomis and Saulteux swore "fidelity and obedience" to the commander. Later, in the course of the summer, the tribes in the region of Michilimackinac confirmed their attachment to France.[13]

France had not been dismayed by d'Anville's failure. On the contrary, encouraged by her victory at Raucoux and the capture of Madras, she decided to reinforce her Canadian colony. Early in 1747 a squadron of seven warships was assembled; it was to convoy six merchant vessels belonging to the West India Company, and twenty-six others, of which nineteen were bound for Canada and the rest for the West Indies. The fleet was under the command of La Jonquière who would take up his duties as Governor. London had received information on these preparations, and on May 14 the French fleet, which had left port four days earlier, encountered an English squadron of seventeen ships under Admirals Anson and Warren. The fleets went into action at Cape Ortegal about three o'clock in the afternoon, and, although opposed by a greatly superior force, La Jonquière fought valiantly until seven o'clock. Then, as the ships, with torn sails and battered rigging, could not hope to escape from the close-range pounding of the enemy's guns, they lowered their flags. The ships bound for Canada had managed to escape during the battle, but nine others were hunted down and captured.[14]

The news of La Jonquière's capture reached France in June. The Marquis de La Galissonnière was appointed as temporary governor and in September he arrived in Quebec to relieve Beauharnois. During his long period of twenty-one years in office, Beauharnois had served the country well, devoting all his intelligence and his solid wisdom to its present problems, but always conscious of its great future possibilities.[15]

La Galissonnière was fifty-four years old. He already knew Canada as, on three different occasions in the course of a distinguished career in the navy, he had spent some time in Quebec. He was "a small man, slightly deformed," with a pleasant manner. In his intelligent and dynamic person a remarkable philosophical and scientific knowledge was allied with high political concepts and vast projects for colonial expansion. His first act was to inform himself as to the state of affairs in New France and, having done this, he then made a report in which the King's councillors in Versailles were forcibly reminded of the prime importance of Canada. La Galissonnière agreed that the colony was a cause of expense to the mother country. But, he argued, if France shirked the responsibility of exploiting its possibilities and resources, she would lose its rich fisheries, its trading fleet, the sailors trained in its ships, a considerable and growing overseas trade and a whole population of valiant fighters. Other colonies, he continued, doubtless produced wealth more rapidly; but the prolific Canadian people produced men, the greatest wealth of all. He became indignant at the very thought of the "abandonment" which "threatened a colony so valuable and so full of loyal zeal."[16]

La Galissonnière immediately took steps to renew the treaty with the four Iroquois nations. He also maintained the system of war parties, although he admitted that "these quick forays irritate the enemy without weakening him." But, he added, "Attack is our strong point; it is our only means of ridding ourselves of fear here in the colony." In order to protect St. Frédéric, the most advanced and therefore the most seriously threatened of the forts, he opened a road between Montreal and St. Jean on the

Richelieu and built a palisaded fort at St. Jean itself. With these improvements, it would be possible to get help to Fort St. Frédéric in two days.[17]

Once again Canadian events were shaped by events in Europe. After Cumberland's defeat at Lawfeld by the Maréchal de Saxe, after the capture of Berg-op-Zoom (nicknamed the Virgin because it had never been taken) and the siege of Maestricht in 1747, England and Holland agreed to participate in peace parleys. In April 1748 they approved articles of a cease-fire agreement. This news reached Quebec at the beginning of August, and peace was finally signed at Aix-la-Chapelle on October 18.[18]

After her victories in Holland and in India, France could have obtained a favorable treaty. But, moved by a vainglorious desire to negotiate "like a prince and not like a merchant," Louis XV abandoned his conquests in Flanders and restored Madras to the English. He even agreed to expel the Pretender, Charles Edward, from France. All that he asked in return was that Ile Royale be restored to France, and that two English hostages guarantee the execution of this article. The treaty did not even fix Canada's frontiers in Acadia or on the Ohio. These were to be settled later by a commission representing the two powers. The terms of the treaty angered the people of France and gave rise to a new formula for expressing the acme of scorn: "As stupid as the peace."[19]

The English authorities did not even wait for the boundary commission to come into being; instead, they tried immediately to make good their longstanding territorial claims. In October 1748, before the peace terms were known, Mascarene sent Colonel Gorham to obtain a declaration of submission from the inhabitants of Beaubassin, and to exact an oath of allegiance from twenty or thirty Acadian families at St. John, although they were living in French territory. In 1749 La Galissonnière answered this provocation by sending Boishébert with a detachment to St. John to oppose by force of arms any English infiltration from Boston or Annapolis.[20]

In Virginia a company was formed for the colonization of the Ohio country, and in February 1749 London granted a tract of land to the company on condition that a fort be built for the protection of colonists. In making this grant, England was violat-

ing the Treaty of Aix-la-Chapelle and invading French territory.
At the same time the merchants of New York, Pennsylvania and
Virginia continued to trade in the region of the Great Lakes,
and even built posts in the Ohio valley. In order to halt this
illegal advance, the Governor of Canada sent out a detachment
composed of 230 regulars, militia and Indians, under the command of Céloron de Blainville.

Setting out from Lachine on June 15, 1749, Céloron visited
Forts Frontenac and Niagara, and then proceeded, by way of
Lake Erie, to Detroit. At various points along his route, he
buried lead plates bearing the arms of France. Then, having
accomplished his mission to reaffirm France's rights, he returned
to Montreal where he arrived on November 10. In the course of
his conversations with various tribes, he learned that they preferred to establish trade relations with English merchants, whose
goods were of better quality and cheaper than the corresponding
French articles.[21] Also in June 1749 La Galissonnière had undertaken the construction of a new fort, La Présentation
(Ogdensburg). It was situated half-way between Lakes St. Francis
and Ontario, in a strategic position for keeping watch over the
western territory and cutting off unauthorized trade. There was
also an Iroquois mission at the post under the direction of the
Sulpician François Piquet.[22]

On the Atlantic coast, France made all haste to re-establish
pre-war conditions. On July 12, 1749 a new governor, Captain
Charles des Herbiers of the Royal Navy, formally repossessed
Louisbourg. After a siege and three years of British rule, the
town was in lamentable condition; most of the houses were in a
state of dilapidation, as were the hospital and even the church,
which had served as barracks for the army of occupation. Fish
houses had been destroyed around Louisbourg, as well as at Port
Toulouse and the other outports. The energetic Governor and
the *Commissaire-ordonnateur,* Prévost, found some sort of lodging for the two thousand inhabitants who had come back with
them from France, as well as for the twelve hundred members of
the garrison, and the Acadians (about one hundred) who had
joined the colonists. For the first year, the authorities provided
food for the population, buying cattle from Acadia and corned
beef from Boston.[23]

Fishermen immediately began to build small boats for themselves, or to buy schooners from the English, and vessels from France soon joined the local fleet. In 1750 the fish were very abundant, and the following year 95,580 quintals of fish and 955 barrels of oil were marketed, with a total value of 2,026,200 *livres*.[24] Thirty-six ships arrived from France and 35 from the West Indies in 1752, but, as a result of the famine of 1751, only a few cargoes of flour and meat were sent from Canada.[25]

In spite of prohibitions from both mother countries, trade between the colonies grew and flourished. The New Englanders sold the foodstuffs without which the new French population could not have survived: fresh and salt meat, flour, vegetables and fruit. They also provided lumber and sailing vessels. In 1750 seventeen New England vessels dropped anchor in Louisbourg harbour. In exchange for their cargoes, the Anglo-Americans took tafia, molasses and wine.[26] In 1752 imports into the island reached a total value of some 2,354,022 *livres*, while the figure for exports in 1753 was 2,175,505 *livres*. France and the West Indies took the entire fish catch; New England bought products from the Antilles. These were Cape Breton's important customers; Canada with her small population accounted for only one twentieth of the export trade, buying tafia, tobacco and coffee.[27]

Ile Royale had already taken the first steps in a remarkable economic development, and her population was larger than before the war. In 1752, of a population of 5,845, 1,500 soldiers and 2,674 civilians were concentrated in Louisbourg, while 1,671 were scattered in the island's other small communities.[28]

When it was evident that the colony was well established, with every hope of future growth, the King allowed Des Herbiers to resume his service in the navy. His successor, the Comte de Raymond, was appointed on March 1, 1751 and arrived in Louisbourg at the beginning of August. General Raymond was the first army officer to occupy the post of Governor, which up to that time had been held by naval officers. The innovation did not appear to be a happy one. Raymond was not altogether lacking in positive qualities, but his zeal for activity outstripped his intelligence, and he was vain and tactless. In his desire to impose his authority, he very soon intruded on the functions of the *Commissaire-ordonnateur,* and the ensuing clash between the two highest officials resulted in complete paralysis in the colony's administration. Prévost was a disciple of Bigot, to whom he owed his appointment, and like Bigot he seized every opportunity to use public services for his own private interest. However, although he was the object of criticism and ridicule,[29] his good qualities compensated in some measure for his defects, and he remained in office until the end of the régime.[30]

The fortifications of Louisbourg had been practically ruined by the siege, and Versailles, realizing how important it was to maintain the strength of Canada's bastion, decided to rebuild them. Plans were drawn up by the engineer Franquet, and in 1752 work was begun. It advanced so slowly, however, that in 1758, when the threat of war had already been hanging over Louisbourg for two years, the fortifications were still incomplete.[31]

Chapter Nine
ANGLO-FRENCH RIVALRY IN THE OHIO VALLEY

~~~~~~

La Jonquière and Bigot in Quebec. Frontiers strength-
ened in Acadia and the West. The Governor's inter-
ests in the fur trade. Contraband trade carried on by
the Désauniers sisters at the Sault mission. Death of La
Jonquière. Strategy of Duquesne. Forts in the Ohio
valley. English counter-measures. Washington's attack
on Jumonville. Surrender of Fort Necessity. Resigna-
tion of Duquesne.

~~~~~~

In 1749 France's colonial administration passed into new hands.
Maurepas, whose satiric temper had evoked the displeasure of
Madame de Pompadour, had shown little persistence in carrying out the ideas which he conceived. His successor, Rouillé,
devoted all the resources of a less brilliant but more disciplined
intelligence to the duties of his office.

La Jonquière had been liberated by the Treaty of Aix-la-
Chapelle. In August 1749 he finally rejoined his post and was
received in Quebec with the ceremony befitting his office. As his
boat approached the landing stage, guns boomed and church
bells rang out while the crowds on the wharf shouted their wel-
come. Tall and stiff in red coat and gold braid, preceded by his
servants dressed in green livery and carrying rifles, the new governor presented an imposing figure as he stepped ashore to be
greeted by La Galissonnière and Mgr. de Pontbriand. La Jonquière had won a reputation for courage amounting almost to
foolhardiness, but his brusque and tactless manners were those
of a soldier rather than of a well-educated and polished gentleman. Moreover, he soon showed symptoms of the disease from
which so many of Canada's governors had suffered—greed for
wealth and the desire to use the office of governor and the fur
trade to satisfy that greed.[1]

The honest and progressive Hocquart had been recalled a year earlier from his post as Intendant. To replace him, François Bigot was transferred from Louisbourg where he had made use of his office to carry on very profitable commercial operations. In Quebec, Bigot immediately made a great show of zeal and competence, attacking existing abuses and setting himself the task of bringing order out of confusion in an administration where, he wrote, private individuals were serving their own interests at the state's expense. This introductory report promised well and made an excellent impression in Versailles.[2]

After consulting La Galissonnière, La Jonquière adopted the latter's policy of opposing by force "any British encroachment." In the autumn (1749) he dispatched the Chevalier de La Corne with a small detachment to guard the Isthmus of Chignecto, constantly threatened by the English who claimed it as a part of Nova Scotia. The following year the Governor sent Boishébert to rebuild the fort on the St. John River.[3] He also collaborated with Bigot to send food to the Acadians who emigrated from the English territory of Merligouèche to the Isthmus of Chignecto and Ile St. Jean. These emigrants were unwilling to take the oath of allegiance which Nova Scotia's new governor, Cornwallis, was again demanding, the unmodified oath which did not recognize their right to remain neutral in case of war with France.[4]

La Galissonnière adhered strictly to the Indian policy of his predecessors whose constant aim, since the Montreal treaty of 1701, had been to keep the Iroquois neutral. In two meetings, held in 1750 and 1751, he won the support of the Cayugas and the influential Onondagas.[5] In 1750 he ordered the construction of Fort Rouillé on their hunting grounds north of Lake Ontario. This fort, protected by a palisade and defended with a garrison, was also a trading post. Its site on the Toronto portage had been chosen in order to intercept the hunters who were in the habit of taking their furs down by this route to the English post of Chouaguen.[6] In the Ohio valley where, for the moment, trade rather than sovereignty was the burning question, officers at the French posts were instructed to put an end to the activities of English traders and to drive them out of French territory. They had already been expelled by Céloron, but had reappeared the following year.[7]

The situation in the West presented further cause for worry.

Because they were able to offer goods of excellent quality at low prices, the English agents were beginning to undermine the loyalty of the Indian allies. From the Ohio to the Miami country plots were being hatched against the French. In June (1750) La Jonquière took measures to snuff out this disaffection and to protect French trade: Michilimackinac was strengthened and a fort was built at Sault Ste. Marie. In the autumn of the same year the Governor and the Intendant built a fort at the foot of the Niagara portage and provided it with a palisade and a garrison, as well as a warehouse. The following year La Jonquière renewed the treaty which had been signed in 1701 by the Iroquois and the Western Nations.[8]

La Jonquière was hardly installed in office before he began to seek ways of satisfying his love of money. As the beaver trade obviously brought in considerable profits, he asked to be granted a trading post as a concession. This Rouillé refused, at the same time pointing out how very improper it would be for the highest dignitary in the country to be engaged in such a commercial enterprise. But the Minister's rebuke fell on deaf ears. The Governor, who knew how profitable were the affairs of Bigot and his agents, took good care not to interfere with existing abuses.[9] On the contrary, since the Minister refused his request for a trading post, he appropriated two, the post of la Mer de l'Ouest and that of la Baie des Puants. At the same time he installed in them two of his own henchmen, Le Gardeur de Saint-Pierre and Marin. He entered into partnership with Bigot and recommended for promotion Bigot's chief confederates, Péan and Bréard. Moreover, to his own secretary, Grasset de Saint-Sauveur, who was notorious for his shameless cupidity and his illegal dealings, he granted the "exclusive right to sell brandy" to the Indians. The profits from this monopoly could easily be shared.[10]

Some of La Jonquière's activities redounded to the advantages of his country as well as to his own, for example, the very close supervision which he maintained in order to prevent furs from being taken to Albany or Chouaguen. This careful check uncovered the fact that at the Sault mission the two Desauniers sisters, in agreement with Father Tournois, had had a trading store and had carried on contraband trade for years. Using as intermediaries the Indians of the village, who naturally had an interest in the transaction, they exchanged furs for merchandise

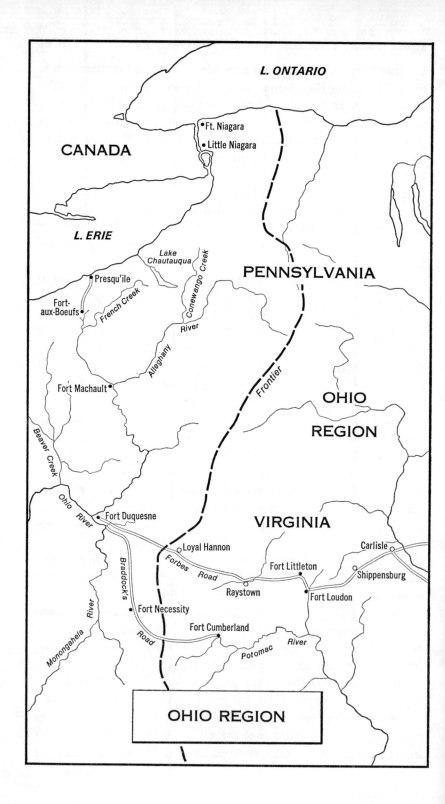

L. ONTARIO

CANADA

• Ft. Niagara
• Little Niagara

L. ERIE

Lake
Chautauqua

Conewango Creek

PENNSYLVANIA

• Presqu'ile
Fort-
aux-Boeufs •

French Creek

River

Alleghany

OHIO

REGION

Frontier

Fort Machault •

Beaver Creek

Ohio River

Fort Duquesne •

VIRGINIA

○ Loyal Hannon

Forbes Road

Carlisle ○

Fort Littleton

Shippensburg ○

Braddock's

Raystown

Fort Loudon

Monongahela River

Road

Fort Necessity •

Fort Cumberland •

Potomac River

OHIO REGION

from New York.[11] In 1742 Maurepas had issued instructions for the store to be closed and three years later had ordered that its proprietors be evicted.[12] But the Jesuits had succeeded in preventing the execution of the order, and La Jonquière's investigations revealed that operations were still being carried on. Father Tournois became worried. After soliciting an audience for his Iroquois, he composed a harangue which they recited to the Governor and which proclaimed their right to trade with the English colonies. La Jonquière rated the envoys soundly and dismissed them, whereupon the disconcerted Indians asked to speak to him in private and told him the whole story of the Jesuit's scheme. It was, they said, the Desauniers ladies who carried on the business with the connivance of the missionaries. On May 29, 1750 La Jonquière ordered the Desauniers and Father Tournois to leave the mission village, an order which was later approved by Versailles.[13] The sisters did not give in without a struggle, but went the following year to present a protest to the Minister in person. Their petition for permission to remain in business was refused, and the episode was closed when in 1752 Rouillé issued a formal order expressly forbidding them to reopen their store.[14]

In Versailles, the Jesuits and the Desauniers ladies accused the Governor of "having appropriated the beaver trade," while in Quebec merchants and officers protested against the goings-on of La Jonquière and his secretary. As it was impossible to ignore these repeated accusations, Rouillé brought up the matter in a letter to the Governor. In carefully impersonal phrases he intimated that he had received "general complaints that trade at the posts was being monopolized by a private company." The Minister knew how exacting the Governor's standards were; "he was sure that he would tolerate no abuse" and he assured the Governor "that these recriminations had made no impression" on the reputation which he enjoyed. At the same time it was rumoured at Versailles that La Jonquière had been instructed not to dabble "in government supplies or shipbuilding." Wounded to the quick by the insinuations which he recognized under the camouflage of fine phrases, he defended himself with as much dignity as he could muster. He thanked the Minister for his confidence and deplored the vagueness of the accusations. He was even rash enough to put his office at stake. Protesting that "self-interest was incompatible with his character," he asked the Minister to "procure his recall from His Majesty." This was a fatal step; far from opposing the request, Rouillé seized upon it, expressed regret that the state of the Governor's health did not permit him to remain in Canada and informed him that he would be free to leave as soon as a successor arrived to relieve him. In short, the Governor was being recalled. It was a fact that he was very ill, and his illness must have been still further aggravated by royal disfavour. He died on March 17, 1752 at the age of sixty-seven years. During a career of fifty years in the navy, La Jonquière had served in twenty-nine campaigns and fought in nine battles. After a state funeral, he was buried in the church of the Récollets, beside Frontenac, Callières and Vaudreuil.[15]

On the death of La Jonquière, the direction of affairs was taken over by the Governor of Montreal, Charles Le Moyne, Baron de Longueuil. His father, the first Baron de Longueuil, had become temporary governor in 1725 on the death of Vaudreuil and had solicited an appointment as Governor. Like his father, the younger Le Moyne had rendered eminent services to his country and, following his father's example, he presented himself as a candidate for the office of Governor-General. But Versailles ignored his request as it had ignored his father's, and probably for the same reason: he was a Canadian, and he might be inclined to favour his very numerous relations. In March 1752 the King appointed a naval officer, the Marquis Duquesne de Menneville. Duquesne was a tall, fine-looking man with a proud and haughty bearing. He was an authoritarian and a strict disciplinarian, whose sound judgement was matched by complete confidence in his own opinion. He was unmarried but fond of the society of women. Although he felt the need to improve his modest fortunes, he never sought to procure wealth "by scandalous means."[16]

When Duquesne disembarked in Quebec in July 1752, he was the bearer of very specific instructions: not only was he enjoined to prevent illicit trade on the part of the English, but he was to take every means to drive them out of the Ohio region. For their intrusions threatened to make very serious inroads on the country's trade, and even to cut off communication between Canada and Louisiana. As for the Indians whom the English had succeeded in turning against the French, the Canadian policy must not be to eliminate them by encouraging inter-tribal wars, but rather to restore peace among the tribes.[17]

These last instructions were inspired by the serious situation which had developed in the West. In 1752, when the allied Indians under Cadet de Langlade attacked the band of the anglophile chief La Demoiselle at Fort Miami south-west of Lake Erie, they captured eight English traders with their stocks of furs. Longueuil also reported incidents more disturbing to Canada: warriors of four different tribes had killed some ten Frenchmen during the year 1751.[18] In order to ward off the threat of invasion and to prevent more serious trouble later, Duquesne decided to take offensive action. As a first step in preparation for an expedition, he tightened up the discipline of the regular marines. As well as the regulars, the colony had 165 companies of militia with a total strength of 11,628 men. Orders were issued for these companies to be drilled every Sunday, and militia officers were enjoined to carry their swords and to wear the gorgets which were the insignia of their authority. Two special companies, made up of *bourgeois* of Montreal and Quebec, wore "scarlet uniforms with white vests and cuffs." The distinction of wearing such a uniform, the only one to be authorized during the French régime, flattered the vanity of the wearers, who were glad to pay for the honour. It was in deference to the same human weakness that Duquesne made another exception and appointed as officers of the Montreal and Quebec companies members of the nobility who were not already serving in the forces.[19]

To protect the Alleghany frontier and bar the way to the English in that region, Duquesne adopted the ambitious and costly strategy of establishing a chain of forts between Lake Erie and the Ohio. A start was made on the project during the summer of 1753. Captain Marin, who was chosen to lead a force of sixteen hundred regulars and militia, had already won the esteem of the Indians. The party went up Lake Ontario and built a fort at Presqu'île on the south shore of Lake Erie. They then built a portage road to Rivière-aux-Bœufs (French Creek) where they built a second fort. From Rivière-aux-Bœufs they pushed on twenty leagues to the post of Venango (Warren) at the site of an Indian village where the English had built a forge and a store.[20]

Marin, however, was not able to complete his project by building the final fort on the Ohio. The water in the Rivière-aux-Bœufs was too low for canoes; soldiers and militiamen alike were at the point of exhaustion after their labour of road-building and portaging. Five hundred of them had scurvy. Marin himself, who was sixty-three years old, fell ill and died on October 29. Captain Le Gardeur, who succeeded him in the Ohio command, detailed garrisons to the three new posts, and the other members of the expeditionary force returned to Montreal where they arrived, gaunt and exhausted, in November.[21]

Four hundred men had died in the course of the operation which, thanks to the dishonest manipulations of Bigot and his accomplices, had cost 4,000,000 *livres*. It was a heavy price to pay for success. The mission did, however, accomplish its object: the palisades of three forts now barred the way to any English advance, and the western Indians, profoundly impressed by such a show of military force and interpreting it as a sign of French superiority, adopted the French cause, for the moment at least, and gave it their help and support.[22]

The French operation caused a great stir in the English colonies, especially in Virginia. On October 31, (1753), after taking cognizance of Virginia's complaints, Governor Robert Dinwiddie dispatched a rather boastful and inexperienced young officer, George Washington, with a letter to Le Gardeur at Fort-aux-Bœufs. The letter protested against the presence of the French and claimed that the territory was an English dependency. To this spy disguised as a diplomat Le Gardeur replied that, in that region, he recognized no other rights except those of France and that he would maintain those rights in their entirety.

Le Gardeur's proud words did not end the matter, however.[23] In March (1754) Dinwiddie sent Captain Trent to erect a fort at the junction of the Alleghany and the Monongahela, but a French detachment under Le Mercier appeared on April 17 and, after driving out the English occupants, began to erect Fort Duquesne on the same site.[24] A few days later Washington, who was on his way with two companies of sixty men each, to reinforce Trent, learned of the presence of a second French contingent in the region. At dawn on May 28 he joined the band of Chief Demi-Roi of the Mingo Indians and entered into a joint agreement with him to "strike together," that is, to make an armed attack on the French.[25]

Washington's information was correct. On May 23 Contre-cœur, who was in command at Fort-aux-Bœufs, had heard of the errand on which Washington was engaged and had sent Ensign Jumonville with thirty Canadians to summon him to "withdraw peacefully" from French territory. On the evening of the 27th, the French contingent camped in a valley. The next morning, about eight o'clock, Washington succeeded in surrounding the camp on one side with his militiamen, and on the other with his Indian allies. As soon as he became aware that their presence had been observed, he gave the order to fire. The Canadians scarcely had time to seize their arms, or Jumonville to brandish his summons, before the Indians opened fire from the other side. Jumonville and nine of his men were killed in the cross-fire. The enemy then rushed on the camp and captured twenty survivors, while the Indians scalped the dead. Only one man, the runner Monceau, escaped towards Fort Duquesne.[26]

By an act until then unheard-of among civilized nations, Washington, in peace time and without any warning, had shot men who had the same right as he to be where they were. After the courteous reception which the French had given him on his spying mission to Fort-aux-Bœufs, and after the peaceful summons to evacuate Canadian territory presented by these same Frenchmen, Washington's action may well be termed "murder," as it was in contemporary reports; the defence presented in his journal of the expedition in no way invalidates the term.[27]

This brutal act of aggression started a chain of reactions leading straight to the Seven Years' War. And yet, when the news reached France, Versailles merely expressed "distress" at the incident and asked the Court of St. James's for an explanation. Meanwhile the authorities in Quebec were advised to remain on the defensive as long as possible.[27a]

After having struck his blow, and in the expectation of French reprisals, Washington started work two days later on a palisaded fort which he named Fort Necessity. In Canada, his unprovoked attack aroused the deepest indignation. It was "murder," wrote Duquesne, and "could be washed out" only with blood. Contrecœur, who was of the same opinion, charged Louis Coulon de Villiers with the mission of punishing the English. On July 3 six hundred French and one hundred Indians invested Washington's fort, defended by five hundred men with nine guns. Both sides opened fire, and the battle continued through a long day of rain. In the evening the Indians seemed disposed to withdraw. Accordingly, Villiers invited the English to surrender in order, as he said, to avoid further loss of life and the risk of torture at the hands of the savages. Daunted by the prospect of possible Indian cruelty, Washington accepted the proposal, and the capitulation was signed at eight o'clock in the evening by candle light. The garrison was allowed to withdraw from the fort with the honours of war. Washington promised to restore the members of Jumonville's detachment who were being held prisoner, and two hostages, Captains Van Bram and Stobo, were to remain in French hands until this condition was carried out. The next day the English, "still haunted with terror of the savages," decamped so fast that they abandoned two flags. The garrison had lost eighty men in killed and wounded, while French casualties had been limited to two killed and one wounded. Before leaving for Fort Duquesne, Villiers and his men dismantled the guns and destroyed the fort, as well as several English storage depots in the region.[28]

After the defeat of Washington, the western Indians, who had gone over to the English, hastened to Fort Duquesne where they professed penitence for their infidelity and offered their services to Contrecœur. Even the Five Nations, whose warriors had rallied in large numbers to the British flag, reaffirmed their intention to remain neutral in case of war.[29]

After two years in Canada, Duquesne was not very happy. Acting in the interests of public discipline and morality, he had banished a number of convicted lawbreakers and imprisoned members of the militia for failing to carry out orders. These measures were unpopular with the naturally unsubmissive Canadians, and their excessive severity brought down on the Governor a severe rebuke from Versailles. Duquesne was also on bad terms with Bigot. Bigot complained that the Governor encroached on the Intendant's judicial domain; but his real grievance was that the Governor's indiscreet supervision cut down the trading profits of the Intendant and his clique. To make matters worse, Versailles refused to allow the Governor to participate legally in the fur trade and rejected his application for a concession at Temiscaming. For all these reasons, Duquesne petitioned the King to allow him to resume his service in the navy. This permission was granted in 1754; he would be free to leave Canada as soon as his successor, M. de Vaudreuil, arrived in Quebec.[30]

Duquesne's departure caused few regrets, and his last impressions were unhappy ones. He was especially hurt at the discourtesy of Vaudreuil, who did not write to him after his appointment, and he went to Montreal in order to avoid being present at his successor's reception in Quebec. Before leaving Quebec for France, however, he made a point of saying a good word for the Canadian people. No people in the world, said the departing governor, could equal Canadians in zeal and service to their country.[31]

Chapter Ten

FOUNDING OF HALIFAX AND EXPULSION
OF THE ACADIANS
1749-1763

*Fidelity of the Acadians to France. Plan for expulsion
denied. Founding of Halifax. Refusal of unqualified
oath. Burning of Beaubassin. Construction of Fort
Lawrence. Siege and capture of Beauséjour. The oath
again rejected. Lawrence organizes the deportations.
Dispersal of Acadians in English colonies. Fate of the
displaced Acadians. Further deportations. Re-estab-
lishment of Acadians who take the oath. Profits from
the sale of confiscated cattle. Creation of a legislative
assembly. Increase in Nova Scotia's population.*

After the Treaty of Utrecht had established her in possession
of Nova Scotia, England had good reason for opposing the emigration of the Acadians. Their immediate departure would ruin
the country, whereas, if they remained, she hoped to win over
the younger generation.[1] But the hope proved illusory, since the
Acadian population remained faithfully attached to France. In
1730 Philipps appeared to have solved the problem, but duplic-
ity could not provide a permanent solution, and with the mother
countries at war, the difficulties of the situation again became
apparent. Carrying out their part of a French plan for recon-
quest, a Canadian force besieged Annapolis and inflicted a defeat
on the English at Minas. Certain missionaries, especially the
Abbé Le Loutre, following instructions from Versailles, incited
the Indians to hostile acts and exhorted the Acadians to collab-
orate in the French invasion. The Acadians themselves continued to claim their right to remain neutral, even after the
signing of the Treaty of Aix-la-Chapelle, and England found
herself once more faced with the Acadian problem.[2]

90

The Acadian population numbered about thirteen thousand. Although they lived in the hope that the country would be re-conquered by France, they refused to participate in any action against the English. In this, they followed the advice of certain of their curés, such as Fathers Desenclaves, Chevreux and Min-iac. When they provided supplies for the French troops, they justified this action in the eyes of the English authorities by pro-ducing documents ordering them to do so "on pain of death."[3] Mascarene, who was not deceived by this plea of coercion, re-ported that, while no more than a score of Acadians had violated their neutrality, he could not count on the fidelity of the popula-tion in the event of a French invasion.[4] Concluding that they would remain French as long as there were French missionaries among them, he proposed that an attempt be made to win their allegiance to the Crown, and that in case of failure they should be deported.[5] In August 1746 London's official adviser, Shirley, recommended that the priests should be replaced by French Protestant ministers, and that Protestant converts should receive preferential treatment. The following July he suggested that the French inhabitants of Beaubassin should be deported to New England and that their lands should be distributed among one thousand British colonists.[6] The old idea of deportation was being revived.

Rumours of plans for expulsion spread alarm among the Acadians. Realizing that such a fear might well be the deciding factor in their choice of allegiance if the threatened invasion became a reality, Shirley hastened to allay their anxiety. A letter written in French and circulated among them assured them that no deportation was contemplated. In 1747 a royal proclamation published the same message in London: His Majesty had "no intention of expelling the French inhabitants"; on the contrary, he promised to maintain them in the full possession of their rights.[7]

It was in this Machiavellian spirit that England, once the war was over, made a decision of prime importance. Abandoning for the moment any thought of deportation, she decided to combine British colonization with a new attempt to win over the Acadian population. At the same time she would build a fort in the colony capable of resisting any French attack. These were the instructions given to Colonel Edward Cornwallis who was appointed Governor of Nova Scotia in March 1749 and who stepped ashore at Chebucto Bay in June. He was followed by a convoy of 14 ships bearing 2,576 colonists. The emigrants were to be supplied with food for one year, and their lands were to be exempt from taxation for ten years. The work pressed rapidly forward; trees were felled and houses built, and the settlement was surrounded by a protecting palisade. In July the Governor created an administrative council, and in October the post, now the capital of the province, was named Halifax, in honour of the President of the Board of Trade.[8]

The existence of such an important new establishment immediately modified the Acadian situation. On July 14, less than a month after taking office, Cornwallis issued a categorical proclamation. He informed the Acadians that, in spite of their lack of "good will" during the war, the King graciously consented to grant them once more possession of their lands and freedom to practice their religion, but "only on condition that they take the oath of allegiance, with the obligations that it entails." In a letter dated August 1, the representatives of the Acadians asked for a renewal of their exemption from bearing arms in case of war. Cornwallis refused this request and at the same time ordered that the oath be taken before October 15. The Acadians replied in September that "they could not accept the new oath" since it contradicted the one they had taken in 1727 which exempted them "from bearing arms." They were all "ready to leave the country rather than accept it."[9] When their determined attitude was reported in London, the Governor was instructed to refrain from any coercion, and the question remained in abeyance.[10]

In October 1749 the Acadians in their distress appealed to Louis XV, begging him to obtain for them the rights which Philipps had recognized. But London rejected every proposal, even refusing to alter the time limit set by Cornwallis.[11] Still obdurate, the Acadians applied for grants of land in the territory claimed by France between St. John and Baie Verte.[12] France's policy was directed towards a double goal: to make use of the influence of the missionaries in order to stir up the Micmacs "secretly" against the English, and to encourage the Acadians to emigrate. And this policy had been bearing fruit. Although the incorrigible Abbé Le Loutre had had a price on his head ever since 1747, it was at his instigation that in September 1749 the Micmacs attacked the post at Canso;[13] and Acadians were emigrating to Ile Royale, to Ile St. Jean, and into the Isthmus of Chignecto.[13a]

Meanwhile the English continued to carry out acts of war. In April 1750 Colonel Lawrence led an armed force to Beaubassin, with the object of expelling the French from the shores of Chignecto Bay. When the English troops appeared, La Corne evacuated the villagers, under military escort, to the north shore of the Missaguash River, at the same time signifying to Lawrence that he would resist any intrusion into French territory. On May 2 Le Loutre's Indians set fire to the village and the church, and, in the face of determined opposition from French and Indians, Lawrence withdrew.[14] In the course of the summer, two supply ships were seized by the English, and in August the *Saint-François* was attacked and captured.[15] On September 12 Lawrence returned to Chignecto with a stronger force and erected Fort Lawrence on the site of Beaubassin. The Acadian population signified its opposition to this English occupation by burning six villages in the region and moving into French territory. Most of the fifteen hundred Acadians who emigrated at this time went to Ile St. Jean, whose population increased to about two thousand.[16]

Thus, during the years 1749 and 1750, incident followed incident. French and English forces kept up a cold war interrupted occasionally by hot episodes, while Le Loutre's Indians raided English settlements and killed and scalped English settlers.[17] In October 1750 Captain Howe was the victim of an act of treachery on the part of the Micmac, Etienne Bâtard, who lured the English officer away from the fort by displaying a white flag as if asking to parley. As the two men were talking, Howe was shot down by Indians in ambush. The incident provoked an exchange of protest between the courts of England and France, with reiteration of their respective claims in the region.[18]

In spite of such violent episodes, the situation gradually became somewhat calmer.[19] Raymond, the new governor in Louisbourg, established satisfactory relations with Hopson, the new governor in Halifax.[20] In December 1752 Hopson wrote to London to ask for instructions concerning the unqualified oath. He had taken no action in the matter, for he was convinced that the Acadians would maintain their refusal to subscribe to it. If he forced them, they would leave the country, and the country could not do without them. In March 1753 London answered that it would be most imprudent to impose the oath while the country was in a peaceful state. It was for the Governor to choose the moment for requiring the oath and the manner in which the requirement should be met. In the course of 1753 tensions had been reduced to such a degree that some Acadians considered accepting the English allegiance unreservedly. Le Loutre, however, used every means to induce them to emigrate into French territory, even threatening those who returned to the English zone with destruction of their property at the hands of the Indians.[21]

While Hopson was devoting himself whole-heartedly to the organization of his province, whose population, swelled by immigration, had now reached 4,200, the Indians resumed their guerilla warfare against the English. Their hostility, fanned by Le Loutre, was an obstacle in the path of better Franco-English relations. In the summer of 1753 a party of Indians appeared at Fort Beauséjour with eighteen scalps. Since an Indian scalp was worth ten pounds sterling in Halifax, Le Loutre could not refuse these and he bought them at 100 French *livres* for each scalp.[22]

On October 1753 Hopson was forced by illness to return to England. For the time being the province was to be administered by Colonel Lawrence, an enterprising, ambitious and headstrong officer.[22] In December Lawrence suggested to the British authorities that the question of the oath should be settled once and for all, but in April 1754 he was advised not to alarm the Acadians, nor risk driving them out of the province.[23] At this time the Ohio valley was being claimed by both the French and English, and both parties to the dispute were arming. The atmosphere was charged with the possibility of war when Lawrence wrote to the Minister, Robinson, that a policy of tolerance would prove illusory, and that the Acadians, in possession of the best land and under the influence of their "incendiary" clergy, were an obstacle to the progress of the country. He concluded that, if they refused to take the oath, it would be better to rid the province of their presence. Shirley, who was once more Governor of Massachusetts, wrote in the same aggressive vein. In May (1754) he proposed that an attack should be launched against the French forts in Acadia, and Robinson approved the suggestion, even though England and France were at peace.[24]

Without delay, Shirley and Lawrence embarked on preparations for an expedition, and on June 2, 1755 thirty-seven ships under the command of Colonel Monckton lowered their sails two leagues from Fort Beauséjour. Information about the fort had been sold to the enemy by its secretary, Thomas Pichon. It was defended by 150 soldiers, had 27 guns, and was well provided with food and ammunition. The garrison had just been reinforced by 240 Acadians, the only body of militia ever recruited in Acadia. Militia companies had been created by the simple expedient of conferring "the title of captain or officer on the most important person in each settlement." With the Acadians were the Abbé Le Loutre and his Indians. A contemporary described the commander of the fort, Du Chambon de Vergor, as a man who knew "how to turn a crank," but who was the "dullest fellow I ever met in my life." He had been Bigot's "master of ceremonies," and his wife had been Bigot's mistress. The Intendant had procured the post of commander for his protégé and had advised him, in characteristic fashion, to get all the profit he could from it. Vergor, who had "no talent for war," was quite incapable of organizing the defence of the fort. The English opened fire on June 13, and during the next two days a few cannon shots were exchanged. But little attempt was made to organize an effective resistance, and when three officers were killed by the explosion of an English bomb, the Acadians, already shaken, became completely demoralized.

On June 15 and 16 the Acadians revolted and announced their intention of leaving and, with "one voice," demanded that the commander surrender. A council of war was held and, in spite of vigorous opposition from the Abbé Le Loutre and Lieutenant Jacau de Fiedmont who had tried vainly to put a little spirit into the half-hearted defence, it recommended capitulation. Accordingly, after a "velvet siege" of only four days, Vergor offered to surrender the fort to Monckton. The terms of the capitulation which was signed on June 16 guaranteed the honours of war to the combatants and pardon to the Acadians, "since they had been forced to take up arms on pain of death."

The next day, Villeray, with his force of twenty men, accepted the same conditions and surrendered his palisade at Gaspereau on Baie Verte.[25]

When he saw that surrender was inevitable, the Abbé Le Loutre left the fort. He managed to make his way to Quebec, where the Governor and the Bishop roundly condemned his interference in military matters. The Minister, on the other hand, confirmed his approval of Le Loutre's policy, and ordered that the commanders responsible for the inadequate defence of Beauséjour and Gaspereau be tried by court martial. When the trial was held in September 1757 in Quebec, both men were exonerated. The verdict was fully justified in the case of Villeray, whose conduct was beyond reproach, but Vergor escaped condemnation for incompetence only through the influence of Bigot, who pulled strings and manipulated memoranda and evidence in favour of his protégé.[26]

Having disposed of the threat presented by Beauséjour, Lawrence immediately dispatched three ships, under Captain Rous, to Fort St. John, the last French fort in Acadia. On June 21, 1755 the ships dropped anchor before the fort whose commander, Boishébert, realizing that his force of thirty men could not defend their stockade against the greatly superior numbers of attackers, set fire to the post and withdrew to a position farther up the river.[27]

With the capture of Beauséjour and St. John, the Acadian population had lost its only French protection, and Lawrence, now free of opposition, decided to liquidate the Acadian problem. In his mind, the choice was clear: he must either bring the Acadians to accept absolute allegiance to England, or get rid of them altogether. During July (1755) delegations from Minas, Annapolis, Piziquid and Rivière-aux-Canards solicited from the Council of the province the right to take the oath in its old form which exempted them from military service. The Council answered that if they refused unrestricted allegiance they would cease to be British subjects and would have to leave the country. The Acadians, adamant in their attachment to their nationality and in their refusal to accept an oath binding them to fight against their mother country, asked for time to make the necessary preparations for their departure. On July 28 the Council decreed that their refusal left only one course open: deportation to the English colonies.[28]

Once the decision was made, Lawrence set to work to organize the expulsion. He ordered fort commanders to assemble the inhabitants and "to get them on board ship by force or by ruse." They were to be allowed to take their money and their personal effects with them. He then sent a letter to the neighbouring governors, informing them that the exiles would be arriving in their colonies, and suggesting that they should make useful workers of them.[29]

During August and September, senior officers—Monckton at Beauséjour, Winslow at Grand-Pré, Handfield at Annapolis and Murray at Piziquid—gathered the people of their respective regions and held them in forts or churches or camps to await the arrival of transports.[30] Soldiers everywhere tore families from their homes and burned houses, barns and churches.[31] Emptied of its people, Acadia presented a desolate spectacle of smoking villages and farms. Life had gone even from the fields, for the cattle had been rounded up and were being held, at least so it was said, for the province.[32]

Some Acadians succeeded in eluding the troops. Those who could do so took refuge in the neighbouring forests. At Chepody, Aulac and Cobequid almost all the people escaped to the woods before the soldiers arrived. On the Petitcodiac, Boishébert, with a force of a hundred Acadians and Indians, drove off the English detachment after inflicting on them a loss of twenty men. In October eighty-six captives escaped from Fort Lawrence through a trench which they had dug under the wall.

In September transports in Chignecto Bay, Minas Basin and Annapolis harbour began to take on their human cargo. No attempt was made to keep families together. The exiles were crowded on the ships at a rate of two for each unit of tonnage. Each person was given supplies for a week: five pounds of flour, two pounds of bread, a pound of beef and some beans.[33] At Grand-Pré, Winslow was ready to take the first men aboard on September 10. The young lads refused to go without their fathers. The officer gave the order to fix bayonets, and the soldiers, thus armed, forced the obdurate youths to march. Jostled by the troops, "praying, singing, wailing," the men moved slowly forward, while all along the way "women and children on their knees prayed and lamented loudly."[34]

From September to December (1755) heartbreaking scenes of eviction, burning and spoilation were repeated, while embarking Acadians were subjected to brutal treatment from soldiers and arrogant severity from certain officers. Some 6,941 persons were deported during the expulsion which an Acadian euphemism calls "the great disturbance," but which was carried out, as history reveals, "with a harshness and a disregard for the rights of humanity for which there can be no justification or excuse."[35] The cost of the explusion must be counted, not only in human suffering but in material losses, which were enormous. In the single village of Grand-Pré, the English seized 5,000 head of cattle and burned 255 houses and 431 barns.[36]

In October London received a letter from Lawrence containing a report of the deportation. The Minister did not answer until March 23 of the following year and this was his significant comment: "We do not doubt that your conduct in the matter will meet with His Majesty's approval." In fact, the King had already given evidence of such approval: on December 8 (1755) Lawrence had been appointed Governor of Nova Scotia. Not only had his conduct been approved, it had been rewarded with promotion.[37]

In Europe, the event was scarcely noticed and evoked no comment. Still more surprising, France presented no protest to England and expressed no indignation in her correspondence with Canada. This silence appears to indicate France's acceptance of the contemporary code of political morality: the Acadians being British subjects, England had the right to deal with them as she saw fit. This right was explicitly recognized in 1763 when France disclaimed any intention of intervening in the matter.[38]

One ship of the deportation fleet was seized on the high seas by twenty-five exiles who sailed it into the harbour at Fort St. John.[38a] The others, forty-five in all, reached the ports to which they were bound, and discharged their human cargo in Massachusetts, Connecticut, Maryland, New York, Pennsylvania, Virginia, Carolina and Georgia. The immigrants were most unwelcome in the colonies. Not only were they enemies and Catholics but they would be the cause of needless expense. Nevertheless, Maryland asked its people to help them for the sake of "humanity and Christian charity," and Connecticut agreed to "install" them as well as possible, while New York and Massachusetts passed laws authorizing the use of their services. Vir-

ginia and Carolina, on the other hand, hastened to ship them off
to England where they remained for several years in captivity
before being repatriated to France after the Treaty of Paris
(1763). Georgia allowed "displaced persons" to build ships in
which two hundred of them made the long and difficult journey
up the coast and back to Acadia.[39]

The Acadians who escaped deportation took refuge wherever
they could. Some settled on the site of Fort St. John, some crossed
the strait to the Ile St. Jean; other larger groups established
themselves in the region between Shediac and Miramichi, where
they received some supplies and other help from Canada. The
most obstinate managed to stay and live in the forest near their
homes; some even ventured to go back to their farms. Almost all
of them lived through years of intense moral and physical suffering.[40]

Between 1755 and 1757, at least two thousand refugees succeeded in reaching Quebec.[40a] Meanwhile the deportations went
on. In April 1756 Lawrence seized two hundred persons at Cape
Sable and shipped them off to Boston. In 1758, after the capture
of Louisbourg, Amherst sent troops to round up the population
of Ile St. Jean. Some 3,500 persons were captured and sent to
France, where they were granted a state subsidy of six *sous* a day
for each adult and three for each child. Finally, in 1762, on
Belcher's orders, 400 Acadians from Chignecto were deported to
Boston.[41] When, at the end of the war, large numbers of Acadian prisoners were sent from England to France, they were settled more or less successfully in Poitou and Belle-Isle and at
Cayenne in French Guiana. In 1764 the King sought permission
from England to repatriate the last of the French inhabitants of
Acadia, but London was no longer willing to deprive its colony
of these valuable workers.[42]

In the course of the deportations which were carried out
between 1755 and 1762, 11,000 Acadians out of a total of 15,500
were exiled from their country. In 1764 Belcher recommended
the expulsion of the 2,000 who still remained in the province.[43]
But in July 1764 England decreed that, now that peace was
restored, Acadians who took the oath of allegiance would be
allowed to re-establish themselves in the country. Many still refused obstinately to live under the British flag, and of these, 600
men, women and children emigrated at their own expense to the

French West Indies. Those who remained, or who returned from exile, accepted British rule and Nova Scotia's offer of free land to each member of a family, with the result that 2,600 Acadians were once more living in the farming districts of the province in 1763.[44]

After the evictions had been duly carried out, London began to make inquiries about the thousands of head of cattle which had been seized in the name of the Crown. An investigation revealed that there was no record of sale in the provincial accounts. It appears that the contractors who had provisioned the transports, Apthorpe, Hancock, Baker and Saul, had helped themselves to the cattle without paying a penny to the Public Treasury. A contemporary witness even accused Lawrence of having participated in this "great piece of dishonesty." This evidence supports the statement made by the Board of Trade that the Governor had intervened in public contracts involving similar "frauds." Whatever may be the truth about this apparent misappropriation of the Acadians' cattle, it was the result, and not a cause, of the expulsion.[45] Moreover, it was not the first such irregularity to raise doubts in London as to the Governor's honesty. As early as 1756, the ministers had urged the establishment of a legislative assembly in Halifax, and although they professed almost complete confidence in Lawrence's integrity, it was obvious that they wanted to put a check on illegal administrative practices. The assembly was created, in spite of Lawrence's opposition, and the opening of the first British parliament in Canada took place in Halifax on October 20, 1758.[46]

In 1756 London returned to its project of settlement. After the capture of Quebec, and after the conclusion of a peace treaty with the Micmacs in 1762, settlers poured into the province from Ireland and from the English colonies in America. Between 1752 and 1763, the population increased three-fold, from 4,203 to 12,998. This latter figure included 2,600 Acadians who resettled in the province.[47] In this period of fourteen years since the founding of Halifax, Nova Scotia, the British province in Canadian territory had shown remarkable development and progress, demographically, economically and politically.

Chapter Eleven

COLONIZATION: RENEWED EFFORTS
1713-1756

Inadequate population. Engagés. *Delinquents:* fils de
famille *and salt-smugglers. Married and discharged
soldiers. Prisoners of war and English deserters. Immigration statistics. Natural increase. Mission Indians.
Negroes and Indian slaves.*

After thirty years of war, the Treaty of Utrecht opened the
way for a new phase of growth, but there still remained obstacles
to the expansion which was to mark the final period in Canada's
history as a French colony. The country had not yet recovered
from the failure of the *Compagnie du Canada,* nor from the
financial losses caused by a fifty per cent reduction in the value
of its card money. Still more serious, its economy was in the
hands of an intendant, Bégon, who continued to pursue a policy
of personal gain until his recall in 1726.

Action was taken immediately, however, to remedy the population shortage which was Canada's essential weakness; for in
1713 the whole vast country had only 18,119 inhabitants.[1] "The
very small size of Canada's population," wrote Vaudreuil,
"causes every undertaking to fail. It is difficult to find permanent
or daily workers, and they have to be paid exorbitant wages."
Realizing that this paralysing lack of manpower made all
progress impossible, he sent an urgent plea to France for colonists. He proposed that an active campaign be undertaken to
find emigrants in the provinces. If there were no volunteers, he
would be willing to accept prisoners, provided these were chosen
from certain categories: contrabanders, salt-smugglers and other
such delinquents. These were not, after all, dangerous criminals
or hardened offenders. The Intendant added his suggestion that
they should borrow an idea from New York and introduce

101

Negro slaves into Canada. But these ideas were considered impractical. It was pointed out that Negroes brought up in a tropical climate could not stand Canada's winter; and that the colony's long unguarded frontiers would be an invitation to paroled prisoners to escape.[2]

Instead of acting on these suggestions, the King decided to return to the earlier system whereby *engagés* agreed to emigrate to America and to bind themselves by contract to a master, generally for a period of three years, after which time they were free to settle in the country if they wished to do so. To help finance this operation, an order of March 20, 1714 obliged shipowners and captains of ships going to Canada to transport from three to six *engagés*, according to the tonnage of their vessels. The price of the passage would be paid later by the employer of the *engagé*. This procedure, useful and practical in conception, would have produced better results if regulations for inspection on departure and arrival had been more strictly enforced. In fact, regulations were frequently evaded by captains with the connivance of the port commissioners. In 1723 the colony received only one third of the *engagés* claimed by the captains as passengers.[2a]

Although the results of the system of arranged passages were somewhat meagre, it was used more or less regularly up to, and even during, the War of the Austrian Succession. After that, it began to decline and in 1758 it ceased to operate. To supplement this official emigration administered by officers of the Crown, *engagés* were recruited privately almost every year for colonists who needed workers or servants, while from time to time special conditions or circumstances encouraged individuals to emigrate on their own initiative. Relations and friends came to join settlers already established, civil servants were appointed to major or minor posts in the administration, and commercial agents were sent out by a score of French business houses. The number of immigrants in all these categories—*engagés,* servants, free emigrants—remained small, and varied from year to year. Over a period of forty-four years, from 1714 to 1758, these sources provided a total of about fifteen hundred settlers.[3]

Such a thin trickle of immigrants had little or no effect on the labour shortage. Vaudreuil and Bégon continued to importune the French authorities, who finally withdrew their opposition to the idea of penal colonization and who, in 1721, ruled that shipowners could transport prisoners to the colony, instead of *engagés*.[4] The following year the system came into full operation, with emigrants drawn from two distinct categories of delinquents: *fils de famille* and condemned law-breakers.

Pontchartrain probably remembered that he had set a precedent in 1712. In that year the Sieur de Cassin, who had contracted an "unfortunate marriage," was dispatched to the colony to become Canada's first *fils de famille*. It was not, however, until 1722, when two such immigrants arrived in Quebec, that the procedure was followed with any regularity. The following year six *fils de famille* and a few law-breakers constituted a small group of penal settlers. The *fils de famille*, young men who had turned out badly, were taken from the Hôpital Général in Paris or picked up by police officers armed with *lettres de cachet* procured by the offenders' parents. The charge against them was generally licentious conduct. Six of these young men came to the colony in 1723, four in 1726 and fifteen in 1729, a number of this last group with appointments to serve in the colonial troops.[5]

The exiles were usually left free after their arrival in the colony. When some of them justified their reputation as undesirables and malefactors, Mgr. de Saint-Vallier, the Intendant and the inhabitants in general protested so vigorously that, in 1730, the King decided to abandon the system of deporting France's black sheep.[6] The principle was established that henceforth Canada would not be asked to accept them as colonists; but in an absolute monarchy exceptions to the principle were always possible. Almost every year between 1730 and 1749, one, two, or three *fils de famille* were deported to Canada. The total number of such exiles can be estimated at about eighty. Most of them were young, between eighteen and twenty-five years of age; most came from good families, some from noble or distinguished ones. Among them there were three noblemen, eight chevaliers, two lawyers and three law students. There were also, curiously enough, a Protestant, Groulx, and a missionary, the Sieur Esprit. Some of these unwilling colonists received remittances from their families, twenty-six served in the army, about a dozen became itinerant country schoolmasters.

There were also three notaries, two attorneys and two civil servants. Fifteen of their number were allowed to return to France,
while a few deserted either by sea or by way of the English
colonies.[6a]

The colony appears to have kept and assimilated only about
forty *fils de famille*. These included some incorrigible wrong-
doers, but Beauharnois was speaking of the majority when, in
1738, he expressed the opinion that "young men of this kind
change when they get here." In a small community, where
healthy moral standards are the rule, escapades are neither encouraged nor condoned, and the young exiles probably learned
fairly soon to conform. It is difficult to discern any ill effects
arising from the practice of deportations. On the contrary, some
of the *fils de famille* not only proved their own worth, but
founded families whose members contributed to the strength of
the country.[6b]

It was the second category of delinquents, the condemned
law-breakers, that constituted the principal source of penal emigration, authorized in an order of January 14, 1721. A first con-
signment of twenty-four prisoners in 1721 was followed by a
second, of fifty, in 1724. On their arrival, some were incorporated into the army or bound by contract to farmers. Those
who remained free roamed the country, "pilfering and stealing,"
and as a result of complaints which poured in on the Minister, it
was decided that no more prisoners would be deported to Canada. Notwithstanding this decree of 1726, a shipload of twenty-
seven convicts reached Quebec in 1728. The Minister hastened
to explain, however, that even if they were "not very respectable
people," they had at least "not been convicted of serious crimes."
There were among them, for instance, three poachers and a wife-
beater. But whatever their degree of "honesty" or disreputabil-
ity, they were considered undesirable, and both the Governor
and Intendant expressed a preference for salt-tax offenders.[6c]

In France, the state held a monopoly on the sale and distribution of salt. Salt was subject to both import and excise duty,
and, as the rate of taxation varied considerably from province to
province, contraband trade flourished. But violators of the salt
laws were not essentially criminals. They were in the same class
as poachers, or those persons in the modern world who evade
taxes on tobacco and alcohol. They defrauded the state of one

specific revenue, but that did not prevent them from being hard-working and reliable in other respects.

The mother country had then no difficulty in complying with the request of Beauharnois and Hocquart, and the summer of 1730 saw the first salt-smugglers, a group of twenty-six, disembark in Quebec. The Governor and the Intendant decided which were to be enrolled in the army and which were to be placed with employers who had asked for them. When put to work, they carried out their service so well that Quebec asked for more of the same kind, and the following year Maurepas supplied sixty-four, of whom four were taken into the troops, while the others were distributed among the inhabitants.[7] Everyone was so pleased with them that Mgr. Dosquet asked to have some for his seigniory. From that time until 1743, the arrival of the salt-smugglers in Quebec was almost an annual event. Then, after an interruption of several years, one last group of nine was sent out in 1749. Unlike the *engagés*, who could return to France on the expiry of their three-year contract, the salt-smugglers were deported to Canada for life. They were paid at the rate of 100 *livres* a year by their employers. Most of them were young and healthy, and the majority were unmarried. However, about a dozen arrived with wives, and the wives of some fifteen others, with their children, joined their husbands later.[8]

Canada's penal settlers, of whom, according to the most reliable sources, there were some seven hundred, were almost all salt-law violators, with a sprinkling of poachers and contrabanders, and were chosen from among "the most recommendable" and the best workers in their fraternity.[8a] It is difficult to estimate the exact number of those who remained permanently in the country. Although an official supervision was maintained, and penalties for desertion ranged from six months in prison to life service in the galleys, desertions were reported from time to time throughout the period. If we estimate at two hundred the loss by desertion and to the troops, we may assume that some five hundred salt-smugglers settled in the country. Some of them found employment in the towns, but most were farm workers and would become tenant farmers. They appear to have filled the colony's requirements in manpower, which Beauharnois estimated at four hundred in 1731; for in 1743, the last year in which they are mentioned in the official correspondence, only ten were requested for the following year.[8b] Moreover, since no complaints were recorded against them, we must conclude that this group of almost a thousand persons, counting the women and children, made a useful contribution to the country's population and economy.[9]

Another means of increasing the population was the settlement in the country of soldiers who had completed their term of garrison duty. A precedent for military colonization had been set in 1668 when the Carignan regiment was disbanded. At that time Colbert had ruled that married men or men about to be married could remain in the colony. After the peace of Utrecht, Vaudreuil recommended that existing restrictions be eased so that more soldiers might marry and settle in Canada.[9a] However, as it was important to keep the companies up to strength, troopers were discharged only when they could be replaced by recruits from France, and those who wished to marry and settle had first to obtain the Governor's consent. Many of them would have liked this new life, for a soldier's pay was meagre and his ration consisted of only a pound and a half of bread and four ounces of salt pork a day. But it sometimes happened that Vaudreuil delayed the necessary permission for years in order to keep his best men. The Bishop protested that such refusals encouraged immorality and illegitimate births, and, as a result of his protests, Beauharnois pursued a more generous policy in this respect. In 1734, in order to regularize procedure, the King ruled that soldiers should be free to marry after three years of service.[10]

The door was thus opened wide to soldier settlement. Troopers "make good farm workers," wrote La Galissonnière in 1747; "we couldn't discharge too many married soldiers." Accordingly, in 1750 his successor, La Jonquière, made use of the opportunity provided by the arrival of 1,000 recruits to release 233 married soldiers. To the men must be added the officers from France who married Canadians and established families in Canada. They were a small group, but their social contribution was large in proportion to their numbers. Existing records allow us to estimate at about 1,600 the number of persons established through soldier settlement in the period between the Treaty of Utrecht (1713) and the capitulation of Quebec (1759).[11]

Rather surprisingly, there were some English settlers in Canada, most of them prisoners captured during raids on the neighbouring colonies. In May 1710 almost eighty men and women were granted letters of naturalization, and when prisoners were exchanged after the Treaty of Utrecht, a certain number of English prisoners preferred to remain in Canada rather than return to their own country. Two girls entered religious orders; Mary Silver joined the sisters of the Hôtel-Dieu in Montreal, and Mary Wheelwright the Ursulines in Quebec. Later, a few Englishmen settled in Montreal where they were allowed to farm, but not to engage in trade.[12] Deserters from the Nova Scotia garrisons provided still another British element in the population of Canada. Thirty English, Irish and Scots deserters came ashore in Quebec in 1750. Some signed on with ships' captains, some moved on to the West Indies; thirty-three remained in Quebec where they were employed as day labourers in the shipyard. Others followed this first contingent, but Bigot's estimate of five hundred British deserters in the colony is probably an exaggeration. They were no more desirable than are most soldiers who go over to the enemy, but the Minister recommended that they be allowed to stay in the country and to work as artisans in the towns or as farm labourers. In 1757 Vaudreuil deported to France forty-six Irish deserters who had worked on the fortifications of Quebec and who might give information to the enemy.[13] Official records provide evidence that some of these British immigrants remained in the colony. In 1754 a certain Joseph Brown figures as a member of Jumonville's militia detachment in Montreal, and in 1761 Gage tried to assemble "English and other" prisoners and deserters in Montreal.[14]

A few approximate figures will allow us to form an idea of the volume of immigration between the Treaty of Utrecht (1713) and the Seven Years' War (1756). Fifteen hundred *engagés*, 80 *fils de famille*, 700 salt-smugglers and 1,600 soldiers make a total of 3,880 persons. To these must be added the women and children who accompanied the men, as well as one or two hundred English and Irish and a few hundred individuals who do not appear in the official records. The total for the period of 33 years lies somewhere between 4,000 and 5,000, a very meagre contribution, especially when we consider that this thin trickle of emigrants came from a country with a population of 20,000,000.[14a]

Fortunately for Canada, the astonishing fertility of her people compensated for inadequate immigration. Between 1714 and 1734, the population doubled, rising from 18,964 to 37,716. The figure recorded 20 years later, 55,000, is probably incorrect. One would expect to find that the population had again doubled, and the total of 76,172, reported by Amherst in 1761, would indicate that this was indeed the case. We should, therefore, probably accept Amherst's figure as a maximum for the French régime. Montcalm quotes a census giving the total as 82,000, but this total no doubt included the troops as well as the civil population.[15]

It must not be forgotten that there were Indians within the settlements. These natives, who were said to be "domiciled," lived in villages under the direction of missionaries. The oldest of the villages, Lorette, situated a few miles from Quebec, was a hundred years old. In the region of Three Rivers, Abenakis had established villages at Bécancour and St. François-du-Lac. The Sulpicians directed the Mountain mission which, originally founded on the slope of Mount Royal, was later transferred to the Lake of Two Mountains. The mission at Sault St. Louis was served by the Jesuits, as were the remaining Indian villages. The population of the missions varied from year to year, between a maximum of three thousand and a minimum of twelve hundred. The attempt to teach the Indians French ways was a complete failure, and the premium offered to encourage Franco-Indian marriages proved ineffectual as an incentive. Indeed, in the light of experience in the Illinois country, Franco-Indian marriages came to be considered "dishonourable," and the children of such unions remained little savages. Of the different tribes who lived in daily contact with settlers, only the Hurons spoke a little primitive French. For all the others the services of an interpreter were required. The only useful services performed by these "domiciled" Indians were those of guides and auxiliary troops against the English, and a high price was paid for these services. Each year, from 30,000 to 60,000 *livres'* worth of supplies, merchandise and munitions were distributed as "King's gifts." In wartime, this expense increased at least five-fold.[15a]

To complete our picture of the colony's population, we must add a few dozen Negroes who appeared over the years, as well as a few hundred Indian slaves, known as Panis, from the name of a tribe from the Lake region which supplied most of them.[15b]

The population of the towns grew in proportion to that of the country in general. Towards the end of the régime the rate of increase in the towns was above average. Quebec, the capital and seaport, had, with its suburbs, a population of 4,613 inhabitants until about 1745 when work on the fortifications attracted people from the country to the town. The exodus became so serious that Bigot forbade country dwellers to "come and establish themselves" in the town without written permission, but this order did not halt the increase in the population, which reached a total of 8,000 in 1754. The population of Montreal, the centre of the western fur trade, increased from about 2,500 in 1739 to 4,000 in 1754, while the figure for Three Rivers practically doubled, rising from 273 in 1739 to 600 in 1754.[15c]

Chapter Twelve

ECONOMIC EXPANSION

1713-1756

Distribution of seigniories and new settlements. Agricultural progress. Ginseng and tobacco. Shipbuilding and bounties. Ships for the navy. Iron mines and works at St. Maurice. Seal and porpoise fisheries. Weaving. Export of board, sheathing and masts. Hatmaking; demolition of Canadian equipment. The fur trade and its various methods of exploitation. Increase in trade: Canada, the West Indies, France. Public finance. Tax proposals.

During the twenty years following the Treaty of Utrecht, Canada's population doubled, and the increase in population forced Versailles to modify a land policy which had been adopted in 1716. At that time, as some seigneurs were unwilling to concede farms except at exorbitant rents and some farmers were leaving a part of their land unbroken, it was decreed that no more seigniories would be granted. But as the population increased more land was brought under cultivation until finally there was no land available for new farms in the existing seigniories. Consequently, in 1729 Louis XV revived the practice of creating seigniories, and this policy continued to be followed until the end of the régime.[1]

Earlier concessions had been limited to the land bordering on the St. Lawrence, which served as a highway linking them to the three towns in the colony. Now, since there was very little unoccupied land on the river, the Governor and the Intendant created a second belt of seigniories behind the older ones.[1a] Moreover, since the peace had removed the danger of Anglo-Indian raids, Beauharnois and Hocquart decided to make grants of land along the Richelieu and on Lake Champlain as far as St.

Frédéric where they would have the protection of a fort in case of war. Accordingly, some twenty domains were allotted to officers and other influential persons between 1731 and 1748. But the results of the experiment were disappointing both to seigneurs and to officials. Settlers were discouraged by the distance of the proffered homesteads from the towns and the difficulty of communication. Some thirty farms were taken up, but the farmers had hardly sown their first wheat when the War of the Austrian Succession forced them to withdraw into the shelter of the colony. Settlement had not yet been resumed when the Seven Years' War intervened and brought about the conquest of the country. It is for this reason that the seigniories on the Richelieu do not appear in the censuses of Canada.[1b]

Another new settlement had a happier history. As Beauharnois and Hocquart were looking for land for *engagés*, discharged soldiers and especially sons of established land-holders, their eye fell upon the Chaudière, a tributary on the south shore of the St. Lawrence. Land in this region seemed to offer every advantage: it was near Quebec, to which the river provided transport, and the soil was so fertile that the district was christened New Beauce. Seven seigniories were created and quickly attracted settlers. In 1739 New Beauce and Sault-à-la-Chaudière counted 317 tenants and homesteaders whose 579 *arpents* of fields produced wheat, peas, oats, barley and even tobacco. Progress was sometimes hampered here as elsewhere by the uncertain course of events, but Beauce continued to grow and at the end of the French régime had a population of about 800.[1c]

Another successful venture reanimated the post at Detroit whose population had shrunk to 34 in 1721. After repossessing a part of Lamothe-Cadillac's seigniory and converting it into a royal domain, Vaudreuil and Bégon leased holdings directly, thereby initiating a procedure which was followed by Beauharnois and Hocquart, and which resulted in a population increase of 100 per cent. In 1749 La Galissonnière gave further encouragement to settlers by supplying them with transport, food supplies for eighteen months, tools and animals. This aid to migration was continued with the King's approval by La Jonquière, and under its influence the population of Detroit increased by more than 500 in 1751.[1d]

The opening of new seigniories after 1729 was a great stimulus to the country's rural economy. Whereas in 1721 the 26,146 *arpents* under cultivation yielded a crop of 282,700 bushels of wheat, in 1739 the acreage was trebled, and the production had risen to 634,605 bushels. In the same period the number of horned cattle increased from 23,888 to 38,821, and the increase in flax production, from 54,650 pounds to 127,219 pounds, was remarkable. Hemp was the only product which declined. Starting at 2,100 pounds in 1721, it reached a peak of 5,384 in 1739, though with the help of a royal subsidy. Then, as the price was allowed to fall, production also declined until it reached a minimum after 1746.[1e]

For a few years the colony carried on a flourishing trade in ginseng, which had been discovered by Father Lafitau about 1715. The Chinese attributed valuable medicinal properties to ginseng root and paid a high price for it. At first the Canadian price was one or two *livres* a pound, but as it rose rapidly to twenty-five *livres*, there was a rush to find and harvest the precious plant. In order to hasten delivery and payment, someone conceived the idea of drying the root in an oven instead of keeping it outdoors in the shade, and by this means they were able to ship 500,000 pounds in 1751. But the Chinese considered that the artificial drying destroyed the virtue of the plant. They refused to buy it, and large stocks remained unsold in La Rochelle. An order of 1752, directing that the root be harvested in the autumn in order to assure "good quality," was received too late, and the ginseng market was lost to Canada.[1f]

As there was an import duty on French tobacco, Canadian farmers began to cultivate the native plant some time before 1700 and the tobacco crop became an important one, increasing from 48,038 pounds in 1721 to 166,054 in 1734 and 215,932 in 1739. An attempt was made to export tobacco, but at their maximum, exports did not exceed 32,000 pounds, the figure for 1744. The strong flavour of the Canadian tobacco leaf was an effective obstacle to competition in foreign markets, but it suited local taste, so that, although Canadians were inveterate smokers, only limited quantities of tobacco had to be imported.[1g]

Ever since Talon had established his shipyards, people had been aware that the colony possessed, in her forests and their by-products, the essential raw materials for a profitable industry. Shipbuilding had been virtually abandoned, however, with the last of Colbert's economic programmes for Canada, and had remained dormant during the war years. It revived after the peace of Utrecht and became still more active during the intendancy of Bégon. With nine good-sized ships under construction in 1728, the industry continued to prosper. In 1731, in order to encourage it still further, Hocquart recommended, and the King granted, bounties of 100 to 500 *livres* according to tonnage, and as a result twenty-one ships were launched in two years. After that, the rate of construction slackened somewhat, although oak from Lake Champlain and pine from the Richelieu still found a market. On the recommendation of Hocquart, the King decided to establish royal yards in Quebec, and a site was chosen in 1731 on the right bank of the St. Charles, a few yards from the Intendant's palace. The enterprise came within the province of the Intendant, but it was under the immediate direction of an assistant builder, M. Levasseur, who had been sent out from France with a number of carpenters. Several well-built, sturdy ships were launched, and in 1739 the keel was laid down for a five-hundred-ton merchantman, the *Canada*, which was launched on June 4, 1742. When it reached France after its maiden voyage, the *Canada* was considered "so well built," and its performance at sea had been so impressive, that Levasseur was congratulated by the Minister and promoted to the grade of master builder.[2]

Encouraged by this success, the King agreed in 1745 to transfer the yards to the *Cul-de-sac* in the lower town in order to facilitate the work. Between 1745 and 1756 the new shipyard produced seven frigates and other vessels, of which the largest, the *Algonquin*, carried seventy-two guns. But enthusiasm for the Canadian ships began to be tempered by doubts. Opinion in Brest was critical of the *Algonquin*, and the navy's experts complained of the poor quality of the wood in the frigates *Caribou* and *Saint-Laurent*. Bigot, who was anxious to transfer the control of the yards to his partners, seized the opportunity to point out that they were a great expense to the Royal Treasury. In the light of these opinions, the King decided to halt construction on big ships pending further reports. However, although no further royal orders were received, shipbuilding remained active. The services of Levasseur, who had been appointed *Inspecteur* of woods and forests, were available to the industry until the end of the French régime.[2a]

Although the search for minerals had gone on ever since Talon's day, only one mineral-based industry was established, the St. Maurice Iron Works, which smelted the iron discovered near Three Rivers in 1670. Tests showed that in quality the St. Maurice ore compared favourably with Swedish iron, but the mine was not exploited until 1732, when the King granted Poulin de Francheville a privilege and a subsidy of 10,000 *livres.* The first ingots were cast in 1733, but on the death of Francheville in November of that same year work was stopped.[3]

In 1737 a new company was set up by Olivier de Vézins, and, with the help of a loan of 100,000 *livres* from the Royal Treasury, work was resumed. The iron works manufactured such household necessities as nails, axes, iron pots and stoves, and they also provided iron to be used in shipbuilding. Unfortunately, the industry was badly managed and proved uneconomical. In 1743 the company declared itself bankrupt, with a debt to the Crown of 192,602 *livres,* and on May 1, 1743 the foundries became a part of the royal domain. Reopened under new and better management, they employed 120 workmen and produced between 300,000 and 400,000 pounds of iron a year. In 1747 they began to cast cannon balls and even cannon. Some of this production showed a balance of profit, but the industry as a whole continued to be a burden on the Royal Treasury.[4]

The courage and enterprise of individuals who tried to establish slate and tile industries were not rewarded with the success which they deserved. Dr. Sarrazin's slate works at Grand-Etang, near the Notre-Dame hills, failed in 1734, although they had been subsidized by means of royal purchases. The tile yard which, after years of planning, M. de Meloises opened in Quebec in 1734, maintained a precarious existence until the outbreak of the Seven Years' War.[5]

The colony's efforts to process its own tar met with greater success. After a series of attempts inspired by various intendants from Talon to Raudot, the industry had finally become established at Baie St.-Paul before 1712, and in 1720 it was able to supply all the colony's needs. After 1734, under its competent French director, M. de Chevigny, it made rapid strides. Plants were established at Kamouraska and Sorel, and by-products, pitch and resin of excellent quality, were exported to France.[6]

Even with the St. Lawrence at their doors, and lakes within

easy reach, Canadians limited their fishing to easy and profitable seal- and porpoise-hunting. In 1724 seventeen porpoise-fishing stations were strung out at intervals between Ile Verte and Tadoussac, and the following year one hundred porpoises were taken. But as the number of fishing stations increased, the size of the catch diminished. After 1732, although fishing continued at a number of points, most of the stations were abandoned.[7]

Seals were valuable both for their skin and their oil. Seal-hunting was carried on chiefly on the Labrador coast, where Augustin de Courtemanche had established a post at Baie des Esquimaux in 1706. In 1711, abandoning this station, he moved with a few French families and a band of Montagnais Indians to Baie Phélypeaux. In 1714 he was appointed Commander of the Coast, a post in which he was succeeded in 1717 by his son-in-law, Martel de Brouage. Brouage, continuing the good work begun by Courtemanche, built up a thriving fishing industry. New posts were established, and exports to France and the West Indies were maintained until the end of the régime. In 1744 nine stations on the north shore produced eighteen hundred barrels of oil. In the course of the years, Canadian fishing smacks were joined by French schooners which had come to fish cod in the Gulf, and whose masters were glad to be able to take advantage of the protection offered by the post against marauding Eskimos.[8]

After the sale of Madame de Repentigny's establishment in 1713, little commercial weaving was done, although silk and wool stockings were manufactured until 1731 in the workshop which Brother Charron had established in the Hôpital Général in Montreal. The policy of Versailles was generally to discourage such experiments. In 1748 this policy was stated explicitly when it was announced that new manufactures should be introduced only when they did not interfere with those of the mother country. Since they had no incentive to develop a weaving industry, the farmers' wives used their wool to make their own homespun cloth and to knit stockings. The Sisters of the Congregation also were famous for their skill in weaving.[9]

Except to meet local needs and to supply wood for shipbuilding, little effort was made to exploit the great wealth of the country's forests. As part of the economic activity stimulated by Talon, a small quantity of wood was exported, but this trade was interrupted after his departure from Canada. It was revived by Quebec merchants, but only after the Treaty of Utrecht. The Governor of Montreal, Claude de Ramezay, who established a lumber business at Baie St.-Paul in 1713, signed a contract in 1721 to supply planks, sheathing and masts to the navy. After the death of Ramezay in 1724, the business was continued, under his wife's direction, until 1726.[10]

The Intendant, Dupuy, seemed to be endowed with the gift of prophecy when, in 1727, he made the following statement in connection with the lumber trade: "We must regard wood as Canada's natural product, replacing furs, of which the supply is everywhere diminishing." In that same year, he signed a five-year contract for lumber with the seigneur of Terrebonne, the Abbé Lepage. Although orders for masts were discontinued because they were difficult to transport, Bégon's mills were providing the navy with sheathing in 1733. Wood continued to be exported without licence until 1756 when Bigot introduced the requirement of a specific permit from the Intendant, probably with the intention of monopolizing profits for his partners of the *Grande Compagnie*.[11]

An attempt had been made to develop a secondary industry from the fur trade by setting up a small workshop for manufacturing beaver hats. But in 1717 the King refused to license such a business, since the West India Company held the beaver monopoly. In 1735 the three hat-makers who made and sold between twelve hundred and fifteen hundred straw and felt hats a year in the colony, asked permission to export half-finished beaver hats to France. The Minister's violent reaction to such a dangerous proposal resulted in drastic orders which reached Quebec the following year. Not only was it forbidden to make hats of any kind, but hatters were required to demolish existing plants, thus eliminating competition with the French trade. The work of destruction was duly carried out under official supervision. It constitutes the most extreme example in practice of the draconian principle, reaffirmed by Versailles in 1748, that only those manufactures which did not compete with French industry could be allowed to operate in Canada. In this respect, England's policy was similar to that of France; the manufacture of hats, and even of iron nails, was prohibited in the British colonies.[12]

After the Treaty of Utrecht, as before, the fur trade continued to be the most important factor in the country's economy. The monopoly was exercised by the Aubert company until December 1717. In January 1718 it passed into the hands of the *Compagnie d'Occident* which was to enjoy the privilege of "receiving, to the exclusion of all others," beaver skins from the colony. The King reserved to himself the right to regulate the price and the quantity of skins. The following year the *Compagnie des Indes* absorbed the *Compagnie d'Occident* and took over the monopoly which it held until the end of the French régime.[13] To regulate the fur trade, the system of *congés* or trading licences had been reintroduced in 1716. The Governor sold twenty-five annual permits at 250 *livres* each and distributed the proceeds to officers' widows and needy families. The system was once more abolished in 1719, but after being finally re-established in 1726 it continued to operate until the conquest.[14]

The country, from Tadoussac to the Saskatchewan, was divided into trading regions, each with its post whose chief officer was chosen in one of three ways. Some posts were obtained through influence or as a reward for service, others were leased to the highest bidder. In both these cases, the commander of the post, who might also be commander of the region, was absolute master in his own domain, and the system made it possible for some individuals, especially commanders of posts, to make enormous profits. In the third case, that of posts such as Toronto, Frontenac and Niagara, where profits were small or non-existent, the Crown assumed responsibility for administration and exploitation.[15]

Whoever they might be, licence-holders and post commanders pursued the same end: to realize the greatest possible profit. And the method which they followed was generally to bring pressure to bear on the Indian traders, to buy their furs at the lowest price possible and to sell them manufactured articles at a very high one. The rapacity of licensed traders helped to stimulate the illicit traffic carried on by *coureurs de bois* and mission Indians. English merchants abetted the law-breakers by selling iron pots and the highly prized red blankets at prices thirty per cent lower than those which prevailed in Montreal. Moreover, in Albany it was easy to obtain brandy for barter, whereas Mgr. Dosquet declared the sale of liquor a sin, on which judgment was reserved for his own tribunal.[16]

Partly because of an increase in the price of fur, partly perhaps because persistent smuggling invited closer supervision,
the fur trade continued to increase in volume and in value.
Until 1725 the yearly fur harvest brought in about 60,000 skins.
In 1726 the number of skins jumped to 135,000 and in 1730 to
164,000. By 1737 it had dropped again to about 134,000 and in
the following years it remained approximately the same. By 1744
the value of the furs had reached 1,500,000 *livres* a year, and
during the following years it sometimes exceeded 2,000,000
livres. Thus the fur trade occupied the first place in the Canadian economy right up to the end of the French régime.[17]

The traffic continued to be carried on by means of *voyageurs*
or *coureurs de bois* whose services were hired by contract to
entrepreneurs. From Montreal, where they loaded their canoes
with merchandise including all the brandy they could obtain by
legal or fraudulent means, they went up the Ottawa and on to
the different posts, which were strung out, hundreds of miles
apart, from Lake Ontario to the Saskatchewan. A year or two
later, they came back with their cargoes of furs, following the
same route by river and lake and back-breaking portage. It was
an arduous and exhausting life, but it held many attractions. In
France, the apprentice setting out on his *tour de France* looked
forward eagerly to the joys of travel and freedom from the rule
of a master. How much more exciting for the young Canadian
was the prospect of a *tour de la Nouvelle France* during which
he would see vast new country and live among the Indians, far
from the moral restraints of family and parish.[18]

Trade in general, as well as the fur trade, expanded rapidly
after the peace of Utrecht, more especially as a result of the
founding of Louisbourg. The new colony had to be supplied
with food and wood, and it was soon to become an important
centre of exchange for products from France, the West Indies
and Canada. Increases in the poulation and in the volume and
variety of products were also factors in the expansion of trade.
Progress in this sphere can be measured by the creation of the
Exchange in Montreal in 1717. Canada's first modest Exchange
had been established in Quebec in 1708. Each of the exchanges
had the privilege of electing one of its members to speak in the
name of all and to make to the Governor-General and the Intendant "the representations which may be necessary for the good

of their commerce." More than professional recognition, this right was a political gain allowing businessmen to exercise a certain influence in the economic direction of the country.[19]

As the years went by activity increased in the port of Quebec. In 1724 twenty ships came into the harbour; there were more than fifty in the last years of the régime. The colony continued to import goods from France in ever-increasing quantities: woven materials, shoes, hardware, groceries, wines and brandy. From the Antilles came tropical products: rum, molasses, coffee, sugar and tobacco. Even Ile Royale contributed a few shiploads of coal or cod. In exchange, Canada exported flour, peas, wood, and sometimes vegetables and meat. Ships from her shipyards were also sold abroad.[20]

In 1730 the value of imports was 1,419,415 *livres,* that of exports 1,398,327. Although the figures, both for imports and for exports, varied from year to year, the general tendency was towards a marked increase. Thus, in 1748 imports and exports had attained the respective values of 2,483,486 and 2,396,642 *livres.* No exact figures are given in the intendants' reports, but we may judge from them that imports almost always exceeded exports. Only three times in a period of thirty years, from 1730 to 1760, did exports represent the greater value. On the other hand, it sometimes happened that the value of imports was three times that of exports. A financial balance was established, however, chiefly through the sale of raw materials and services to the Crown, which assumed all military expenses and all the expenses of economic, political and social administration. Hocquart remarked in 1743 that Canadian merchants received less than half the profits from Canadian business. In 1755 the situation had not changed since Machault reported that Canadian businessmen were not rich enough to provide for the country's needs. Profits went into the pockets of the French merchants and their agents in the colony. Fourteen French companies carried on three quarters of the country's business, while the West India Company held the fur monopoly, and Versailles maintained and directed the shipbuilding and mining industries. Thus lack of capital and of scope for initiative prevented the development in Canada of a true bourgeoisie which might have controlled and directed the country's trade and commerce.[21]

In the period from 1713 to the conquest, there was no fundamental change in the structure of the budget, which continued to include the same categories of expenses: soldiers' pay, maintenance of fortifications, administrative salaries, public works, subsidies to industry, gifts to the Indians.[22] An analysis of yearly statements shows that from 1714 to 1726 sums expended by the Crown in Canada remained "very modest, scarcely exceeding 360,000 *livres*" a year. In the course of time, with increased needs, disbursements followed a rising curve which passed from 550,000 *livres* in 1741[23] to 1,000,000 in 1744, and to 2,000,000 during the War of the Austrian Succession. In 1752, as a result of four years of profiteering by Bigot, the war figure itself was doubled. Prospects of a new war brought a further rise, and when it came, the Seven Years' War, combined with the malversation of the Intendant and his gang, brought the country's expenses to the enormous total of 19,000,000 *livres* in 1756 and 30,000,000 in 1759.[24]

Meanwhile receipts were drawn from two principal sources, import and export duties and profits made by the King's warehouses.[25] Receipts from these sources increased steadily from 50,000 *livres* (1713) to 120,000 *livres* (1740). After that, with commercial expansion and higher taxes, the total rose to 335,000 *livres* in 1757.[26]

Even if we disregard the period during which Bigot's scandalous operations sent expenses to astronomical heights defying all comparison with previous budgets, the public accounts of the colony are evidence that receipts did not at any time equal expenses. The Royal Treasury made up a deficit which increased progressively from 100,000 *livres* in 1740 to 960,000 *livres* in 1747,[27] and which, in spite of the imposition of higher duties in 1747 and 1748, continued to increase during the final years of the French régime.

The King's accountants in Versailles were disturbed by this deficit and the impression it created of a colony which was an ever heavier charge on the mother country. On several occasions the Minister considered the possibility of levying a tax on the colonists. In 1713 Pontchartrain proposed that Canadians should contribute, in money or in kind, to the country's running expenses. Again in 1733, Maurepas suggested that the habitants should pay taxes proportionate to those which were levied in France, and that the taxes should be paid in wheat or other

products. These plans, which remained abortive, were followed
in 1742 by a proposal to subject every city and country dweller
either to a head or a property tax. This proposal too was abandoned when the Governor and the Intendant pointed out that
the country was very poor, and that revenues from the taxes
would not compensate for the expense of collecting them. Finally, in 1754, one final, futile attempt was made to elaborate an
effective plan for a general head tax. The scale of payment was
graduated from one to sixty *livres* according to the financial
capacity of the individual. The estimated yield, from a modest
average contribution of four *livres*, would have been 225,
842 *livres* for Canada's population of 55,000.[28] But this scheme
for direct taxation went the way of all its predecessors. Canadians remained exempt from all taxes except import and export
duties, and Versailles had to pay an annual deficit until the end
of the régime.[29]

Chapter Thirteen

ADMINISTRATION AND SOCIAL INSTITUTIONS
1713-1760

~~~~~~

The Governor superior to the Intendant. Restrictions on the functions of the Superior Council. The machinery of government. Social structure: clergy, nobility, third estate. Membership of each of the three orders; their function. Public institutions. Progress of the country under Hocquart. Military situation.

~~~~~~

As the colony grew in population and in wealth, changing needs and circumstances determined its evolution in other respects. Thus, while no formal change was made in the triple structure of administration, with Governor, Intendant and Sovereign Council, special conditions brought about a change in practice. The acrimonious disputes on questions of protocol, which had exasperated Louis XIV and resulted in the recall of Frontenac, were only the first in a long succession of such feuds. Champigny quarrelled with Callières, and Raudot senior was at odds with Vaudreuil, who did not always agree with Bégon. Rivalry with the Governor and, still more, ambition on the part of the Intendant, reached a climax with Dupuy, who disparaged, defied, and finally rejected, the Governor's authority. This time, Versailles became angry enough to take action; the Intendant was dismissed and replaced by a *commissaire-ordonnateur,* thus ending the dual authority and proclaiming once and for all the absolute supremacy of the Governor.[1]

From that time forward, no intendant made any pretension to absolute supremacy even in his own sphere. After his promotion to the intendancy in 1731, Hocquart took the initiative in introducing a number of new ideas, but he was always careful not to encroach in any way on the domain of the Governor. Bigot, who was as intelligent as he was unprincipled, and who was less interested in adding to the Intendant's prestige than in deriving gain from his office, was skilful enough to interest the governors La Jonquière, Duquesne, and especially Vaudreuil, in his dubious operations, and in effect, to direct the authority which governed the country. When Montcalm wrote that the highly centralized authority in the colony resides "in two, you might almost say one" man, the one man was the Intendant. This was so true that it was Bigot who framed the articles of the capitulation of Montreal.[1a]

The Superior Council, which was subordinate to the two highest dignitaries, had, on occasion, exercised certain political powers, powers which it had lost by a royal decision of 1685. In 1714, when the Council ventured to try to resume its former prerogative, Vaudreuil and Bégon immediately informed its members that discussion of matters of general administration was to be initiated only when the Governor and the Intendant were present. In 1726 a specific directive marked the limitations of the Council's functions; the King reminded the councillors that in them resided only "a part of his authority to render justice; it is to that duty that they must devote themselves." Henceforth, the Council's political function was strictly that of an auxiliary. The Governor and the Intendant were free to consult it, and might allow it, when they were present or simply with their permission, to make policy decisions and regulations. In practice, it was limited to its function as a court of appeal.[2]

The machinery of administration was very simple, with three courts of justice in Quebec, Montreal and Three Rivers. Subordinate to these were a small number of seigniorial courts, a police tribunal and an office of roads. Later there were added an admiralty court, an office of the controller of the Ministry of Marine and an office of clerks of the Treasurer-General of the Ministry of Finance. To these must also be added the posts of administrator of the King's domain, director of shipbuilding, inspector of woods and forests, inspector of fortifications and captain of the port of Quebec. Each of these services had its own personnel of secretaries, writers, store-keepers and clerks. The total number of civil servants in all these groups was no more than 218 during the last years of French rule.[3]

Under an authoritarian government which was itself subject to the authority of Versailles, the social structure of the country

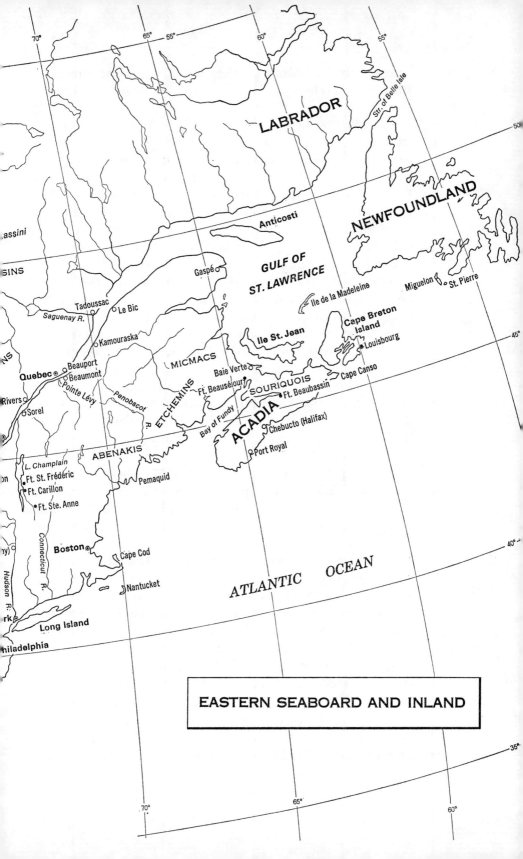

LABRADOR

Str. of Belle Isle

NEWFOUNDLAND

Anticosti

GULF OF
ST. LAWRENCE

assini

SINS

Gaspé

Tadoussac   Le Bic

Saguenay R.

Ile de la Madeleine

Miquelon   St. Pierre

Ile St. Jean

Cape Breton
Island

Kamouraska

Louisbourg

MICMACS

Baie Verte

Beauport

Quebec   Beaumont

Pointe Lévy

Ft. Beauséjour

Cape Canso

NS

SOURIQUOIS

Ft. Beaubassin

Rivers

Penobscot

ETCHEMINS

Sorel

R.

ACADIA

Bay of Fundy

Chebucto (Halifax)

ABENAKIS

Port Royal

L. Champlain

Ft. St. Frédéric

on

Pemaquid

Ft. Carillon

Ft. Ste. Anne

Connecticut R.

ny)

Boston   Cape Cod

Hudson R.

Nantucket

ATLANTIC   OCEAN

rk

Long Island

hiladelphia

EASTERN SEABOARD AND INLAND

did not change. Although they were seldom mentioned, the three orders—clergy, nobility, and third estate—continued to exist.[3a]

The first of these orders, the clergy, had 124 parishes under its direction at the end of the régime. Partly because there were not enough priests, and partly because the tithes did not suffice to pay a priest's salary, one third of the parishes had to be served by non-resident curés. Only forty-four parishes were entirely self-supporting; the others could count on a supplementary grant from the Royal Treasury. For the King regularly allotted subsidies to clergy and religious communities according to their needs, just as in the past he had granted to the Jesuits, the Sulpicians, the Quebec Seminary, the Ursulines and the Hospital Sisters, vast seigniories which yielded rich revenues. The only curés whose charges were permanent were those of Notre-Dame in Montreal and Notre-Dame in Quebec. Elsewhere parish priests were transferable at the discretion of the Bishop. Canada's 163 priests included 84 seculars, 30 Sulpicians, 25 Jesuits and 24 Récollets. Of this number 82 had been born in France, and 81 in Canada. Since the members of the latter group were drawn from the humbler social classes, while those of the former had enjoyed superior educational and cultural advantages, effective direction of the clergy was exercised by the French priests. The Bishop was always French.[4] In 1737, when the name of Canon Lotbinière was proposed, the King refused to appoint a "Canadian bishop." The reasons alleged were the "proud and hasty" temper of Canadian priests and their tendency "to independence and insubordination."[5]

The King gave generous help to the Church, although it was subject to his control and his decisions. He exercised his prerogative by appointing bishops and other high dignitaries, by fixing tithes and by directing religious communities in matters such as their rules, their number, and even their habits. He supervised the conduct, sermons and pastoral instructions of the clergy and threatened with sanctions those who were guilty of the slightest deviation. Times had indeed changed since 1663. Colbert and Talon had started the process of change by undermining the theocracy established by Mgr. de Laval and the Jesuits, and Louis XIV had contributed to it by openly reprimanding Mgr. de Saint-Vallier. In the eighteenth century, the prestige and influence of the Bishop and the clergy were at such a low ebb that in 1732 a royal order authorized the searching of religious houses, although their privilege exempted them from such treatment, and religious cases were removed from the ecclesiastical tribunal and judged by civil courts. The Church, in the person of Mgr. de Pontbriand, suffered another setback in the affair of the Protestant merchants. Invoking a law which barred Protestants from the country, the Bishop had asked that those already in Quebec be expelled, but, on the advice of Vaudreuil and Bigot, the King took no action.[6]

The second class, the nobility, unlike the nobility of France, was allowed to engage in trade. Its members were privileged to wear swords, but even when they appeared before the Council, their rank was strictly honorary and carried no political implications. At the mid-century, the nobility counted about two hundred heads of families. Most of them possessed seigniories, and for most of them service in the marines was a family tradition. Their great ambition was to command a post in the West, where fortunes could be made in the fur trade, whether licensed or contraband. Some, however, preferred to seek appointments in the administration or the courts. Those who could do so continued the practice of their fathers and grandfathers by engaging directly or indirectly in some form of business. A list drawn up at the end of the régime records that among twenty-two officers, twelve were rich or very rich, while six had remained poor. A contemporary adds the comment that, even though luxury was unknown, seigneurs had the means required to "keep up their dignity."[7]

Whatever their degree of wealth, the nobles represented a social élite. The authorities consulted them on matters of general interest in official meetings called for the purpose. The people recognized in them the prestige of rank, education or command. The degree of deference accorded to the nobility differed with individuals and circumstances, but when some seigneurs tried to increase their profits by imposing illegal or excessive obligations on their tenants, the unpopularity provoked by such exploitation tended to redound upon the class as a whole.[8]

The lowest order, the third estate, included the whole population with the exception of the nobility and the clergy. Within this order the recognized leaders were the officers of justice and the merchants. In religious ceremonies only the members of the first of these groups continued to occupy a place of honour; but the experience of the merchants and their numbers gradually made them the dominant influence, and the third estate finally assumed the significant name of *Corps du Commerce*. When delegations were sent to make representations to the authorities, the nobility and the clergy merely supported the third order, while the "merchants' syndic," a layman and a commoner, became the colony's "representative." Thus after the theocratic ascendancy of Mgr. de Laval, and a period of aristocratic influence, at the end of the French period it was the deputy of the people who spoke in the name of the country.[9]

The function of people's representative existed, however, only by virtue of the authorities' consent, for Canadians had no political rights. The only ways open to them for the expression of ideas or complaints were meetings called by, or permitted by, the authorities, and petitions to the King, the Minister, or the Governor and the Intendant. We should not, however, conclude with Raynal, Tocqueville and Parkman that Canada was subjected to completely despotic rule.[10] The royal authority did in fact maintain the principle of absolutism, but, in Canada still more than in France, the theoretically absolute power of the King was exercised in a true spirit of justice, tolerance and even benevolence. On several occasions, Versailles reminded the senior officials in the colony of the respect they owed to the liberties of its citizens, and contravened orders which overstepped the powers of the officials who had issued them. On the other hand, governors and intendants often persuaded the French authorities to modify or rescind certain decisions which were inopportune. There were even cases where petitions from the colonists led ministers to postpone the execution of royal orders. Official documents offer abundant proof that, thanks to the reasonable spirit which prevailed on both sides of the Atlantic, the colony was not oppressed under absolute rule.

Another indication of a tendency towards liberalism is to be seen in the royal permission, granted in 1717, for the establishment of Exchanges in Quebec and Montreal. This permission was granted in compliance with a petition presented by the merchants of the two towns. At the same time each of the two trade exchanges was accorded the privilege of electing a delegate to speak "in the name of all" and to make representations to the Governor and the Intendant. Thus a way was opened officially for the expression of public opinion. In one other respect Canadians were placed on an equal footing with their French cousins during this period. On two occasions distinguished Canadians had been excluded from the office of Governor-General, but in 1755 Vaudreuil de Cavagnal became the first native son to be chosen by the King as his representative in Canada.[11]

Before the end of the seventeenth century the colony had been provided with the social services considered essential at that time. Quebec, Montreal and Three Rivers had hospitals and homes for the sick and the aged. They also had schools for boys and convents for girls. There were schools in a certain number of rural parishes while the trade school at St. Joachim trained artisans and taught Latin to future seminarists. In Montreal the Jesuits and the Sulpicians gave Latin courses. In Quebec candidates for the priesthood were enrolled in the junior seminary, where the Jesuits had a course in theology as well as the traditional classical curriculum. The royal school of hydrography taught mathematics and navigation to future officers and sailors, and French lawyers gave lectures on law which were attended by candidates for the magistracy.[12]

Public assistance was maintained by subsidies. Victims of every kind of misfortune appealed to the compassion of the Royal Treasury whose bounties were administered by the Intendant. Illegitimate and abandoned children were supported at the rate of ten *livres* a month; help was given to victims of accidents or disasters, poverty or famine.[13]

To sum up the situation at the mid-century: under an authoritarian and paternalistic government, too often timid and lacking in vision, the population of the country was growing steadily and its economy was expanding. This progress must be attributed in large part to Hocquart, who, in so far as he was allowed to do so, devoted all his energies and his superior intelligence to the task of developing the potentialities of the colony. At the same time, under the influence of local ways and economic conditions, an equalization of classes was gradually taking place.

Ever blacker clouds on the international horizon warned that open conflict was imminent. When it came, Canada, with a military force quite inadequate for such a task, would have to defend an immense territory stretching from Quebec to the far western posts. A corps of 2,700 marines, most of whose officers were Canadian, constituted the permanent garrison. In 1755 Versailles sent reinforcements consisting of about 6,000 regulars. The members of this force—officers and men—were French and took precedence over those of the colonial force. The militia provided services and troops. At full strength, it counted 15,912 men but as they could not all serve at once without paralysing the life of the country, the effective strength even in moments of crisis was not much more than half the total number. In 1753, for the first time, a militia detachment received its own colours, colours which in a few years would have seen their baptism of fire.[14]

Chapter Fourteen
BIGOT'S RÉGIME.
HOSTILITIES BEFORE THE DECLARATION OF WAR
1755-1756

A Canadian Governor, Vaudreuil. Bigot's malversations. The Grande Société. Bigot praised by Vaudreuil. Commission on the boundaries of Acadia. English policy in America. Attack and capture of the Alcide and the Lys. Battle of the Monongahela and defeat of Brock. Dieskau repulsed at Lake George. Montcalm in command. War parties against the English colonies.

In January 1755 Duquesne was succeeded by Pierre de Vaudreuil de Cavagnal, who assumed the honorary title of Marquis, although the same title was already held by the head of the Vaudreuil family. A fellow officer, Potot de Montbeillard, who had reasons of interest for seeing good points in Vaudreuil, said of him that he was "sensible" though "not brilliant," and that he was "noble and generous but equally ignorant of the laws of civil and of military government." He added that the Governor was conscious of his authority and had a "head for his task," but that he was lacking in firmness and had less confidence in French officers than in the Canadians who were his compatriots and sometimes his relations. Vaudreuil was a native of Quebec. After serving as an officer in the marines, he was named Governor of Three Rivers in 1733. In 1742 he was promoted, through family influence, to the post of Governor of Louisiana. On his return to Quebec in 1755 he was warmly welcomed, partly because he was Canada's first Canadian Governor-General, and partly because it was hoped that he would bring back the "happy days" of his father's administration. He still possessed the seigniory of Vaudreuil, although, to his great chagrin, the illicit trade carried on by his farmers for his benefit had been suppressed by Beauharnois in 1742 before his departure for Louisiana.[1]

When Vaudreuil arrived in Quebec in June 1755, his colleague Bigot had already been in office seven years, during which time he had made use of his quite exceptional talents to perfect a remarkable system for despoiling the Royal Treasury, and to acquire a virtual monopoly of the country's trade. Not only was Bigot intelligent, perspicacious and hard-working, but he had a real genius for business, and he used his knowledge of the intricacies of the administrative machine to make it work for his profit. He appropriated for himself and for La Jonquière a share in the fur trade, and he had already formed a business partnership with a shipowner in Bordeaux, Gradis, and the Controller of Marine in Quebec, Michel Bréard.[2] The most notorious among his accomplices were the "triumvirate," Hughes Péan, Joseph Cadet and Brassard Descheneaux. Péan, who was Brevet-Major of the city of Quebec, was "a born tradesman" rather than a soldier. It was said of him that "all his good qualities consisted in the charms of his wife." Madame Péan had become the Intendant's mistress, and to this relationship her husband owed contracts which brought him enormous profits. Cadet was a butcher "without education of any kind," but he was "the most industrious, the most active and the most knowing" of agents where buying and selling were concerned. Descheneaux was the son of a shoemaker, and had been educated by a notary. He was Bigot's secretary, and his "keen and penetrating mind," combined with his knowledge of intendancy business, made him indispensable in the organization and direction of the Intendant's profitable deals. This *Grande Société*, as it was called, grabbed every contract in which the government was a party. Each time that the administration needed supplies, Bigot informed his partners, who bought up the articles in question and sold them to the state at a profit of 100 per cent, of which a large proportion went to the Intendant. In 1750 his revenue from this particular kind of transaction was 200,000 *livres*. In the case of wheat, the Company bought the crop from the farmer at a very low price. Then the Intendant issued an order fixing a much higher price and, in his official capacity, bought the partners' whole stock, whatever its quality, at this increased rate. In

the same way, shipping contracts "which were very profitable"
were reserved for the ships belonging to the profiteers. They
"even managed to sell the same merchandise several times over to
the King and to make him pay a higher price for it each time."
As headquarters for its many and various operations, the group
maintained two stores, one in Quebec and the other in Montreal.
The common people, who well knew what sort of business was
transacted in them, called the shops "the rogues."[3]

As early as 1751, the Minister accused Bigot of paying more
than current market prices for supplies which he bought in the
King's name. Year after year, Rouillé complained of abuses in
the awarding of contracts and of mounting expenses, and each
complaint was a reprimand for the Intendant. In 1754 the Minister went further and mentioned names of persons who were
exercising a monopoly in the buying and selling of flour and
other goods. The Intendant was requested to supply satisfactory
"clarification" of these matters.[4]

At this point Rouillé was replaced by Machault at the Ministry of Marine, and Bigot thought it wise to present himself in
person to the new minister. After disposing of Rouillé's charges
of maladministration, he proposed to seek an appointment as
Intendant of Rochefort. Accordingly, he went to France, where
he had another silent partner in the person of the Sieur de La
Porte, chief clerk in the Ministry of Marine. With the help of
this ally, Bigot completely won the confidence of Machault, who
decided to ignore his request for an appointment in France and
to send him back to Quebec. Bigot's mission had been more
successful than he could have dared to hope. By renewing his
appointment, the Minister had set the seal of approval on his
previous record and had left him free to add to it. Thus armed
with an endorsement of his past conduct, the Intendant returned to Canada and resumed more vigorously than ever the
profitable business of malversation.[4a]

"The high hopes which had been entertained" that the new
governor would put an end to administrative embezzlement
and illicit monopolies "soon vanished." The budget for 1755
marked an increase of 2,000,000 *livres* over the previous year,
and the Minister threatened to "abandon" the country if expenses could not be reduced, but the Governor had nothing but
praise for Bigot, whose extraordinary talents, zeal and energy

had no equal.[5] Vaudreuil wrote in this vein to the Minister even though he was quite aware of Bigot's misappropriations, and it is significant that contemporaries place the beginnings of the Governor's fortune and that of his secretary Grasset de Saint-Sauveur in 1755.[6]

Vaudreuil had received definite instructions in respect to Canada's relations with the English colonies: he was to adopt a defensive policy; but, if the English initiated any offensive action beyond the Alleghany frontier, he was to "use all force" against them, specifically at Oswego. For, after the conclusion of peace, the problem of frontiers in the disputed territories of Acadia and the Ohio kept coming to the surface. The Treaty of Aix-la-Chapelle had not fixed these frontiers, but had referred the question to a commission whose members were La Galissonnière and Silhouette for the French and William Shirley and William Mildmay for the English. The commission met in Paris in 1750, and at intervals until 1754, without arriving at any conclusion. While the French limited Acadia to that part of the peninsula which lay south of a line running from Minas to Canso, the English claimed all the mainland east of the Penobscot River and north to the St. Lawrence. With both parties presenting such unreasonable claims, the commission might accumulate any number of briefs and documents, but its deliberations were bound to end in failure.[7] In the Ohio valley the English refused to recognize the Alleghany frontier and claimed a region which had been recognized as French ever since the time of Cavelier de La Salle. They based their claim "on the rights of the Iroquois," who were, they alleged, their subjects, although the Iroquois had no rights in the region and recognized no foreign sovereign.[7a]

It seemed obvious that no agreement would be reached on either of these disputed frontiers. At the same time the question was being asked in Europe whether England really desired a peaceful solution to territorial disputes which might lead to war. Within a period of sixty years England's economic structure had changed. By a series of steps, two of which were the Navigation Act (1660) and the Commerce Act (1689), this agricultural people had been changed into a nation of shopkeepers. As the country's commerce expanded, its merchant marine increased ten-fold, providing a "nursery" for seamen in a navy whose power was becoming more formidable every day. England, now transformed into a mercantile and marine nation, could not live without foreign markets, preferably markets in the undeveloped countries—America, the West Indies, India—in each of which a rival, France, was already installed.[8]

The French in America were a special source of irritation. Not only did they dispute the frontier in Acadia, where they tried to limit the English to a narrow coastal region, but they closed the fur routes to the West and claimed the valley of the Ohio. The Anglo-American colonies were more conscious of frustration even than the mother country. Threatened with being hemmed in along the Atlantic seaboard, New York, Virginia and even Pennsylvania had for years been sending merchants and settlers into French territory. The Governor of Virginia dispatched militia to build posts and forts for the defence of settlers. In 1754 the colonies held a congress in Albany with the intention of combining their forces against the common enemy; but no agreement was reached and no action was taken. Versailles was aware both of movements in the colonies and of the campaign being carried on in London by financial and commercial interests with the aim "of attacking Canada simultaneously from every side with superior forces." All these schemes were being promoted with the tacit consent of the "English government at a time when it was assuring France of its most pacific intentions."[9]

In this situation the capitulation of Fort Necessity was a great blow to Great Britain. In September 1754, still protesting that her one aim was to protect her possessions, she entrusted to General Edward Braddock the organization of the campaign which was being prepared, and in January 1755 two regiments were dispatched to Virginia from Ireland. Far from limiting him to defensive action, Braddock's secret instructions directed him to organize attacks against Niagara, St. Frédéric, Beauséjour and the forts on the Ohio. Since the French victories at Fontenoy and Lawfeld, the Duke of Cumberland had not ceased to fan the spirit of revenge, and for two years England had been preparing to take the offensive in New France on all fronts.[10]

In spite of mounting proofs of a war policy in England, Louis XV still hoped that an open break might be avoided. However, in May 1755, not wishing to be caught unawares, he sent a squadron of 18 ships to Canada. The fleet, under the command of Dubois de La Mothe, included 3 frigates armed for war, and carried a force of 3,150 men. Two of its 6 battalions were destined for Louisbourg. These defensive preparations provoked an English decision to dispense with the formality of a declaration of war and to open hostilities immediately. Accordingly, while the two countries were at peace, secret instructions were transmitted to Admiral Boscawen ordering him to intercept and capture any French transports which he might meet.[11]

On June 7, when he was south of Newfoundland, Dubois de La Mothe sighted the enemy squadron. He escaped with most of his fleet into the gulf, but three of his ships, the *Alcide,* the *Lys* and the *Dauphin Royal,* were cut off from the others by fog. The following day, when the fog lifted, they sighted eleven English ships. As one of them, the *Dunkirk,* was bearing down on the *Alcide,* Captain Hocquart seized a megaphone and shouted: "Are we at war or at peace?" To which Captain Howe replied: "At peace, at peace." But when the *Dunkirk* was within half a pistol-shot its guns opened fire on the *Alcide,* which was also attacked by four other ships, including the flagship. The *Alcide* replied with "heavy fire from guns and muskets," but with eighty men killed or wounded, his cannon out of action and his rigging shot to pieces, Hocquart had finally to surrender to Boscawen. The *Lys,* caught in a cross-fire, fought for two hours before lowering her flag. Only the swifter sailing *Dauphin* made good her escape and succeeded in reaching Louisbourg. Three hundred and thirty soldiers from the regiments of La Reine and Languedoc were captured in this unjustifiable attack. The English aggression aroused great indignation in Paris, but, when Louis XV instructed his ambassador to the Court of St. James's to lodge an official protest, the incident was attributed to a misinterpretation of royal instructions.[12]

The English also assumed the offensive on land, this time on American soil. Braddock had received information on conditions at Fort Duquesne from a certain Captain Stobo who had taken advantage of his position as hostage to act as a spy, and in June (1755), armed with this information, he set out to destroy the French post. From Fort Cumberland on the Potomac he marched to the recently rebuilt Fort Necessity, and from there he advanced, with a force of almost 2,000 soldiers and militia, to attack Fort Duquesne, 3 leagues away. On July 8, informed of the English expedition, the commander of the French fort, M. de Contrecœur, ordered Liénard de Beaujeu to lead a detachment against the enemy. The force was made up of 37 officers, 72 regulars, 146 militiamen and 637 Indians, a total of 892 men.[13]

The following day, July 9, as Braddock's troop was advancing through a forest, Beaujeu spread out his Indians along both sides of the road with orders not to show themselves until he had made his frontal attack. He disposed his 200 soldiers and militiamen in ranks of 15 and when the English army appeared, at about eleven o'clock, he ordered them to open fire with their rifles. The English replied with a disciplined fusillade, opening their ranks after each discharge in order to allow the artillery to come into action. The combined fire demoralized the irregulars, accustomed to guerilla tactics, and they fell back in confusion. At the third discharge Beaujeu was killed and Captain Dumas took command. At that moment the Indians, who were hidden by the trees, opened fire on the English from both sides. Their shooting was irregular, but "not a single shot missed its mark." Disconcerted by this rain of fire from an invisible enemy, Braddock's soldiers broke their formation and, by trying to attack on both sides of the road, paralysed their own frontal action. Dumas was quick to seize the opportunity to regroup his forces and renew his attack. The English fought with "the most stubborn courage," but their compact formation made it impossible for them to manœuvre in the dense forest, and "whole ranks fell at once." Battered by fire from French and Indians, their squares faltered and broke. Braddock had five horses killed under him, and, as he strove heroically to rally his troops, he himself fell, mortally wounded. The French force charged the enemy while the Indians came out from behind the trees brandishing their tomahawks and uttering terrifying war whoops. Under the "indescribable fury" of their assault, the English regulars broke ranks, retreated and fled to Fort Necessity.[14]

The battle had lasted 5 hours, and the French had lost 24 dead and 16 wounded. English losses amounted to 997 men, of whom about 600 were killed. Among the dead was "General

Braddock's mistress, beautiful as Love. Mounted on a magnificent horse . . . she was killed, fighting beside her lover." The
victors salvaged a great deal of war material from the battle-
field: mortars, rifles, ammunition and utensils. The next day,
they pursued the enemy to Fort Necessity, only to find that the
fort had been evacuated and set on fire. General Braddock's
trunks, which were still intact, contained his instructions and
plans for campaigns against St. Frédéric and Niagara. They also
contained the letters, written by Captain Stobo while a hostage
in Quebec, which had supplied information about the French
colony.[15]

Before receiving the news of the victory of the Monongahela, Vaudreuil had formed a plan to capture Oswego (Fort
Chouaguen), the English trading station and offensive outpost
at the entrance to Lake Ontario. But before his plan could be
realized he learned that New York had an army of 4,400 men
ready to march against Fort St. Frédéric, at the head of Lake
Champlain. In order to meet this immediate threat he assembled an army of 3,000 men and dispatched them under the
command of Baron Dieskau with instructions to attack and
repulse the English force.[16]

Dieskau, who had served under the Maréchal de Saxe, had
the reputation of being "credulous, stubborn and uncompro-
mising in his opinions" and of commanding his troops "in the
German fashion." On September 4 he set out from Fort St.
Frédéric with a force of about 600 Canadians, 600 Indians and
230 regulars. His plan was to surprise Fort Edward on the
Hudson, but on the evening of the 7th, learning that a force of
3,000 men under Colonel Johnson was encamped at the head of
Lake George, he decided to attack the camp.[17] The next day,
September 8, the troops surprised an advance guard of 400 English and savages which they assailed and pursued to within
sight of Johnson's army. Then, without giving his men time "to
get their breath," Dieskau gave the order for an assault on the
camp, which was strongly entrenched behind a barrier of carts
and boats. The Canadians advanced in open formation, but the
mission Iroquois, having recognized some Mohawks among the
English, refrained from joining the other warriors in the French
ranks. The exchange of fire went on actively for two hours before the superior force of muskets on the English side stopped

the French sixty yards from the camp. Dieskau, fighting in the front lines, had three bullets in his legs, but he refused to allow himself to be carried to the rear and instructed Montreuil, his adjutant, to lead the regulars in the assault on the camp. However, when their Indian allies retired from the field, the Canadians were also forced to withdraw. Finally the whole force retreated, leaving Dieskau a prisoner in the hands of the enemy.[18]

The expeditionary force returned to the colony. Soldiers, militia and Indians all blamed Dieskau, whose rash action in ordering 1,500 men to attack a camp defended by 3,000 had compromised the success of the expedition. On the other hand, all agreed that the Canadians and the regulars had fought bravely. In the two engagements the French casualties had been 103 wounded and 132 killed, while the English had lost about 400 men. The capture of Dieskau made the French defeat a great victory in the eyes of the English, and Vaudreuil could not forgive Montreuil for not recapturing his general "by force."[19]

Dieskau's setback did not suffice to counterbalance the victory of the Monongahela, nor did it prevent Vaudreuil's success in maintaining the neutrality of the Five Nations and the friendly disposition of the western tribes. The Governor also strengthened the outer defences of the colony. He increased the garrisons at Frontenac and Niagara and, as a deterrent to attacks on Fort St. Frédéric, he erected Fort Carillon at the entrance to Lake Champlain.[20]

After the capture of the *Alcide* and the *Lys*, and Braddock's expedition, England continued her naval aggression on a grand scale. During October and November 1755, while the two nations were still at peace, Admirals Boscawen and Hawke captured three hundred French merchant vessels and six thousand seamen. In December Louis XV presented a note to George II protesting these "acts of piracy," and demanding restitution of the prizes and their crews. In January London answered with a communication accusing France of building forts in British Acadia and on the Ohio, and of arresting English fur traders. Since French troops had been sent to Canada, England affirmed her right, by virtue "of the principle of defence," to seize ships of the French navy, and George II refused to disavow his officers' acts.[21]

Even in the face of the facts, Louis XV maintained his peace policy and, refusing stubbornly to declare war, limited his action to strengthening Canada's defences. In March 1756 he appointed the Marquis de Montcalm as Field-Marshal in command of the forces in New France. Montcalm was a small man, but his expressive face and his wise and witty conversation made him an attractive figure. His native intelligence had been cultivated in the course of a wide classical education and in his profession as an officer in the army. For on this point we must reject the allegations of his only detractor, the incompetent Montbeillard, who was not an impartial witness. Montbeillard had been one of Bigot's accomplices in plundering the Royal Treasury, and he could not forgive Montcalm for having denounced the Intendant's fraudulent manœuvres. Montcalm had fought with distinction in several campaigns and had been wounded five times.

Montcalm's second-in-command, the Chevalier de Lévis, while not a man of exceptional abilities, was endowed with qualities which were very valuable in an officer: "experience, good sense, judgment and decision." As aide-de-camp the commander-in-chief chose Antoine de Bougainville, a young man whose studies had included both literature and mathematics and who was warmly recommended by Madame de Pompadour. Montcalm was directed to conform in every detail to the orders and instructions of the Governor-General, except in cases of unforeseen emergency. He disembarked in Quebec at the beginning of May with his troops, two battalions from the regiments of La Sarre and Royal Roussillon.[22]

During the winter and through the spring of 1756, Vaudreuil, resorting to guerilla tactics, sent Indian war parties to raid English settlements. The Indians took no prisoners, but killed everyone they encountered—men, women and children. Georgia, Carolina and Virginia were ravaged by this "cruellest form of war," and Lieutenant de Villiers attacked and burned Fort Grandville, six miles from Philadelphia. In May the Sieur de Léry, with six hundred men, captured Fort Bull, thirty leagues from Oswego, which was defended by a garrison of about two hundred men. The wife of one of the commanders was about to be burned at the stake, but at the last moment she was ransomed by a French soldier for four hundred *livres*. The soldier wrote to Vaudreuil that "he had saved the most beautiful English woman you could ever see," and asked that his money be repaid or that he be allowed to marry her. It may be assumed that Vaudreuil granted the necessary permission.[23]

Chapter Fifteen
FIRST HOSTILITIES IN THE SEVEN YEARS' WAR
1756-1757

Declaration of war. England's naval superiority. Siege and capture of Chouaguen by Montcalm. Friction between French and Canadian officers. Trial of Stobo. Siege and surrender of Fort William Henry. The so-called massacre of prisoners. Vaudreuil's prejudice against Montcalm. Cadet appointed commissary-general. Abuses, famine, rationing. Extravagance and frivolity in official circles.

While Vaudreuil's preventive raids in America were keeping the English colonies in a state of alarm, changes were being effected in the political map of Europe. England was determined to make the conquest of Canada the first objective of the conflict already in progress, and, in order to achieve this end, she required an ally who would engage French forces on the continent and at the same time protect Hanover for George II. Her diplomats pointed out to Frederick II the danger of maintaining a secret pact with Russia, whose long-term policy was opposed to the expansion of Prussia. In January 1756 Frederick signed a treaty which, while dissipating the Russian threat, betrayed his engagements with France and made him England's ally and his army England's army in Europe. In May, in order to protect herself, France carried out the "reversal of alliances" whereby she became the ally of Austria, her former rival and the sworn enemy of Prussia. In April France had answered England's acts of piracy by sending an armed force to invade Minorca, which surrendered the following month. War was formally declared, by England on May 17, and by France on June 16. The French proclamation denounced "Great Britain's violations of international law."[1]

France thus found herself engaged in a conflict which she had to fight both on the European and on the American fronts. Great Britain, on the other hand, could leave the continental struggle to her Prussian ally and confine her operations to American territory, while the Channel protected her own soil from the danger of invasion. She was also favoured in war overseas, for her naval superiority made it possible for her to send her armies to America, and at the same time to block the passage of French reinforcements. When hostilities began, England could muster 100 armed transports and frigates against 81 French ships in the same categories. The disproportion between the English and French populations in America was still more striking: 1,000,000 in the first case, 70,000 in the second.[2]

The presence of Montcalm's 2 battalions and 400 recruits for the marines encouraged Vaudreuil to revive his plan to capture Fort Chouaguen on the Oswego River, and, after some hesitation, an expedition was finally organized under the leadership of Montcalm. Although they did not know it, conditions in the English colonies were rather favourable for the attackers. In April Shirley, the man of action, was recalled from Massachusetts and replaced by the uncertain and hesitant Loudoun. The change of leadership was followed by disputes between the British command and the colonial officers who claimed equality of rank with their fellow officers in the British regiments, and as a result of these difficulties the campaign against St. Frédéric had to be postponed.[3]

Meanwhile the French expedition under Montcalm set out and reached Chouaguen on August 9. It included 1,550 regulars with about 1,500 militia and 250 savages. There were 3 forts in the group at the entrance of the Oswego River: Fort Ontario, which was protected by a stockade, the principal fort known as Old Chouaguen, a fortified house with a solid defence wall, and Fort George, a small picket fort. They were defended by 1,134 regulars and militia under the orders of Colonel James Mercer.[4]

On August 12 Montcalm invested Fort Ontario, and the Canadians and Indians opened fire on the walls. All the next day the enemy kept up a brisk fire, but in the evening Mercer ordered the garrison to withdraw to Fort George. On the 14th, French artillery was brought into action against Chouaguen. During the day the walls were battered by French balls, and the

English guns answered with equally heavy fire. At nine o'clock a detachment of Canadians and Indians under Rigaud de Vaudreuil carried out Montcalm's order to ford the river. Wading through water up to their waists, they occupied the shore and isolated the fort. Mercer was preparing to counterattack when he was killed by a cannon ball. Colonel Littlehales assumed command of the fort, but, as the besiegers were bringing up a fresh battery, he called a council of war which voted in favour of capitulation. Terms were quickly arranged and were signed by Montcalm at eleven o'clock on August 14 (1756).[5] Unfortunately, the surrender was followed by certain disorders. Although orders were given to stave in the rum barrels, some Indians managed to become intoxicated and to perpetrate a certain number of violent acts before Montcalm stopped them with presents of the value of 10,000 *livres*. Other Indians looted the fort and killed "a few soldiers" who tried to escape into the woods.[6]

Chouaguen was taken at a cost to the French of a relatively small number of casualties: 6 dead and 24 wounded. English losses were much heavier: 152 dead, about 30 wounded, and 1,640 prisoners. As well as the colours of 5 regiments, the victors captured an enormous quantity of booty, including 7 vessels, 137 cannon, 23,000 pounds of powder and 2 granaries with their stock of provisions.[7]

During the next few days, the troops razed the three forts, and Montcalm erected a cross bearing the inscription: *In hoc signo vincunt.* On August 17 the army embarked for its return voyage to Montreal. There the clergy chanted a solemn *Te Deum* and the whole town rejoiced. Verses were written to celebrate the victory, which was also recorded in a chronicle published in France and circulated the following year in Quebec.[8]

This exploit was carried out in spite of a certain friction in the defence forces which went back to Dieskau's campaign. The hardy colonial officers, formed in the school of raids and surprise attacks, had little liking for the elegant French officers and their European strategy. When Montcalm extolled the land army and its "incredible spirit," Vaudreuil also sang its praises to the Minister of War, and recognized the military genius of Montcalm. But with the same pen he wrote to his own Minister of Marine that the land troops "did not distinguish themselves to the highest degree." He attributed credit for the victory to himself, his brother Rigaud, and the other Canadian officers, and he even claimed that the French officers mistreated militiamen "with sword or stick in hand." Bougainville later gave a very highly coloured picture of these differences when he reported that officers from France and from Canada seemed to belong to "different, even hostile, nations."[9]

So dismayed were the Anglo-Americans by the fall of Chouaguen that Loudoun abandoned his plan of an expedition against Fort St. Frédéric and decided to remain on the defensive.[10] Another beneficial result of Montcalm's victory was that it confirmed the neutrality of all the Iroquois nations except the Mohawks, and fortified the loyalty of the various western tribes, who continued to harass settlements in the English colonies from Maryland to Virginia.[11] In Canada, a poor harvest created near-famine conditions and a smallpox epidemic took a heavy toll of lives.[12] In Montreal Vaudreuil had Captain Stobo brought to trial. Stobo, who, according to his own admission, had violated his obligation as a hostage and given military information to the enemy, was tried by court martial on November 8, 1757 and sentenced to death. His sentence was later commuted, but he was held as a prisoner in Quebec until he escaped in April 1759.[12a]

In Great Britain, the indomitable Pitt, who had sworn to conquer America, ordered Loudoun to undertake the siege of Louisbourg. But when Vice-Admiral Holbourne's fleet dropped anchor in Halifax harbour in July 1757, it was already too late. The French had been informed of the plan and a French fleet of twenty-three ships was mounting guard off Louisbourg. When scouts brought news of this development to Halifax, Loudoun returned to New York.

After Chouaguen, Vaudreuil's next target was Fort William Henry at the entrance to Lake George, which he proposed to surprise by a winter attack. In February he assembled a detachment of fourteen hundred Canadians and Indians and appointed his brother, Rigaud de Vaudreuil, who according to Machault and Duquesne, was more courageous than intelligent, to command the expedition.[13] The little army travelled sixty leagues on snowshoes, living on salt pork and bread, and sleeping on the snow under canvas shelters and wrapped in bearskins. On March 18 they reached the fort, only to find it strongly fortified. As Rigaud's force was too weak to attempt an assault, he withdrew after burning everything—skiffs, boats and stores—that had been left outside the fortifications.[13a]

In July Vaudreuil, who knew that Loudoun was immobilized in Halifax, dispatched a second and much more imposing force to attack Fort William Henry. Montcalm, already posted at Carillon, was given command of an army of about 8,000 regulars, militia and Indians. On August 3 this army laid siege to the fort, a walled enclosure 300 feet square, well provided with guns and supported by an entrenched camp. Colonel Munro commanded the defending garrison of 2,400 men. Montcalm summoned the commander to surrender and so avoid possible torture at the hands of the Indians, but Munro rejected the summons. As the bearer of Munro's message passed through the enemy's lines, an Indian shouted a threat which was later to be made good: "Defend yourself well then; for if I take you, no quarter for you."[14]

During the next two or three days, although the French positions were under heavy fire, Montcalm succeeded in establishing two batteries. On August 7 scouts intercepted a message from Colonel Webb at Fort Edward informing Munro that he could not expect any help and that he must surrender under the most favourable terms obtainable. After reading the letter, Montcalm sent it on to Munro, who thanked him for it. The exchange of fire continued throughout the following day, but on August 9 Munro hoisted the white flag and offered to surrender. The terms of capitulation granted the honours of war to the garrison which was to be taken under French escort to Fort Edward. The sick and the wounded were to remain under the protection of General Montcalm. The losses amounted on the English side to 80 killed and 120 wounded, and on the French side to 17 killed and 40 wounded. The victors also captured 43 pieces of artillery, 25,000 pounds of powder and large quantities of provisions.[15]

The surrender was followed by a most unfortunate incident. Before the capitulation, Montcalm, hoping to prevent the possibility of Indian looting and cruelty, had persuaded the chiefs to promise that "their young men would commit no disorder." His envoy Bougainville had also urged the English to pour out

Habitants playing cards, from a painting by C. Krieghoff

Mme Elisabeth Bégon

Mme Angélique Péan

Marquis de Montcalm

General Jeffery Amherst

Habitants dancing a minuet, from a painting by Heriot

their stocks "of wine, brandy and all intoxicating liquors." When, at dawn the next day, August 10, the prisoners set out for Fort Edward with an escort of 200 French soldiers, the Indians swarmed around them. Some of the Indians forced their way into the abandoned camp and killed about 15 wounded men in the hospital tents. As the number of victims grew, the terrified English soldiers, hoping to pacify the savages, gave them their arms and their uniforms. Some of them even gave them their gourds filled with rum and, as they drank, the Indians become more and more arrogant. A group of Abenakis, in a rage of vengeance for the betrayal which their nation had recently suffered at the hands of the people of Boston, attacked the rear of the column. The English were carrying rifles with bayonets fixed, but they offered no resistance, and the Indians stripped them of everything: arms, equipment, clothes. In the course of this orgy of looting, they killed "about a dozen soldiers" and captured five or six hundred. The French escort, "at the risk of their lives," gave the prisoners what protection they could. Some soldiers were wounded in the attempt. Alerted by the clamour, Montcalm and Lévis, officers and interpreters, missionaries and Canadians all hastened to the help of the English, and by their combined efforts succeeded in calming the Indians' frenzy. Montcalm ransomed four hundred prisoners whom he provided with clothes and sent four days later to Fort Edward. The Indians, still loaded with booty and still holding two hundred prisoners, took the road to Montreal, where Vaudreuil displayed a singular lack of firmness and courage. Instead of punishing the culprits, he merely "scolded them for having violated the terms of surrender" and persuaded them to accept a ransom of two barrels of brandy for each of their prisoners.[16]

The campaign had ended with a public display of weakness on the part of the Governor. The Intendant, with Vaudreuil's help, was to make it a source of scandalously dishonest profit for himself. Although the booty from Fort William Henry was the immediate responsibility of the Governor, Vaudreuil allowed the Intendant to sell it to his accomplice, the purveyor Cadet, at one-tenth of current prices. "It is easy to believe," concluded an anonymous memoir-writer, "that these prices were not contrary to the interests of the *société*."[16a]

In the English colonies "the massacre of Fort William

Henry," as it is called, provoked a great surge of indignation. Violent articles in the press were enlivened with horrible, and fictitious, details of torture. The French were accused of having reached "the height of perfidy and cruelty" on the orders of "the most Christian King," and of having violated the sacred engagement of surrender.[17]

How serious was this so-called massacre? About fifteen wounded men, seventeen at most, were killed in their beds. In the course of the pillaging "about a dozen were killed." This is Bougainville's figure, and it is corroborated by "several English officers" who affirmed that the Indians "killed no more than ten or twelve men" and that Montcalm took all the prisoners, officers and men, under his protection. At Fort William Henry, in spite of Montcalm's advice to the defenders and in spite of all his precautions, a maximum of twenty-nine persons were killed by Indians. For this regrettable incident the English were partly to blame, and in any case it was not the wholesale slaughter which political propaganda and outrageously distorted accounts have enshrined in history. On the contrary, historical evidence allows us to affirm that the "massacre" of Fort William Henry was not a massacre in the true sense of the term.[18]

With Fort William Henry in French hands, Montcalm refused Vaudreuil's suggestion that he should go on to attack Fort Edward. He agreed with his officers that such an expedition would encounter "invincible obstacles." The journey between the two forts, although short, entailed a portage of six leagues over which artillery would have to be transported without horses, and large-scale defections could be expected among the Indian fighters. Montcalm also reminded Vaudreuil of his own order to release the militiamen for the harvest, lest in their "frenzy" to be home they go "without leave." Accordingly, after razing the fort, the army embarked for Carillon where a *Te Deum* was sung to celebrate the victory.[19]

Vaudreuil, whom Lévis classed among the armchair generals "who conceive bold plans in their studies," maintained his own opinion in this matter. His report to Versailles was critical of Montcalm's failure to attack Fort Edward and his neglect of the superior talents of Rigaud de Vaudreuil. It even implied that if Montcalm had listened to the advice of the Governor's brother no prisoners would have been murdered. In his reply, the Minister not only dismissed Vaudreuil's charges but reprimanded him for his frequent complaints about the French troops and his insinuations that Montcalm had "less zeal and courage" than Lévis. His final comment, amply justified, was presented in the form of a query: could it be possible that these constant complaints were symptomatic of a certain "prejudice" on the Governor's part?[20]

Montcalm, for his part, was loud in his praises of the Canadians. "What a people," he wrote, "waiting to be called upon! They are all naturally intelligent and courageous." Speaking of himself, he recognized the existence of a difficult situation in Canada and asked no other favour than to be recalled if the Minister considered that Lévis or some other general would be more successful than he.[21] Fortunately, the antagonism between French and Canadians was limited to the officers. It was reported that "the troops live in the closest union with the Canadians." Montcalm ordered his young officers to deal gently with the local people, and any harshness "was immediately punished with the utmost severity." The French soldiers took kindly to life in the colony. Many of them (eighty in 1757) married Canadian girls, and some of them, while still in service, started work on farms. Montcalm encouraged such arrangements and recommended that, when peace was established, there should be no limit on the number of soldiers allowed to stay as settlers in the country.[21a]

The war in Europe had started auspiciously for France with the capture of Minorca (May 1756) and the defeat of Frederick at Kolin (June 1757), but these victories were followed by the rout of the French army at Rossbach in November 1757 and that of the Austrians at Leuthen in December.[22] In France court intrigues resulted in the removal of Machault from the Ministry of Marine in February 1757. His successor, the mediocre and hesitant Moras, was himself replaced in June 1758 by a tired septuagenarian, Admiral Massiac; and when, five months later, Massiac retired in his turn, the helm was taken over by Nicolas René Berryer, a former lieutenant-general of police.

Thanks to the military successes achieved under the leadership of Montcalm, the people of Canada were quite confident of their ability to resist any attack. The capture of Forts William

Henry and Oswego renewed once again the loyalty and support of the Indians, who kept up their raids on the English colonies.[23] Even the Iroquois, with the exception of the Mohawks, fought on the side of the French. The country's economic condition, however, gave cause for grave concern. The *Grande Société,* run by Bigot and his partners, continued to monopolize government contracts and to draw exorbitant profits from them. In 1756, on the recommendation of the Intendant, the Minister granted the contract for supplies of food to a commissary-general who was none other than Joseph Cadet, the most active of Bigot's confederates. The contract was signed without question by Vaudreuil in October 1756, and was to come into force the following year. In the course of the autumn, as supplies did not arrive from France, the contractor and the *Grande Société* bought up cattle and food supplies, including wheat which was already scarce as a result of poor harvests. The price of wheat was fixed by order at five or seven *livres* a peck. The clique in the *Grande Société* bought it at this price and sold it at twenty-six *livres.* This manœuvre resulted in great expense to the Royal Treasury, while the townspeople were reduced to a state of near famine. Montrealers were allowed a daily ration of half a pound of bread with which they ate horsemeat. When angry housewives protested to Vaudreuil, he cut them off rudely and told them that if they returned to the attack "he would have them all put in prison, and half of them hanged." The soldiers of the garrison refused to eat horsemeat until Lévis' threats forced them to do so. Horsemeat was introduced into the French-Canadian cuisine in the guise of *bœuf à la mode.* Montcalm set an example by serving it to his guests. At his table bewigged officers and ladies in panniers ate horsemeat patties, horse fillets cooked on the spit, horse tongue with onions and ragout of horse.[24]

In the course of the winter, as the food crisis became more acute, the bread ration was cut to a quarter of a pound a day. In Quebec, in April (1758), it was reduced to two ounces. Even at exorbitant prices there was not enough beef to supply a quarter of the need; "without poultry, vegetables, sheep or calves" the capital was "on the point of dying of hunger." Bigot had 1,500 horses slaughtered to feed the poor and he later distributed "a quarter of a pound of salt pork and half a pound of cod per day." At the same time food prices soared; butter went from eight *sous* to twenty-five, and sugar from twenty to fifty *sous*. At the beginning of May Montcalm reported that some people were "reduced to eating grass." A few days after these words were written the tragic situation was relieved by the arrival of eight ships from France with seven hundred barrels of flour which broke the famine and put an end to rationing.[25]

Meanwhile neither the dangers of war nor famine were an effective deterrent to social frivolity and pleasure-seeking. However, under the careful supervision of Madame de Vaudreuil, the Governor's receptions were simple and their number was kept to a minimum. As commander-in-chief, Montcalm did the honours for the army by inviting the ladies of Quebec society to his table with his officers. But it was Bigot, with a fortune amassed by despoiling the people and robbing the Royal Treasury, who set the example of ostentatious and extravagant entertaining. His banquets, where as many as eighty guests gathered around tables set with magnificent silver, were followed by concerts or balls. Violins played for the dancers until dawn, while stakes ran high at the gaming tables. One night the Intendant himself lost 1,500 *louis* (36,000 *livres*) in an hour. In this whirl of social excitement elegant ladies and handsome officers found many opportunities for flirtation and amorous adventure. Bigot's mistress, Madame Péan, distributed smiles and favours to her little court. Péan found consolation with Madame Pénissault, the reigning beauty of the day, until she transferred her affections to the Chevalier de Lévis. The seductive widow Clavery and pretty Madame Melin shared the attentions of Captain de Roquemaure. The common people were affronted and scandalized by all this dissipation, which the clergy also deplored and condemned. The Sulpician curé of Montreal denounced the "infamous . . . balls and picnics" which could not but lead to "immodest conduct and fornication." Mgr. de Pontbriand interdicted a Jesuit, Father Bonnécamp, and a Récollet, Father Valérian, because they had absolved ladies of the sin of dancing during carnival.[26] Madame Bégon, reporting that Madame de Beaucour "used her body as she saw fit," roundly condemned her conduct and that of women who followed her example. We must not, however, take any of these imputations too seriously. Even in this period of extravagant dissipation, conjugal infidelity was the exception.

Montcalm, whose own friendship with Madame de Beaubassin was common knowledge, recognized that Canadian women "were more anxious to have admirers than lovers."[26a]

In the unnatural conditions of war, with its enormous costs, there was an abnormal growth in economic activity. Increased forces and frequent military expeditions required greater and greater provisions of food and munitions. At the same time the elimination of the English depots at Chouaguen increased the volume of furs on the Canadian market. The need for transport, both within the colony and beyond its shores, doubled the work of shipyards, which continued to launch fighting ships, as well as merchantmen and smaller schooners.[27]

Anxiety about the military situation, corruption in the administration, exploitation of the country people, food shortages, social frivolity, these are the elements which constitute the uneasy and lowering atmosphere of the colony at the end of 1757, when the sky was dark with the threat of a renewed English offensive.

Chapter Sixteen

THE SURRENDER OF LOUISBOURG
AND THE VICTORY OF CARILLON
1758

~~~~~~

The great English offensive. Amherst and Boscawen at Louisbourg. Resistance and surrender. Abercromby's expedition against Fort St. Frédéric. Victory of Montcalm at Carillon. Bradstreet captures Fort Frontenac. Grant repulsed at Fort Duquesne. Fort Duquesne abandoned and occupied by Forbes. Excesses of the Grande Société. *Weakness of Vaudreuil. Inflation. Weakness of Canada's defensive situation.*

~~~~~~

In the spring of 1758, after three years of war and the victories of the Monongahela, Chouaguen and Fort William Henry, Canada found herself in a situation of great danger. Although Vaudreuil made laudable efforts to bolster the confidence of the Canadian people, he was not himself strong enough to clean up the administration and put it back on a sound basis. Far from restraining the excesses of Bigot and the *Grande Société*, he praised the Intendant for his zeal and his great talents.[1]

Another serious source of danger lay in the strained relations existing between Montcalm and the Governor. Vaudreuil complained constantly to Versailles about the commander-in-chief, and suggested to the Minister that he should be recalled and replaced by Lévis, while Montcalm criticized Vaudreuil's double-dealing and his lack of decision. The dissension between the two men was so well known that a New York newspaper made reference to it. Both men sincerely desired to assure the safety of their country, but it was unfortunate that in this moment of grave danger for Canada two posts of great responsibility were occupied by men so completely incompatible in temperament and ideas.[2]

In England Pitt, the real leader of the Cabinet, rallied the King, the Parliament and the whole nation in support of his vigorous war policy. Pitt was determined to win America for Britain's political and commercial empire, and he was convinced that the war to achieve this end would be fought in America. Accordingly, a plan was mapped out early in 1758. Attacks would be directed at three outposts on the perimeter of New France: Fort Duquesne in the west, Fort St. Frédéric in the centre and Louisbourg in the east. As Louisbourg was to be the first of these targets, a powerful naval and military expedition was at once set on foot. Admiral Boscawen commanded the fleet of 39 warships, with 1,842 guns and 14,000 men, which anchored on May 27 in Gabarus Bay, 6 leagues from Louisbourg. The warships were followed by 150 transports carrying 13,152 soldiers. General Jeffery Amherst, who had been recalled from active service in Germany to take up this new command, was known as a methodical and determined tactician.[3]

Louisbourg was badly situated for defence. The town was surrounded by higher ground, and its apparently solid fortifications were no stronger than the inferior mortar which had gone into their construction. Governor Drucourt's defence force included 3,000 regular soldiers, 2,600 seamen, and three or four hundred militia. The land forces were supported by five warships under the command of Admiral des Gouttes.[4]

On June 8 three detachments, one of them commanded by a young brigadier, James Wolfe, made a first landing and drove the French soldiers from the entrenchments at Coromandière back into the town. The following days were spent by the landing parties in building roads and setting up batteries, while the defenders tried to hamper their movements with artillery and rifle fire. The warships in the harbour contributed little to the defence of the town. Only Captain Vauquelin of the frigate *Aréthuse* seemed aware that the naval force had its part to play, and constant fire from her thirty-six guns seriously impeded the enemy's progress until July 6 when she was put out of action. The town also was within range of the four new batteries which disabled the *Aréthuse*. For the next two weeks, it was subjected to bombardment which demolished houses and fortifications and set fire to barracks and ships in the harbour. During this intense shelling the Governor, officers and soldiers all displayed great fortitude, while Madame Drucourt set an example of courage for the townspeople by appearing every day on the ramparts and firing three cannon shots. But the French defence was gradually weakening.[5]

On July 9 a sortie caught a part of the invading army by surprise, and it fell back under the attack. But reinforcements prevented the French from exploiting their success and forced them to retreat from their position. No further sorties were attempted, and as more and more cannon were put out of action, the defence of the town itself became less and less effective. The enemy's powerful naval artillery and shore batteries were breaching the ramparts. In a matter of days, the entrance to the port would be open, and the English fleet could fire at close range on a town unable to resist an assault. On July 26 the Governor, on the advice of a council of war, offered to surrender. But when Boscawen denied them the honours of war, the garrison refused to accept such insulting terms and resolved to fight to the end. Thereupon, the *Commissaire-ordonnateur* pointed out the futility of such a decision. Houses and fortifications were in ruins. Defence was impossible, and further bombardment and assault would bring more suffering to the civilian population of 4,000 and the 1,200 sick and wounded. Convinced by this argument, Drucourt agreed to capitulate that very day, to the intense chagrin of the soldiers of the Cambis regiment, who broke their rifles and burned their own colours.[6]

The surrender of July 26 gave England Ile Royale and the neighbouring Ile St. Jean. The prisoners of war, 5,637 soldiers and sailors, were to be taken to England, while the 4,000 inhabitants of Louisbourg would be repatriated to France. The English captured 11 flags, 235 pieces of artillery, and large stocks of provisions and munitions. The siege cost France 102 dead and 237 wounded, in comparison with enemy losses of 170 killed and 354 wounded. The once imposing fortress presented a pitiful spectacle of destruction and ruin, but its excellent situation made it useful as a base until 1760 when, on orders from Pitt, it was "totally demolished and razed."[7]

The attacks on Carillon and St. Frédéric, which constituted the other part of Pitt's plan, were organized more slowly. Although Abercromby received his commission as Commander-in-Chief on March 4, it was four months later that the army dis-

embarked at the foot of Lake George a few miles from Fort
Carillon. The force included 6,367 regulars and 9,024 colonial
militiamen, as well as artillery units.[8]

In comparison with this impressive army, the French forces
were very weak. Refusing to believe his own territory was being
invaded, Vaudreuil had been imprudent enough to send a contingent, under Lévis, to attack Corlaer. Consequently, Montcalm had only 3,660 men: 3,260 regulars, 250 militia and 150
Indians, to defend Carillon against a force of 15,000. He would
have to compensate for his weakness by skill in defence. On July
6 he chose a position on a crest of land between Fall River and
the forest, about a quarter of a mile from the fort. On this
height, which commanded both frontier roads, he built entrenchments "made of tree trunks piled one on top of the other.
These felled trees with the stumps of their branches sharpened
into spikes gave the effect of *chevaux de frise.*" On the 8th, at
dawn, the troops took up their posts. The regulars occupied the
whole line, with the marines and the Canadians forming a reserve force on the right. Lévis, who arrived during the morning,
was to command the right, and Bourlamaque the left. Montcalm himself remained in the centre so that he could reach
any part of the line which might be hard pressed.[9]

Advised by his engineer that the time was right to capture
the enemy's position before he had time to reinforce it, Abercromby gave the order to march, and at noon the army de-
bouched opposite the French lines. The grenadiers, scouts and
light troops advanced and opened a brisk fire on the abattis.
They were followed by the regulars who advanced in successive
waves to the assault. One column attacked the centre, and two
were directed against the left, where Bourlamaque was in command. The fourth column, attacking Lévis' forces on the right,
was composed of grenadiers and Scottish highlanders who
charged repeatedly in the face of heavy fire. With each charge
they gained ground, and when their advance was finally halted,
the men at the head of the column were within fifteen feet of
the abattis. As they retreated, they were harassed by fire from
the Canadians who had been held in reserve on the flank. After
this first repulse, the English forces re-formed and attacked the
centre so fiercely that Lévis had to supply reinforcements from
the right, while Montcalm brought up the reserves. On the left

also, where the first two columns were making desperate efforts to dislodge the defenders, Montcalm had to answer several calls for help from Bourlamaque. The battle lasted, with hard fighting and displays of great courage on both sides, until six o'clock. Then the British tried one last valiant bayonet charge against the centre and the left, but it too was repulsed. At seven o'clock, disconcerted by the enemy's stubborn resistance and shaken by heavy casualties including the loss of several officers, the English beat a retreat to their fortified camp.[10] There they were safe from pursuit since Montcalm could not risk exposing his forces in an attack on an entrenched army three times the size of his own. The next day he strengthened his position in anticipation of another attack, but Abercromby did not venture to renew the battle. During the day, with his troops still at their stations, Montcalm ordered that a *Te Deum* be sung. He also erected a cross bearing the following inscription:

> Quid dux? quid miles? quid strata ingentia ligna?
> En signum! En victor! Deus hic, Deus ipse triumphat.

A French paraphrase made specific reference to the forces engaged. The following is an English rendering of the French text:

> Christian, it was not Montcalm with his wisdom,
> Nor these felled trees, nor the exploits of these heroes
> That deceived the hopes of the English and threw them into
>   confusion:
> It was the arm of God, it was Christ victorious on this cross![11]

French casualties in the battle of Carillon were 104 killed and 273 wounded, while the English lost 551 dead and 1,356 wounded. The victory, over a truly formidable army of invasion, brought joy to the population and "for the moment, saved Canada." It had been won by the stubborn courage of the French soldiers, marines and Canadian auxiliary troops. The English admitted the superiority of their adversaries: "We attacked you fiercely, but your defence was better than our attack." The battle could not have been won without the special talents of Montcalm. Lévis was the first to acknowledge the outstanding leadership of his commander-in-chief, and his praise of Montcalm was echoed by everyone, as Vaudreuil himself informed the Minister. The victory was celebrated in Paris

on October 1 with a *Te Deum,* cannon salvos, fireworks, and
free wine and dancing in the streets.[12]

The defeat at Carillon did not, however, prevent the English from taking the offensive at other points. On August 24
Colonel John Bradstreet, who had crossed Lake Ontario with a
force of 3,000 men, took up a position before Fort Frontenac.
This key post for the "up country" was defended by a garrison
of only 80 men; it had been consistently neglected by Vaudreuil
who refused to recognize how vulnerable it was to attack. When
the English artillery opened fire, Commander de Noyan ordered his men to answer, but the fortification was soon breached
and the guns disabled. After a resistance which lasted three
days, De Noyan had no choice but to surrender, and the victors,
after removing enormous stocks of furs, munitions and provisions, demolished the fort. Vaudreuil had finally dispatched reinforcements, but news of the capitulation reached the relief
force when it was still in Lachine.[13]

To the south, the English successfully carried out their
project to capture Fort Duquesne, the one French obstacle to
their advance in the Ohio valley. An army of 6,000 regulars and
militia under General Forbes was assembled at Loyalhanna in
Pennsylvania. On September 14 the vanguard of this force, 838
men under Major Grant, was driven back by the garrison of
1,000 commanded by Captain de Ligneris. This first defeat
halted the English offensive for a time, but it was resumed two
months later when Forbes and his army advanced to within six
leagues of the fort. Thereupon, de Ligneris, acting upon orders
from Vaudreuil, evacuated the garrison which he divided between Detroit and Presqu'île. On November 24, after blowing
up the fort, he withdrew with 200 men to the neighbouring
post of Machault. The following day, Forbes took possession of
the site which he renamed Pittsburg in honour of Pitt.[14]

Before and after the capture of Duquesne and Frontenac,
the English had been engaged in parleys with the Indians, and
their military successes had weakened the western Indians' allegiance to the French.[15] Still more serious, in December 1758
New France found herself isolated from Louisiana and confined
to the St. Lawrence valley. There remained only four points,
Quebec, St. Frédéric, Montreal and Niagara, at which she could
offer effective resistance to the powerful invasion which was

being prepared by England as a prelude to total conquest. At the same time the colony itself was torn by internal dissension. The victory at Carillon had not sufficed to create harmony between French and Canadian officers. The former, triumphant at having beaten the English with little help from the Canadians, maintained that in the war which was now upon them European tactics must prevail, while the Canadians still wanted to fight a war of raids and swift surprise attacks.[16]

The ideas of the two commanders at the summit reflected a similar opposition. Vaudreuil wanted to hamper the English offensive by raids on their settlements, while Montcalm recommended defensive tactics, with the strength of the colony concentrated in solid positions on its periphery. The Governor suggested that Montcalm should be replaced by Lévis, and immediately after the victory Montcalm would have been willing to accept this way out of a difficult situation. However, a later letter to the Minister reveals his conviction that his duty lay in Canada. "The colony's affairs are going badly," he wrote, and "it is for me to try to improve them." In a desire to reduce the friction which could not but be detrimental to the country, he sent his envoy Bougainville to Vaudreuil with "orders to destroy, if it were possible, this ferment of discord."[17] Bigot intervened with the same motive. In a secret dispatch to the Minister he summed up in a few phrases the distinctive qualities of the two men: "The first [Montcalm] has gained distinction as a good general, vigorous and active, zealous in the service of his country, careful in every detail. The second [Vaudreuil] can do anything he likes with the Indian nations, and he is perfectly familiar with the methods of war as it is waged in this country."[18]

At the same time Vaudreuil's constant criticisms of Montcalm finally made some impression in Versailles, and in December (1758) a memorandum on the subject was presented to Louis XV. The report recognized that Vaudreuil was not sufficiently "military minded" to lead the country, but it also posed the question whether it might not be wise to recall Montcalm. The memorandum was sent back from the King's cabinet with this item in the minutes: "All things considered, this change should not take place since M. de Montcalm is needed in the present circumstances."[19]

The civil administration was also in a state of disarray. Here the Intendant was directly responsible for the staggering increase in expenditures. Admonitions from Versailles had no effect on Bigot, even when accompanied, as they were after 1754, by thinly-veiled accusations of dishonesty. Realizing that it would not be easy to replace him in war-time, the Intendant made the country's defence an excuse for everything. All his energies were directed towards one end: "to make a great fortune for himself and his confederates," with the collaboration of Péan and Cadet, and with the connivance of the Governor's secretary, Saint-Sauveur. A whole methodical and voracious system of malversation, fraud and swindling, in every sector of the country's affairs, made the budget leap from 8,000,000 *livres* in 1756 to 13,000,000 the following year, and to 24,000,000 *livres* in 1758.[20]

"The Intendant and his *Société*," wrote Désandrouins, "are the first to profit at the expense of the State and private citizen. He is obviously involved in every deal and he favours his creatures, even to the point of making it possible, with a stroke of his pen, for them to make immense fortunes." The King bought nothing directly. When any particular product was needed, Bigot saw that it was acquired by one of his favoured friends, who then sold it to the Intendant at a profit of seventy per cent. At the trading posts, Bigot's agents sold for their own benefit and at exorbitant prices not only goods belonging to the State but even the King's gifts to the Indians. During a small-pox epidemic among the Indians, they entered expenses of 1,000,000 *livres* in the Treasury accounts, without any explanation as to how the money was spent. Contractors made use of the King's workmen and entered in their own accounts wages which they had not paid. In winter they burned tools and carts so that new ones would have to be bought in the spring. The craze for riches spread to employees in the posts and warehouses. In two years a purveyor's clerk made 100,000 crowns. "Contaminated by example, the simple habitants, once so honest, no longer scruple to rob the King." As an excuse for their conduct they offered the proverb: "At Easter our good King forgives all." Even quite honest persons, "fresh from France, tend to adopt this reasoning." French officers—an artillery major, Montbeillard, an adjutant, La Pause, an army surgeon,

Arnoux—amassed fraudulent profits. Even in respectable circles, those who could not make use of their position to enrich themselves at the expense of the public purse were considered rather stupid. This lack of conscience was by no means general, however. The clergy, and public opinion in general, denounced all this scandalous official dishonesty. Dufy Desauniers and many others like him maintained their standards of integrity and refused the bribes which they were offered as enticement to join the band.[21]

Bigot and his confederates found their richest field for exploitation in military budgets: expenses of posts, gifts to the Indians, equipment and maintenance of troops, costs of war parties. All these items were the responsibility of the Governor who certified all orders and receipts in connection with them. And yet, for four years Vaudreuil had been "weak" enough, as the Minister put it, to allow every sort of irregularity and to sign documents authorizing the most scandalous peculation. Although he was aware of Bigot's manœuvres, and in spite of Berryer's warnings, he continued to defend the Intendant against "his jealous accusers." Even in 1759 he declared his certainty that no one had the King's interest more at heart than Bigot. It is hard to understand that a man in Vaudreuil's position could make such a statement. What is infinitely more serious, however, is that the Governor authorized misappropriations in favour of his own family. Désandrouins affirms that among the fraudulent certificates which he signed was one for 500,000 *livres* in favour of his brother Rigaud. Désandrouins adds that the expense incurred was actually only 30,000 *livres,* and that even Bigot thought it wise to reduce to 200,000 *livres* the sum authorized for payment. To cover an outlay of 10 *livres* by his son-in-law, Le Verrier, whom he had appointed commandant at Michilimackinac, Vaudreuil signed a certificate for 10,000 *livres.*[22]

The *Grande Société* did not stop at robbing the King; it also despoiled the simple country habitants, commandeering their wheat, with the help of armed force if necessary, and paying the minimum price fixed by Bigot. Its agents seized, again by force if necessary, any articles which might be useful in their business transactions; and Cadet, "acting despotically," attributed to these articles "prices which best suited the interests of the *Soci-*

été," and which represented one third of their real value. In answer to complaints from the parishes, Vaudreuil promised to see that justice was done, but "the poor defrauded habitants" had no redress. In the region of St.-Sulpice, the Abbé Richer denounced the *Grande Société* from the pulpit in a sermon in which Vaudreuil and Bigot "were placed in their true light."
22a

As a result of Bigot's system, prices rose constantly from year to year. The necessities of life cost eight times more at the beginning of 1759 than in 1755. The inhabitants were alarmed at this inflation in prices and the corresponding drop in the value of money. In 1759 money had lost one third of its value, and a *louis d'or,* nominally worth 20 *livres,* could be sold for 30 *livres.* People hoarded gold and silver pieces and refused to sell unless they were paid in coin. Bigot finally issued an order fixing a prison term and a fine of 1,000 crowns as a penalty for refusal to accept paper money. Meanwhile official society and the Intendant's circle continued their gay and extravagant round of balls and excursions, supper parties and gambling.[23]

In this troubled and insecure atmosphere, faced with the certainty of a powerful invasion, Montcalm and Vaudreuil were agreed on one point at least: the gravity of the peril which threatened Canada. The danger was increased by inadequate stocks of necessities of every kind. The country was short of munitions and trading goods. A poor crop had caused "great misery" in Quebec, while the country's stock of food was barely sufficient for two months. Realizing how very urgent was the need for help, Montcalm secured Vaudreuil's agreement to entrust his aide-de-camp Bougainville and commissioner Doreil with a mission to "inform the Minister of Marine with complete frankness on the whole situation." Accordingly, on November 11, 1758 the two messengers embarked for France. But at the same time, Vaudreuil sent word to the Minister that these delegates were "Montcalm's creatures," and that they did not know the colony well enough to give a complete picture.[24]

English and French warships in Louisbourg harbor, July 26, 1758.

Quebec City at the time of cession.

The Bishop's Palace, Quebec City.

Battle of the Plains of Abraham, September 13, 1759.

Chapter Seventeen

THE ENGLISH OFFENSIVE AND
THE BATTLE OF THE PLAINS OF ABRAHAM

~~~~~~

Bougainville in Versailles. French policy: to maintain a foothold in Canada. Failure of the plan to invade England. The English invasion force under Wolfe and Saunders. Siege of Quebec. Bombardment. Montcalm repulses Wolfe at Montmorency. Capture of Niagara. St. Frédéric abandoned. The English scale the heights above l'Anse-au-Foulon. The Battle of the Plains of Abraham. Victory and death of Wolfe. Montcalm mortally wounded.

~~~~~~

The year 1759, which was to be Canada's *année terrible*, began in an atmosphere of alarm and crisis. Montcalm's victories had in no way weakened England's stubborn determination to drive France from American soil, and plans were being laid for two powerful invasions, one under Wolfe, against Quebec, and the other, under Amherst, against Montreal.[1]

As early as January, Versailles was fully informed on these plans. Doreil and Bougainville had also revealed the lamentable state of Canada, starved for troops, munitions and food supplies. But the new Minister of Marine, to whom Bougainville made his report, was quite incapable of understanding or dealing with the situation. Nicolas René Berryer was a former Lieutenant-General of Police, a man of limited intelligence whose rough, hectoring manner betrayed his earlier occupation. He was ignorant, presumptuous and stubborn and his appointment as Minister had been Madame de Pompadour's reward to him for supplying her with information about her enemies. Such a man could not comprehend the importance of maintaining Canada as a barrier against English domination in America. His answer to Bougainville's plea for help was that "you don't try to save

163

the stables when the house is on fire." Bourgainville did, however, win support from Madame de Pompadour who "was then Prime Minister." Speaking in a "committee of ministers," she supported the young officer's plan for the colony and promised to contribute 2,000,000 *livres* for its execution, but she did not succeed in her effort to have the plan adopted.[2]

After studying a large number of memoranda on the defence of Canada, the ministers in Versailles arrived at a decision which was tantamount to abandoning the country to its own resources and the military genius of Montcalm. The Minister of War informed the commander-in-chief that France could supply neither troops nor any other help, and this for two reasons: lack of resources and risk of interception by British fleets. In these conditions, continued the Minister, the only possible course was to concentrate the defence within a limited zone so that the different posts could help and support one another. The essential thing was to hold at least a part of the country for France so that territory temporarily lost might be recovered when peace was signed. For if the whole country was conquered it would be impossible to regain possession of any part of it.[3]

Although the King's intention was to hold Canada, Versailles adopted the policy of providing only the most meagre supply of munitions, food and other necessary goods, and only a few hundred recruits. Choiseul hoped to help and relieve Canada by an operation which would engage the would-be conqueror's forces elsewhere. He had conceived a foolhardy scheme to invade England and thus to make sure that her troops could not be sent abroad. The first step in this operation was to be a junction between the Brest and Toulon fleets; but the venture was a complete failure. On August 17 and 18 (1759) the Toulon squadron, commanded by Admiral La Clue, was defeated by Boscawen off Lagos on the coast of Portugal; and three months later, at the battle of Quiberon, the fleet from Brest suffered the same fate at the hands of Admiral Hawke within sight of the Breton coast.[4]

On May 13, fifteen transports escorted by two frigates under Kanon and Vauquelin had reached Quebec with all the relief in men and supplies that the colony was to receive from the Minister: four hundred recruits, munitions, and six thousand tons of food supplies. At the same time the army purveyor, Cadet, unloaded twenty thousand tons from his own ships so that the troops, at least, would be sure of their rations. The King tried to compensate for the inadequacy of his help with a generous distribution of promotions. Vaudreuil received the Grand Cross of the Order of St. Louis, Montcalm was promoted to Lieutenant-General, and Lévis to Field-Marshal. Only protocol, which did not allow a field-marshal to hold this rank, prevented Louis XV from creating Montcalm Marshal of France. Moreover, in a secret dispatch dated January 28, 1759, the King repeated a decision made earlier, that in the event of Vaudreuil's death Montcalm was to assume the post of Governor-General of Canada. Berryer also transmitted an order to Vaudreuil and Bigot to consult Montcalm not only on military matters but in any administrative question concerning the country's safety. The pre-eminence of Montcalm's service and talents, in comparison with those of the Governor and Intendant, was recognized in every possible way.[5]

All the prisoners captured during the winter and spring had the same story to tell: the English plan was to besiege Quebec and, at the same time, to send two other armies to attack the colony, one by way of Lake Champlain and the other by Lake Ontario. The Indians confirmed Colonel Johnson's statement that this was the plan to be followed. But, in spite of these repeated warnings, Vaudreuil remained irresolute, and it was not until April that he finally decided on a plan of campaign: to hold Fort Machault on the Ohio and to fortify Niagara. It was no part of his strategy to strengthen Quebec or to reinforce its garrison, for he remained convinced that no attack would be made on the town. He was still in Montreal when, on May 14, Bougainville informed him that an expedition had left England for Canada. On May 20 he addressed a letter to all captains of militia instructing them that all able-bodied men must be ready to march at the first order. "Aware of the cruel treatment they would suffer at the hands of the English," he exhorted the habitants to defend their property, their wives and their religion. "For my part," added the Governor, "I will never surrender, for I know full well what dangerous results such a course would have for all Canadians."[6]

Finally convinced of the imminence of the danger, Vaudreuil agreed that the commander-in-chief should be in the capital, and Montcalm arrived in Quebec on the evening of May 22.

The next day the first ships of the British squadron were reported at St. Barnabé, sixty leagues down the river. On the 24th, the Governor ordered to the capital the troops from Montreal and Three Rivers. All the country people above Kamouraska were instructed to leave their farms, with their wives and farm animals, and seek protection at Pointe-Lévis or in the woods. Meanwhile Montcalm had established his headquarters at La Canardière on the outskirts of Quebec, and, in order to prevent any attempt at a landing on the unprotected eastern flank of the town, had started to throw up a line of entrenchments with redoubts and cannon all along the river from Beauport to Montmorency.[7]

Fortunately, the situation of Quebec, on the high promontory between the St. Lawrence and St. Charles rivers, was an excellent one for defence. The Plains of Abraham, to the left of the city, were protected on the river side by an escarpment apparently impossible to scale. The ramparts were armed with guns and mortars, and the lower town was defended by four batteries commanding the harbour. Montcalm's fighting force was made up of regular soldiers, marines and militia, in all about 13,718 men. In their zeal to defend their country, Canadians flocked to Quebec; old men of eighty and children of twelve presented themselves for service. Boys from the Jesuit school formed a company which was nicknamed the *Royal-Syntaxe*. The Bishop exhorted the population to fight for the freedom of their country, and curés contributed their tithes to the Royal Treasury.[8]

On May 26 the enemy's entire fleet was anchored off the Island of Orleans. The following day they landed 8,000 men and established themselves at St. Laurent. An English force was encamped in the heart of Canada.[9] Vice-Admiral Charles Saunders was in command of the fleet of 49 warships armed with 2,000 pieces of artillery and manned by 13,750 seamen. This formidable armada convoyed 193 troopships with an army of 11,333 English regulars and colonial militia under the command of General James Wolfe. Saunders was an able and intelligent naval officer and a man of wise judgment. On the other hand, Wolfe, a young man of thirty-two who had already had a brilliant career, had the qualities of a tactician rather than a strategist, and proved to be impressionable, stubborn, and easily aroused to anger.[10]

The day after the first landing, Wolfe signed a manifesto and had it posted throughout the rural districts. The notice, written in French, promised the people that, provided they did not take up arms, their property and their religion would be respected. If, however, they persisted in fighting, they must expect that their churches and houses would be destroyed in reprisal for Franco-Indian atrocities in the English colonies.[11]

On May 29 Vaudreuil launched eight fire-ships in an effort to destroy a part of the enemy's fleet, but the fire was lighted when the target was still a whole league away and the attempt was a failure. The incident was, however, very profitable for Cadet and his company, who had supplied the fire-ships at the exorbitant price of 80,000 *livres* per ship.[12]

During the month of June Montcalm continued to fortify the Beaufort-Montmorency line. In the last days of June, although his men were under fire from the guns of Quebec, Monckton succeeded in establishing batteries at Pointe-Lévis, and on July 12 the first English cannon balls fell on Quebec. During the following days an intense bombardment destroyed several houses, the cathederal and the cathedral presbytery. In reply the French kept up their fire against the English batteries and made another unsuccessful attempt to attack the fleet with fire-ships.[13]

On July 9, setting in motion an offensive against the Montmorency-Beaufort positions, Wolfe had established a camp of 4,000 men on the left bank of the Montmorency River. From there English batteries shelled the French positions on the right bank. When the bombardment failed to achieve its objective of provoking a sortie, Wolfe took the initiative and attacked. At nine o'clock on July 31 forty guns on shore and the cannon of three supporting ships under Saunders opened fire on the French entrenchments. The French guns answered and a violent artillery duel followed. Meanwhile boats were landing troops on the beach. About five o'clock, Wolfe, who had been wounded and who was still aboard one of the ships, gave the order for the assault. The vanguard of 2,500 grenadiers charged and captured the first redoubts on the shore, and then tried to scale the slopes below the entrenchments. Lévis' troops had been reinforced by Montcalm, and the deadly artillery fire which they poured down from above decimated the attacking force. With torrential rain and sticky mud impeding their movements, even the legendary courage of the grenadiers could not hold out against cannon ball and grapeshot. They had already suffered heavy losses when, at seven o'clock, Wolfe gave the order to retreat. The battle of Montmorency had been lost and had cost the lives of 500 men.[14]

While Quebec was being successfully defended, French arms and diplomacy suffered a series of defeats in other sectors of the colony. In June the Iroquois nations declared in favour of the English. On June 6 the Chevalier de La Corne and his detachment of 1,000 men were repulsed by Haldimand at Oswego. At Niagara, Pouchot, with a garrison of 486 men, put up a brave resistance against Prideaux's 4,000 regulars before capitulating on June 26 with the honours of war. In the east, Amherst set out from Fort Edward with an army 12,000 strong to attack Fort Carillon. Following instructions from Vaudreuil, Bourlamaque immediately withdrew with his garrison of 2,300 men to Fort St. Frédéric. On July 26 Hébécourt blew up the fort at Carillon. On July 31 Bourlamaque set the fuse to a mine which destroyed Fort St. Frédéric. The French garrisons from Carillon and St. Frédéric concentrated their forces on Ile-aux-Noix, which subsequently became a fortified post barring the invasion route by the Richelieu. Meanwhile Amherst, established in Fort St. Frédéric, which he had rebuilt, was planning the next steps in his campaign.[15]

Defeated at Montmorency, the English resumed their destructive bombardment of Quebec. On August 9 bombs set fires which destroyed the church and 135 houses in the lower town. The devastation added to the difficulties of provisioning, and flour became so scarce that the bread ration of "ordinary people" was only a quarter of a pound per day. Priests increased their gifts of charity, while houses were broken into by burglars in search of food. The situation remained extremely critical until September when a shipment of wheat arrived from Montreal.[16]

While he continued to batter Quebec with artillery fire, Wolfe was also engaged in a campaign of terrorism designed to crush any resistance on the part of the country people. For he hated the "Canadian vermin," whom he accused of committing "unheard-of cruelties." On July 25 a proclamation was posted on the door of the church at St. Henri. By a strange error Wolfe refused to admit that militiamen were combatants recognized by law and declared that Canadians who refused to lay down their arms were "unworthy" of his generosity. Consequently, acting, as Montcalm said, "in a ferocious spirit," he ordered that their houses should be destroyed and that only churches should be spared. Beginning on August 14 with St. Antoine, seven parishes from Château-Richer to Baie St.-Paul were put to the torch. On August 23 the curé of St. Joachim, M. de Portneuf, and nine parishioners were massacred; the priest was scalped and the church burned. In September the English continued their campaign of destruction by burning all the houses between Montmorency and Cap Tourmente.[17]

In his proclamation at St. Henri, Wolfe expressed his indignation at the scalpings of which the Indians had been guilty and threatened reprisals against his prisoners. Wolfe forgot that in June his Rangers had scalped French soldiers, and that in July they had massacred in cold blood some captured children whose cries might have betrayed their presence.[18]

On July 18 Wolfe and Saunders had succeeded in sending four vessels up the river beyond Quebec. After the battle of Montmorency, others were added to their number. To meet this threat, Montcalm sent Bougainville with a strong detachment to guard the coast, and during August three attempts at landing were repulsed. In September, from Cap Rouge, three leagues above Quebec, where he was mounting guard with a force of two thousand men, Bougainville followed the movements of an English squadron sailing up and down the river. It appeared to be looking for a possible landing place; in reality it was acting as a decoy, keeping Bougainville's army engaged while the real assault was to be made on Quebec.[19] The forces defending the capital had already been reduced. Early in July, after the fall of Fort Niagara, Vaudreuil had become alarmed for the safety of Montreal and had sent Lévis with eight hundred men to guard the upper St. Lawrence.[20]

At the end of August, Wolfe, to his great chagrin, had not succeeded in drawing Montcalm into battle, and Saunders was urging him not to delay the departure of the fleet too long. On September 10, as Wolfe was exploring the shore with his glass, he discovered at l'Anse-au-Foulon, less than two miles above

Quebec, a sort of trail by which it might be possible to scale the heights and reach the Plains facing the town. The next day he signed orders for an attack on September 13. In order to throw the defence off the scent, he bombarded Quebec throughout the day of the 12th, while ships manœuvring near Pointe-aux-Trembles immobilized Bougainville's detachment.[21]

At two o'clock in the morning of the 13th, the English boats, filled with soldiers, rowed to the foot of the cliff. To the sentry's challenge, "Who goes there?" Captain Fraser answered, "France," adding in perfect French, "These are the provisions from Montreal." The sentry accepted the explanation since, as a deserter had informed the English, provision boats were expected that very day. Having successfully passed the sentry, the boats rowed on. The men leaped ashore and started their climb with Wolfe at their side. At the Foulon guard post, the commander, Vergors, and his thirty men, who had been asleep, were suddenly awakened. They fired a few ineffectual shots, but were quickly captured or put to flight. The day before, Montcalm had asked permission to station a battalion at Foulon, but Vaudreuil had answered: "We shall see about it tomorrow." Finding the way open before it, the English army climbed up in long files and advanced on to the Plains of Abraham. At dawn, Wolfe assigned the men to their battle positions and ordered them to load their rifles with two bullets, but not to fire until they were within forty paces of the enemy. There were 4,285 combatants, and they had two cannon.[22]

When rifle shots were heard from l'Anse-au-Foulon, the alarm was sounded, and Montcalm went at once to reconnoitre the position of the enemy. The uneven ground concealing some of the troops led him to suppose that the force was still small enough to be repulsed if it were attacked immediately. When he consulted his officers, some suggested that, as Bougainville's troops were only seven miles away and probably already on the march, they should wait for them and take the enemy between two fires. Others advised an immediate attack before the English could be reinforced. Montcalm finally decided that he must dislodge the English before they became entrenched. Unfortunately, he did not know that some of the troops on which he was counting had been held on Vaudreuil's orders "at the bridge over the little river." Forgetting in his impatience what stubborn fighters the English could be and remembering only that he had so far triumphed over their stubbornness, Montcalm led out on to the Plains all the troops he could muster, regulars, marines, militia and Indians. As he rode out, he said to his aide-de-camp, "We cannot avoid a battle. The enemy is entrenching himself. If we give him time to establish himself we shall never be able to attack with our small body of troops. Is it possible," he asked himself, "that Bougainville does not realize this?"[22a]

At eight o'clock 3,500 men occupied a battlefront stretching from the river to the Ste. Foy road. The English, drawn up in two lines, awaited the French advance. On seeing the English in battle formation, Montcalm disposed his troops in three columns of six ranks each, the second and third ranks being made up of Canadians and marines. While his orders were being carried out, the general rode up and down the lines encouraging his men. Then, having given the order to advance, he led his cheering army into battle. Canadians on the wings fired on the English flanks from the bushes and cornfields where they were concealed. After first giving ground, the enemy returned a steady fire which forced the irregulars to withdraw into the shelter of the bushes. When the English were within range, the Canadians and the marines in the third rank fired "without waiting for orders." Then, according to their custom, they "lay flat on the ground to reload." This manœuvre disrupted "all the battalions," while on the flanks the militiamen withdrew to a position in the bushes. The regulars continued their advance and opened fire on the still-motionless redcoats. When the French force was within forty paces of the English line, an order rang out and a massive volley mowed down the first rank of Montcalm's army. The French answered with spasmodic fire which was met by a methodical fusillade directed against front and flank. Under the hail of bullets, the French line wavered and broke. Then, as Wolfe gave the order for the bayonet charge, the French troops turned and fled in confusion towards the town.[23]

Wolfe had already been struck by a bullet in his wrist and by another in the groin. Now, in the moment of victory, a third bullet pierced his lung. He died without regaining consciousness, but knowing that his audacious tactics had been crowned with victory. Montcalm, still trying to rally his fleeing army, was wounded in the hip and in the stomach. With his wounds still undressed, he was carried on horseback to the town, where consternation reigned.[24] The battle had cost the French 1,200 killed and wounded, and the English about 660.

An eyewitness relates Vaudreuil's part in the engagement. In the course of the action "he appeared on the hill in a carriage; the sight of him only intensified the rout, and he himself decamped immediately and crossed back by the bridge over the little river."

On the Plains, the English pursued the fugitive soldiers. The Canadian riflemen fought courageously against them in two skirmishes on the Ste. Foy road and at the St. Jean gate, but they were driven back. Although Bougainville had not received Vaudreuil's message until nine o'clock, at eleven his detachment had completed its seven-mile march and arrived in sight of the Plains. Then, as the enemy advanced on his small force, Bougainville withdrew with his men to Lorette.[24a] In the short space of an hour or two the battle of the Plains of Abraham had been lost and won and the fate of New France decided.

Although mortally wounded, Montcalm did not forget the fate of his soldiers. He found the strength to write the new English commander, Townshend, and to recommend to "his kindness" the "sick and wounded" who had fallen into the hands of the enemy.[24b] He died the following day, and his death brought sorrow to the army, the French population and the Indians. War, "the grave of the Montcalms," had taken one of the most fascinating figures in Canadian history, a man whose brilliant intellect and broad vision were guided by a strong sense of duty. The four victories, Chouaguen, William Henry, Carillon and Montmorency, which he had won with a tiny army, bear witness to his unique military talents.[24c]

After the battle, Vaudreuil, forgetting former animosity, sent a message of sympathy to Montcalm: "I cannot repeat too often how deeply grieved I am at your wounds. . . . No one could be more deeply concerned than I who have felt so closely attached to you for so many years." A few weeks later, however, on October 30, he sent the Minister a letter in which he poured out a whole series of accusations against the general who had died on the field of honour, accusations which are refuted by the facts and by documentary evidence. Forgetting that Montcalm had himself asked to be recalled, he accused him of having wanted to become Governor-General from the moment of his arrival in Canada. With this end in view, continued the Governor, Montcalm had spread "discord among the troops," tried "to corrupt the most virtuous subjects" and "tolerated pillaging by soldiers" in the rural districts. Vaudreuil had the audacity to attribute to a signally courageous officer the incredible intention of "razing Quebec" and the even more improbable suggestion that, in the King's interest and "in order to save the colony," the Governor should agree to surrender.[25]

The explanation of this accumulation of false accusations is not, as has generally been believed, Vaudreuil's hatred of Montcalm. Its object was, rather, to distract attention from his own fatal error in ordering too early, and without necessity, the capitulation of Quebec, a capitulation for which he now expected to be blamed by Versailles as he had been blamed by Lévis. He admitted as much himself when he said that he was "in despair at being obliged" to write this letter. However, he continued, "I feel the loss of Quebec too deeply to hide its cause from you." It was in order to disengage his own responsibility in the matter that he attributed the fault to the general who was no longer there to answer false charges.[26]

Let the testimony of Foligné suffice to answer for Montcalm: "Never was a general more beloved by his troops or more universally mourned. A man of superior mind, he was generous, gentle, affable, familiar with everybody, and he had won the confidence of the whole colony." Another colonist added that his loss "was felt deeply by the State, and still more by all Canadians."[27]

Chapter Eighteen
VICTORY OF STE. FOY
AND CAPITULATION OF MONTREAL
1759-1760

Retreat of the army to Jacques-Cartier. Capitulation of Quebec. Seat of government transferred to Montreal. Victory of Ste. Foy and siege of Quebec. Arrival of English ships. French convoy destroyed at Restigouche. Three armies under Amherst before Montreal. Vaudreuil capitulates. Departure of the French troops. Trial of Bigot and his associates. Liquidation of the King's debt. Treaty of Paris.

With the battle lost, Montcalm wounded, and his second-in-command, Sénezergues, a prisoner, the army was in a state of utter confusion. Vaudreuil, who was quite incapable of effective leadership, allowed the disorderly mob of troops to retreat towards the St. Charles River and the bridge at La Canardière. Instead of ordering Roquemaure to rally the men in the face of the enemy, he held a council of war and accepted without question its advice to retreat to Jacques-Cartier. In his panic, he sent instructions that same day, September 13, to Ramezay, who was in command in Quebec, that as soon as provisions ran short he was to show the white flag; he was not to wait for the enemy to take the town by assault. Vaudreuil even included in his dispatch the terms of surrender that Ramezay was to propose. For the fact was that in March 1758 Vaudreuil, constitutionally a defeatist, had asked for instructions from Versailles as to the terms of surrender which he should solicit.[1]

Quebec was in a sorry state, with 180 houses burned to the ground and a large number of others ruined or damaged by bombs. Two churches had been destroyed, and three others were no more than empty shells. To feed a garrison of 2,200 men and a civil population of 3,800 including 2,600 women and children, there remained a provision of 15,000 half-rations which melted away during the next two days while the English landed troops and guns in preparation for an assault. Threatened with famine and touched by the pleadings of their women, the citizens urged the commander to surrender the fort. Accordingly, on September 15 Ramezay called a council of war. Two days later, following its decision and Vaudreuil's instructions, he submitted his conditions for surrender to General Townshend, who had replaced Wolfe. Townshend had not yet set up a single battery, and he was naturally both delighted and surprised at an offer for which there was no justification. That night La Rochebeaucour's cavalry succeeded in bringing a hundred bags of biscuit into Quebec. They promised that further help would follow, but, with a complete lack of intelligence, Ramezay informed them that it was too late; M. Joannès was already parleying with the English. He could not recall his envoy unless the English refused certain conditions, in which case he would break off negotiations. The English, however, were only too glad to accept the proposed terms, and the following day, September 18, Saunders and Townshend signed the capitulation which granted the honours of war to the garrison and guaranteed property rights and religious freedom to the population. About nine o'clock three companies of grenadiers took up their stations at the gates of the town, and at half-past three the English troops took possession of Quebec. The siege had lasted sixty-eight days.[2]

Meanwhile, on the morning of the 17th, Lévis had arrived from Montreal at Jacques-Cartier, where the army was encamped under the command of the Governor. Lévis frankly stated his opinion that it was a gross blunder to abandon Quebec, whereupon Vaudreuil sent a hasty message to Ramezay ordering him to hold the fort and informing him that provisions and a relief army were on the way. When he received the answer that negotiations had now gone too far to be broken off, Vaudreuil, quite forgetting that he had himself given the order to surrender, blamed Ramezay for giving up Quebec so quickly. The troops were at St. Augustin, four leagues away from Quebec, when they learned that the town was already in the enemy's hands. They therefore returned to Jacques-Cartier, where they began to build a frontier fort.

On the night of October 4 an English raid was carried out right in the heart of the colony. Taking advantage of the disorganized state of French defences, Major Robert Rogers and a troop of militia made a bold attack on the Abenaki village of St. François-du-Lac, where they killed about thirty men and captured thirty women and children. Then, after pillaging and burning the village, they withdrew without having met any effective opposition. Admiral Saunders did not want to expose his ships to the risk of spending the winter in the frozen St. Lawrence. Accordingly, when their services were no longer needed, he gave the order for departure, and on October 12 they set sail for their home ports. After the English fleet had left, five of Cadet's ships succeeded in slipping past Quebec one dark night and escaping to France. They carried dispatches from Vaudreuil and Bigot urging upon Versailles the country's vital need of reinforcements and help.[3]

In England, news of the capture of Quebec was received with the greatest enthusiasm, and the King declared a day of national thanksgiving. General Murray, now Governor of the city of Quebec, applied himself immediately to the task of fortifying the approaches to the town. He also managed to find some sort of quarters in the ruined capital for his garrison of 7,690 men. Early in November he issued a proclamation inviting Canadians to accept the "equitable" sovereignty of England. If they took up arms, they must expect to be treated with "all the severity of a justly irritated army." In order to guard against any French offensive, he stationed detachments in the churches of Ste. Foy and Vieille-Lorette. Facing this frontier, the French established posts at St. Augustin and Pointe-aux-Trembles which were supported by the fort at Jacques-Cartier. During the winter, each camp kept a watchful eye on the other; there were a few skirmishes between English and French detachments, and rumours kept reaching Murray that Lévis was preparing to attack in the spring.[4]

The Governor had taken up residence in Montreal with the Intendant, the Bishop and the members of the Sovereign Council, and the provisional capital teemed with activity in this hour of supreme crisis. Supplies of beef and pork had run out, there was very little flour, the troops were on very short rations, and food prices had tripled. Acting under Vaudreuil's orders, Cadet's agents went out into the country districts with an escort of soldiers and commandeered as many cattle as they could find. Inflation in the town and the confiscation of food in the rural communities caused great hardship, but the people did not complain and thought only of saving the colony. "Let the King take anything we have," they said, "if only Canada is saved."[5]

As they prepared an expedition to recapture Quebec, Vaudreuil and Lévis used persuasion, and, where necessary, force, to gather stores and munitions into the common stock. They even succeeded in getting supplies from Jacques-Cartier, where a "scandalous commerce" between English and French had been established. At the same time the *Grande Société* was as active as ever. Among the useless articles which it sold at enormous profit were 300,000 *livres* worth of moccasins. In March 1760 troops and militia were assembled in Montreal. On April 16 Vaudreuil sent a message ordering the militiamen from the Quebec district to join Lévis' army and threatening with death any who refused to serve. At the same time he granted an amnesty to those who had taken the oath of allegiance which Murray demanded, or who had provided services to the occupying force.[6]

The army left Montreal on April 20 and on the 24th it was encamped at Pointe-aux-Trembles, where the escorting ships supplied it with munitions. On the 26th it set out for Quebec, and that same night Murray was informed of its movements by a French artilleryman who had been rescued from an ice cake floating down the river. The following day Lévis entered Ste. Foy after driving out an English detachment. Before retreating, the English soldiers had set fire to the church in which they were quartered.[7]

On April 28, about eight o'clock, Murray led out his men and the two armies took up their positions on the Plains between the river and the Ste. Foy road. The 5,000 French combatants, including 2,400 militia, were opposed by 3,860 English soldiers with 22 guns. The English army stood in two ranks on sloping ground, with its back to the town. The French, a little lower down, were drawn up in files of four. The first encounter took place at the Dumont house on the Ste. Foy road. French grenadiers made a bayonet charge and dislodged a detachment of Scottish Highlanders, but the Highlanders rallied and returned to the attack, brandishing their claymores as they advanced. The

house changed hands several times, but the French finally remained in possession. Meanwhile the two armies advanced to
within rifle shot of one another. English bullets and grapeshot
riddled the French left, forcing it to give ground. The English
right then advanced down the slope, and as the French troop was
being decimated by its steady fire, the order to retreat was given.
But a fiery Bearnais, Captain Dalquier, refusing to obey the
order, rallied his marines and charged the enemy. "No, lads," he
shouted, "you don't retreat when you are twenty paces from the
enemy. Fix bayonets and charge!" The sudden bayonet charge
surprised the English right and halted its advance. Murray had
two horses killed under him as he directed his infantry fire
against the French centre, forcing it to retreat to the shelter of
the trees. Lévis rode throughout his lines ordering the movements of his troops, rallying them at weak points and urging
them on to the attack. The two armies vied with one another in
courage and tenacity. Then, as the French right stretched out
beyond the enemy's line, Lévis ordered Poulariès to make a left
turn and a bayonet charge. Whereupon, regulars and Canadians
attacked with such spirit that the English left broke and fled, and
when Murray's right and centre followed their lead the flight became a rout. The French troops pursued the fleeing army so
closely that, if they had not received the order to halt, they might
have entered the city.[8] Thus, the battle of Ste. Foy, the last
battle of the campaign, was a French victory. On the French
side it cost 198 killed and 640 wounded, while the English lost
259 killed and 820 wounded.

Instead of launching an immediate attack on the fort, while
the garrison was demoralized by defeat, Lévis made preparations
for a regular siege. The next day his soldiers began to dig
trenches for batteries, but they made slow progress in their task
of digging frozen ground under constant fire from the ramparts.
Moreover, the real test of strength would be made elsewhere.
Besiegers and besieged alike kept their eyes fixed on the river,
knowing full well that the first ships to arrive, whether French
or English, would decide the fate of Quebec. On May 9 the
frigate *Lowestoffe* sailed into the harbour and fired a twenty-
one gun salute to the British flag flying above the fortress. The
enthusiasm of the garrison knew no bounds; cannon salvos accompanied by cheers from the soldiers went on all day. Two days

later Lévis, still hoping to see French vessels appear, opened fire with his feeble batteries. Four more days passed; then, on the evening of the 15th, two English warships, the *Vanguard* and the *Diana,* dropped anchor before Quebec.[9] The fate of Canada was sealed.

The next day the French vessels, convoyed by the frigate *Atalante,* under the command of Vauquelin, left l'Anse-au-Foulon and proceeded up the St. Lawrence as far as the Cap Rouge River, but at Pointe-aux-Trembles the escort was attacked by the *Vanguard* and the *Diana.* After two hours of fighting, the *Atalante* was lying on her side, riddled with cannon balls and helpless to defend herself. Her powder was exhausted, her commander and most of her men were wounded, but Vauquelin, still refusing to surrender, waited with rifle in hand for the enemy to board his ship. Finally, the English boarding party lowered the flag which Vauquelin had refused to strike. When the French commander reached Quebec, Murray expressed great admiration for his gallant adversary and paid him all the honour due to such valiant resistance.[10]

Now that the enemy's ships had arrived, Lévis realized the futility of attempting to reduce Quebec by siege. On May 16 he withdrew his forces to the camp at Jacques-Cartier, and then to Montreal, where Vaudreuil could consult him as to further measures to be taken. Bougainville and Pouchot were already at their posts on Ile-aux-Noix and Ile Lévis, ready to defend the Richelieu route and the foot of Lake Ontario. Meanwhile a squadron under the command of Lord Colville had reached Quebec with reinforcements, thus making the fortress safe against any attack.[11]

In February (1760) France had at long last decided to send help to Canada, and on April 10 five ships convoyed by the frigate *Machault,* under Captain La Giraudais, sailed out of the harbour of Bordeaux. The fleet carried four hundred soldiers commanded by Dangeac, as well as munitions and food supplies, but even this modest convoy arrived too late. On May 15, at the entrance to the Gulf, La Giraudais learned that the English squadron was ahead of him. He therefore led his little fleet into the Baie des Chaleurs and proceeded up the bay to the Resti-gouche. When his presence was reported to the English, five English vessels under the command of Commodore Byron were sent in pursuit. Between June 27 and July 8, the French ships were battered and finally sunk by English artillery fire, while the crews escaped overland. La Giraudais had sent the Versailles dispatches to Vaudreuil as soon as he had reached the Baie des Chaleurs, and answers had been sent to him by a messenger who covered the distance between Montreal and the Restigouche in thirteen days. Vaudreuil's dispatches were delivered to the Minister by La Giraudais, who arrived in France in September after crossing the ocean in an Acadian schooner.[12]

In the colony, which could no longer hope for help from the mother country, events moved swiftly. On May 26 Murray published a proclamation promising pardon to militiamen who had taken up arms, on condition that they redeem their past misdeeds with conduct beyond reproach. If they submitted, the King of England would guarantee their property and freedom to practise their religion; let them therefore avoid further suffering from war and famine by laying down their arms. On June 21 the oath of allegiance was administered to the inhabitants of St. Nicolas, and on July 2 the citizens of Quebec, who had been evacuated before the siege, were permitted to return to the city.[13]

On Murray's orders, a fleet of thirty-five ships with three thousand men was equipped, and on July 14 it set sail for Montreal. At various places on the way up the river, copies of the pardon proclamation were given to the militia captains. The people of several parishes came to take the oath of allegiance and were treated "gently" by the soldiers. On August 15 Murray issued an order to his troops prescribing the death penalty for looting and for violence against women. On the 22nd he ordered that fire be set to all the houses on the river bank near Sorel, for a distance of three miles. An attack had been carried out there by French militia and regulars, and the militiamen were informed that this was their punishment for taking up arms; for Murray, like Wolfe, ignorant of military custom, refused to recognize the right of the inhabitants to defend their homes. A few days later, when the landing party was opposed by the Varennes militia, he instructed his soldiers to loot, and "girls and women were violated, something that had never happened in the whole course of the war."[14]

As Murray's fleet advanced up the river, Bourlamaque, who was guarding the banks, ordered his troops to fall back on Montreal. Thereupon, his soldiers, especially those who had Canadian wives, no doubt, "deserted in large numbers, while the militia returned to their homes."

Having met almost no opposition, Murray led his force right up to the gates of Montreal and on September 7 established a camp to the east of the town.[14a] While the fleet from Quebec was on its way up the river, an army of 3,400 men under Colonel William Haviland came down the Richelieu, and on August 14 turned the destructive fire of its batteries on the Ile-aux-Noix post. On August 27, as Bougainville had only 1,100 men and rations for 2 days, he carried out instructions previously given by Vaudreuil and retreated before Haldimand's advancing army, which encamped at Longueuil on September 6.[15]

A third and much more powerful army was invading the colony from a base at Oswego, where the commander-in-chief, General Amherst, had assembled 9,750 militia and regulars and 600 Indians. The fort on Ile Lévis, with its garrison of 400 men commanded by Pouchot, surrendered on August 24, after a siege of 8 days. Amherst continued on his way down the river and on September 7, just as Murray was hemming in Montreal from the east, established his camp on the lower slope of the mountain overlooking the town. Meanwhile all available French troops from every quarter of the colony had gathered in Montreal, ready to fight under Lévis' orders.[16]

The situation was desperate. Montreal, the colony's last stronghold, was surrounded, and its only fortification was a plain stone wall, while pitted against its defending force of three thousand men was a besieging army eighteen thousand strong. In the rural districts, where the only alternative to submission was death, the terrorized habitants were swearing allegiance to the British Crown. In Montreal itself, the number of defenders was being reduced by desertions, chiefly among militiamen and marines, although some of the deserters were regular army men who had married Canadian wives. The western tribes and the Iroquois, including those living at the missions, had cast in their lot with the English.[17]

Faced with this desperate situation, Vaudreuil called a council of war which met on September 6 at eight o'clock in the evening, and at which Bigot was present as the official responsible for the commissariat. The council decided unanimously on surrender, and terms for capitulation were prepared and read in the course of the meeting. The following day Bougainville submitted the terms to Amherst, who agreed to almost all of them, but refused to grant the troops the honours of war. This humiliation, explained Amherst, was the penalty exacted for the barbarous raids against English colonies in which the French had participated. Lévis and the other officers urged Vaudreuil to reject such an insulting condition and to resort to arms in order to obtain more honourable terms. Their reaction was only natural, and Vaudreuil sympathized with it, but realizing that resistance was tantamount to mass suicide he wisely rejected the officers' proposal. The following day, September 8, the Governor signed the articles of capitulation, and Lévis ordered the colours to be burned so that they should not be handed over to the enemy. The same day, a detachment of English troops under Colonel Haldimand took possession of Montreal. Three days later Amherst was guest of honour at the Governor's table, but Vaudreuil "had not succeeded in persuading a single army officer to dine with him."[18]

So ended Canada's struggle to retain possession of her own territory, a struggle which had gone on for five years, and during which regular soldiers and militia had fought with constant courage and enthusiasm, and the civilian population had made great sacrifices. For Vaudreuil's surrender meant much more than the surrender of Montreal: it meant that the British forces were taking possession of the whole of New France, from Labrador to the Western plains. The articles of capitulation included guarantees of property and freedom to practise the Catholic religion, but the rights of the Jesuits, the Récollets and the Sulpicians, and the question of maintaining French laws were left to royal decision.[19]

By virtue of another condition of surrender, the French troops were transported to France on board English ships. Vaudreuil chose as travelling companion the great profiteer and former butcher, Joseph Cadet, while Lévis was accompanied by his dear friend Madame Pénissault. The country had one compensation in its dark hour. Won over by the advantages and benefits of life in a friendly country and freedom from the drudgery of army routine, about one third of the French soldiers chose to remain in Canada. Lévis estimated their numbers at 509 marines and about 500 soldiers. Some of them had already married Canadian wives, and their group was a precious addition to the country's population. On the other hand, the large body of civil servants from France and the French merchants and business representatives returned to France with their families. It was their departure which gave rise to the legend of an exodus of the classes which had provided the colony's leaders.[20]

As for the Canadians themselves, they refused to leave their native land, although the terms of surrender left them free to do so. Naturally Canadian officers in the marines went to France with their companies, but more than half of them came back to Canada later. Notwithstanding repeated affirmations based on a misinterpretation of facts, statistics and documents prove conclusively that Canada's élite did not emigrate. Not only the rural and urban population as a whole, but clergy, administrative leaders, seigneurs, officers of justice, merchants and leading citizens remained and took root in the country. Far from thinking of emigrating, Canadians, leaders and common people alike, had only one fear, that they might be "expelled from their native land, as the Acadians had been."[21]

After the capitulation, the English adopted a policy of tolerance and liberalism towards the population. On September 22, 1760 Amherst issued a proclamation announcing freedom of commerce and the maintenance of French laws. Since the occupation authorities paid hard cash for everything they bought, the average citizen found himself in a favourable position, while at the same time he hoped that the fleur-de-lis would return with peace. He was beset, however, by one haunting worry. During the summer of 1760, Vaudreuil and Bigot had announced that the payment of bills of exchange was deferred either to six months or to eighteen months after the declaration of peace, and that short-term payments would be met as circumstances permitted. Now that the officers of administration had left the country, what was to become of these promises? This was the question that was worrying the whole population.[22]

Haunted by the fear of losing the fruit of their labours and their savings, the people, who had already suffered much, vented their indignation in denunciations of Bigot. They swore "eternal hatred" and reviled him for being "the real cause of the loss of the colony," while the clergy regarded him as the "destroyer of religion." In the same spirit, the people "cursed" Vaudreuil for his weakness, for his flight after the defeat of the Plains of Abraham, and his premature order for the surrender of Quebec. The last words of a popular bit of doggerel mourned the fate of the people of Canada:

> Ils sont réduits à de si grands maldeuils
> Par la faute du marquis de Vaudreuil.[23]

In France, the conquest of Canada, which for the last two years had been almost a foregone conclusion, caused some stir in the military world, where there was some speculation as to the possibility of recapturing the country. But public opinion was completely indifferent. For years, colonies in general, and New France in particular, had been the butt of criticism from intellectuals, encyclopedists and journalists. Even Montesquieu, generally so clearsighted in his political views, was in favour only of commercial colonies, such as the West Indies, whose products supplemented those of France. He spoke out strongly against colonies like Canada which required settlers; these, in his view, depopulated the mother country without offering any compensating advantage. Voltaire, the most influential and famous publicist of the day, and a shareholder in the India Trading Company, was interested only in India, and sensible of its loss. After the fall of Pondichéry he wrote: "All my joy is over." On the other hand, he always underestimated the importance of Canada, which he considered "the most hateful country in the world." He even suggested "selling it to England in order to get rid of it." When he thought of those "acres of snow" with their bears and their beaver he kept insisting that "France can be quite happy without Quebec."[24]

Nor must we forget that in Europe the transfer of a people from one sovereignty to another was at the time accepted international practice. In the cases of Savoie, Alsace, Silesia and Poland, annexation of territory occasioned neither surprise nor protest nor regret.

Civil servants and ministers were equally unmoved by the loss of a colony which had been the cause of "enormous expense." Only the world of trade realized its value and its possibilities. The boards of trade of the maritime cities, St. Malo, Marseille, La Rochelle, Nantes, Dunkerque, Bayonne and Bordeaux, pleaded eloquently for its return to France. Berryer reprimanded Vaudreuil for giving up the country after having assured him so often that he could hold it. The King too expressed his displeasure that the Governor had disregarded Lévis' proposal that they try, by means of one final feat of arms, to obtain more honourable terms of surrender.[25]

As the ministers became conscious of criticism from army and business sources, they looked for a scapegoat who might distract attention from themselves and bear the brunt of public indignation. An order dated December 12, 1761 instructed the lieutenant-general of police to bring to trial the "authors of abuses, monopolies and acts of extortion and misappropriation committed in Canada." A judiciary commission was appointed, and, with the help of informers and documents already in the hands of the authorities, a list of fifty-five suspected offenders was drawn up. Among the accused were the Governor, the Intendant, senior civil servants, officers, clerks and store-keepers. Vaudreuil and Bigot, with any others who happened to be in France, were sent to the Bastille.

In such cases, rumour always exaggerates the sums involved, but an officer present at the trials gave the following estimates in *livres* of the fortunes acquired by the most important of the accused: Vaudreuil, Governor-General, 23,000,000; Bigot, Intendant, 29,000,000; Cadet, Purveyor-General, 15,000,000; Péan, Troop Major, 7,000,000; Saint-Sauveur, Secretary to the Governor, 1,900,000; Lotbinière, engineer and the Governor's nephew, 1,400,000; Bréard, Controller of the Treasury, 2,000,000; Pénissault, Assistant Purveyor, 1,900,000. The first nineteen were named, and the amount of their gains was listed. To this list must be added the subordinates not designated by name, with an estimated total of 31,600,000 *livres*, as well as eighteen of Cadet's clerks reputed to possess 400,000 *livres* apiece. These sums represent, in round figures, the fortunes of Canada's so-called "forty millionaires" who might more properly be called "the forty thieves."[26]

The great trial lasted two years, and when, on December 10, 1763 judgment was finally pronounced, the discrepancies between sentences showed clearly that family and feminine influence, as well as hard cash, had been at work behind the scenes. Those who belonged to the aristocracy, or who had powerful friends, escaped scot free. Thus Vaudreuil and his nephew de Lotbinière, des Méloises and Boishébert were exonerated. But heavy sentences were pronounced against the commoners whose names appeared high on the list of culprits. Bigot, the spirit of malversation personified, was spared the death sentence, but was exiled for life and required to make restitution of 1,500,000 *livres*. Cadet, Pénissault and Maurin were banished for nine years and required to pay 600,000 *livres* each. Madame Pénissault "had been fortunate enough to attract the interest of the Duc de Choiseul," and, through her influence, means were found to help her husband make his payments. She herself was later granted a pension of 4,000 *livres*. Madame Péan had already used her intimate relations with Bigot in her husband's interest, and it was apparently through her good offices that he was given a light prison sentence of six months. He was also to make restitution of 600,000 *livres*. Bigot took refuge in Switzerland, where he continued to live in comfort, although all his appeals against his sentence were rejected. He died in Neuchâtel on January 12, 1778.[27]

After the trial of the 40 millionaires came the settlement of the King's debt in Canada. It amounted to about 90,000,000 *livres* in bills of exchange, paper money and securities. When all deeds and documents had been examined by the appropriate bureau, the King's decisions in the matter were incorporated in an order which was published on June 29, 1764. Bills of exchange issued in France before 1759, and those issued for the account of the army in 1760, would be paid in full. But the value of the other bills of exchange was reduced by one half and that of paper money by three quarters. The amount of the King's debt was thus fixed at 45,607,000 *livres,* while the Royal Treasury was to receive 8,000,000 *livres* by way of restitution. The King's creditors would receive 37,000,000 *livres* in bearer notes with interest at four per cent. This represented a very heavy loss for the Canadian people, who had already been ruthlessly despoiled by the Bigot-Cadet crew.[28]

It is all too obvious that, under Bigot and his triumvirate, corruption and misuse of public funds wrought havoc in Canada's economy. It must be recognized, however, that their operations did not reduce the military strength of the colony in any way. Thanks to Bigot's intelligence and energy, and to Cadet's skill in organization, the troops were supplied throughout the war with the food and munitions they required. But an all-embracing system of peculation, misappropriation, and falsification of records sent the costs of these services to astronomical heights. Bigot and his clique were not responsible for the loss of Canada; but they looted the colonial treasury, destroyed all standards of public honesty and squeezed the entire population. The chain reaction which they set in motion continued even after their disappearance from the Canadian scene, and resulted finally in terms of settlement of the royal debt which wiped out a large part of the people's savings.[29]

Chapter Nineteen
1763

English policy: annexation of Canada. Conciliation and respect for existing institutions. Benefits of the occupation. The people adopt the attitude dictated by circumstances. Hopes that the country may be restored to France. Course of the war. The Family Pact. Loss of the West Indies. Failure in Newfoundland. Peace preliminaries. Canada or Guadeloupe. Treaty of Paris. Canada no longer French.

While proceedings were being carried on in Paris against Bigot and his associates, Amherst and his aides were organizing a military administration of Canadian territory.[1] England was determined not only to win a military victory in Canada but to hold the country after the peace,[1a] and immediately after the capture of Quebec her generals had begun to put into effect a policy designed to conciliate the population. On September 22 (1759) Monckton, who had become commander-in-chief, assured the Canadians that they would enjoy full property and religious rights "without the least hindrance from the English." The one condition was that they should take the oath of allegiance. Monckton's successor, Murray, exhorted them to accept "a just government" and warned them "to expect the most severe treatment" if they offered armed resistance. This was no empty threat, since in February (1760) he had burned down the houses of Pointe-Lévis whose owners had not informed him of the presence of a French contingent. By a strange contradiction, the English, while recognizing American militia as fighting units, refused the same status to their Canadian counterpart. It was in this atmosphere of protection for those who submitted and took the oath, and of "bloody vengeance" on those who offered resistance, that Murray carried on the administration in the region of Quebec until the capitulation of Montreal.[1b]

Two weeks after the surrender of Montreal, the commander-in-chief, Amherst, laid the bases of a provisional administration for the country. As Governor of Quebec, Murray would continue to administer that region, while General Gage and Colonel Burton were appointed governors of Montreal and Three Rivers respectively. Each governor was to have exclusive jurisdiction within his own region, but all three were subordinate to the authority of the general-in-chief, whose headquarters would shortly be established in New York. A proclamation issued by Amherst on September 22 repeated the order that all arms were to be surrendered to the new authorities. Commerce would be "open to all and free of tax," and all goods and services provided by the population would be paid for at once and "in specie." Amherst "enjoined his soldiers to live in harmony and understanding" with the inhabitants, and recommended to the latter that they should "treat the troops as brothers and fellow citizens." Finally, he assured all Canadians that they would "enjoy the same privileges as British subjects."

These were the broad lines of the military administration approved by the King. The governors, whose task it was to apply the policy, provided themselves with French-speaking secretaries, of whom one was Swiss and the others were Huguenots.[2] Each governor invested the former captains of militia with power to judge, without charge, cases which might be submitted to them, and to settle "any differences which might arise among the inhabitants." Appeals from their decisions could be made to the military authority in the district and, finally, to the Governor.[3] The English also appropriated the succession of the King of France in the seigniorial system by requiring that seigniorial rents be paid and by authorizing the recovery of land from tenants who had not fulfilled their obligation to establish homesteads. The clearest indication that Britain did not consider the possibility of restoring Canada to France lies in the fact that in April 1762 seigniories carved out of the former French concession of La Malbaie were granted to two British officers.[4]

Not content with merely leaving Canadian ways of life unchanged, Amherst tried to win over the people by improving the conditions in which they lived. After the capture of Montreal, when the war had left the town starved of the ordinary necessities, he addressed an appeal to the governors of the English colonies for "all kinds of food and refreshments." In December merchants and agents arrived from New York and Massachusetts with a great variety of goods which they exchanged for furs and other products. As trade increased, the habitants had the satisfaction of being paid once more in coin, which they hoarded.[5]

Murray showed his care for the well-being of the "new subjects" of King George in several ways. In October he asked the Abbé Briand, the Vicar-General of Quebec, for a list of the needy families in the district. He then asked the merchants and the officers and men of the garrison to subscribe to a relief fund. Each soldier agreed to give one day's ration a month. In February 1761 Murray and Gage worked together to arrange for the purchase of grain in the Montreal region and for its distribution to farmers in the Quebec district who had no seed grain for their spring sowing.[6]

The policy of benevolence towards the population, maintenance of its institutions, and help for its needs, was warmly approved by George III, who praised the "kindness and benignity" of the governors. The Canadians, wrote the King in March 1762, "are now subjects of His Britannic Majesty" and they have the right "to enjoy all the advantages" pertaining to that estate. At the same time he forbade "anyone whatsoever to offend them by insulting remarks on their language, costumes, manners, customs or country, or by uncharitable and unchristian reflections upon the religion which they profess."[7]

Since in 1761 Canadians were already classed as British subjects, the authorities decreed that public mourning should be observed for the death of George II. Curés were ordered to drape their churches in black, and the people were instructed to wear black clothes and crêpe hatbands. On the same principle, the accession of George III, the King's marriage, and even victories over the armies of France, were proclaimed to the people of Quebec as occasions for rejoicing.[8]

Did the administration of the occupying power, judicious, skilful and almost always sympathetic, achieve its aim of reconciling a French Catholic population to a foreign Protestant monarchy? The administrators themselves agreed that it did.

Murray was convinced that the Canadians, reassured as to their freedom to practise their religion, "would quickly become good and faithful subjects of His Majesty." Burton declared that "the inhabitants, and especially the peasants, seemed very pleased with their change of masters." Haldimand expressed the opinion, obviously coloured by wishful thinking, that "the people would be reduced to despair by the sight of a French fleet and French troops."[9]

French documents provide no confirmation of these subjective and partial statements. It is true that Canadians benefited by the abolition of military service and obligations. They were also delighted to have their markets well supplied with merchandise and to be paid for their products in gold and silver and not in paper money.[9a] A Citizens' Address of 1764 stated that the maintenance of their institutions allowed them to remain as happy and as untroubled "in their religion and the possession of their property" as they had been "before their defeat."[10] The "principal bourgeois and merchants" of Montreal and Three Rivers appeared faithfully at all official ceremonies. It was difficult for them to do otherwise, and in any case self-interest was a powerful motive for such outward gestures of conformity. The rural population lived in exemplary harmony with the troops who were quartered on them. Fraternization led to the establishment of "attachments" between soldiers and the women of the houses in which they were lodged, attachments which were sometimes, though not always, the result of "violence done to women by soldiers and officers." One result of such adventures was a certain number of illegitimate births. Another, and more significant one, was that some fifteen Canadian girls from very good families were married by British army chaplains to English officers. However, to sum up the situation, there is nothing in any of these facts that is not perfectly usual and normal in a long military occupation.[11]

The country's one collective voice, the Church, occasionally made pronouncements associated with political events. In February 1762, on the occasion of the coronation of George III, a solemn *Te Deum* was sung in each of the three towns. For the Vicar-General of Montreal, Abbé Mongolfier, it was an occasion for manifesting "our" joy. The Abbé Perrault, speaking to his parishioners in Three Rivers, sounded a similar note: "You will thus express your attachment and your joy." But the Abbé Briand in Quebec merely invited his flock to "share the joy of the peoples" who already recognized the new King.[12]

None of these formulas is to be accepted at its face value. They are merely diplomatic phrases required by the convention of the time and commanded by the authorities or by circumstance. Indications of the true spirit of the population must be sought elsewhere. Writing in April 1762, Burton defines this spirit quite clearly. "Canadians in general," he announces, "prefer not to speak of the matter, since they flatter themselves with the silent hope" that the country will be restored to France at the end of the war. Gage, for his part, declared that it could not be expected that the population of Canada "would ever manifest for a British sovereign the love and affection" which were felt by his other subjects. Resigned to the presence of an occupying army, Canadians concentrated all their thoughts on the peace "so ardently desired" and the hope "that they might resume their work" in the conditions which had existed before the war. The Treaty of Paris proved that this hope was vain, and in the pastoral letter which he wrote in May, when the terms of the treaty became known in Canada, the Vicar-General of Three Rivers expressed the real feelings of the people: "The event is one which has stirred your deepest emotions; you cannot think of it without sorrow."[13]

Grief, hope, resignation, these were some of the feelings experienced by Canadians between the surrender of Montreal and the Treaty of Paris. When, in preliminaries concluded in November 1762, the fate of the country was revealed, a group of members of the three orders—nobility, clergy and third estate— addressed a petition to George III. They pointed out that they were innocent victims of the disorders which had ruined the country's economy and, since the preliminaries left "no room to doubt that Canada was coming under his rule," they begged the King to procure the dispatch of their merchandise immobilized in French warehouses and the "prompt payment" of their paper money. In the distress and grief of the moment, the Canadians' first thought was not for problematical rights in the future; it was to salvage the remnants of their economic resources and thus establish some basis of security for their material needs.[14]

After the capitulation of Montreal, the concourse of military and political circumstances had set the final seal on the fate of Canada. In November 1759 vague peace parleys had been opened, but they had remained abortive, and after the death of George II the war went on with no decisive gain on either side. The French victory at Clostercamp in October 1760 scarcely compensated for the defeat the previous year at Minden. In February 1761 Lally-Tollendal surrendered Pondichéry after a siege of seven months, and India fell to the English. In March Choiseul, in a memorandum which revived the proposal for peace, suggested that "the two Crowns should remain in possession of their conquests." This was the first suggestion from France that she might give up Canada. Negotiations were opened in the two capitals, and in July France agreed to cede Canada on condition that England guarantee the inhabitants' right to practise the Catholic religion "according to the Roman rite," and that Ile Royale and Louisbourg be restored to France. In September Pitt promised freedom of religion to Canada "without interruption or molestation," but refused absolutely to give up Ile Royale.[14a]

Meanwhile, in August, Choiseul had tried to improve his country's situation by concluding the "Family Pact" between France and Spain against England. Angered by this alliance, Pitt suspended the peace parleys, whereupon George III, who was completely out of sympathy with Pitt's imperialistic policy and domineering methods, forced his Prime Minister to resign and appointed his former tutor Lord Bute in his stead.[15]

Despite this display of the King's authority, hostilities continued. In February 1762 the English fleets seized Martinique, Granada and Ste. Lucie, and in August they captured Cuba and Havana from Spain, and ravaged the Philippines. In July 1762 the Chevalier de Ternay, with a squadron of four vessels, attacked and captured St. John's. But this wasteful diversion of naval strength served no useful purpose since the fort was recaptured by the English in September.[15a] The war had now lost its *raison d'être*. England had attained her objective, the possession of Canada and India; she could afford to give some consideration to her people who were groaning under a load of debt, and to her commerce which was in a state of stagnation. On the continent, Hanover was safe, and Prussia had annexed Silesia. On the other side, France, Spain and Austria had exhausted their financial resources and realized that they could not reverse the military situation. All Europe yearned for the end of hostilities and relief for the growing distress of its peoples. Negotiations were resumed, and preliminary conditions were signed at Fontainebleau on November 3, 1762.[16]

In England, as peace conditons were under discussion, a curious debate was carried on in newspapers and pamphlets as to which of the two French possessions, Guadeloupe or Canada, England should insist upon keeping. The argument in favour of Guadeloupe was that the island's exports in sugar and cotton were worth 1,000,000 pounds sterling, whereas Canadian furs did not bring in one-tenth of that sum. But financial circles, and still more, the pressure of opinion in the American colonies, tipped the balance in favour of Canada.[16a]

A few months later, on February 10, 1763, England, France and Spain signed the Treaty of Paris which ended the Seven Years' War. The treaty was written in French, and only one of its twenty-five articles dealt exclusively with Canada. By article IV, Louis XV ceded to England the whole territory of New France from Ile Royale to the western plains. For his part George III granted to Canadians the right to practise the Catholic faith "in so far as the laws of Great Britain allow." The inhabitants could leave the country at any time within a period of eighteen months, and those who emigrated could sell their property to British subjects. France retained only the tiny islands of St. Pierre and Miquelon, and French fishermen retained the right to fish on the Newfoundland banks and to dry fish on the northern shores of the island. In the West Indies, Martinique, Guadeloupe, and three small neighbouring islands were restored to France.[17]

The people of Canada were informed of their fate in May when the governors published the Treaty of Paris. Conquered by force of arms and ceded by treaty, New France was now subject to Great Britain after two centuries under the French flag.[18]

Chapter Twenty
REVIEW AND RETROSPECT

~~~~~~

Discoveries. Trading companies. Royal rule and colonization. Period of peace and expansion. Wars and final conquest. Causes of French failure to hold Canada: inadequate population; hostility of English colonies; France's continental policy. England's strength: superior naval power; her position as an island fortress.

~~~~~~

At the end of the French régime, the names Canada and New France were no longer distinctive, but were used indiscriminately to designate France's Laurentian colony, whose history went back two and a half centuries.[a] Its beginnings can be traced to the arrival of Breton fishermen on the Grand Banks in 1504. These fishermen were also the first French fur-traders. In 1524 Verrazano named the country New France, and ten years later Cartier discovered the St. Lawrence valley, where he reported the existence of gold and diamonds. A first attempt at settlement under the leadership of Roberval was abandoned in 1543 when Cartier's diamonds proved to be "false." French ships continued, however, to pursue the fur trade in the St. Lawrence. Half a century later, two posts were established, one under La Roche on Sable Island, and the other under Chauvin at Tadoussac, but these too were short-lived.

In 1603 Henry IV adopted a colonization policy; companies of merchants would undertake to recruit settlers and in return would be granted property and a trading monopoly. As a result of this scheme de Monts led a group of settlers to Acadia in 1604, and in 1608 Champlain founded Quebec and Canada. A succession of trading companies followed, but since none of them wanted to reduce its profits by the expenses of colonization, the colony was nothing more than a trading factory. This situation continued until the creation of the Company of New France in 1627. Although Richelieu's failure to provide an escort for its fleet resulted in initial disaster, the Company made the first systematic effort to colonize the country by means of seigniorial grants.[1]

The efforts of the Company of New France met with only partial success, and in 1663 a population of some 2,500 lived under constant threat of reduction by Indian raids. At this time the Company was abolished, Canada was brought once more under royal administration, and Colbert initiated a programme of subsidized emigration and aid to industry and commerce which was carried out by Talon.[2] After Talon's return to France in 1672 the country had to rely on its own resources, of which the most stable and valuable was the fur trade. It had to defend itself against Iroquois raids which continued until the great peace of 1701, while hostilities in America resulting from two European wars ended only with the signing of the Treaty of Utrecht in 1713.

For Canada, the Treaty of Utrecht marked the beginning of 30 years of peace (1713-43). The population, which in 1713 had reached 18,000, was increased during the following years by the immigration of *engagés* and salt-smugglers and by soldier settlement. Thanks to a phenomenally high birth rate, the population doubled in each of two twenty-year periods, and in 1760 stood at 75,000. The years following 1713 brought renewed strength and activity to the country's economy. Its growth became more marked with the opening of new seigniories, the development of shipbuilding, the exploitation of iron mines, and especially with the increase of land under cultivation. Unfortunately, Hocquart's intelligent and honest administration was followed by the reign of Bigot and his gang whose systematic abuse of trust disrupted the economy and caused financial havoc. To a country already weakened internally, the Seven Years' War brought invasion by powerful English forces, while English fleets dominated the sea and cut off help from France. The last military engagement in Canada resulted in a French victory, but the inevitable end came when an English fleet sailed up the river to Montreal. The surrender of Montreal to the armies of General Amherst completed the conquest of Canada which the Treaty of Paris confirmed three years later.[3]

So ended the political existence of France's oldest and largest colony in America. The conquest, which had been a threat ever since the expedition of Phipps three quarters of a century earlier (1690), may be attributed to three main causes: an inadequate population, hostility on the part of the English colonies and France's continental policy.

There were several reasons for the slow rate of settlement in Canada. Before 1627 the trading companies were unwilling to pay the costs of colonization, especially since they feared that settlement of the country would be detrimental to the fur trade. After 1633 the Jesuit *Relations* unconsciously discouraged potential colonists. Tales of Indian cruelty doubtless achieved their object of winning moral and financial support for the Jesuit missions, but they were less likely to attract European settlers to the country.[4] Moreover, even the French peasant or artisan whose interest was aroused by the prospect of a freer and more independent life in a new country might well be daunted by Canada's climate, its ice-bound isolation for six months of the year, and its distance from France. With the advent of the royal régime an effort was made to stimulate emigration by means of financial aid—an effort too soon abandoned by a king ambitious for supremacy in Europe and unwilling to divert young men from his armies to his Canadian colony. The vast territory in which Talon dreamed of founding an empire received only four thousand immigrants in ten years of state-aided colonization. Even during the long peace that followed Utrecht, France, entirely preoccupied with the need for economic recovery at home, sent only a thin trickle of emigrants to Canada, although she could easily have sent "four hundred persons every year" from certain provinces where land was so scarce that the peasants had to cultivate "mountain tops."

There were also subsidiary factors militating against the growth of Canada. The West Indies presented a powerful counter-attraction, evidenced by its population of 40,000 at a time when Canada had only 10,000 inhabitants. Martinique and Guadeloupe had a pleasant climate and could be reached more easily. They had also a very flourishing trade. Whereas Canadian exchanges barely reached a total of 10,000,000 *livres* a year, the figure for the West Indies was 200,000,000 *livres*. Not only did the islands have the advantage of a pleasant climate, but their

most important export, sugar cane, was an article of common
consumption. Canada's furs, on the other hand, suffered a
double disadvantage: they were a luxury article, and their distribution was controlled by a monopoly.[5] Considering Pitt's
unshakeable determination to conquer Canada at any price,
100,000 more Canadians, including 25,000 potential militiamen,
might not have prevented the final disaster, but they might have
made it possible to prolong the struggle and perhaps to obtain
more favourable conditions at a time when England had not yet
made a final choice between Canada and Guadeloupe.[6]

A second impediment to Canada's free development was the
inveterate and growing antagonism of the English colonies on
her frontiers. The first English settlers had sought a land where
they would be free to practise their religion. They had been
fortunate in finding a country whose soil was fertile, which was
easy of access, and which was near the Acadian fishing banks. As
a result, their colonies expanded rapidly. Farming, fishing and
contraband trade with the West Indies were the basis of a profi-
able trade among provinces and between the provinces and the
mother country. At the beginning of the eighteenth century,
when Canada's population numbered 20,000, that of the English
colonies was already 350,000. At the time of the conquest the
corresponding figures were 75,000 and 1,500,000.[7]

Though comparatively few in number, the French in America presented a serious obstacle to the realization of English
ambitions; for they claimed the right to exclude English fishermen from Acadian waters and their posts barred the routes to
the western fur country. The English saw a solution to their
difficulties in the expulsion of the French from the continent,
and they made repeated attempts to achieve this end. Two unsuccessful expeditions were launched against Quebec, and Port
Royal was captured four times in fifty years. When Canadians
retaliated with cruel and devastating attacks on the English frontier settlements, the "barbarous papists' " raids added a motive
of hatred to the British colonists' lust for territory. When Quebec built a chain of forts in the Ohio valley in order to hem in
the English along the Atlantic seaboard, the colonists rose in
their wrath and dispatched an army, under Braddock, to attempt
the conquest of the West. Louisbourg, after having been captured by the English and restored to France, was finally reduced

by an overpowering invasion force. For all the seaboard colonies from Massachusetts to Virginia, the watchword was that the Canadian wall barring their expansion must be destroyed. Their collective hatred, supported by the influence and help of the capitalists and shipowners of the mother country, became the driving force of the British will to conquer Canada. If the antagonism of the neighbouring colonies had been a little less obsessive, Canada might perhaps, like Louisiana, have been spared massive invasion and conquest, at least for the time being.[8]

The third cause of Canada's downfall is to be found in the policy of Versailles. After following for a very brief time Colbert's plan for colonization, Louis XIV inaugurated a policy of continental supremacy and expansion. Instead of colonists, he enlisted soldiers. Historical and geographical influences necessarily placed the field of the King's action on the Rhine, and at a time when he was occupied in consolidating his position by the annexation of Artois and Franche-Comté, it was natural that he should be less interested in the territory around the Great Lakes. It is easy to understand that in the triumph of Nymwegen he might continue to be hypnotized by his continental ambitions and lose sight of the future empire which Talon envisaged in America. It is less easy to understand why he disregarded d'Iberville's warning against British domination of America or Callières' scheme to capture Boston and New York. Not only did the King fail to provide means to stimulate Canada's economy, to send more colonists and to grant more generous subsidies; when the resources of his kingdom were almost exhausted by the wars which his policy had provoked, he even threatened to abandon a colony which took money from the royal coffers. Finally, the noble ambition to establish a Bourbon on the throne of Spain cost New France the loss of Acadia, Newfoundland and Hudson Bay.

These important losses were followed by the creation of a new colony on Ile Royale; but rather than a colony in the true sense of the term, Louisbourg was a military wall intended to halt England's expansion. Still obsessed with its European strategy, Versailles spent millions of *livres* on the fortifications of Louisbourg which might have been used to strengthen Canada's economy and to increase her population. When France became

involved in the European conflict, Louis XV exhausted her
strength fighting on the continent and sent pitifully inadequate
help to her colonies, with the result that Louisbourg was
captured during the War of the Austrian Succession, and that at
the end of the Seven Years' War Pitt could boast that he had
conquered Canada in Germany.[9]

France's policy, which could not be avoided but which was
followed too exclusively, was all the more futile since England,
entrenched in her island fortress, was free to strike at points
which she herself chose. Canada fell because France, a continental power, was obliged to fight in Europe, whereas England's
naval superiority made it possible for her to concentrate her land
forces in America and at the same time prevent any French help
from reaching Canada. Thus the British navy was the decisive
factor in the final victory. The French poet Lemercier symbolized
England's strength in a neoclassic image:

Le trident de Neptune est le sceptre du monde.[10]

From the beginning of the eighteenth century, the continental policy of Louis XIV and Louis XV prevented them from
taking more than a minor interest in Canada, and from giving
the country more than the most meagre help. The royal attitude
was reflected in that of the Minister of Marine, who became more
and more exasperated as the colony drained the treasury. It was
also in agreement with public opinion, which had been misled
by the short-sighted anti-colonial theories of the encyclopedists.
All these influences working together led straight to the sacrifice
of the Canadian "stables" when "the house," the mother country,
was on fire.

New France ceased to exist as a political entity in 1763, but
its 75,000 citizens remained in the country. Although they were
haunted by the memory of the Acadian deportation, neither the
clergy nor the leaders among the laymen deserted the colony,
and the population, following their example, remained rooted in
the soil of Canada.[11] For these descendants of pioneers of whom
the first had arrived more than a century earlier, Canada was the
"land of their forefathers," the country which gave them a good
life, free of servitude; they would not desert her in the hour of
defeat.

Chapter Twenty-one
CANADA AT THE TIME OF THE CESSION

Population. Physical and moral characteristics of the people. Conditions in the towns and in the country. The élite. Economic and political situation in Canada. Life in the seigniories. The towns; Quebec, Montreal, Three Rivers. Canadian society: its defects and its good points. Social gatherings and distractions. The intellectual and social qualities of Canadian women. Emergence of a new human type, the Canadian: his characteristics; his past achievements; elements of promise for his future.

At the date of the cession, Canada's whole vast territory had only 75,000 inhabitants, of whom 13,000 lived in the country's three towns and 62,000 in rural communities. Whether townsmen or country dwellers, all displayed similarities in thinking, manners and language, which gave the people a specific character of its own.[1]

This sturdy young race owed its origins, for the most part, to the industrious and progressive provinces of northern and western France, from Picardy to Saintonge. Living in a harsh but healthy climate, in a country where long winters were followed by hot summers, where work was hard and communication difficult, these descendants of French forefathers acquired a degree of vigour and endurance which astonished European visitors. "Canadians," observed one officer, "are well built, big, strong, skilful in handling rifle and axe." Brave and able fighters, in peace they were hospitable, obliging, industrious and jovial. Theirs was an essentially healthy morality and they were sincere believers, although their piety was expressed in the outward practices of Catholicism and was seldom a deeply spiritual experience, and their devoutness did not always exclude superstition.

201

There is no reason to suppose that any of them showed lean-
ings towards Jansenism. Two Jansenist priests who appeared
briefly between 1712 and 1718 left no mark. Under the direction
of their bishops and curés, and of the seminaries in Quebec and
Montreal, the faithful consistently professed and practised a
comprehensive and orthodox doctrine. In worldly affairs, however, observers remarked that they were crafty, grasping, boastful, and disrespectful of the King's rights and property. But the
foreigner who reported that their taste for tobacco and brandy
led to idleness was certainly biased.[1a]

If, on the one hand, Canadians did not work well together,
on the other, they did not indulge in tale-bearing or informing.
They all shared a horror of discipline and a passion for independence "to such a point that you couldn't get servants." Moreover, the possession of their own lands with hunting and fishing
rights, and the knowledge that they were under the special protection of the Intendant encouraged them to adopt egalitarian
manners. "They are all Monsieur and Madame, be they peasants
or gentlemen, peasant women or great ladies." Travellers expressed the opinion that the country people were "made of finer
stuff than the peasants of France; they were more intelligent and
less rustic." Murray declared that Canadians were "perhaps the
bravest and best race upon the globe," frugal, moral and industrious. Observers agreed that the women, who were "pretty
rather than beautiful," were "witty in conversation," and that in
intellectual development they were superior to the men. The
master of the house recognized the competence of the mistress
and always consulted her before concluding any important matter. In their desire to be attractive, the women lavished a great
deal of care of their clothes and their coiffure, and they loved
pleasure and wordly distractions, but at the same time they were
deeply "attached to their husbands and their children." They
were also excellent housekeepers, and they maintained pleasant
social relations with the other members of their community.
"The whole population is very polite," reported one traveller;
they speak "the same French as we do, with an accent as good as
the one you hear in Paris."[2]

Conditions of life in the country differed in important aspects from those in the city. Urban shopkeepers and artisans had
a fairly easy and comfortable life, at least until all food supplies

were cornered by the *Grande Société;* but the unskilled workers and day labourers, who constituted a lower class, went through periods of austerity, privation and poverty. On the other hand, the country people, with their fields of grain, their cattle and their gardens, and with fish and game at their door, lived in real comfort which the women enhanced still further with the products of their spinning wheels and looms. The houses, usually of wood and with steep sloping roofs, sometimes thatched, were generally small and were heated by enormous fires or by big iron stoves. They were lighted by tallow candles or by porpoise-oil lamps. The men wore their hair in pigtails, and the "parish dandies" sported "embroidered hats and shirts with cuffs." Many of them had their own horses and rode to church with their sweethearts riding pillion. In Montcalm's opinion Canadian freeholders were "very comfortable" and lived like minor noblemen in France.[2a]

There were also differences between country and city dress. The townsman followed the European fashion, with three-cornered hat, "French" shoes, knee breeches with stockings, and a coat which came down to his knees. The coats were of velvet or silk cloth or wool drugget, according to the social class or the purse of the wearer, and they ranged from deep red to light brown. By contrast, the countryman's costume was quite distinctive: long trousers, a woollen coat, hooded and belted and fastened with tapes, moccasins and a tuque, blue or red depending on whether he lived in the Montreal or the Quebec region. On feast days the farmer's wife wore a white cap and a coloured bodice. Below a short skirt she wore French shoes and sometimes silk stockings. In the towns, the ladies followed the Paris fashions, which naturally reached Canada a little late. Bodices were tightly fitted above wide panniered skirts of striped or flowered silk. On their heads women wore embroidered caps or fine lace mantillas with the ends knotted loosely in front. They brought out the beauty of their skin with rouge and patches, but they did not use rouge on their lips.[3]

The population of Canada, limited though it was, included a class of leaders equal to their task. This class was made up of about 400 long-established families whose heads may be grouped in the following categories: 131 seigneurs, of whom some were commoners; 106 gentlemen and notables; 119 merchants; 22

lawyers and 13 doctors. There were also about 40 notaries, but there had been no barristers since 1667 when Louis XIV had decreed "that it was not to the colony's advantage to admit any."[4] When the Court or the Governor wished to sound out the opinion of the country, the assembly which they consulted was composed of representatives chosen from these groups which also provided the delegates charged with presenting petitions to the King, the Minister, the Governor or the Intendant.[5]

The individuals constituting this upper class lived on a very modest scale. A report from Raudot before 1713 and one from Versailles after Utrecht comment on their condition of near-poverty. Even in 1732, after the economic recovery of the country, Hocquart speaks of their "slender resources." Their situation did, however, improve noticeably with the increase in population and production. By 1740 most of them were in easy circumstances, and an increase in duties on wines and brandy in 1747 is an indication of continuing prosperity. In 1751 Bonnefons reported that these leading citizens were still not wealthy, although their material condition continued to improve. All those who could do so "participated in trade with the up-country." In this trade, in which they were often partners of the Governor or the Intendant, officers and merchants soon made fortunes. Under the impetus of their wealth and the ill-gotten gains of the Péan-Cadet-Descheneaux triumvirate, the bourgeois of Montreal and Quebec adopted habits of luxury and prodigality which reached the proportions of a public scandal during the last decade of the French régime.[6]

Improved economic conditions had very little effect on those seigneurs who preferred the life of a country gentleman to that of the city. In their simple wooden manor houses looking out on the river, they were content with a peaceful, monotonous family life whose only distractions were hunting, fishing and visits from family and friends, who brought news from the cities and from France. Occasionally some religious or seigniorial festival interrupted the even course of their days. The feast of the patron saint of the parish was a holiday. High mass was celebrated, and the seigneur, in court dress and occupying the place of honour, made the offering of blessed bread. But the most outstanding religious ceremony was the visit of the Bishop. In the church, decked for the occasion with spruce boughs, the prelate celebrated a pontifical mass and preached a moving sermon. The children of the parish were then confirmed, and the day ended with a ceremonial dinner at the manor house.

Two red-letter days, not specially marked on the church calendar, were St. Martin's day and May day. On November 11 all the farm carts in the parish converged on the manor house, where the tenants paid their seigniorial dues. Bags of grain were deposited at the door, capons and chickens were handed over, money was counted out piece by piece on the big table— all this in accordance with the terms of the contract. A more joyous occasion was the seigniorial festival when the maypole was planted before the door of the manor house. A tall fir tree was brought up, already stripped of its branches and bark and with a weathercock attached to its tip. As soon as it was in place, the young people made the trunk a target for their rifle shots, shouting loudly as they performed this "baptism." The seigneur then served a feast of meat, sweet cakes and brandy, after which the party ended with singing.[7]

Although the population of the colony had increased, it still had only three small towns. Quebec, the capital and seaport, was beautifully situated on a promontory and was surrounded by solid ramparts armed with cannon. Its eight thousand inhabitants were proud of their upper town with its church spires piercing the sky and its handsome buildings. Particularly noteworthy were the Governor's residence, the Château St. Louis, the palace of the Intendant, the Hôtel-Dieu and the Hôpital Général; and among the religious buildings, the Cathedral, the Bishop's palace, the Jesuit college and the Ursuline convent. Tall stone houses surmounted by broad chimneys lined the steep, narrow streets. The lower town was more modest, but its central square boasted a statue of Louis XIV, and while it was surrounded on three sides by shops, the fourth side was occupied by the pretty chapel which bore the proud name of Notre-Dame-des-Victoires.[8]

Quebec was the capital, but the Governor and the Intendant spent a period of residence each year in Montreal, the gateway to the West and the country's great fur market. The town, pleasantly situated between the river and the tree-covered mountain, stretched out along the river bank. It was protected only by a narrow stone wall and a small citadel. The visitor would have seen some fine private mansions, the château de Vaudreuil, the

château de Ramezay and the château de Bécancour. He would
also have admired the religious establishments, the parish
church, the Seminary of St. Sulpice, the Récollet monastery and
the Jesuit residence and chapel.[8a] Three Rivers, situated half-
way between Quebec and Montreal, still had only six hundred
inhabitants. It served as a transport centre for the St. Maurice
ironworks, and its birch-bark canoes were reputed to be the best
in the country. The only buildings of any interest in Three
Rivers were the modest Governor's residence, the graceful Ursuline convent and the simple Récollet church.[8b]

The three towns were linked by the King's highway, and the
journey between them was made in several stages in post carriages with one or two horses. Travellers paid twenty *sous* per
mile and per horse. As there were no inns along the route, they
spent the night "in the houses of the better farmers" who, according to Bougainville, "dispensed hospitality in noble fash-
and made the traveller pay "even more nobly and at an
arbitrary rate." But we must not forget that Bougainville was a
senior officer; Bonnefons assures us that, in the case of passengers in more modest circumstances or of private soldiers, "you
receive from all Canadians thoughtful and generous hospitality,
which protects you from the risk of hunger and thirst, or cold in
winter . . . and everything is urged upon you so insistently that
you can hardly refuse without offending.[9]

The visitor's interest in Montreal or Quebec was not limited
to their fine sites and buildings. The streets of both cities presented a picturesque and colourful scene. People of every rank
and social category met and mingled on the wooden sidewalks.
There were officers with coloured coats, velvet vests and gold-
edged tricornes; gentlemen or *bourgeois* in grey or plum-
coloured suits and braided hats; soldiers in white uniforms with
red, blue or green lapels, and gaiters to their knees; working
men in knee breeches and short jackets, with their hair in pigtails; ladies in full skirts, with powdered hair and lace caps;
working women with short skirts, coloured blouses and embroidered bonnets. Around the shops one might see countrymen
in blanket coats and occasionally a few half-naked Indians with
painted faces and a blanket over one shoulder. Carts creaked by
with their horses harnessed in tandem, while elegant ladies in
high-wheeled calèches made play with their fans.[10]

In the course of the year, the towns followed a sort of social calendar. Protocol required that the year should begin with the New Year's Day calls. One observer remarked that in Canada such visits "grew like grass," whether their motive was official obligation, friendship, or mere inquisitiveness. The Mardi Gras carnival was the signal for a whole series of celebrations, often extravagant or unusual ones: hay-cart rides, drawing-room plays, balls which continued into the small hours of Ash Wednesday, champagne dinners and all-night stag parties ending with onion soup.[10a]

The great event of the summer was the arrival of ships from France with the year's mail, answers to the letters which had been written the previous autumn before the river was closed by ice. As well as family letters, the ships brought dispatches from Versailles announcing decisions, subsidies and appointments which affected the whole life of the colony. They also brought young officers, who were likely to be snapped up as husbands by the attractive Quebec girls before the rival beauties of Montreal even had a chance to see them.

When occasion offered, the towns held public celebrations. News of a royal birth or a victory elicited an order for the *Te Deum* to be sung in the churches. The religious ceremony was followed by a military review, with salvos of artillery fire. In the evening candles were lit in all the windows, the Governor gave a banquet, and there were fireworks for the people. The arrival of a new governor was marked by a great military and religious reception attended by all Quebec. For everyday amusement, the men disdained skittles and bowls, but they played chess, and the idlers spent their time in the taverns (of which there were very few). The ladies had their own distractions. They went driving, played cards or dice, and took dancing lessons. In the winter, there were skating and sleighing parties on the river.[11]

Travellers observing the members of the ruling class were struck by the mixture in them of optimism and immaturity, vigour and presumption. Some considered them "affable and sociable," others "generous and obliging," but often lacking in strength of character. Their education had generally been neglected, but since they were "quite intelligent," one observer concluded that, "with better instruction," they would be "capable of understanding the sciences and exercising the charges required by the administration of a state."[12] A certain number of them acquired a broad, general and professional education. These were the jurists, doctors, engineers, botanists, architects, geographers. Readers in search of information made use of the school libraries or of private libraries belonging to wealthy individuals. The constant succession of officers, priests and high officials from France kept the colony informed on literary and scientific matters, while missionaries and officers returning from the West contributed to their knowledge of ethnography and geography. According to the Swedish scientist Peter Kalm, there was a greater interest in letters and science in Canada than in the more populous English colonies. Plays were presented in both Quebec and Montreal. Nuns, such as Mother Andrée Duplessis and priests, such as the Abbé La Tour, compiled valuable annals; ladies, such as Madame Bégon, wrote lively letters, and versifiers composed songs, lampoons and laments. The Abbé Marchand even wrote a mock-heroic poem, and Jean Taché composed a *Tableau de la mer*.[13]

Reports all agree that the ladies were distinguished by their elegant figures and their graceful carriage. They were generally very intelligent, and their intelligence was enhanced by natural vivacity and a good education. They loved pretty clothes and they liked to be admired. Many French officers lost their hearts to attractive Canadian girls, although Montcalm openly expressed his disapproval of "stupid marriages" contracted between officers and girls from poor families. According to one observer, the women of Montreal, although they had not had received as complete an instruction as that given in the Ursuline convent, were more serious than their Quebec sisters. He added that they were more beautiful and prouder. The Quebec woman, mocking and frivolous, had more free and easy ways. She followed the Paris fashions as faithfully as possible and was a charming conversationalist. In short, she was a "true French woman in her education and her manners."[14]

Montcalm knew these men and women well and was himself an intelligent observer. A few lines from his private diary sum up the opinion of this very competent judge: "Quebec has impressed me as a town with an air of breeding; and I do not believe there are a dozen in France whose society is superior to that of Quebec."[15]

In the short history of this young people, the processes of evolution had already produced a new human type, the Canadian. Adapting themselves to a new climate, a different social environment and different requirements, sons and grandsons of French emigrants were exposed to experiences and developed reactions which progressively modified their mental attitudes and their racial behaviour. The Canadian had proud, unconquered Indians for his neighbours and brothers. His own ears were attuned to the call of the great open plains and virgin forests. With the air that he breathed he absorbed a taste for adventure, the spirit of liberty and a passion for independence. After a period of twenty years during which they were free of financial responsibility towards the Church, Canadians agreed to pay tithes but only at a rate that met with their approval. Such insubordination towards ecclesiastical authority was unknown in France; and the Canadian displayed the same sense of independence in his capacity as landholder. Master in his own right of his parcel of land, he did not recognize, as the French peasant did, "submission" to his seigneur. In the same spirit, he protested against the imposition in Canada of any of the numerous taxes for which peasants were liable in the mother country. Minor symptoms betraying the existence of a distinct Canadian personality were the self-importance of the men, which prevented them from going into service, and the vanity of the women who aped the manners of high society ladies. Even the language of Canadians marked them off from their French cousins. They kept the accent of France, but their speech was larded with sea terms, Indian words and picturesque expressions of their own invention.

This specifically Canadian character showed itself even in military matters. For the marines and the militia, war was a succession of raids and attacks from ambush, "Indian war." They resisted the European idea of war in the open field to which their French officers tried to convert them.[16]

Canadians were then impenitent individualists, often stubborn and boastful, and proud of having directed their own existence and kept their country free over a period of a hundred years. During this time their society, almost untouched by outside influences, had developed an unusual degree of egalitarianism. Levelling from the top came about as nobles of greater and lesser degree, dignitaries and seigneurs, associated with *bourgeois* in trading enterprises and married their partners' daughters. At the same time, the levelling process was going on from the bottom, as merchants and even simple tenant farmers acquired seigniories and thus moved up a step on the social ladder. The result was the gradual emergence of a one-class society.

Although the country had become a distinct entity, it had not yet achieved an autonomous existence. In every department it was completely subject to the authority of the mother country. Its public finances were dependent on the Royal Treasury; its administrators were sent out from France; the capitalists who exploited its resources were French shipowners and traders; and its religious life was directed by a French bishop. Canada was, nonetheless, moving towards an undeclared emancipation. Native sons had won appointments as district governors; one of them had recently been named to the highest post in the country, that of Governor-General. A Canadian candidate was considered for the episcopacy, and a good half of the clergy and of the Superior Council were of Canadian origin, as were the majority of marine officers. In the business world, Canadian traders and officers received a large share of the profits from the fur trade. In short, Canada was on the way to taking possession of its own essential activities when the supreme disaster struck.

But, although it was suddenly arrested, the work accomplished in New France was one of remarkable economic, political and social value. In a territory isolated from the mother country a few thousand colonists had taken root in the soil, explored vast regions, created an economy, sown crops and built villages. Under the authority of Versailles, they had developed a stable government and created public welfare services. They had evangelized the natives, established racial equality, encouraged the improvement of social conditions, and founded an ethnic group comparable to others of the age. In the course of the years, they had defeated the Indians at their own game of guerilla warfare and they had repulsed numerous English invasions. The last battle fought by troops of New France in Canada, the battle of Ste. Foy, was a French victory.

From the moment when the publication of the "preliminaries of peace" denationalized them and transformed them into British subjects, the people of Canada faced the catastrophe with resolution and courage. With the help of the clergy they organized themselves under their leaders, *bourgeois* and seigneurs, and sent a deputy from the colony to petition their new sovereign for guarantees of the survival of their French Catholic society.[17]

As the people of Canada took up the broken thread of their lives, their hearts were heavy with sorrow and mourning, but they still retained pride in the past, confidence in their leaders, and faith in Providence. These unquenchable sparks of loyalty were to inspire and determine the social and political evolution of the Canadian people under foreign domination.

APPENDICES

DOCUMENTS

TREATY OF UTRECHT[1]

April 16, 1713

X. The said most Christian King shall restore to the Kingdom and Queen of Great Britain, to be possessed in full right forever, the bay and streights of Hudson, together with all lands, seas, sea-coasts, rivers and places situated in the said bay, and streights, and which belong thereunto, no tracts of land or sea being excepted, which are at present possessed by the subjects of France. All which, as well as any buildings there made, in the condition they now are, and likewise all fortresses there erected, either before or since the French seized the same, shall within six months from the ratification of the present treaty, or sooner, if possible, be well and truly delivered to the British subjects, having commission from the Queen of Great Britain, to demand and receive the same, entire and undemolished, together with all the cannon and cannonball which are therein, as also with a quantity of powder, if it be there found, in proportion to the cannon ball, and with the other provision of war usually belonging to cannon. It is however provided, that it may be entirely free for the company of Quebec, and all other subjects of the most Christian King whatsoever, to go by land, or by sea, whithersoever they please out of the lands of the said bay, together with all their goods, merchandizes, arms and effects of what nature or condition soever, except such things as are above reserved in this article. But it is agreed on both sides, to determine within a year, by commissaries to be forthwith named by each party, the limits which are to be fixed between the said Bay of Hudson, and the places appertaining to the French; which limits both the British and French subjects shall be wholly forbid to pass over, or thereby to go to each other by sea or by land. The same commissaries shall also have orders to describe and settle, in like manner, the boundaries between the other British and French colonies in those parts.

XI. The abovementioned most Christian King shall take care that satisfaction be given, according to the rule of justice and equity, to the English company trading to the Bay of Hudson, for all damages and spoildome to their colonies, ships, persons, and goods, by the hostile incursions and depredations of the French, in time of

---

[1] *A collection of all the Treaties of Peace, Alliance and Commerce Between Great Britain and other powers. From the Treaty signed at Munster in 1648 to the Treaties signed in Paris in 1783* (London, 1785), II, pp. 34-37.

peace, an estimate being made thereof by commissaries to be named at the requisition of each party. The same commissaries shall moreover inquire as well into the complaints of the British subjects concerning ships taken by the French in time of peace, as also concerning the damages sustained last year in the island called Montserat, and others, as into those things of which the French subjects complained, relating to the capitulation in the island of Nevis, and castle of Gambia, also to French ships, if perchance any such have been taken by British subjects in time of peace. And in like manner into all disputes of this kind, which shall be found to have arisen between both nations, and which are not yet ended; and due justice shall be done on both sides without delay.

XII. The most Christian King shall take care to have delivered to the Queen of Great Britain, on the same day that the ratification of this treaty shall be exchanged, solemn and authentic letters, or instruments, by virtue whereof it shall appear that the island of St. Christophers is to be possessed alone hereafter by British subjects, likewise all Nova Scotia or Acadia, with its ancient boundaries, as also the cities of Port Royal, now called Annapolis Royal, and all other things in those parts, which depend on the said lands and islands, together with the dominion, propriety, and possession of the said islands, lands, and places, and all right whatsoever, by treaties, or by any other way obtained, which the most Christian King, the crown of France, or any the subjects thereof, have hitherto had to the said islands, lands, and places, and the inhabitants of the same, are yielded and made over to the Queen of Great Britain, and to her crown for ever, as the most Christian King does at present yield and make over all the particulars abovesaid; and that in such ample manner and form, that the subjects of the most Christian King shall hereafter be excluded from all kinds of fishing in the said seas, bays, and other places, on the coasts of Nova Scotia, that is to say, on those which lie towards the East, within 30 leagues, beginning from the island commonly called Sable, inclusively, and thence stretching along towards the South west.

XIII. The island called Newfoundland, with the adjacent islands, shall from this time forward, belong of right wholly to Britain; and to that end the town and fortress of Placentia, and whatever other places in the fair island, are in the possession of the French, shall be yielded and given up, within seven months from the exchange of the ratifications of this treaty, or sooner if possible, by the most Christian King, to those who have a commission from the Queen of Great Britain, for that purpose. Nor shall the most Christian King, his heirs and successors, or any of their subjects, at any time hereafter, lay claim to any right to the said island and islands, or to any part of it, of them. Moreover, it shall not be lawful for the subjects of France, to fortify any place in the said island of Newfoundland, or to erect any buildings there, besides stages made of boards, and huts necessary and usual for drying of fish; or to resort to the fair island, beyond the time necessary for fishing, and drying fish. But it shall be allowed to the subjects of France, to catch fish, and to dry them on land, in that part only, and in no other besides that, of the said island of Newfoundland, which stretches from the place called cape Bonavista, to the northern point of the said island, and from thence running down by the western side reaches as far as the place called Point Riche. But the island called Cape Breton as also all others, both in the mouth of the river of St. Lawrence, and in the gulph of the same name, shall hereafter belong of right to the French, and the most Christian King shall have all manner of liberty to fortify any place, or places there.

XIV. It is expressly provided, that in all the said places and colonies to be yielded and restored by the most Christian King, in pursuance of this treaty, the subjects of the said King may have liberty to remove themselves within a year to any other place, as they shall think fit, together with all their moveable effects. But those who are willing to remain there, and to be subject to the kingdom of Great Britain, are to enjoy the free exercise of their religion, according to the usage of the Church of Rome, as far as the laws of Great Britain do allow the same.

XV. The subjects of France inhabiting Canada, and others, shall hereafter give no hindrance or molestation to the Five Nations or cantons of Indians, subject to the dominion of Great Britain, nor to the other natives of America, who are friends to the same. In like manner, the subjects of Great Britain shall behave themselves peaceably towards the Americans who are subjects or friends to France; and on both sides they shall enjoy full liberty of going and coming on account of trade. As also the natives of those countries shall, with the same liberty, resort, as they please, to the British and French colonies, for promoting trade on one side, and the other, without any molestation or hindrance, either on the part of the British subjects, or of the French, but it is to be exactly and indistinctly settled by commissaries, who are, who ought to be accounted the subjects and friends of Britain or of France.[1]

TAXES IMPOSED IN 1747 AND 1748[1]

Decision of the King's Council concerning an increase for a period of three years of the import duties on wine, brandy, and tafia; January twenty-third, one thousand seven hundred and forty-seven.

The King being informed that after repeated representations by the inhabitants of the town of Quebec, in Canada, the Sieurs Beauharnois, Governor and Lieutenant-General for His Majesty, and Hocquart, Intendant of the said country, have caused work to be

[1]*Edits et Ord.*, I, p. 588.

done on a surrounding wall and other subsidiary works for the defence of the aforementioned town, and that the expenses incurred up to the present have been acquitted with His Majesty's funds by the clerks of the treasurers general of the Marine in the said colony; until he can make a general definitive arrangement, which he will make as light a burden as possible for the inhabitants of the aforementioned colony, His Majesty has resolved to order provisional and temporary increase in the duties which are levied on the wines and liquors imported into the said country.

Having received and considered the opinion of the Sieurs Beauharnois and Hocquart on this matter, and having heard their report, the King, being in his Council, has ordered and orders that for three consecutive years, counting from the day of registration of the present order, the import duty of nine *livres* which is collected on each cask of wine imported into Canada will be collected at the rate of twelve *livres,* that the gallon of brandy which pays sixteen *sous,* eight *deniers,* will pay one *livre,* four *sous,* and that the duty on a cask of tafia, now fixed at fifteen *livres,* will be paid at the rate of twenty-four *livres.*

It is His Majesty's wish that for each of the three years a special account be kept of the revenue from the aforementioned increase on the aforementioned liquors in order that he may give appropriate orders for its disposal.

His Majesty orders the Governor, his Lieutenant-General, and the Intendant, each in his own capacity, to execute this order, which will be registered by the Superior Council in Quebec.

Decreed at a meeting of the King's Council of State at Versailles, his Majesty being present, the twenty-third of January, one thousand seven hundred and forty-seven.

Signed: Phelypeaux

The order of the King's Council of State given above was registered, as required by the King's Attorney-General and in accordance with the order bearing the date of this day, by us, Chief Clerk of the Council, undersigned, June twenty-sixth, one thousand seven hundred and forty-seven.

A royal edict concerning the imposition of import and export duties on all merchandise entering or leaving Canada, payable by every class of person according to the statement and tariff of the said duties attached to the aforementioned edict.[1]

Louis, by the grace of God, King of France and of Navarre, to all those present and to come, greeting:

The help of every kind which, since the beginning of this war, we

[1] *Edits et Ord.,* I. pp. 591-94.

have sent to our colony of Canada, to defend it against the threat of
enemy action, has had the effect which might have been expected: it
has served to stimulate still further zeal and courage of which the
inhabitants have given proof at all times; and the enemy was forced
not only to abandon his plans for conquest of the colony, but to
defend his own country against raids by our troops and our militia.
But the measures necessary for this success were carried out at a cost
so considerable that we find ourselves obliged to require the commerce and people of the country to bear part of it. It was with this
object that, pending the general and definitive arrangement which
will be made when all the circumstances are known, we ordered, by a
decision of our Council dated January 23, 1747, that for a period of
three years duties should be increased on wine, brandy and tafia
imported into Canada, and that the product of this increase should
be used for the repayment of special disbursements which had been
made and which might be made from our funds for the fortification
of Quebec, undertaken in 1745 at the repeated instance of the inhabitants of that town. And since the revenue from this increase in
duties would not suffice to meet all these expenses, and as it is just
that taxes for them be generally divided among all inhabitants and
the commerce of the colony, we have judged, after careful consideration of all the different arrangements proposed to us, that none is
more suitable than the imposition on merchandise which has heretofore been free of import and export taxes, of a duty whose modesty
is in accord with our constant care to grant favourable treatment to
this colony.

Moved by these considerations, and others, with the advice of our
Council, and in our own certain knowledge, full power and royal
authority, we have, by the present edict signed by our hand, declared, decreed and ordered, and we do declare, decree and order the
following articles; this is our pleasure:

Article I. There will be levied for our profit in our colony of
Canada, a duty of three per cent on all merchandise of any kind
imported into the said country of Canada, whether it be brought
from France or from other French colonies; excepted from this order
are wine, brandy, tafia, liqueur wines and brandy liqueurs, which
will not be subject to the three per cent import duty, but which will
continue to pay the duties which they have paid or been required to
pay up to the present, with the increase on the aforementioned wines
and liquors fixed by the order of our Council of State on January
twenty-third, 1747.

II. In like manner, a duty of three per cent will be levied in our
aforementioned colony of Canada on all merchandise originating in
the colony, and exported to France or other French colonies, with
the exception of moose hides which will continue to pay the export
duty at present levied upon them.

III. Wheat, flour, biscuit, peas, beans, corn, oats, vegetables, salt beef and pork, fat, butter and other such foodstuffs produced in Canada and exported to France, the French islands in America or any other of our colonies, will not be subject to the export duty ordered in the preceding article.

IV. The foodstuffs and merchandise which are dispatched from Quebec to equip fishing and fur-trading vessels in the St. Lawrence River will also be exempt from the aforementioned export duty and the product of such fishing and trading delivered in our city of Quebec shall in like manner be exempt from the import duty ordered by the first article.

V. It is our will also that rigging of all kinds and salt imported into the said colony be exempt from the import duty ordered by the first article; in like manner, horses, ships built in Canada, shingles, oak for shipbuilding, masts, stave-wood, spruce boards, hemp and salt herring are exempt from the export duty ordered in article II.

VI. The import and export duties, as set in the first and second articles, will be paid in cash at the office of our domain in Quebec, by all persons without exception or privilege, save only mendicant priests; they will be paid in money current in the colony of Canada according to the tariff ordered in our Council and hereto attached under the seal of our chancellery, beginning on the day of publication of the present order in the aforementioned city of Quebec.

VII. It is our wish that, in order to ensure the collection of the said import and export duties, all captains and masters of vessels and boats landing in Quebec be required to present themselves at the office of our domain within twenty-four hours of their arrival, and to make a true and exact declaration of the merchandise constituting their cargo, or to furnish receipts and bills of lading from the ports in France from which they sailed.

VIII. We forbid any captain or merchant to leave Canada without first making a general declaration at the office of our domain of all the merchandise constituting his cargo and obtaining there the necessary receipts and bills of lading.

IX. In like manner, we forbid any merchant or other individual to have any merchandise placed on board or unloaded from a vessel or boat without first having obtained a permit from the office of the domain and made his own declaration.

X. All the aforementioned declarations, whether of captains and masters or of merchants and other individuals shall be made in the form prescribed by section two of the order fixing the conditions for the leasing of royal farms, February 1687, of which we ordered the execution in Canada by a decision of our Council dated June 9, 1722; the order includes a statement of penalties for its violation.

XI. We order that the aforementioned declarations be checked by the clerks of the domain, and that violators be prosecuted according to the terms of the same section of the aforementioned order, and to this effect we desire that the aforementioned clerks carry out all necessary examinations and verifications as well as searches in the vessels and boats and anywhere that such searches may be necessary.

XII. Under the same penalties, we forbid captains and masters of vessels and boats, merchants and other individuals to discharge cargo except at wharfs of the Place du Cul-de-sac in the Lower Town of Quebec.

XIII. Merchandise may not be loaded on or unloaded from vessels or boats or transferred from one boat to another except by written permit and in the presence of a clerk of the domain.

XIV. We desire further that our letters patent of the month of April 1717, regulating trade for French islands and colonies, and made applicable for Canada by an order of our Council of the eleventh of December following, together with the regulations forbidding foreign trade and trade in or the use of contraband or prohibited merchandise, be executed in Canada according to their form and tenor, and that in case of violation the penalties therein stated be applied.

We also command our armies and loyal subjects constituting our Superior Council in Quebec to have this edict read, published and registered, and to cause its content to be maintained and observed according to its form and tenor; this notwithstanding all edicts, declarations, ordinances, regulations and other documents running contrary to it, all such orders having been nullified and being nullified by the present edict; we enjoin our governors, our generals in command and superior officers, our intendants and junior commissaries, and all other officials on whom this duty may fall, to execute this ordinance and to cause it to be executed; for such is our pleasure; and in order to establish this as a fixed and permanent law, we have caused our seal to be placed on it.

Given in Versailles in the month of February, in the year of grace one thousand seven hundred and forty-eight, and of our reign the thirty-third.

Signed: Louis

At one side, visa Daguesseau
and lower down,

By the King's order

Signed: Phelypeaux

And sealed with the great seal on green wax, with knots of silk.

CENSUS OF CANADA, 1713[1]

Names of towns and seigniories	Churches	Men over 50 years of age	Men under 50 years of age	Married women and widows	Unmarried men over 15 years of age	Boys under 15 years of age	Unmarried women over 15 years of age	Girls under 15 years of age	Houses and Cabins
			←——MARRIED——→			←————UNMARRIED————→			
Quebec City and suburbs	7	33	249	343	162	388	239	405	257
Malbaie			1	1		2		4	1
Baie St. Paul, Cap Tourmente									
Ste. Anne	5	45	130	195	120	220	130	216	170
Château Richer									
Ange Gardien									
Beauport and village	1	23	46	66	77	87	29	107	56
Notre Dame des Anges		18	16	27	36	50	45	30	30
Charlesbourg, Petit Auvergne, St. Bernard	1	14	22	34	32	30	35	36	34
Saint Romain and Petit St. Antoine									
Nouvelle Laurette, Grand St. Antoine	1	14	5	18	9	31	6	38	18
Dorsainville County, Bourg Royale		5	25	29	11	47	11	35	25
St. Jean, St. Michel, Sillery	3	6	23	30	21	47	9	57	30
Cap Rouge, Gauderville, Champigny	1	10	35	40	33	45	28	47	38
De Maure	1	8	30	35	35	47	25	40	36
Neuville, Pointe aux Ecuroeuils	1	25	52	70	85	110	35	122	75
Portneuf and Deschambault	1	8	20	27	20	60	10	45	30
Les Grondines and Lachevrotière	2	10	22	34	26	72	14	59	33
St. Pierre	4	54	184	216	174	238	150	255	180
Ste. Famille									
St. François, St. Jean, St. Laurans									
Ile aux oies et aux grues		2	6	7	10	12	8	15	8
Rivière du Loup and Lebicq		1	3	4	6	10	5	7	4
Bouteillerie, Rivière Ouelle, Kamouraska	2	12	30	48	27	85	17	90	52
Grande Ance		8	16	28	15	50	8	44	24
Rivière des trois Saumons, Bonsecours, Vincelette, Port Jolly, Rivière Dusud	1	15	24	46	27	87	20	96	48
Ladurantais, Beaumont, Berthier	3	20	60	83	58	118	63	130	83
Côte de Lauson and Vincenne	2	22	70	85	62	110	58	120	85
Tilly, Ste. Croix Becquet	2	9	35	38	46	73	26	70	38

[1] Arch. Col. Série G, vol. 461.

Names of towns and seigniories	Churches	MARRIED			UNMARRIED				Houses and Cabins
		Men over 50 years of age	Men under 50 years of age	Married women and widows	Unmarried men over 15 years of age	Boys under 15 years of age	Unmarried women over 15 years of age	Girls under 15 years of age	
Bonsecours and Charet		5	5	10	11	3	8	6	10
Lotbinière, and Rivière du Chesne	1	8	13	21	17	22	12	28	20
Gouvernement des Trois-Rivieres									
Les Trois Rivieres et Banlieue	3	17	20	51	49	50	60	52	48
Rre Duloup Baye St Antoine Tonnancour	2	4	25	25	7	33	9	31	25
Sainte Anne	1	11	30	40	26	60	20	44	50
Batiscans	1	18	34	55	68	90	37	82	52
Champlain et gentilly	1	12	29	45	56	75	25	70	40
Cap Lamadeleine	1	2	10	11	19	21	9	23	11
Rivière puante Becancourt et marsollet		4	15	17	8	27	8	30	19
Saint François	1	8	21	29	21	45	12	50	27
Gouvernement de Montréal									
Villemarie Lamontaigne	8	118	252	405	234	530	358	647	399
Berthier et Lisle dupas	1	8	34	42	27	63	13	82	42
Lavalterie et dautray	1	3	15	15	3	10	5	18	15
Repentigny	1	4	30	28	8	46	11	43	32
Lachesnais		3	27	27	2	38	4	40	30
Isle Jesus	1	5	28	34	7	37	3	46	32
Isle Ste Theraise		5	10	15	20	20	18	25	15
Isle Bouchard ou dejourdy		1	27	11	12	17	2	12	20
pointe autremble et bas de lisle / St François et St Martin	1	30	30	65	40	107	49	120	63
La Riviere des prairies	1	5	30	34	18	67	15	53	38
Riviere St pierre, La Chine	2	12	60	89	28	150	28	162	84
Le haut de lisle	2	3	35	35	26	77	15	71	37
Sorel	1	5	12	17	13	41	12	28	19
St Ours	1	4	9	14	14	22	8	22	16
Contrecoeur	1	4	25	30	25	41	13	43	30
Vercheres		2	27	26	7	35	6	38	27
Cap Varenne et St Michel	1	6	15	19	20	42	16	30	17
Boucherville	1	29	58	88	66	125	47	109	88
Tremblay et longueuil	1	8	35	47	22	118	20	94	46
Prairie de la madelaine et St Lambert	1	10	49	65	32	100	16	125	70
Chateauguay		4	10	11	10	12	6	14	12
Isle St paul		3	3	4	6	8	3	7	4
Chambly		2	16	11	7	17	2	18	16
	74	725	2143	2940	2321	4168	1841	4331	2859

CANADA'S MILLIONAIRES[1]

Beginning of their fortune in Canada		Gain in livres	Date of return to France

ARMY

1755	The Marquis de Vaudreuil, Governor General (A part of his fortune came from Louisiana)	23,000,000	1760
1737	Saint-Luc La Corne, Captain of Marines, A famous Indian interpreter	1,200,000	1760
1754	Lotbinière, Engineer, nephew of M. de Vaudreuil	1,400,000	1760
1755	Le Mercier, Artillery Commander	1,800,000	1759
1752	Péan, Colony Major, triumvir, one of the associates in the Army Purveyor's company	7,000,000	1758
	Total for the military section:	35,000,000	

FINANCE

1749	Bigot, Intendant (A part of his fortune was made in Louisbourg, where he was commissaire during the last war.)	29,000,000	1760
1758	De Vilers, Controller	1,200,000	1760
1758	Martel, Chief Writer	1,900,000	1760
1737	Varin, Commissaire in Montreal	4,000,000	1758
1749	Bréard, Controller	2,200,000	1758
1750	Martel, Supervisor of stores in Montreal	2,500,000	1758
1750	Estèbe, Supervisor of stores in Quebec and Member of the Conseil Supérieur	1,700,000	1758
1755	Landrième, Writer, acting as Commissaire in Canada	900,000	Remained in Canada
1753	Saint-Sauveur, Secretary to M. de Vaudreuil	1,900,000	Remained in Canada
1754	Descheneaux, Secretary to M. Bigot, Intendant	2,000,000	Remained in Canada
	Total for finance:	79,000,000	

COMMISSARIAT

1757	Cadet, Purveyor-General	15,000,000	1760
1757	Corpron, his agent	1,200,000	1760
1757	Pénissault, Sub-contractor for provisions	1,900,000	1760
1757	Maurin, Sub-contractor for provisions	1,900,000	1760
	Total for the Commissariat:	20,000,000	
	Total for Commissariat and Finance:	99,000,000	

Everything that I have said in this memorandum has been presented without passion and with the strictest regard for truth. I have refrained from including certain statements, partly in an effort to be as generous as possible, and partly from fear of making myself appear ridiculous by advancing facts which might seem incredible to fair-minded readers.

---

[1] *Rapport de l'archiviste de la province de Québec*, 1924-25, "Mémoire du Canada," pp. 196-98.

ARTICLES OF CAPITULATION OF MONTREAL[1]

Between their Excellencies Major General Amherst, Commander in Chief of his Britannic Majesty's troops and forces in North America, on the one part, and the Marquis de Vaudreuil, Sc. Governor and Lieutenant General for the king in Canada, on the other.

Article Ist.

Twenty-four hours after the signing of the present capitulation, the British General shall cause the troops of his Britannic Majesty to take possession of the Gates of the town of Montreal: and the British Garrison shall not enter the place till after the French troops shall have evacuated it.—"The whole Garrison of Montreal must lay down their arms, and shall not serve during the present war. Immediately after the signing of the present capitulation, the King's troops shall take possession of the gates, and shall post the Guards necessary to preserve good order in the town."

Article IId.

The troops and the militia, who are in Garrison in the town of Montreal, shall go out by the gate of Quebec, with all the honours of war, six pieces of cannon and one mortar, which shall be put on board the vessel where the Marquis de Vaudreuil shall embark, with ten rounds for each piece; and the same shall be granted to the Garrison of the Three Rivers, as to the honours of war.—"Referred to the next article."

Article IIId.

The troops and militia, who are in Garrison in the Fort of Jacques Cartier, and in the Island of St. Helen, and other forts, shall be treated in the same manner, and shall have the same honours; and these troops shall go to Montreal, or the Three Rivers or Quebec; to be there embarked for the first sea port in France by the shortest way. The troops, who are in our posts, situated on our frontiers, on the side of Acadia, at Detroit, Michilimaquinac, and other posts, shall enjoy the same honours, and be treated in the same manner.—"All these troops are not to serve during the present war, and "shall likewise lay down their arms; the rest is granted."

Article IVth.

The militia after evacuating the above towns, forts and posts, shall return to their habitations, without being molested on any pretence whatever, on account of their having carried arms.— "Granted."

---

1 Adam Shortt and Arthur G. Doughty, *Documents relating to the Constitutional History of Canada* (Ottawa, 1907) I, pp. 21-9. The terms requested are presented at the beginning of the paragraph; the answer is presented within quotation marks at the end of the paragraph.

Article Vth.

The troops, who keep the field, shall raise their camp, drums beating, with their arms, bagage and artillery, to join the garrison of Montreal, and shall be treated in every respect the same.—"These troops, as well as the others, must lay down their arms."

Article VI.

The Subjects of his Britannic Majesty, and of his most Christian Majesty, Soldiers, Militia or Seamen, who shall have deserted or left the service of their Sovereign, and carried arms in North-America, shall be, on both sides pardoned for their crime; they shall be respectively returned to their country; if not, each shall remain where he is without being sought after or molested.—"Refused."

Article VII.

The Magazines, the artillery, firelocks, sabres, ammunition of war, and, in general every thing that belongs to his most Christian Majesty, as well in the towns of Montreal and Three Rivers, as in the forts and post mentioned in the Third article shall be delivered up, according to exact Inventories, to the commissaries who shall be appointed to receive the same in the name of his Britannic Majesty. Duplicates of the said Inventories shall be given to the Marquis de Vaudreuil.—"This is every thing that can be asked on this article."

Article VIII.

The Officers, Soldiers, Militia, Seamen and even the Indians, detained on account of their wounds or sickness, as well as in the hospital, as in private houses, shall enjoy the privileges of the cartel, and be treated accordingly.—" The sick and wounded shall be treated the same as our own people."

Article IX.

The British General shall engage to send back, to their own homes, the Indians, and Moraignans, who make part of his armies, immediately after the signing of the present capitulation, and, in the mean time, the better to prevent all disorders on the part of those who may not be gone away, the said Generals shall give safe-guards to such persons as shall desire them, as well in the town as in the country.—"The first part refused. There never have been any cruelties committed by the Indians of our army: and good order shall be preserved."

Article X.

His Britannic Majesty's General shall be answerable for all disorders on the part of his troops, and shall oblige them to pay the Damages they may do, as well in the towns as in the country.— "Answered by the preceding article."

Article XI.

The British General shall not oblige the Marquis de Vaudreuil to leave the town of Montreal before .... and no person shall be quartered in his house till he is gone. The Chevalier de Levis, Commander of the land forces and colony troops, the Engineers, Officers of the Artillery, and Commissary of war, shall also remain at Montreal till the said day, and shall keep their lodgings. The same shall be observed with regard to M. Bigot, Intendant, the Commissaries of Marines and writers, whom the said M. Bigot shall have occasion for, and no person shall be lodged at the Intendant's house before he shall take his departure.—"The Marquis de Vaudreuil, and all these gentlemen, shall be masters of their houses, and shall embark, when the King's ship shall be ready to sail for Europe; and all possible conveniences shall be granted them."

Article XII.

The most convenient vessel that can be found shall be appointed to carry the Marquis de Vaudreuil, M. de Rigaud, the Governor of Montreal, and the suite of this General, by the straitest passage to the first sea port in France; and every necessary accommodation shall be made for them. This vessel shall be properly victualled at the expence of his Britannic Majesty: and the Marquis de Vaudreuil shall take with him his papers, without their being examined, and his equipages, plate, baggage, and also those of his retinue.— "Granted, except the archives which shall be necessary for the Government of the country."

Article XIII.

If before, or after, the embarkation of the Marquis de Vaudreuil, news of Peace should arrive, and, that by treaty, Canada should remain to his most Christian Majesty, the Marquis de Vaudreuil shall return to Quebec or Montreal; every thing shall return to its former state under the Dominion of his most Christian Majesty, and the present capitulation shall become null and of no effect.—"Whatever the King may have done, on this subject, shall be obeyed."

Article XIV.

Two ships will be appointed to carry to France, le Chevalier de Levis, the principal officers, and the staff of the Land forces, the Engineers, officers of Artillery, and their domestics. These vessels shall likewise be victualled, and the necessary accomodation provided in them. The said officers shall take with them their papers, without being examined, and also, their equipages and bagage. Such of the said officers as shall be married, shall have liberty to take with them their wives and children, who shall also be victualled.—

"Granted, except that the Marquis de Vaudreuil and all the officers, of whatever rank they may be, shall faithfully deliver to us all the charts and plans of the country."

Article XV.

A vessel shall also be appointed for the passage of Mr. Bigot, the Intendant, with his suite; in which vessel the proper accomodation shall be made for him, and the persons he shall take with him: he shall likewise embark with him his papers, which shall not be examined: His equipages, plate, baggage and those of his suite: this vessel shall be victualled as before mentioned.—"Granted, with the same reserve, as in the preceding article."

Article XVI.

The British General shall also order the necessary and most convenient vessels to carry to France M. de Longueuil, Governor of Trois Rivieres, the staff of the colony, and the Commissary of the Marine; they shall embark therein their families, servants, baggage and equipages, and they shall be properly victualled, during the passage, at the expence of his Britannic Majesty.—"Granted."

Article XVII.

The officers and soldiers, as well as of the Land-forces, as of the colony, and also the Marine Officers, and Seamen, who are in the colony, shall be likewise embarked for France, and sufficient and convenient vessels shall be appointed for them. The Land and sea officers, who shall be married, shall take with them their families, and all of them shall have liberty to embark their servants and baggage. As to the soldiers and seamen, those who are married shall take with them their wives and children, and all of them shall embark their haversacks and baggage, these vessels shall be properly and sufficiently victualled at the expence of his Britannic Majesty. —"Granted."

Article XVIII.

The Officers, Soldiers and the followers of the troops, who shall have their baggage in the fields, may send for it before they depart, without any hindrance or molestation.—"Granted."

Article XIX.

An hospital ship shall be provided by the British General, for such of the wounded and sick officers, soldiers and seamen as shall be in a condition to be carried to France, and shall likewise be victualled at the expence of his Britannic Majesty. It shall be the same with regard to the other wounded and sick officers, soldiers and sailors, as soon as they shall be recovered. They shall have liberty to carry with them their wives, children, servants and baggage; and the said soldiers and sailors shall not be solicited nor forced to enter into the service of his Britannic Majesty.—"Granted."

Article XX.

A Commissary and one of the King's Writers, shall be left to take care of the hospitals, and whatever may relate to the service of his most Christian Majesty.—"Granted."

Article XXI.

The British General shall also provide ships for carrying to France the officers of the supreme council, of justice, police, admiralty, and all other officers, having commissions or brevets from his most Christian Majesty, for them, their families, servants and equipages, as well as for the other officers: and they shall likewise be victualled at the expence of his Britannic Majesty. They shall, however, be at liberty to stay in the colony, if they think proper to settle their affairs, or to withdraw to France whenever they think fit.— "Granted, but if they have papers relating to the Government of the country, they are to be delivered up to us."

Article XXII.

If there are any Military officers, whose affairs should require their presence in the colony till the next year, they shall have liberty to stay in it, after having obtained the permission of the Marquis de Vaudreuil for that purpose, and without being reputed prisoners of war.—"All those whose private affairs shall require their stay in the country, and who shall have the Marquis de Vaudreuil's leave for so doing, shall be allowed to remain till their affairs are settled."

Article XXIII.

The Commissary for the King's provisions shall be at liberty to stay in Canada till next year, in order to be enabled to answer the debts he has contracted in the colony, on account of what he has furnished; but, if he should prefer to go to France this year, he shall be obliged to leave, till next year, a person to transact his business. This private person shall preserve, and have liberty to carry off, all his papers, without being inspected. His Clerks shall have leave to stay in the colony or go to France; and in this last case, a passage and subsistence, shall be allowed them on board the ships of his Britannic Majesty, for them, their families, and their baggage.—"Granted."

Article XXIV.

The provisions and other kind of stores, which shall be found in the Magazines of the commissary, as well in the towns of Montreal, and of the Three-Rivers, as in the country, shall be preserved to him, the said provisions belonging to him, and not to the King; and he shall be at liberty to sell them to the French and English.—"Every thing that is actually in the magazines, destined for the use of the troops, is to be delivered to the British commissary, for the King's forces."

Article XXV.

A passage to France shall likewise be granted, on board of his Britannic Majesty's ships, as well as victuals to such officers of the India company as shall be willing to go thither, and they shall take with them their families, servants and baggage. The Chief agent of the said Company, in case he should chuse to go to France, shall be allowed to leave such person as he shall think proper till next year, to settle the affairs of the said Company, and to recover such sums as are due to them. The said chief agent shall keep possession of all the papers belonging to the said company, and they shall not be liable to inspection.—"Granted."

Article XXVI.

The said company shall be maintained in the property of the Ecarlatines, and Castors, which they may have in the town of Montreal; they shall not be touched under any pretence whatever, and the necessary Licences shall be given to the Chief Agent, to send this year his Castors to France, on board his Britannic Majesty's ships, paying the freight on the same footing as the British would pay it.—"Granted, with regard to what may belong to the company, or to private persons; but if his Most Christian Majesty has any share in it, that must become the property of the King."

Article XXVII.

The free exercise of the Catholic, Apostolic, and Roman Religion, shall subsist entire, in such manner that all the states and the people of the Towns and countries, places and distant posts, shall continue to assemble in the churches, and to frequent the sacraments as heretofore, without being molested in any manner, directly or indirectly. These people shall be obliged, by the English Government, to pay their Priests the tithes, and all the taxes they were used to pay under the Government of his most Christian Majesty.— "Granted, as to the free exercise of their religion, the obligation of paying the tithes to the Priests will depend on the King's pleasure."

Article XXVIII.

The Chapter, Priests, Curates and Missionaries shall continue, with an entire liberty, their exercise and functions of cures, in the parishes of the towns and countries.—"Granted."

Article XXIX.

The Grand Vicars, named by the Chapter to administer to the diocese during the vacancy of the Episcopal see, shall have liberty to dwell in the towns or country parishes, as they shall think proper. They shall at all times be free to visit the different parishes of the Diocese with the ordinary ceremonies, and exercise all the jurisdiction they exercised under the French Dominion. They shall enjoy the same rights in case of the death of the future Bishop, of which mention will be made in the following article.—"Granted, except what regards the following article."

Article XXX.

If by the treaty of peace, Canada should remain in the power of his Britannic Majesty, his most Christian Majesty shall continue to name the Bishop of the colony, who shall always be of the Roman communion, and under whose authority the people shall exercise the Roman Religion.—"Refused."

Article XXXI.

The Bishop shall, in case of need, establish new parishes, and provide for the rebuilding of his Cathedral and his Episcopal palace; and, in the meantime, he shall have the liberty to dwell in the towns or parishes, as he shall judge proper. He shall be at liberty to visit his Diocese with the ordinary ceremonies, and exercise all the jurisdiction which his predecessor exercised under the French Dominion, save that an oath of fidelity, or a promise to do nothing contrary to his Britannic Majesty's service, may be required of him.—" This article is comprised under the foregoing."

Article XXXII.

The communities of Nuns shall be preserved in their constitutions and privileges; they shall continue to observe their rules, they shall be exempted from lodging any military; and it shall be forbid to molest them in their religious exercises, or to enter their monasteries: safe-guards shall even be given them, if they desire them. —"Granted."

Article XXXIII.

The preceeding article shall likewise be executed, with regard to the communities of Jesuits and Recollets and of the house of the priests of St. Sulpice at Montreal; these last, and the Jesuits, shall preserve their right to nominate to certain curacies and missions, as heretofore.—"Refused till the King's pleasure be known."

Article XXXIV.

All the communities, and all the priests, shall preserve their moveables, the property and revenues of the Seignories and other estates, which they possess in the colony, of what nature soever they be; and the same estates shall be preserved in their privileges, rights, honours, and exemptions—"Granted."

Article XXXV.

If the Canons, Priests, Missionaries, the Priests of the seminary of the foreign Missions, and of St. Sulpice, as well as the Jesuits, and the Recollets, chuse to go to France, a passage shall be granted them in his Britannic Majesty's ships, and they shall have leave to sell in whole, or in part, the estates and moveables which they possess in the colonies, either to the French or to the English, without the least hindrance or obstacle from the British Government.—They may take with them, or send to France, the produce of what nature soever it be, of the said goods sold, paying the freight, as mentioned in the XXVIth. article; and such of the said Priests, who chuse to go this year, shall be victualled during the passage, at the expence of his Britannic Majesty; and they shall take with them their baggage.— "They shall be masters to dispose of their estates and to send the produce thereof, as well as their persons, and all that belongs to them to France."

Article XXXVI.

If by the treaty of Peace, Canada remains to his Britannic Majesty, all the French, Canadians, Acadians, Merchants and other persons who chuse to retire to France, shall have leave to do so from the British General, who shall procure them a passage: and nevertheless, if, from this time to that decision, any French, or Canadian Merchants or other persons, shall desire to go to France; they shall likewise have leave from the British General. Both the one and the other shall take with them their families, servants, and baggage.— "Granted."

Article XXXVII.

The Lords of Manors, the Military and Civil officers, the Canadians as well in the Towns as in the country, the French settled, or trading, in the whole extent of the colony of Canada, and all other persons whatsoever, shall preserve the entire peaceable property and

possession of the goods, noble and ignoble, moveable and immoveable, merchandizes, furs and other effects, even their ships; they shall
not be touched, nor the least damage done to them, on any pretence
whatever. They shall have liberty to keep, let or sell them, as well to
the French as to the British; to take away the produce of them in
Bills of exchange, furs, specie or other returns, whenever they shall
judge proper to go to France, paying their freight, as in the XXVIth
Article. They shall also have the furs which are in the posts above,
and which belong to them, and may be on the way to Montreal; and,
for this purpose, they shall have leave to send, this year, or the next,
canoes fitted out, to fetch such of the said furs as shall have remained
in those posts.—"Granted as in the XXVIth article."

Article XXXVIII.

All the people who have left Acadia, and who shall be found in
Canada, including the frontiers of Canada on the side of Acadia,
shall have the same treatment as the Canadians, and shall enjoy the
same privileges.—"The King is to dispose of his ancient Subjects: in
the mean time, they shall enjoy the same privileges as the Canadians."

Article XXXIX.

None of the Canadians, Acadians or French, who are now in
Canada, and on the frontiers of the colony, on the side of Acadia,
Detroit, Michillimaquinac, and other places and posts of the countries above, the married and unmarried soldiers, remaining in Canada, shall be carried or transported into the British colonies, or to
Great-Britain, and they shall not be troubled for having carried
arms.—"Granted, except with regard to the Acadians."

Article XL.

The Savages or Indian allies of his most Christian Majesty, shall
be maintained in the Lands they inhabit; if they chuse to remain
there; they shall not be molested on any pretence whatsoever, for
having carried arms, and served his most Christian Majesty; they
shall have, as well as the French, liberty of religion, and shall keep
their missionaries. The actual Vicars General, and the Bishop, when
the Episcopal see shall be filled, shall have leave to send to them new
Missionaries when they shall judge it necessary.—"Granted except
the last article, which has been already refused."

Article XLI.

The French, Canadians, and Acadians of what state and condition soever, who shall remain in the colony, shall not be forced to

take arms against his most Christian Majesty, or his Allies, directly or indirectly, on any occasion whatsoever; the British Government shall only require of them an exact neutrality.—"They become Subjects of the King."

Article XLII.

The French and Canadians shall continue to be governed according to the custom of Paris, and the Laws and usages established for this country, and they shall not be subject to any other imposts than those which were established under the French Dominion.— "Answered by the preceding articles, and particularly by the last."

Article XLIII.

The Papers of the Government shall remain without exception, in the power of the Marquis de Vaudreuil and shall go to France with him. These papers shall not be examined on any pretence whatsoever.—"Granted, with the reserve already made."

Article XLIV.

The papers of the Intendancy, of the offices of Comptroller of the Marine, of the ancient and new treasurers, of the Kings magazines, of the offices of the Revenues and forges of St. Maurice, shall remain in the power of M. Bigot, the Intendant; and they shall be embarked for France in the same vessel with him; these papers shall not be examined.—"The same as in this article."

Article XLV.

The Registers, and other papers of the Supreme Council of Quebec, of the Prévoté, and Admiralty of the said city; those of the Royal Jurisdictions of Trois Rivieres and of Montreal; those of the Seignorial Jurisdictions of the colony; the minutes of the Acts of the Notaries of the towns and of the countries; and in general, the acts, and other papers, that may serve to prove the estates and fortunes of the Citizens, shall remain in the colony, in the rolls of the jurisdictions on which these paper depend.—"Granted."

Article XLVI.

The inhabitants and Merchants shall enjoy all the privileges of trade, under the same favours and conditions granted to the subjects of his Britannic Majesty, as well as in the countries above, as the interior of the colony.—"Granted."

Article XLVII.

The Negroes and panis of both sexes shall remain, in their quality of slaves, in the possession of the French and Canadians to whom they belong; they shall be at liberty to keep them in their service in the colony or to sell them; and they may also continue to bring them up in the Roman Religion—"Granted, except those who shall have been made prisoners."

Article XLVIII.

The Marquis de Vaudreuil, the General and Staff Officers of the landforces, the Governors and Staff officers of the different places of the colony, the Military and Civil officers, and all other persons who shall leave the colony, or who are already absent, shall have leave to name and appoint Attornies to act for them, and in their name in the administration of their effects, moveable and immoveable, until the peace; and, if, by the treaty between the two crowns, Canada does not return under the French dominions, these officers, or other persons, or attornies for them, shall have leave to sell their manors, houses, and other estates, their moveables and effects, &c. to carry away or send to France, the produce thereof, either in bills of exchange, specie, furs or other returns, as is mentioned in the XXXVII Article.—"Granted."

Article XLIX.

The inhabitants, and other persons, who shall have suffered any damage in their goods, moveable or immovable, which remained at Quebec, under the faith of the capitulation of that city, may make their representations to the British Government, who shall render them due justice against the person to whom it shall belong.—"Granted."

Article L. and last.

The present capitulation shall be inviolably executed in all its articles, and bonâ fide, on both sides, nothwithstanding any infraction, and any other pretence, with regard to the preceding capitulations, and without making use of reprisals.—"Granted."

POSTSCRIPT.

Article LI.

The British General shall engage, in case any Indians remain after the surrender of this town, to prevent their coming into the towns, and that they do not, in any manner, insult the subjects of his Most Christian Majesty.—"Care shall be taken that the Indians do not insult any of the subjects of his Most Christian Majesty."

Article LII.

The troops and other subjects of his Most Christian Majesty, who are to go to France, shall be embarked, at latest, fifteen days after the signing of the present capitulation.—"Answered by the XIth Article."

Article LIII.

The Troops and other subjects of his Most Christian Majesty, who are to go to France, shall remain lodged and incamped in the town of Montreal, and other posts which they now occupy, till they shall be embarked for their departure: passeports, however, shall be granted to those who shall want them, for the different places of the colony, to take care of their affairs.—"Granted."

Article LIV.

All the officers and soldiers of the troops in the service of France, who are prisoners in New-England: and who were taken in Canada, shall be sent back, as soon as possible, to France, where their ransom or exchange shall be treated of, agreeable to the cartel; and if any of these officers have affairs in Canada, they shall have leave to come there.—"Granted."

Article LV.

As to the officers of the Militia, the Militia, and the Acadians, who are prisoners in New-England, they shall be sent back to their Countries.

Done at Montreal, the 8th of September, 1760.

Signed: Vaudreuil

Granted except what regards the Acadians. Done in the Camp before Montreal, the 8th September, 1760.

Signed: Jeffery Amherst

ORDER FROM GENERAL AMHERST[1]

By His Excellency Jeffery Amherst, Esquire, Field Marshall, Commander in Chief of the troops and forces of His Majesty the King of Great Britain, in North America, and His Governor General for the Province of Virginia, etc., etc., etc.

Be it known, that we have constituted and appointed Mr. Gage, Brigadier of the King's armies, Governor of the town of Montreal and of its dependencies; and that in like manner we have appointed

---

1 Shortt and Doughty, *Documents relating to the Constitutional History of Canada* (Ottawa, 1907) I, pp. 32-33.

Mr. Burton, Colonel of His Majesty's troops, Governor of Three Rivers and its dependencies.

That all the inhabitants of the Government of Three Rivers who have not yet given up their arms, are to give them up at the places named by Mr. Burton.

That for the better maintenance both of good order and police in each parish or district, their arms shall be delivered up to the officers of militia; and if thereafter there shall be any of the residents who desire to have them, they must ask for a permit from the governor, to be signed by the said governor, or by his subdelegates, so that the officer of the troops, commanding the district in which these persons are residing, may know that they have the right to carry arms.

That according to our instructions, the governors are authorized to nominate to all posts vacant in the militia, and may begin by signing commissions in favour of those who have lately enjoyed such posts under His Most Christian Majesty.

That in order to settle amicably as far as possible all differences which may arise amongst the inhabitants, the said governors are charged to authorise the officer of militia commanding in each parish or district, to hear all complaints, and if they are of such a nature that he can settle them, he shall do so with all due justice and equity; if he cannot decide at once, he must send the parties before the officer commanding the troops in his district, who shall in like manner be authorised to decide between them if the case is not sufficiently serious to require its being brought before the Governor himself, who in this, as in every other case, shall administer justice where it is due.

That the troops, in the towns as well as in their cantonments, are provided for by the King in kind, and that it is expressly ordered that they shall pay for all that they buy from the inhabitants in ready money and specie.

That all proprietors of horses, carts or other vehicles who shall be employed, either by the troops, or others, shall likewise be paid in specie for each journey, or by the day, when they shall have been thus engaged, and the latter shall be according to the tariff and at the rate of ten shillings, money of New York, per day for each cart or sleigh carrying a thousand pounds weight, and a horse by the day at the rate of three York shillings.

Master of posts shall be careful neither to let out nor furnish to any one soever, without a written order from us, or from the Governors Gage, Murray, or Burton, either horses or carriages belonging to the offices of the said posts, and those to whom they shall be furnished, as above stated, shall pay for a horse at the rate of 17 cents, money of New York, for every three English miles or French league; those who shall take a horse and carriage shall pay double, but two persons shall be allowed to go in it.

That the meagre support which Canada has received from France for the past two years having exhausted her wealth, her supplies, and her necessaries, we have for the common good both of the troops and the habitant, given orders in our letters, to the different governors of the English colonies nearest to Canada, to post up and publish notices to their colonists to repair hither with all sorts of provisions and supplies, and we flatter ourselves, that we shall see this project carried out without delay; and, as soon as it is done, everyone will be notified so that he may have his share in it, at the current rates, and without duty.

Trade will be free to everyone without duty, but merchants will be obliged to take out passports from the governors, which will be furnished them gratis.

As it is specially enjoined on the troops to live with the habitants in harmony and good fellowship, we likewise recommend the habitant to receive and treat the troops as brothers and fellow-citizens. It is further enjoined upon them to hearken to and obey all that is commanded them, whether by us or by their governors, and those having authority from us and them; and so long as the said habitants shall obey and conform to the said orders, they shall enjoy the same privileges as the ancient subjects of the King, and they may rely on our protection.

We desire and require that our present ordinance be read, published and posted in the usual places.

Given at Montreal, the 22 September 1760, signed by our hand and sealed with the seal of our arms.

Signed: Jeffery Amherst

PETITION FOR BRITISH INTERVENTION TO SECURE PAYMENTS OF THE CANADA PAPERS[1]

Most humble and respectful address of the citizens of the Town of Montreal to His Britannic Majesty

SIRE:

The citizens of the town of Montreal in Canada venture to take the liberty of prostrating themselves at the foot of Your Throne, fully persuaded that there dwells the sanctuary of justice and the temple of all virtues.

The preliminaries of peace signed in the month of November last between Your Majesty and their Most Christian and Catholic Majesties leave us no longer room for doubt that Canada being about to become part of your territories, we are to become your subjects. It is in this capacity that we have recourse to the most generous and magnanimous of Kings. Kindly father of his people, we flatter ourselves that he will deign to listen to the tale of our misfortunes.

1 Adam Shortt, *Documents relating to Canadian Currency, Exchange and Finance during the French Period* (Ottawa, 1925) II, pp. 969-71.

The scourges of war and famine, long before the surrender of Canada, afflicted its unfortunate inhabitants, expenditures of funds multiplied beyond reason had, long before its downfall, spread about an extraordinary quantity of paper; companies as avaricious as they were powerful, were formed. All the trade was captured, and the merchants of Canada were helpless onlookers at business which should have been theirs. Would to Heaven that the ministry of France had been earlier informed as to these injustices! It would have imposed a check on abuses so antagonistic to the welfare of a colony!

These same merchants had made purchases of goods in France in the years 1757 and 1758. The fear of these running risks on the sea in time of war led them to take the resolution to await more favourable circumstances. They adopted the expedient of leaving their goods in warehouses, until peace was restored. This peace, so dear to them and so much desired, aroused the hope of commencing their labours anew; but vain hope, Canada passed under the dominion of Your Majesty.

From this time, paper money, the only kind which circulated in the country, became totally discredited and entirely useless. The suspension of the payment of bills of exchange brought upon us the last blow; in a word, all classes and conditions of the people found themselves and are finding themselves in terrible distress, and in a situation most deplorable. The public markets are filled to overflowing with goods and chattels absolutely necessary to maintain the existence of our families.

In the midst of these misfortunes, the wise and generous governor of this town has stretched out a helping hand to those most heavily stricken; kind-hearted and compassionate, he has reckoned his days by his good deeds; such men do honour to humanity; it is to be hoped that we may keep him for a long time.

Still, the future casts dread over the people of Canada. What will become of them if the payment of their money is deferred? What will become of their families? The rural labourer will find at least in the fertility of the soil, a reward for his labours; he will live, but, more unfortunate than he, the inhabitants of the town will have no resources; they will do everything in their feebleness to assist one another, because they suffer in common.

The truly Royal heart of Your Majesty is touched at the sight of this feeble portrayal of our misfortune; it pities the fate of so many unfortunates. Permit us, then, Great King, to seize this moment to obtain your favorable notice. Deign to interest yourself in the prompt payment of our paper; long enough and too long have we suffered without complaining; we are not the authors of the disorders which have perpetrated in the finances of Canada; and nothing can be more just than to discriminate between the innocent and the guilty.

Deign also, to grant us permission to bring from France our merchandise which was purchased long since, and which will become a total loss if it lies longer in warehouses. This object is not so considerable as to be able to prejudice, in the least, the trade of your old subjects; no abuses can creep in on account of the precautions which will be taken to send out nothing that our agents cannot prove to have been purchased in the former period.

We humbly beg Your Majesty to be so good as to grant us your royal protection. If our submission, our zeal and the ardent wishes which we cherish for you are sufficient to merit it there are no people in the universe who are more entitled to it than most humble and faithful subjects of Your Majesty.

[Signed]

The Body of the Clergy:

Montgolfier, Vic. Gen.
Sr. Simon, Superior of the C.G.N.D.
Sister Catherine Martel, Superior of the *Hotel Dieu* of St. Joseph.
M. M. Lajommerat, Widow Youville, Directress of the General Hospital

The Body of the *Noblesse*:

Dailleboust de Cuisy
Le Chevalier Dailleboust Dargenteuil
La Corne St. Luc
La Valtrie

Desrivières Beaubien
Count Dupré

The Body of the Merchants:

Ignace Gamelin
Mézière
Hervieux Fils
Hervieux
Nevue Sevestre
Lacoste Fils
Jacques Hervieux
Saint-George Dupré
Gauetreu
Pierre Ranger
F. Perrin
Renard Menard
Netille
R. Duvuagn (sic)
Dufy Desauniers
Réaume
Bondy
Desrivières Lamoinodière
D. Bazy
Curot
Sanguinet

Legras
Courraud Lacoste
Amoid
Js Le Guillon
Frs. Lhuillier chevalier
Léchelle
Le Cte Dupré Fils
Le Pailleur
Carignant
Lemoine
Bourassa
Du Bartzsotz
Pilet
Jean Veillat
Toussains Baudry
Moran
Le Febvre
J. Deshautel
Jacques Vigé
L. Prudhomme
Mesière

F. Papin	Cheneville
Du Chouquet	St. Disier
Estève	Giasson
Viger	Sibenberger
Jean Décary	Marechessau
Fs Germain	Hery
Panet	Pier Leduc
Pre Desaunier	P. Pillet
Le Grand	P. Hervieux
Courthiau	Cenedeville

TREATY OF PARIS[1]

The definitive Treaty of Peace and Friendship between his Britannick Majesty, the Most Christian King, and the King of Spain. Concluded at Paris the 10th day of February, 1763. To which the King of Portugal acceded on the same day. (Printed from the Copy.)

In the Name of the Most Holy and Undivided Trinity, Father, Son, and Holy

Ghost. So be it.

Be it known to all those whom it shall, or may, in any manner, belong,

It has pleased the Most High to diffuse the spirit of union and concord among the Princes, whose divisions had spread troubles in the four parts of the world, and to inspire them with the inclination to cause the comforts of peace to succeed to the misfortunes of a long and bloody war, which having arisen between England and France during the reign of the Most Serene and Most Potent Prince, George the Second, by the grace of God, King of Great Britain, of glorious memory, continued under the reign of the Most Serene and Most Potent Prince, George the Third, his successor, and, in its progress, communicated itself to Spain and Portugal: Consequently, the Most Serene and Most Potent Prince, George the Third, by the grace of God, King of Great Britain, France, and Ireland, Duke of Brunswick and Lunenbourg, Arch Treasurer and Elector of the Holy Roman Empire; the Most Serene and Most Potent Prince, Lewis the Fifteenth, by the grace of God, Most Christian King; and the Most Serene and Most Potent Prince, Charles the Third, by the grace of God, King of Spain and of the Indies, after having laid the foundations of peace in the preliminaries signed at Fontainbleau the third

---

1 Shortt and Doughty, *Documents relating to the Constitutional History of Canada*, I.

The English version of the Treaty of 1763 is taken from the Collection of Treaties compiled by the Hon. Charles Jenkinson, afterwards Lord Liverpool, and which appeared under the following title:—"A Collection of all the Treaties of Peace, Alliance, and Commerce, Between Great-Britain and other Powers. From the Treaty signed at Munster in 1648, to the Treaties signed at Paris in 1783. By the Right Hon. Charles Jenkinson. In three Volumes." The Treaty of 1763 is contained in Vol. III, pp. 177-97.

of November last; and the Most Serene and Most Potent Prince, Don Joseph the First, by the grace of God, King of Portugal and of the Algarves, after having acceded thereto, determined to compleat, without delay, this great and important work. For this purpose, the high contracting parties have named and appointed their respective Ambassadors Extraordinary and Ministers Plenipotentiary, viz. his Sacred Majesty the King of Great Britain, the Most Illustrious and Most Excellent Lord, John Duke and Earl of Bedford, Marquis of Tavistock, &c. his Minister of State, Lieutenant General of his Armies, Keeper of his Privy Seal, Knight of the Most Noble Order of the Garter, and his Ambassador Extraordinary and Minister Plenipotentiary to his Most Christian Majesty; his Sacred Majesty the Most Christian King, the most Illustrious and Most Excellent Lord, Caesar Gabriel de Choiseul, Duke of Praslin, Peer of France, Knight of his Orders, Lieutenant General of his Armies and of the province of Britanny, Counsellor of all his Counsils, and Minister and Secretary of State, and of his Commands and Finances; his Sacred Majesty the Catholick King, the Most Illustrious and Most Excellent Lord, Don Jerome Grimaldi, Marquis de Grimaldi, Knight of the Most Christian King's Orders, Gentleman of his Catholick Majesty's Bedchamber in Employment, and his Ambassador Extraordinary to his Most Christian Majesty; his Sacred Majesty the Most Faithful King, the Most Illustrious and Most Excellent Lord, Martin de Mello and Castro, Knight professed of the Order of Christ, of his Most Faithful Majesty's Council, and his Ambassador and Minister Plenipotentiary to his Most Christian Majesty.

Who, after having duly communicated to each other their full powers, in good form, copies whereof are transcribed at the end of the present treaty of peace, have agreed upon the articles, the tenor of which is as follows:

Article I. There shall be a Christian, universal, and perpetual peace, as well by sea as by land, and a sincere and constant friendship shall be re-established between their Britannick, Most Christian, Catholick, and Most Faithful Majesties, and between their heirs and successors, kingdoms, dominions, provinces, countries, subjects, and vassals, of what quality or condition soever they be, without exception of places or of persons: So that the high contracting parties shall give the greatest attention to maintain between themselves and their said dominions and subjects this reciprocal friendship and correspondence, without permitting, on either side, any kind of hostilities, by sea or by land, to be committed from henceforth, for any cause, or under any pretence whatsoever, and every thing shall be carefully avoided which might hereafter prejudice the union happily re-established, applying themselves, on the contrary, on every occasion, to procure for each other whatever may contribute to their mutual glory, interests, and advantages, without giving any assistance or protection, directly or indirectly, to those who would cause any prejudice to either of the high contracting parties: there shall be a general oblivion of every thing that may have been done or committed before or since the commencement of the war which is just ended.

II. The treaties of Westphalia of 1648; those of Madrid between the Crowns of Great Britain and Spain of 1667, and 1670; the treaties of peace of Nimeguen of 1678, and 1679; of Ryswick of 1697; those of peace and of commerce of Utrecht of 1713; that of Baden of 1714; the treaty of the triple alliance of the Hague of 1717; that of the quadruple alliance of London of 1718; the treaty of peace of Vienna of 1738; the definitive treaty of Aix la Chapelle of 1748; and that of Madrid, between the Crowns of Great Britain and Spain of 1750: as well as the treaties between the Crowns of Spain and Portugal of the 13th of February, 1668; of the 6th of February, 1715; and of the 12th of February, 1761; and that of the 11th of April, 1713, between France and Portugal with the guaranties of Great Britain, serve as a basis and foundation to the peace, and to the present treaty: and for this purpose they are all renewed and confirmed in the best form, as well as all the general, which subsisted between the high contracting parties before the war, as if they were inserted here word for word, so that they are to be exactly observed, for the future, in their whole tenor, and religiously executed on all sides, in all their points, which shall not be derogated from by the present treaty, notwithstanding all that may have been stipulated to the contrary by any of the high contracting parties: and all the said parties declare, that they will not suffer any privilege, favour, or indulgence to subsist, contrary to the treaties above confirmed, except what shall have been agreed and stipulated by the present treaty.

III. All the prisoners made, on all sides, as well by land as by sea, and the hostages carried away or given during the war, and to this day, shall be restored, without ransom, six weeks, at least, to be computed from the day of the exchange of the ratification of the present treaty, each crown respectively paying the advances which shall have been made for the subsistance and maintenance of their prisoners by the Sovereign of the country where they shall have been detained, according to the attested receipts and estimates and other authentic vouchers which shall be furnished on one side and the other. And securities shall be reciprocally given for the payment of the debts which the prisoners shall have contracted in the countries where they have been detained until their entire liberty. And all the ships of war and merchant vessels which shall have been taken since the expiration of the terms agreed upon for the cessation of hostilities by sea shall likewise be restored, bonâfide, with all their crews and cargoes: and the execution of this article shall be proceeded upon immediately after the exchange of the ratification of this treaty.

IV. His Most Christian Majesty renounces all pretensions which

he has heretofore formed or might have formed to Nova Scotia or
Acadia in all its parts, and guaranties the whole of it, and with all its
dependencies, to the King of Great Britain: Moreover, his Most
Christian Majesty cedes and guaranties to his said Britannick Majesty, in full right, Canada, with all its dependencies, as well as the
island of Cape Breton, and all the other islands and coasts in the
gulph and river of St. Lawrence, and in general, every thing that
depends on the said countries, lands, islands, and coasts, with the
sovereignty, property, possession, and all rights acquired by treaty, or
otherwise, which the Most Christian King and the Crown of France
have had till now over the said countries, lands, islands, places,
coasts, and their inhabitants, so that the Most Christian King cedes
and makes over the whole to the said King, and to the Crown of
Great Britain, and that in the most ample manner and form, without restriction, and without any liberty to depart from the said
cession and guaranty under any pretence, or to disturb Great Britain
in the possessions above mentioned. His Britannick Majesty, on his
side, agrees to grant the liberty of the Catholick religion to the
inhabitants of Canada: he will, in consequence, give the most precise
and most effectual orders, that his new Roman Catholick subjects
may profess the worship of their religion according to the rites of the
Romish church, as far as the laws of Great Britain permit. His
Britannick Majesty farther agrees, that the French inhabitants, or
others who had been subjects of the Most Christian King in Canada,
may retire with all safety and freedom whereever they shall think
proper, and may sell their estates, provided it be to the subjects of
his Britannick Majesty, and bring away their effects as well as their
persons, without being restrained in their emigration, under any
pretence whatsoever, except that of debts or of criminal prosecutions: The term limited for this emigration shall be fixed to the
space of eighteen months, to be computed from the day of the exchange of the ratification of the present treaty.

V. The subjects of France shall have the liberty of fishing and
drying on a part of the coasts of the island of Newfoundland, such as
it is specified in the XIIIth article of the treaty of Utrecht; which
article is renewed and confirmed by the present treaty, (except what
relates to the island of Cape Breton, as well as to the other islands
and coasts in the mouth and in the gulph of St. Lawrence:) And his
Britannick Majesty consents to leave to the subjects of the Most
Christian King the liberty of fishing in the gulph of St. Lawrence, on
condition that the subjects of France do not exercise the said fishery
but at the distance of three leagues from all the coasts belonging to
Great Britain, as well those of the continent as those of the islands
situated in the said gulph of St. Lawrence. And as to what relates to
the fishery on the coasts of the island of Cape Breton, out of the said
gulph, the subjects of the Most Christian King shall not be permitted to exercise the said fishery but at the distance of fifteen leagues

from the coasts of the island of Cape Breton; and the fishery on the coasts of Nova Scotia or Acadia, and every where else out of the said gulph, shall remain on the foot of former treaties.

VI. The King of Great Britain cedes the islands of St. Pierre and Macquelon, in full right, to his Most Christian Majesty, to serve as a shelter to the French fishermen; and his said Most Christian Majesty engages not to fortify the said islands; to erect no buildings upon them but merely for the conveniency of the fishery; and to keep upon them a guard of fifty men only for the police.

VII. In order to re-establish peace on solid and durable foundations, and to remove for ever all subject of dispute with regard to the limits of the British and French territories on the continent of America; it is agreed, that, for the future, the confines between the dominions of his Britannick Majesty and those of his Most Christian Majesty, in that part of the world, shall be fixed irrevocably by a line drawn along the middle of the River Mississippi, from its source to the river Iberville, and from thence, by a line drawn along the middle of this river, and the lakes Maurepas and Potchartrain to the sea; and for this purpose, the Most Christian King cedes in full right, and guaranties to his Britannick Majesty the river and port of the Mobile, and every thing which he possesses, or ought to possess, on the left side of the river Mississippi, except the town of New Orleans and the island in which it is situated, which shall remain to France, provided that the navigation of the river Mississippi shall be equally free, as well to the subjects of Great Brtain as to those of France, in its whole breadth and length, from its source to the sea, and expressly that part which is between the said island of New Orleans and the right bank of that river, as well as the passage both in and out of its mouth: It is farther stipulated, that the vessels belonging to the subjects of either nation shall not be stopped, visited, or subjected to the payment of any duty whatsoever. The stipulations inserted in the IVth article, in favour of the inhabitants of Canada shall also take place with regard to the inhabitants of the countries ceded by this article.

VIII. The King of Great Britain shall restore to France the islands of Guadaloupe, of Mariegalante, of Desirade, of Martinico, and of Belleisle; and the fortresses of these islands shall be restored in the same condition they were in when they were conquered by the British arms, provided that his Britannick Majesty's subjects, who shall have settled in the said islands, or those who shall have any commercial affairs to settle there or in other places restored to France by the present treaty, shall have liberty to sell their lands and their estates, to settle their affairs, to recover their debts, and to bring away their effects as well as their persons, on board vessels, which they shall be permitted to send to the said islands and other places restored as above, and which shall serve for this use only, without being restrained on account of their religion, or under any other pretence whatsoever, except that of debts or of criminal prosecutions: and for this purpose, the term of eighteen months is allowed to his Britannick Majesty's subjects, to be computed from the day of the exchange of the ratifications of the present treaty; but, as the liberty granted to his Britannick Majesty's subjects, to bring away their persons and their effects, in vessels of their nation, may be liable to abuses if precautions were not taken to prevent them; it has been expressly agreed between his Britannick Majesty and his Most Christian Majesty, that the number of English vessels which have leave to go to the said islands and places restored to France, shall be limited, as well as the number of tons of each one; that they shall go in ballast; shall set sail at a fixed time; and shall make one voyage only; all the effects belonging to the English being to be embarked at the same time. It has been farther agreed, that his Most Christian Majesty shall cause the necessary passports to be given to the said vessels; that, for the greater security, it shall be allowed to place two French clerks or guards in each of the said vessels, which shall be visited in the landing places and ports of the said islands and places restored to France, and that the merchandize which shall be found therein shall be confiscated.

IX. The Most Christian King cedes and guaranties to his Britannick Majesty, in full right, the islands of Grenada, and the Grenadines, with the same stipulations in favour of the inhabitants of this colony, inserted in the IVth article for those of Canada: And the partition of the islands called neutral, is agreed and fixed, so that those of St. Vincent, Dominico, and Tobago, shall remain in full right to Great Britain, and that of St. Lucia shall be delivered to France, to enjoy the same likewise in full right, and the high contracting parties guaranty the partition so stipulated.

AN ORDER[1]

on the occasion of the Treaty of Paris
for the singing of a solemn Te Deum *in thanksgiving*
for the benefit of peace

June 4 1763

Jean-Olivier Briand, Canon of the Cathedral church of Quebec, and Vicar-General of the diocese in the absence of a bishop.

To the secular and regular clergy and to the faithful of the diocese of Quebec, greetings in our Lord Jesus Christ.

Dearly beloved brethren, let us render solemn thanks to the all-powerful god whom we adore and worship according to the Gospel of Jesus Christ his only son; let us bless his name in a spirit of perfect submission.

---

1 *Mandements, Lettres pastorales et Circulaires des Evêques de Quebec* (Quebec, 1887) II, pp. 168-71.

The peace signed in Paris last February tenth, and ratified on the tenth of the following month, has at last put an end to a cruel war which, dividing almost all the powers of Europe one against the other, had lighted fires and spread the most fearful havoc in the four corners of the earth. You, yourselves have experienced the fatal consequences of this war; I shall not remind you of them on this day consecrated to the expression of our gratitude, when our one desire is to render thanks to God who has granted us the priceless gift of peace, that peace so ardently desired and which for so many years had been the object of our prayers both public and private. Not all our prayers have received the answer that we had desired, since Canada with all its dependencies has been irrevocably ceded to the British Crown; but trust, dearly beloved brethren, in the care of divine Providence whose guidance is often so much the more merciful as it thwarts our natural desires and inclinations. Have we not a manifest proof of this in the conduct of our conquerors towards us?

The surrender of Quebec left you at the mercy of a victorious army. At first you were alarmed, frightened, dismayed, and your fears were well founded; you knew what was happening in Germany, and you thought you were about to be victims of like misfortunes. You did not know that an ever-watchful Providence had prepared for you a Governor who, by his moderation, his strict justice, his generous human feelings, his tender compassion for the poor and the unfortunate, and the strict discipline which he maintained among his troops, would dissipate the horrors of war. Where are the oppressive measures, the corruption, the looting, the onerous levies which ordinarily follow victory? Once they had become our basters, did not these noble conquerors seem to forget that they had been our enemies? Did they not immediately concern themselves with our needs and means for satisfying them? You have certainly not forgotten the measures initiated by His Excellency, the illustrious and charitable General Murray, nor the very considerable contributions which he procured for the sustenance of the poor. You have not forgotten his wise and effective precautions against the possibility of famine in the country under his administration.

After such evident signs of God's goodness, must we not be convinced that he has not ceased to love us, and that it depends only upon us to enjoy a happy and durable peace under this new government. Be strict in fulfilling your duties as faithful subjects attached to their prince; and you will have the consolation of knowing a kind, beneficent King, desirous of making you happy, and favourable towards your religion, your attachment to which is for us a source of inexpressible joy.

Moreover, my beloved brethren, this complete and perfect fidelity is more than a means of serving your temporal interests; it is a duty prescribed by your faith.

Saint Paul the Apostle repeats this essential obligation in several places. By evading it you would not only incur the indignation of our lawful sovereign, lose his protection, and be deprived of all the privileges which he has graciously granted to you; you would also be guilty in the eyes of God, the more so since you would run the risk of being deprived of the right to practise our holy and true religion, a right which is granted to us by the treaty of peace. Consider carefully therefore, dearly beloved brethren, how important it is for you to be faithful and submissive subjects; remember that nothing can excuse you from perfect obedience, from scrupulous and conscientious loyalty, nor from an unshakably sincere attachment to our new Monarch and to the interests of the nation of which we have just become a part.

For these reasons, and in accordance with the orders communicated to us by His Excellency General Murray, we have ordered and we now order:

1. That on Tuesday, June 15, about ten o'clock in the morning, a solemn thanksgiving *Te Deum* be sung in the church of the Ursulines in Quebec, now serving as Cathedral and parish church; the secular and regular clergy will take part in the service, as will the Sisters of the diocese.

2. That in the churches of country parishes, a solemn *Te Deum* be sung after vespers on the Sunday following the proclamation of this order.

3. We advise all parish priests of their strict obligation to explain to their people the motives which must inspire obedience and loyalty to the new government, and to make them understand that their happiness, tranquillity, religion and salvation depend upon their obedience.

4. Although public prayers are no longer being offered, we exhort you to continue to raise your hands in supplication to Heaven for the needs of this Church.

This our present order will be read and published from the pulpits of all parish churches on the Sunday immediately following its reception.

Given at the Hôpital-Général, under our seal, that of our secretary, and the seal of the diocese, June 4, 1763.

Briand, Canon, Vicar General

By order of the Vicar General

Hubert, Priest, Secretary,

CENSUS OF CANADA, 1765[1]

Localities	Households	Population	Sex		Married and Widowed			Children and unmarried		
			M	F	M	F	Total	M	F	Total
N. shore of St. Lawrence										
Isle aux Coudres	41	213	101	112	41	41	82	60	71	131
Eboulements	30	149	77	72	30	30	60	47	42	89
Baie St. Paul	88	540	280	260	88	87	175	192	173	365
Petite Rivière	27	152	81	71	26	27	53	55	44	99
St. Joachim	66	362	180	182	66	64	130	114	118	232
St. Féréol	25	125	64	61	25	25	50	39	36	75
Ste. Anne du Nord	64	362	193	169	64	61	125	129	108	237
Château-Richer	87	495	250	245	85	87	172	165	158	323
L'Ange-Gardien	71	418	224	194	71	66	137	153	128	281
Beauport	167	891	451	440	167	165	332	284	275	559
Charlesbourg	235	1,239	631	608	220	235	455	411	373	784
Québec		(8,967*)								
Rivière St. Charles	41	297	146	151	36	41	77	110	110	220
Ste. Foye	75	362	179	183	71	75	146	108	108	216
Ancienne Lorette	189	947	528	419	180	189	369	348	230	578
St. Augustin	151	795	354	441	150	149	299	204	292	496
Pointe-aux-Trembles	125	700	360	340	116	125	241	244	215	459
Ecureuils	57	305	156	149	56	57	113	100	92	192
Cap Santé	153	811	402	409	151	149	300	251	260	511
Deschambault	80	428	203	225	79	80	159	124	145	269
Grondines	50	254	120	134	43	50	93	77	84	161
Ste. Anne de la Pérade	102	563	296	267	112	103	215	184	164	348
Batiscan	130	636	332	304	131	121	252	201	183	384
Champlain	45	228	130	98	46	33	79	84	65	149
St. Maurice	55	273	130	143	60	55	115	70	88	158
Cap de la Madeleine	30	170	90	80	32	24	56	58	56	114
Trois-Rivières	126	644	309	335	130	153	283	179	182	361
Pointe-du-Lac	33	182	91	91	33	35	68	58	56	114
Yamachiche	140	636	332	304	154	133	287	178	171	349
Maskinongé	70	353	189	164	83	70	153	106	94	200
Berthier	136	649	341	308	140	138	278	201	170	371
Petite Riv. de Berthier	80	372	184	188	91	77	168	93	111	204
Isle Dupas	30	178	82	96	32	30	62	50	66	116
D'Autray	62	280	155	125	70	61	131	85	64	149
La Noraye	41	183	94	89	41	37	78	53	52	105
La Valtrie	64	327	173	154	69	59	128	104	95	199
St. Sulpice	105	567	311	256	113	105	218	198	151	349
Repentigny	140	712	376	336	173	134	307	203	202	405
St. Pierre du Portage	209	1,000	528	472	217	201	418	311	271	582
La Chenaye	80	352	179	173	90	70	160	89	103	192
Mascouche	107	542	274	268	124	116	240	150	152	302
Terrebonne	103	540	267	273	116	112	228	151	161	312
Mascouche de Terrebonne	89	436	224	212	105	102	207	119	110	229
Ste. Rose	187	835	421	414	206	186	392	215	228	443
St. François de Sales	42	233	127	106	45	43	88	82	63	145
St. Vincent de Paul	238	1,311	711	600	240	242	482	471	358	829
Sault-au-Récollet	58	257	140	117	58	48	107	82	68	253
Pointe-aux-Trembles	100	459	223	236	104	102	206	119	134	253

[1] *Canada Census*, 1871, IV, pp. 64-67. The census of 1759 gave a total of 75,000 inhabitants, but it has been lost. Figures for some localities are unfortunately missing from the census of 1765 which is reproduced here.

Localities	Households	Population	Sex		Married and Widowed			Children and unmarried		
			M	F	M	F	Total	M	F	Total
Longue Pointe	78	390	209	181	79	77	156	130	104	234
St. Laurent	156	795	411	384	159	142	301	252	242	494
Montreal		(5,733*)								
Lachine	76	423	212	211	76	79	155	136	132	268
Pointe Claire	147	783	419	364	145	136	281	274	228	502
Ste. Geneviève	172	796	404	392	185	171	356	219	221	440
Vaudreuil	83	377	186	191	86	82	168	100	109	209
Ste. Anne	67	325	169	156	72	71	143	97	85	182
Ile Perrot	60	294	157	137	63	59	122	94	78	172
Les Cèdres	56	309	170	139	63	57	120	107	82	189
S. shore of St. Lawrence										
La Prairie	72	366	202	164	77	68	145	125	96	221
Longueuil	129	714	386	328	131	120	251	255	208	463
Boucherville	165	748	374	374	176	157	333	198	217	415
Varennes	232	1,168	617	551	278	218	496	339	333	672
Verchères	186	963	499	464	186	191	377	313	273	586
Contrecoeur	67	371	183	188	69	79	148	114	109	223
Grand St. Ours	44	243	132	111	48	50	98	84	61	145
Petit St. Ours	116	551	309	242	120	106	226	189	136	325
Sorel { partie sur le fleuve	75	332	180	152	87	75	162	93	77	170
Sorel { dans l'intérieur	160	677	363	314	167	144	311	196	170	366
Immaculée Conception	109	555	276	279	112	100	212	164	179	343
Chambly	98	544	282	262	96	93	189	186	169	355
St. Denis	58	312	162	150	62	59	121	100	91	191
St. Antoine	56	309	170	139	70	72	142	100	67	167
St. Charles	87	478	271	207	86	85	171	185	122	307
Yamaska	107	524	277	247	108	97	205	169	150	319
Nicolet	113	510	250	260	110	115	225	140	145	285
St. François du Lac	77	417	211	206	80	79	159	131	127	258
Baie St. Antoine	90	467	247	220	99	96	195	148	124	272
Bécancour	65	332	177	155	72	62	134	105	93	198
Gentilly	34	173	88	85	36	34	70	52	51	103
St. Pierre les Becquets	43	219	110	109	43	39	82	67	70	137
St. Jean d'Eschaillons	32	183	93	90	32	32	64	61	58	119
Lotbinière	75	391	188	203	75	68	143	113	135	248
Ste. Croix	74	369	183	186	73	74	147	110	112	222
St. Antoine	108	559	283	276	108	105	213	175	171	346
St. Nicolas	92	421	209	212	87	86	173	122	126	248
St. Joseph de Lévis	161	802	411	391	142	163	305	269	228	497
St. Henri	72	317	172	145	72	70	142	100	75	175
St. Joseph de la Beauce	94	499	237	262	89	94	183	148	168	316
Ste. Marie de la Beauce	69	357	187	170	69	68	137	118	102	220
Beaumont	81	398	204	194	83	82	165	121	112	233
St. Charles	204	1,073	546	527	204	198	402	342	329	671
St. Michel	170	909	475	434	165	170	335	310	264	574
Isle d'Orléans { St. Pierre	88	471	225	246	85	88	173	140	158	298
Isle d'Orléans { St. Laurent	87	473	242	231	87	83	170	155	148	303
Isle d'Orléans { St. Jean	91	524	264	260	91	90	181	173	170	343
Isle d'Orléans { Ste. Famille	83	457	244	213	77	83	160	167	130	297
Isle d'Orléans { St. François	71	378	185	193	71	67	138	114	126	240

Localities	House-holds	Popula-tion	Sex		Married and Widowed			Children and unmarried		
			M	F	M	F	Total	M	F	Total
St. Vallier	131	676	353	323	128	131	259	225	192	417
Berthier	68	394	197	197	68	67	135	129	130	259
St. François du Sud	104	615	303	312	104	104	208	199	208	407
St. Pierre du Sud	104	597	311	286	104	102	206	207	184	391
St. Thomas	209	1,090	519	571	200	209	409	319	362	681
Cap St. Ignace	110	599	311	288	109	110	219	202	178	380
Islet	108	598	308	290	108	102	210	200	188	388
St. Jean Port-Joly	73	393	191	202	70	73	143	121	129	250
St. Roch	92	560	264	296	88	92	180	176	204	380
Ste. Anne de la Pocatière	114	611	313	298	114	109	223	199	189	388
Rivière Ouelle	139	819	408	411	135	139	274	273	272	545
Kamouraska	157	870	425	445	155	157	312	270	288	558
Rivière-du-Loup	16	68	36	32	16	14	30	20	18	38
Rivages de Resti-gouche	24	93	54	39	24	23	47	30	16	46
Baie des Chaleurs	41	209	114	95	41	33	74	73	62	135
Gaspé	16	109	69	40	27	16	43	42	24	66
	10,660	55,110	28,316	26,794	10,922	10,509	21,431	17,394	16,285	33,679

*Quebec &
*Montréal   14,700-Total   69,810

TABLE II

HOMESTEADS, LAND UNDER CULTIVATION, LIVESTOCK

Localities	Houses	Arpents owned	Bushels of seed sown	Horses	Oxen	Cows	Calves	Sheep	Pigs
N. shore of St. Lawrence									
Isle aux Coudres	40	4,405	445	43	46	30	101	245	92
Eboulements	26	2,355	257	14	2	12	54	109	47
Baie St. Paul	81	10,689	1,130	88	98	94	195	424	255
Petite Rivière	24	8,962	220	24	22	17	56	88	60
St. Joachim	63	10,820	1,396	61	202	142	167	284	187
St. Féréol	23	2,560	357	21	30	24	43	53	40
Ste. Anne du Nord	61	11,551	1,199	59	83	47	130	167	119
Château-Richer	85	9,090	891	50	67	169	115	89	105
L'Ange-Gardien	61	12,635	1,446	61	107	137	153	189	133
Beauport	147	8,854	3,827	175	255	230	370	175	417
Charlesbourg	208	11,702	4,009	208	600	238	509	353	451
Québec	(1,400*)								
Rivière St. Charles	37	3,784	1,287	55	84	53	135	115	129
Ste. Foye	63	5,162	1,659	72	110	84	180	54	146
Ancienne Lorette	170	13,511	3,784	118	236	236	383	267	349
St. Augustin	149	8,212	2,145	110	194	170	259	244	252
Pointe-aux-Trembles	110	7,518	2,114	130	178	229	271	145	261
Ecureuils	54	2,692	802	52	63	64	100	80	119
Cap Santé	131	13,068	2,240	175	133	159	244	272	297
Deschambault	74	7,200	617	91	92	99	151	272	184
Grondines	42	5,824	755	66	28	50	94	89	93
Ste. Anne de la Pérade	102	11,664	2,323	154	154	166	301	401	278
Batiscan	125	9,313	2,390	148	110	147	323	244	347
Champlain	42	5,481	1,257	77	49	87	134	29	156
St. Maurice	55	3,205	809	89	29	67	107	115	184
Cap de la Madeleine	29	3,945	1,019	53	15	71	105	30	116
Trois-Rivières	118	5,830	1,119	100	111	78	231	78	276
Pointe-du-Lac	32	2,070	621	39	32	35	74	2	81
Yamachiche	134	7,861	2,475	177	153	370	280	197	481
Maskinongé	67	7,599	1,129	105	48	146	161	96	213
Berthier	114	7,121	2,496	204	111	156	281	454	436
Petite Riv. de Berthier	78	7,295	1,281	122	41	71	139	254	246
Isle Dupas	30	1,879	688	57	18	68	90	203	134
D'Autray	62	6,674	824	100	49	51	123	91	183
La Noraye	40	4,610	737	73	41	71	89	108	148
La Valtrie	61	3,938	1,236	95	46	102	146	141	194
St. Sulpice	109	8,369	2,892	172	153	205	293	344	434
Repentigny	135	10,877	3,409	292	184	298	355	325	567
St. Pierre du Portage	215	12,763	3,708	287	193	251	423	471	518
La Chenaye	77	8,625	2,495	152	187	200	237	458	407
Mascouche	104	12,418	1,602	143	130	165	196	321	318
Terrebonne	95	5,829	1,284	110	103	119	181	270	308
Mascouche de Terrebonne	85	7,404	1,307	134	79	99	139	240	262
Ste. Rose	173	16,527	2,730	266	222	297	343	767	827
St. François de Sales	39	3,286	1,296	75	105	353	138	311	158
St. Vincent de Paul	226	17,012	3,996	374	357	460	466	714	987
Sault-au-Récollet	59	3,620	1,633	101	171	147	158	34	212
Pointe-aux-Trembles	94	3,179	2,861	169	160	335	343	351	262
Longue Pointe	71	4,207	3,286	139	138	151	239	335	292
St. Laurent	151	10,073	3,810	287	298	253	361	342	495
Montréal	(900*)								
Lachine	75	5,047	1,758	154	144	180	204	143	269
Pointe Claire	145	11,575	4,339	271	322	356	372	428	579
Ste. Geneviève	163	14,264	3,107	245	205	260	310	301	753
Vaudreuil	83	4,892	927	66	70	54	107	20	231
Ste. Anne	64	3,779	1,497	105	92	107	134	89	237

Localities		FARMS				LIVESTOCK			
	Houses	Arpents owned	Bushels of seed sown	Horses	Oxen	Cows	Calves	Sheep	Pigs
Isle Perrot	59	3,908	1,352	92	94	85	150	129	197
Les Cèdres	55	5,398	1,180	91	74	106	102	32	225
S. shore of St. Lawrence									
La Prairie	70	5,185	1,467	124	101	60	178	153	187
Longueuil	124	8,552	2,828	269	200	272	382	160	466
Boucherville	161	25,581	3,004	256	198	221	449	401	407
Varennes	199	26,246	5,642	407	235	329	622	711	535
Verchères	174	20,382	4,595	336	282	382	492	468	587
Contrecoeur	55	6,590	1,183	120	80	129	158	210	349
Grand St. Ours	47	5,057	740	81	34	76	102	137	134
Petit St. Ours	105	10,649	2,031	189	121	137	251	289	330
Sorel { Partie sur le fleuve 71 { dans l'intérieur 148		5,311	767	98	24	60	164	161	229
Immaculée Conception	108	10,125	1,020	149	130	92	196	79	224
Chambly	98	8,766	1,177	156	142	131	232	71	250
St. Denis	58	6,510	1,211	116	124	111	163	107	193
St. Antoine	54	7,376	1,202	107	134	108	156	138	219
St. Charles	87	11,832	1,784	164	137	159	247	198	330
Yamaska	99	10,846	1,046	129	62	92	187	260	278
Nicolet	101	9,233	1,122	101	59	91	195	263	249
St. François du Lac	72	7,821	1,104	128	58	124	254	351	244
Baie St. Antoine	89	11,770	1,075	109	94	81	172	410	250
Bécancour	62	10,432	1,211	92	51	93	204	106	176
Gentilly	34	5,024	378	38	29	27	69	46	80
St. Pierre les Becquets	43	5,351	543	80	32	38	75	115	113
St. Jean d'Eschaillons	30	4,240	436	26	26	30	61	131	70
Lotbinière	72	8,154	551	83	100	98	149	305	164
Ste. Croix	66	5,360	1,233	67	83	66	118	151	111
St. Antoine	99	9,972	1,872	117	115	123	179	191	183
St. Nicolas	74	9,000	1,540	83	101	76	131	166	133
St. Joseph de Lévis	145	16,806	2,023	133	140	106	252	205	291
St. Henri	66	7,900	648	61	49	54	99	114	106
St. Joseph de la Beauce	88	13,728	990	81	80	97	165	247	172
Ste. Marie de la Beauce	68	9,220	785	44	53	37	116	133	112
Beaumont	70	7,428	1,252	71	90	86	114	232	165
St. Charles	197	20,490	1,792	163	132	139	312	406	435
St. Michel	155	14,700	2,261	166	183	178	336	630	375
Isle d'Orléans { St. Pierre	72	9,779	2,071	102	152	184	233	249	219
St. Laurent	77	6,281	2,213	146	134	153	211	233	246
St. Jean	80	10,173	2,028	97	113	144	216	297	227
Ste. Famille	78	7,599	2,274	98	157	190	236	264	244
St. François	58	5,075	1,722	74	121	141	179	268	169
St. Vallier	122	9,538	2,134	158	176	185	319	586	229
Berthier	63	6,156	1,314	87	83	93	173	195	189
St. François du Sud	102	9,076	1,218	117	110	98	205	374	251
St. Pierre du Sud	95	7,346	1,799	145	112	148	260	465	282
St. Thomas	178	10,939	2,264	218	172	192	442	817	508
Cap St. Ignace	99	9,466	1,260	122	105	137	263	671	276
Islet	103	10,955	1,381	117	114	120	215	516	265
St. Jean Port-Joly	68	8,945	755	70	48	60	113	267	161
St. Roch	83	12,997	1,015	101	93	122	209	541	225
Ste. Anne de la Pocatière	107	11,116	1,446	139	57	113	232	510	304
Rivière Ouelle	129	13,249	1,523	144	109	114	286	663	352
Kamouraska	148	22,299	2,282	196	75	154	348	746	496
Rivière-du-Loup	15	2,578	34	15		7	19	33	25
Sauvages de Restigouche Baie des Chaleurs	37			4	5	20	18		
Gaspé	12	7		3		3	6		
	9,930	941,342	179,699	13,488	12,533	14,732	22,748	28,022	28,562

*Québec & { 2,300.—Total 12,230
*Montréal {

BIBLIOGRAPHY

PRELIMINARY NOTE

Some archival collections have been reclassified since the author consulted them, and for this reason references may not always indicate a new title or call number, or a change in numerical order. In such cases the date will serve as a guide and permit the reader to locate the required document.

No attempt has been made to present a complete bibliography of the period studied. This is a task for a professional bibliographer. The lists which follow include only the essential books and collections and those which have been consulted by the author.

DOCUMENTARY SOURCES IN MANUSCRIPT

There are copies or photostats of most of the following series and collections in the National Archives in Ottawa.

FRENCH SOURCES

Archives nationales:

Série E.	Conseil du Roi. I. Conseil des Finances.
Série F²A.	Colonies.
Série F³.	Collection Moreau de Saint-Méry.
Série G.	Administration financière.
Série J.	Trésor des Chartres.
Série K.	Section historique.
Série V⁶.	Grande Chancellerie et Conseils.
Série Z.	Juridictions spéciales et ordinaires.

Archives des Colonies:

Série A.	Actes du Pouvoir souverain.
Série B.	Correspondance ministérielle et Ordres et Dépêches du Roi. Lettres envoyées aux colonies.
Série C¹¹A.	Canada et Dépendances. (Lettres des gouverneurs, intendants, officers et autres.)
C¹¹B.	Ile Royale.
C¹¹C.	Terre-Neuve, Iles de la Madeleine et Saint-Jean.
C¹¹D.	Acadie.
C¹¹G.	Correspondance Raudot.
Série D²C.	Troupes coloniales.
Série F¹A.	Fonds des colonies.
Série F³.	Collection Moreau de Saint-Méry.
Série G¹.	Etat civil des colonies.

Archives de la Marine:

Dépôt des cartes et plans de la Marine.
Manuscrits de la bibliothèque.

Ministère des Affaires étrangères:
  Mémoires et Documents. Amérique.
  Correspondance politique. Angleterre.

Ministère de la Guerre:
  Archives historiques.

Bibliothèque nationale:
  Fonds français.
  Nouvelles Acquisitions.
  Collection Moreau.
  Mélanges Colbert.

ENGLISH SOURCES

Public Record Office:
  B. State Papers: Foreign.
  Treaty Papers.
  C.O. 1. Colonial Papers.
  C.O. 5. America and West Indies.
  C.O. 42. Canada. Original Correspondence.
  C.O. 217. Nova Scotia Original Correspondence.

British Museum:
  Additional manuscripts.
  Haldimand Papers.

CANADIAN SOURCES

National Archives:
  Actes de Foy et Hommage.
  Brown Collection, M. 651.
  Neilson Collection.
  Official Correspondence, Series II.
  Maps Division.
  Nova Scotia State Papers.
  Montreal, Palais de Justice. Ordonnances.
  Montreal, Palais de Justice. Registres judiciaires.
  Trois-Rivières, Pièces judiciaires.

Archives of the Province of Quebec:
  Various series.
  Historical collections.

Private Collections:
  Archives of the Seminary of Saint-Sulpice.
  Quebec Seminary, Letters.
  Letters. Archdiocese of Quebec.
  University of Montreal. Baby Collection.

PRINTED DOCUMENTARY SOURCES

Amherst, Jeffery, *The Journals of Jeffery Amherst,* ed. with introd. by J. Clarence Webster (Toronto, 1931).

Aventures militaires au XVIIIᵉ siècle, d'après les mémoires de Jean-Baptiste d'Aleyrac (Paris, 1935).

Beaumont, Gaston Duboscq de, *Les Derniers jours de l'Acadie. Correspondance et Mémoires: extraits du portefeuille de M. le Courtois de Surlaville* (Paris, 1899).

Bégon, Madame, "Correspondance de Madame Bégon, née Rocbert de La Morandière, 1748-1753," *Rapport de l'archiviste de la province de Québec,* 1934-35.

Bonnefons, Jean-Carmine, *Voyage au Canada dans le Nord de l'Amérique Septentrionale fait depuis l'an 1751 à 1761 par J.C.B.* (Quebec, 1887).

Boucault, Nicolas Gaspard, "Etat présent du Canada (1754)," *R.A.Q.,* 1920-21.

Bougainville, Louis - Antoine de, "Journal," *R.A.Q.,* 1923-24.

Bougainville, "Mémoire de Bougainville sur l'état de la Nouvelle-France, 1757," *R.A.Q.*, 1923-24.

Bourlamaque, François Charles de, "Un Mémoire sur le Canada," *Bulletin des Recherches historiques*, 1919-20.

Brouage, Martel de, "Mémoire de François Martel de Brouage, Comdt pour le Roi à la côte du Labrador, (1678-1729)," *R.A.Q.*, 1922-23.

Le Canada français. Collection de documents inédits sur le Canada et l'Amérique (Quebec, 1888). 3 vols.

Carver, Jonathan, *Travels through the Interior Parts of North America in the years 1766, 1767 and 1768* (London, 1778).

Catalogne, Gédéon de, "Mémoire sur les plans des seigneuries et habitations des gouvernements de Québec, des Trois - Rivières et Montréal," *Bulletin des Recherches historiques*, 1915 (Lévis, 1895-1961).

Collection de Mémoires et de Relations (Société littéraire et historique de Québec, 1840).

Collections and Researches by the Michigan Pioneer and Historical Society (Lansing, 1905). vol. XXIV.

Collection de manuscrits contenant lettres, mémoires et autres documents historiques relatifs à la Nouvelle-France. (Quebec, 1883-85). 3 vols.

Courville, Le Sieur de, *Mémoires sur le Canada depuis 1749 jusqu'à 1760* (Quebec, 1838).

Courville, "Mémoire du Canada," *R.A.Q.*, 1924-25. Attributed to Courville.

Crespel, Emmanuel, *Voyages du R. P. Emmanuel Crespel dans le Canada* (Quebec, 1884).

Cugnet, François Joseph, *Extraits des Edits, Déclarations, Orrdonnances et Règlements de Sa Majesté très chrétienne, des Règlements et Jugements des gouverneurs généraux et intendants, etc.* (Quebec, 1775).

Dargent, Joseph, "Relation d'un voyage de Paris à Montréal, 1731," ed. by the Abbé Arthaud, *Revue d'histoire de l'Amérique française*, vol. I.

Dinwiddie Papers, from the Virginia Historical Collections (Richmond, 1883).

Documents relating to Canadian Currency, Exchange and Finance during the French Period, ed. by Adam Shortt (Ottawa, 1925). 2 vols.

Documents relating to the Colonial History of the State of New York, ed. by W. B. Munro (Albany, 1855-58).

Documents relating to the Constitutional History of Canada, 1759-1791, selected and edited with notes by Adam Shortt and Arthur Doughty (Ottawa, 1911-35). 3 vols.

Documents relating to the Seigniorial Tenure in Canada, 1598-1854, ed. by W. B. Munro (Toronto, 1908).

Doreil, "Lettres de Doreil," *R.A.Q.*, 1944-45.

The Siege of Quebec and the Battle of the Plains of Abraham, ed. by Arthur G. Doughty and C. W. Parmalee (Quebec, 1901). 6 vols. A rich and valuable collection.

Duplessis, Marie-Andrée, "Lettres de la Mère Marie-Andrée Duplessis," *Nova Francia*, 1926-29.

Dupuy, Claude Thomas, "Mémoire de M. Dupuy, indt de la Nouvelle-France, sur les troubles arrivés à Québec en 1727 et 1728 après la mort de Mgr de Saint-Vallier, évêque de Québec," *R.A.Q.*, 1920-21.

Edits, ordonnances royaux, déclarations et arrêts du Conseil d'Etat du Roi, concernant le Canada (Quebec, 1854-56). 3 vols.

Extraits des Archives des Ministères de la Marine et de la Guerre à Paris, publiés sous la direction de l'abbé H. R. Casgrain, Correspondance générale. MM. Duquesne et Vaudreuil, Gouverneurs-Généraux, 1755-60 (Quebec, 1860).

Forbes, John, *Letters of General John Forbes relating to the Expedition against Fort Duquesne*, ed. by Irene Stewart (Pittsburgh, 1927).

Franquet, Louis, *Voyages et Mémoires sur le Canada* (Quebec, 1889).

Franquet, Louis, "Voyage de Louis Franquet aux îles Royales et St. Jean," *R.A.Q.*, 1923-24.

Frye, *Journal of the attack on Fort William Henry*.

Grenier, Fernand, ed., *Papiers Contrecœur et autres documents concernant le conflit anglo-français sur l'Ohio de 1745 à 1756* (Quebec, 1952).

Hendry, Anthony, "From York Factory to the Blackfeet Country. The Journal of Anthony Hendry, 1754-55," ed. by Lawrence J. Burpee, *Proceedings and Transactions of the Royal Society of Canada*, 1907.

Histoire de l'Hôtel-Dieu de Québec (Montauban, 1751). The materials for this history were gathered by Mother Françoise Juchereau de St. Ignace, and the text was written by Mother Marie-Andrée Duplessis de Ste. Hélène. See also *Les Annales de l'Hôtel-Dieu*, ed. by Dom Jamet (Quebec, 1939), a modern edition of the earlier work.

Impartial Account of Co. Bradstreet's Expedition, by a volunteer in the expedition (London, 1859).

Innis, H. A., ed., *Select Documents in Canadian Economic History, 1497-1783* (Toronto, 1929) pp. 1-47.

Inventaire des insinuations du Conseil Souverain de la Nouvelle-France, ed. by P. G. Roy (Beauceville, 1921).

Inventaire des Ordonnances des intendants de la Nouvelle-France, conservées aux Archives provinciales de Québec, ed. by P. G. Roy (Beauceville, 1917). 3 vols.

Inventaire des Jugements et Délibérations du Conseil Souverain, ed. by P. G. Roy (Quebec, 1932-35). 7 vols.

Jérémie, Nicolas, *Relation de la Baie d'Hudson* (Amsterdam, 1720).

Jesuit Relations and Allied Documents, the Travels and Explorations of the Jesuit Missionaries in New France, 1690-1791, ed. by R. G. Thwaites (Cleveland, 1896-1901). 73 vols.

Relations des Jésuites (Quebec, 1858). 3 vols.

Johnstone, Chevalier de, *Mémoires du Chevalier de Johnstone*, Quebec Literary and Historical Society (Quebec, 1915).

Journal du Siège de Québec, published and annotated by Aegidius Fauteux (Quebec, 1922). (Also published in *R.A.Q.*, 1920-21).

Jugements et Délibérations du Conseil Souverain de la Nouvelle-France (Quebec, 1885-1891). 6 vols.

Kalm, Per, *Voyage de Kalm en Amérique* (Montreal, 1880). French translation and summary by L. Marchand.

Kalm, Per, *The America of 1750; Per Kalm's Travels in North America*, ed. by Benson (New York, 1937).

Knox, Captain John, *An Historical Journal of the Campaigns in North America for the years 1757, 1758, 1759 and 1760*, ed. with introd. and notes by Arthur G. Doughty (Champlain Society, 1914-16). 3 vols.

La Grange, Louis Chancels de, "Voyage fait à l'île Royale ou du Cap Breton en Canada," *R.H.A.F.*, (Décembre 1959).

La Pause, "Les Papiers de La Pause," *R.A.Q.*, 1931-32, 1932-33, 1933-34.

La Potherie, Bacqueville de, *Histoire de l'Amérique Septentrionale* (Paris, 1753). 4 vols.

La Tour, Bertrand de, *Mémoires sur la vie de Mgr de Laval* (Cologne, 1761).

Le Beau, C., *Aventures du Sr. C. Le Beau, ou Voyage curieux et nouveau parmi les sauvages de l'Amérique Septentrionale* (Amsterdam, 1758).

Le Gardeur de Saint-Pierre, "Mémoire du Journal de Voyage de Jacques Repentigny Le Gardeur de Saint-Pierre," *Report of the Canadian Archives*, 1886.

Lettre d'un habitant de Louisbourg (à Québec, chez Guillaume le Sincère, à l'image de la Vérite, 1745).

Lettres édifiantes et curieuses écrites des Missions (Paris, 1781). *Missions d'Amérique*, vols. VI-IX.

Lévis, Gaston-François, Chevalier de, *Collection des manuscrits du Maréchal de Lévis*, ed. by the Abbé H. R. Casgrain (Montreal and Quebec, 1889-95). 12 vols. Each volume has its own title. The following are the most important: *Journal des campagnes du Chevalier de Lévis en Canada de 1756-1760; Lettres du marquis de Montcalm au chevalier de Lévis* (Quebec, 1894); and *Journal du Marquis de Montcalm durant ses campagnes au Canada de 1756 à 1759* (Quebec, 1895).

Lévis, Gaston-François, *Journal du Chevalier de Lévis* (Quebec, 1889).

Lévis, Gaston-François, *Lettres du Chevalier de Lévis* (Quebec, 1889).

Louisbourg in 1745: the anonymous *Lettre d'un habitant de Louisbourg*, ed. with an English translation by G. W. Wrong (Toronto, 1897). Contains a narrative by an eye-witness of the siege of 1745.

Malartic, Hippolyte de Maurès, comte de, *Journal des campagnes en Canada, de 1755 à 1760* (Paris, 1890).

Mandements, lettres pastorales et circulaires des Evêques de Québec (Quebec, 1887). 2 vols.

Marchand, Abbé Etienne, *Les Troubles de l'Eglise en Canada en 1728* (Lévis, 1897).

Massicotte, E. Z., *Arrêts, édits, ordonnances, mandements et règlements conservés dans les Archives du Palais de Justice de Montréal, 1653-1725* (Montreal, 1919).

Mémoires des Commissaires du Roi et de ceux de sa Majesté Britannique sur les possessions et les droits respectifs des deux couronnes en Amérique (Paris, 1755-57). 4 vols.

Mémoires et Documents pour servir à l'histoire des origines françaises des pays d'Outre-Mer. Découvertes et établissements, des Français dans l'Ouest et dans le Sud de l'Amérique Septentrionale, ed. by Pierre Margry (Paris, 1879-88). 6 vols.

Memorials of the English and French commissaries concerning the limits of Nova Scotia or Acadia (London, 1756). 2 vols.

Montcalm, Louis Joseph, *Journal du marquis de Montcalm* (Quebec, 1894).

Montcalm, Louis Joseph, *Lettres du marquis de Montcalm* (Quebec, 1894). 2 vols.

Moreau de Saint-Méry, *Lois et Constitutions des colonies françoises de l'Amérique sous le vent* (Paris, 1784). 5 vols.

Navières, Joseph, "Lettres inédites du missionaire Joseph Navières sur le Canada," ed. by Drapeyron in *Revue de Géographie* (Février 1895).

Nouvelle-France, documents historiques. Correspondance échangée entre les autorités françaises et les gouverneurs et intendants (Quebec, 1893). The only volume published. The documents are not well chosen, and their sources are not indicated.

Nova Scotia Historical Society Collection, I, *Journal of Colonel John Nicholson; Diary of John Thomas;* II, *Brown's Papers;* III and IV, *Colonel Wilson's Journal.*

Nova Scotia, *Selections from the Public Documents of the Province of Nova Scotia*, Nova Scotia Archives I, ed. by T. B. Akins (Halifax, 1869).

Ordonnances, Commissions, etc., des Gouverneurs et Intendants de la Nouvelle-France, 1639-1700, ed. by P. G. Roy (Beauceville, 1924). 2 vols.

Panet, J. C., *Journal du Siège de Québec* (Montreal, 1860).

Pichon, Thomas, *Lettres et mémoires pour servir à l'histoire naturelle, civile et politique du Cap-Breton, depuis son établissement jusqu'à la reprise de cette île par les Anglais en 1758* (La Haye, 1760).

Pièces et documents relatifs à la tenure seigneuriale (Quebec, 1854). 2 vols.

Pitt, William, *Correspondence of William Pitt with Colonial Governors*, ed. by Gertrude S. Kimball (New York, 1906). 2 vols.

Pouchot, Pierre, *Mémoires sur la dernière guerre de l'Amérique Septentrionale, entre la France et l'Angleterre* (Yverdon, 1781). 3 vols.

Pradals, Guillaume de, *Un Cadet de Gascogne au Canada. Sept lettres du lieutenant Guillaume de Méritens de Pradals* (Société ariègeoise des Sciences, Lettres et Arts. Foix, 1931).

Proposals for uniting the English Colonies on the Continent of America so as to enable them to act with Force and Vigour against their Enemies (London, 1757).

Reports of the Public Archives of Canada, 1882-1960. These reports contain a number of documents as well as tables of contents of the most important French and English collections in the Archives.

Rapports de l'archiviste de la province de Québec, 1922-1963. This collection contains a great deal of historical material of prime importance.

Raymond, Chevalier de, "Mémoire sur les postes du Canada, 1754," *R.A.Q.*, 1927-28.

Canada Census, 1871, vol. IV. Contains statistical information on the French period.

Récher, Abbé, "Journal du siège de Québec, 1759," *Vie Française*, vol. XIII.

Régne militaire en Canada. Mémoires de la Société historique de Montréal (Montreal, 1870).

Relation par lettres de l'Amérique Septentrionale, ed. by Father C. de Rochemonteix (Paris, 1940). Attributed by the editor to R. P. Sylvy, this relation was drawn up by the intendant Antoine Raudot and is based on contemporary memoirs.

Relations et Journaux de différentes expéditions faites durant les années 1755 à 1760 (Quebec, 1855).

A Scheme to Drive the French out of All the Continent of America (London, 1754).

Shirley, William, *Correspondence of William Shirley, Governor of Massachusetts and Military Commander in America, 1713-1760*, ed. by C. H. Lincoln (New York, 1912). 2 vols.

Stobo, Robert, *Memoirs of Major R. Stobo* (London, 1800).

Stobo, Robert, "Procès de Robert Stobo et de Jacob Van Bram," *R.A.Q.*, 1922-23.

Sulte, Benjamin, "Le Régime militaire 1760-1764," *R.S.C.*, vol. XI.

Les Ursulines de Québec depuis leur établissement jusqu'à nos jours (Quebec, 1863-66). 3 vols.

Les Ursulines de Trois Rivières (1888-1892). 2 vols.

Vezon, Joseph Fournerie de, "Evénements de la guerre en Canada," *R.A.Q.*, 1938-39.

Vienne, François Joseph, "Journal du Siège de Québec, 1759," *R.A.Q.*, 1922-23.

Winslow, Colonel J., *Journal of the Expulsion of the Acadians*. Nova Scotia Historical Society III (Halifax, 1883).

PRINCIPAL SECONDARY SOURCES

Ahern, M. J. and Georges Ahern, *Notes pour servie à l'histoire de la médecine dans le Bas-Canada depuis la fondation de Québec jusqu'au commencement du XIXᵉ siècle* (Quebec, 1925).

America: including Canada, Newfoundland, the British West Indies and the Falkland Islands and Dependencies, ed. by A. J. Herbertson and J.O.R. Howard, *Oxford Survey of the British Empire*, vol. IV (Oxford, 1914).

Anon., *The Private Life of Louis XV* (London, 1781). 4 vols.

Arnoux, Laffrey, *Le Siècle de Louis XV* (Paris, 1796).

Aubert de Gaspé, Philippe, *Les Anciens Canadiens* (Quebec, 1863).

Baby, L.F.G., *L'Exode des classes dirigeantes à la cession du Canada* (Montreal, 1899).

Bailey, Kenneth P.,*The Ohio Company of Virginia and the Westward Movement, 1748-1792* (Glendale, 1939).

Baker, Charlotte Alice, *True Stories of New England Captives carried to Canada during the old French and Indian Wars* (Cambridge, Mass., 1897).

Barbier, *Chroniques de la Régence et du règne de Louis XV, Journal de Barbier* (Paris, 1866).

Barbier, Alfred, *Un Munitionnaire du roi à la Nouvelle-France, Joseph Cadet, 1756-1781*. Société des Antiquaires de l'Ouest, 2nd series, vol. XX (Poitiers, 1899).

Bernard, Antoine, *Le Drame Acadien depuis 1604* (Montreal, 1936).

Bonnault, Claude de, "Le Canada militaire, Etat provisoire des officiers de milice, 1641-1760," *Rapport de l'archiviste de la province de Québec*, 1949-51.

Bonnault, Claude de, *Histoire du Canada français, 1534-1763* (Paris, 1950).

Broglie, Duc de, *La Paix d'Aix-la-Chapelle* (Paris, 1892).

Brebner, J. B., *New England's Outpost. Acadia before the Conquest of Canada* (New York, 1927).

Broadhead, John Romeyn, *History of the State of New York* (New York, 1859).

Bulletin des Recherches historiques (Lévis, 1895-1961).

Burpee, Lawrence J., *The Search for the Western Sea* (Toronto, 1908).

Burt, A. L., *The Old Province of Quebec* (Minneapolis, 1935).

Campeau, R. P. Lucien, "Le Jansénisme en Nouvelle-France," *Analecta Gregoriana*, vol. LXXI.

Campbell, G. G., *The History of Nova Scotia* (Toronto, 1948).

Canada and its Provinces, ed. by Adam Shortt and Arthur Doughty (Toronto, 1917). vol. II.

Caron, Abbé Ivanhoé, *La Colonisation de la Province de Québec* (Quebec, 1923-27). 2 vols.

Caron, Abbé Ivanhoé, *La Colonisation du Canada sous la domination française* (Quebec, 1916).

Casgrain, Abbé H. R., *Guerre du Canada, 1756-60, Montcalm et Lévis* (Quebec, 1891). 2 vols.

Casgrain, Abbé H. R., *Un Pélerinage au pays d'Evangéline* (Quebec, 1888).
Casgrain, Abbé H. R., *L'Ile Saint-Jean-Ile du Prince-Edouard, sous le régime français. Une seconde Acadie* (Quebec, 1894).
Catalogue of pictures, including paintings, drawings and prints in the Public Archives, ed. by J. F. Kenney (Ottawa, 1925).
Chapais, Thomas, *Le Marquis de Montcalm* (Quebec, 1911).
Charland, Thomas Marie, *Historie de Saint-François-du-Lac* (Ottawa, 1942).
Charlevoix, R. P., *Histoire et description générale de la Nouvelle-France* (Paris, 1744). 3 vols.
Colby, Charles William, *Canadian Types of the Old Régime* (New York, 1908).
Concise Account of all the British Colonies in North America (London, 1775).
Crouse, Nillis M., *La Vérendrye, Fur Trader and Explorer* (Ithaca, N.Y., 1956).
Cugnet, F. J., *Traité de la Loi des fiefs, qui a toujours été suivie en Canada depuis son établissement, etc.* (Quebec, 1775).
Daniel, François, *Histoire des grandes familles françaises au Canada* (Montreal, 1867).
Debien, G., "Liste des engagés pour le Canada au XVIIe siècle," *Revue d'histoire de l'Amérique française* (Décembre 1952).
Delalande, J., *Le Conseil souverain de la Nouvelle-France* (Quebec, 1927).
De Longchamps, *Histoire impartiale de la dernière guerre* (Paris, 1888).
Desrosiers, Léo-Paul, *Iroquoisie* (Montreal, 1947).
Dionne, N. E., "Inventaire chronologique des livres publiés dans la province de Québec," *Cahiers des Dix*, vol. V, 1940.
Dussieux, L., *Le Canada sous la domination française* (Paris, 1855).
Eastman, Mack, *Church and State in Early Canada* (Edinburgh, 1915).
Fauteux, Aegidius, "Le S . . . de C . . . enfin démasqué," *Cahiers des Dix*, vol. V, 1940.
Ferland, Abbé J. B., *Cours d'histoire du Canada* (Quebec, 1861-65). 2 vols.
Ferrière, Claude de, *Dictionnaire de droit et de pratique* (Paris, 1755). 2 vols.
Fauteux, Noel, *Essai sur l'industrie au Canada sous le régime français* (Quebec, 1927). 2 vols.
Filteau, Gérard, *La Naissance d'une nation, Tableau du Canada en 1755* (Montreal, 1937).
Fiske, John, *New France and New England* (Boston & New York, 1902).
Frégault, Guy, *La Civilisation de la Nouvelle-France, 1715-1744* (Montreal, 1944).
Frégault, Guy, "La Colonisation du Canada," *Cahiers de l'Académie canadienne française* (Montreal, 1957).
Frégault, Guy, "La Déportation des Acadiens," *R.H.A.F.*, Décembre 1954.
Frégault, Guy, *François Bigot* (Montreal, 1948). 2 vols.
Frégault, Guy, *Le Grand Marquis* (Montreal, 1952).
Frégault, Guy, "Politique et politiciens au début du XVIIIe siècle," *Ecrits du Canada français* (Montreal, 1961).
Gabriel, Charles Nicolas, *Le Maréchal de camp Désandrouins, 1729-1792, guerre du Canada, 1756-60; guerre de l'indépendance américaine, 1780-1782* (Verdun, 1887).
Gagnon, Philéas, *Essai de bibliographie canadienne* (Quebec, 1895 and Montreal, 1913).
Garneau, F. X., *Histoire du Canada* (Paris, 1920). 2 vols.
Gaucher, Delafosse et Debien, "Les Engagés pour le Canada au XVIIIe," *R.H.A.F.*, vol. XIII, 1959-60.
Gaudet, Placide, "The Acadian Fugitives," *The New Brunswick Magazine* (January, 1899).
Gaxotte, Pierre, *La France de Louis XIV* (Paris, 1946).
Gaxotte, Pierre, *Le Siècle de Louis XV* (Paris, 1958).
Gipson, L. H., *Zones of International Friction, North America* (New York, 1954). vol. V, VI, VII.
Giraud, Marcel, *Histoire de la Louisiane française* (Paris, 1953-58). 2 vols.
Godwin, William, *The History of the Life of William Pitt, Earl of Chatham* (London, 1783).
Gosselin, Abbé Amédée, *L'Instruction au Canada sous le régime français* (Quebec, 1911).
Gosselin, Abbé Auguste, *L'Eglise au Canada depuis Mgr de Laval jusqu'à la conquête* (Quebec, 1911-14). 3 vols.
Graham, Gerald, *The Empire of the North Atlantic* (Toronto, 1950).
Graham, Gerald, *The Walker Expedition to Quebec, 1711* (Toronto, 1953).

Grant, W. L., "Canada versus Guadeloupe," *The American Historical Review* (July, 1912).
Groulx, Abbé Lionel, *La Naissance d'une race* (Montreal, 1920).
Groulx, Chanoine Lionel, *Notre belle aventure* (Montreal, 1958).
Groulx, Chanoine Lionel, *Histoire du Canada* (Montreal, 1950-52). 4 vols.
Groulx, Abbé Lionel, *Lendemains de conquête* (Montreal, 1920).
Hamelin, Jean, *Economie et Société en Nouvelle-France* (Quebec, 1960).
Hammang, F. H. *Le Marquis de Vaudreuil* (Bruges, 1938).
Harvey, D. C., *The French in Prince Edward Island* (New Haven, 1926).
Histoire des colonies françaises et de l'expansion de la France dans le monde, ed. by Gabriel Hanotaux and Alfred Martineau. Volume *L'Amérique* by Ch. de la Roncière, J. Tramond, E. Lauvrière and A. Martineau.
Hutchinson, T., *The History of the Colony of Massachusetts Bay* (London, 1765). Second edition.
Innis, H. A., *The Fur Trade in Canada* (New Haven, 1930).
Innis, H. A., *An Introduction to Canadian Economic History, Being the History of the Fur Trade in Canada* (New Haven, 1929).
Innis, Mary Quayle, *An Economic History of Canada* (Toronto, 1935).
Jefferys, T., *The Natural and Civil History of the French Dominions in North and South America* (London, 1760).
Kenney, James F., "The Career of Henry Kelsey," *R.S.C.*, 1929.
Kerallain, René de, *Les Français au Canada. La jeunesse de Bougainville et la guerre de Sept Ans* (Nogent-sur-Rotrou, 1896).
Kingsford, William, *History of Canada* (Toronto, 1887-98). 10 vols.
Labignette, J. E., "Recherches en Suisse sur François Bigot," *R.A.Q.*
Lacour-Gayet, *La Marine militaire sous le règne de Louis XV* (Paris, 1902).
Lanctot, Gustave, "Le Dernier effort de la France au Canada," *R.S.C.*, 1918.
Lanctot, Gustave, *Situation politique de l'Eglise canadienne* (Montreal, 1942).
Lanctot, Gustave, *L'Administration de la Nouvelle-France. L'Administration générale* (Paris, 1929).
Langlois, Georges, *Histoire de la population canadienne française* (Montreal, 1935).
La Roncière, Charles de, *Histoire de la Marine française* (Paris, 1910). 5 vols.
Laut, Agnes, *The Fur Trade of America* (New York, 1921).
Lauvrière, Emile, *La Tragédie d'un peuple. Histoire du peuple Acadien de ses origines à nos jours* (Paris, 1922). 2 vols.
Leblant, Robert, *Un Colonial sous Louis XIV: Philippe Pastour de Costebelle* (Dax, 1935).
Le Jeune, Father Louis-Marie, *Dictionnaire générale de biographie, histoire, littérature, agriculture, industrie, commerce et des arts, sciences, mœurs, coutumes, institutions religieuses et politiques du Canada* (Ottawa, 1931). 2 vols.
Leduc, Gilbert, *Washington and the Murder of Jumonville* (Boston, 1935).
Long, Morden Heaton, *A History of the Canadian People* (Toronto, 1942).
Malchelosse, Gérard, "Faux-Sauniers, prisonniers et fils de famille en Nouvelle-France," *Cahiers des Dix*, 1944.
Malchelosse, Gérard, "Fils de famille en Nouvelle-France," *Cahiers des Dix*, vol. XI, 1946.
Mante, Thomas, *An Impartial History of the Late Glorious War from its Commencement to its conclusion* (London, 1769).
Martin, Ernest, *Les Exilés Acadiens en France au XVIIIe siècle et leur etablissement en Poitou* (Paris, 1936).
Massicotte, E. Z., "Contributions à la petite histoire," *Cahiers des Dix*, vol. IX, 1944.
Maupassant, J. de, *Un Grand armateur de Bordeaux, Abraham Gradis (1699-1780)* (Bordeaux, 1917).
McLennan, J. S., *Louisbourg from its Foundation to its Fall, 1713-58* (London, 1918).
Mémoire contenant le précis des faits avec leurs pièces justificatives pour servir de réponse aux observations envoyées par les ministres d'Angleterre dans les cours d'Europe (Paris, 1756).
Mémoire historique sur la négociation de la France et de l'Angleterre depuis le 26 mars 1761 jusqu'au 20 septembre de la même année (Paris, 1761).
Mémoires des commissaires du Roi et de ceux de Sa Majesté Britannique sur les

possessions et les droits respectifs des deux couronnes en Amérique (Paris, 1755-57). 4 vols.

Moreton, W. L., *The Kingdom of Canada. A General History from earliest times* (Toronto, 1963).

Murdoch, Beamish, *A History of Nova Scotia, or Acadia* (Halifax, 1865-67). 3 vols.

Newton, A. P., "Newfoundland," Chapter V, *The Cambridge History of the British Empire*, vol. VI (London, 1930).

North America: Canada and Newfoundland, ed. by H. M. Ami, *Stanford's Compendium of Geography and Travel*, vol. L (London, 1915).

Pargellis, Stanley, "Braddock's Defeat," *The American Historical Review*, vol. XXI, 1936.

Parkman, F. A., *Pioneers of France in the New World* (Boston, 1897). 2 vols.

Parkman, F. A., *A Half-Century of Conflict* (Toronto, 1898). 2 vols.

Parkman, F. A., *The Old Régime in Canada* (Boston, 1902).

Penhallow, S., *History of the Wars of New England with the Eastern Indians* (Boston, 1726). New edition 1859.

Prowse, Daniel Woodley, *A History of Newfoundland* (London, 1895).

Reasons for keeping Guadaloupe at a Peace, preferable to Canada, explained in five letters from a Gentleman in Guadaloupe to his friend in London (London, 1761).

Sainte-Croix, Guilhem, G. E. J. de Clermont Lodève, Baron de, *Observations sur le traité de paix conclu à Paris, le 10 février 1763, entre la France, L'Espagne et l'Angleterre* (Amsterdam, 1780).

Salone, Emile, *La Colonisation de la Nouvelle-France. Etude sur les origines de la nation canadienne française* (Paris, 1906).

Sargent, Winthrop, *The History of an Expedition against Fort Duquesne in 1755*.

Savelle, Max, *The Diplomatic History of the Canadian Boundary, 1749-1763* (New Haven, 1940).

Schone, *Le Politique Coloniale sous Louis XV et Louis XVI* (Paris, 1907).

Seely, J. R., *The Expansion of England* (London, 1900).

Smith, Philip H., *Acadia. A Lost Chapter of American History* (New York, 1889).

Smith, William, *The History of New York* (Albany, 1914).

Stacey, C. P., "The Anse au Foulon, 1759: Montcalm and Vaudreuil," *Canadian Historical Review* (March, 1959).

Stryenski, *Le Dix-huitième Siècle* (1913).

Sulte, Benjamin, *Les Forges Saint-Maurice*, ed. by Gérard Malchelosse (Montreal, 1920).

Tanguay, Abbé Cyprien, *Dictionnaire généalogique des familles canadiennes depuis la fondation de la colonie jusqu'à nos jours* (Montreal, 1871-90). 7 vols.

Taurines, Gailly de, *La Nation canadienne* (Paris, 1894).

Tessier, Abbé Albert, *Les Trois-Rivières, Quatre siècles d'histoire, 1535-1955* (Trois Rivières, 1954).

Tocqueville, Alexis de, *L'Ancien Régime et la Révolution* (Paris, 1887).

Tramond, Joannès, *Manuel d'histoire maritime* (Paris, 1915).

Traquair, Ramsay, *The Old Architecture of Quebec* (Toronto, 1947).

Trotter, R. G., *Canadian History: A Syllabus and Guide to Reading* (Toronto, 1926).

Trudel, Marcel, *L'Esclavage au Canada* (Quebec, 1960).

Vachon, André, *Histoire du notariat canadien* (Quebec, 1962).

Rameau de Saint-Père, *Une Colonie féodale en Amérique. L'Acadie, 1604-1881* (Paris, 1889).

Rameau de Saint-Père, *La France aux Colonies* (Paris, 1859).

Reid, Allana G., "The Nature of Quebec Society during the French Régime," *Canadian Historical Association Report*, 1951.

Reid, Allana G., "General Trade between Quebec and France during the French Regime," *Canadian Historical Review*, March, 1953.

Renaud, Paul-Emile, *Les Origines économiques du Canada* (Mamers, 1928).

Rich, E. E., *The History of the Hudson's Bay Company*, vol. I (London, 1958-60). 3 vols.

Richard, Edouard, *Acadie* (Quebec, 1916-21). 3 vols.

Rochemonteix, Father Camille de, *Les Jésuites et la Nouvelle-France au XVIIIe siècle* (Paris, 1906). 2 vols.

Rogers, J. D., *Newfoundland*, vol. V, *Historical Geography of the British Colonies* (Oxford, 1911).

Roquebrune, Robert La Roque de, "La Guerre et l'amour au Canada d'autrefois,"
    Les Cahiers reflets, no. 6 (Trois Rivières, 1945).
Roquebrune, Robert La Roque de, Les Canadiens d'autrefois (Montreal, 1962).
Roquebrune, Robert La Roque de, "Uniformes et drapeaux des régiments au
    Canada sous Louis XIV et Louis XV," Revue de l'Université d'Ottawa, juillet
    et septembre 1950.
Roy, Antoine, Les Lettres, les sciences et les arts au Canada sous le régime
    français (Paris, 1930).
Roy, Joseph Edmond, Histoire de la seigneurie de Lauzon (Lévis, 1897-1904). 3
    vols.
Roy, Joseph Edmond, "Des fils de famille envoyés au Canada," R.S.C. (Ottawa,
    1901).
Roy, Joseph Edmond, "Les Intendants de la Nouvelle-France," R.S.C. (Ottawa,
    1903).
Roy, Pierre Georges, Les Petites Choses de notre histoire (Lévis, 1919-25). 5 vols.
Roy, Pierre Georges, Bigot et sa bande et l'affaire du Canada (Lévis, 1950).
Waddington, Richard, La Guerre de Sept Ans (Paris, 1899-1919). 5 vols.
Wallace, W. Stewart, The Dictionary of Canadian Biography (Toronto).
Williams, Catherine, Neutral French exiled from Nova Scotia (Providence, R.I.,
    1841).
Wood, William, The Fight for Canada (London, 1905).
Wrong, G. M., The Rise and Fall of New France (London, 1928). 2 vols.
Wrong, G. M., A Canadian Manor and its Seigneurs (Toronto, 1908).

MAP SOURCES

An Historical Atlas (Toronto, 1927). Edited with an introduction, notes and
    chronological tables, by L. J. Burpee.
Canada: Atlas déscriptif (Ottawa, 1951).
Cartes Maritimes, à la substitution de Valdec, 1727 (The Newberry Library,
    Chicago).
Dumas, Paul E., Cartes géographiques du XVIIIe siècle relatives au Canada
    (Map Division, Public Archives, Ottawa).
Fite, E. D., and Freeman, A., A Book of Old Maps Delineating American History
    from the Earliest Days (Cambridge, 1926).
Kerr, D.G.G., An Historical Atlas of Canada (Toronto, 1961).
List of Manuscript Maps in the Edward E. Ayers Collection (Newberry Library,
    Chicago). Compiled by Clara A. Smith, 1927.
Marcel, Gabriel, Cartographie de la Nouvelle-France (Paris, 1885).
Pinart, A. L., Receuil de cartes, plans et vues relatifs aux Etats-Unis et au
    Canada (Paris, 1893).
Sixteenth Century Maps Relating to Canada: A Check-List and Bibliography,
    with introduction by T. E. Laing (Ottawa, Public Archives of Canada, 1956).
Trudel, Marcel, Atlas historique du Canada français, des origines à 1867 (Quebec,
    1961).

NOTES

ABBREVIATIONS USED

Arch. Can.	Public Archives of Canada
Arch. Col.	Colonial Archives (France)
Arch. Nat.	National Archives (France)
Biblio. Nat.	Bibliothèque Nationale (Paris)
B. R. H.	Bulletin des Recherches historiques
Col. Mss.	Collection de manuscrits contentant lettres, mémoires et autres documents historiques relatifs à la Nouvelle-France
Corr. Pol.	Political Correspondence, Public Archives of Canada
Courville. Memoires	Mémoires de S. . . de C. . .
Docts. N.Y.	Documents relating to the Colonial History of the State of New York
Edits et Ord.	Edits et ordonnances royaux
Jug. et Del.	Jugements et Déliberations du Conseil
N.S.	Nova Scotia State Papers
Ordonnances	Ordonnances, commissions, etc. des gouverneurs et intendants de la Nouvelle-France
R. A. C.	Report of the Canadian Archives Rapport des Archives canadiennes
R. A. Q.	Rapport de l'archiviste de la province de Québec
R. S. C.	Proceedings and Transactions of the Royal Society of Canada
R. H. A. F.	Revue d'histoire de l'Amérique française
Relations	Jesuit Relations (The figure which follows indicates the date of the Relation to which the note refers.)

CHAPTER I

1 *Rapport de l'archiviste de la province de Québec*, 1947-48, "Pontchartrain à Vaudreuil, 31 mai 1713," p. 204; "Vaudreuil à Pontchartrain, 14 novembre 1713," p. 232; "Vaudreuil à Pontchartrain, 16 septembre 1714," p. 270. *Rapport des Archives canadiennes*, 1889, "MM. Raudot à Potchartrain, 4 novembre 1709," p. 213. Augustin-Thierry, *Un Colonial du temps de Colbert, Mémoires de Robert Challes, écrivain du roi* (Paris, 1931).

2 B, 34, *Pontchartrain à Mme de Vaudreuil, 24 avril 1712*, fol. 2; *Pontchartrain à Ramezay, 9 juin 1706*, fol. 68. *R.A.Q.*, 1947-48, "Pontchartrain à Vaudreuil, 4 juin 1713," p. 227; "Vaudreuil et Bégon au Conseil de Marine, 14 octobre 1716," p. 316. *Documents relating to Canadian Currency, Exchange and Finance during the French Period*, ed. by Adam Shortt (Ottawa, 1925) I, n. pp. 128 and 142. B, 27, *Pontchartrain à Ramezay, 17 juin 1705*, fol. 53½.

3 *R.A.Q.*, 1947-48, "Mémoire du roi à Vaudreuil et Bégon, 15 juin 1716," p. 296. B, 13, *Pontchartrain à Lubert, 28 février 1687*, fol. 8. The two major sources of information on this question are M. Guy Frégault, "Essai sur les finances canadiennes," in the *Revue d'histoire de l'Amérique française* (décembre 1958-septembre 1959) and the *Documents* . . . , ed. by Shortt, already cited.

4 "Frontenac à de Lagny, 2 novembre 1695," in Shortt, *op. cit.* I, p. 100.

5 *Ibid.*, "Ordonnance de De Meulles, 8 juin 1685," pp. 68-70; "Ordonnance de Nicolas Dupont, 9 février 1686," pp. 73-75; "Extrait des reponses aux lettres, année 1686," p. 78.

6 *Ibid.*, "Ordonnance de Champigny, 7 janvier 1691," p. 80; "Champigny à Pontchartrain, 10 mai 1691," p. 94; "Champigny à Pontchartrain, 20 octobre

1699," pp. 100-02; "Frontenac et Champigny à Pontchartrain, 26 octobre 1696,"
p. 102; "Pontchartrain à Champigny, 27 mai 1699," pp. 104-06.
    7 *Ibid.*, "Champigny à Pontchartrain, 15 octobre 1700," p. 104; "Mémoire
du roi à Vaudreuil et Beauharnois, 14 juin 1704," p. 126; ". . . 9 juin 1706," p. 154;
"Ramezay à Pontchartrain, 12 octobre 1705," pp. 140-42; "Ordonnance de Raudot,
24 octobre 1705," pp. 144-46.
    8 *Ibid.*, "Pontchartrain à Raudot, 6 juin 1708," p. 178; "Raudot à Pont-
chartrain, 22 octobre 1710," p. 204; "Etat de la nouvelle monnaie de cartes 1710,"
pp. 206-10; "Emission du premier octobre 1711," pp. 210-12; "Mémoire sur le
Canada (1711)," pp. 214-16; "Pontchartrain à Vaudreuil et Raudot, 26 juin
1712," pp. 212-20; "Monnaie de cartes, Historique, 12 avril 1717," p. 384.
    9 *Ibid.*, "Conseil, 3 juillet 1713," p. 238; "Le Ministre à Vaudreuil et Bégon,
23 mai 1714," pp. 266-68.
    10 *Ibid.*, p. 266.
    11 *Ibid.*, "Lettre à M. de Nointel, 8 janvier 1715," p. 286; "Vaudreuil à
Pontchartrain, 16 septembre 1714," p. 272.   *R.A.Q.*, 1947-48, "Vaudreuil à
Pontchartrain, 20 septembre 1714," p. 277.
    12 Shortt, *op. cit.*, "Canada, Monnaie de cartes, 12 mai 1716," I, p. 350;
". . . à Desmaretz, 8 juillet 1716," p. 298; "Mémoire de Vaudreuil, février 1716,"
p. 340; "Monnaie de cartes, Historique, 12 avril 1717," p. 384; "Déclaration du
Roi, 5 juillet 1717," pp. 398-400; "Projet du mémoire du Roi, 5 juillet 1717," pp.
392-96.
    13 *Ibid.*, "Ordonnance du Roi, 12 juillet 1718," pp. 442-44; "Ordonnance
de Vaudreuil et Bégon, 1er novembre 1718," p. 450; "Mémoire du Roi à Vaudreuil
et Bégon, 23 mai 1719," p. 460.
    14 *Ibid.*, "Vaudreuil au Conseil, 31 octobre 1717," pp. 416-18.   C11A, 44,
*Estat abrégé de toute la monnaie de cartes fabriquée au Canada . . . depuis 1702
jusqu'en 1717.*   C11G, 8, *Lettres aux Trésoriers de la Marine, 2 juin 1728*,
fol. 172.
    15 *Edits et ordonnances royaux*, I, "Arrêt et Déclaration du Roi concernant
la Régence du Royaume, 12 septembre 1715," pp. 348-49.   *R.A.Q.*, 1947-48,
"Le Conseil de Marine à Vaudreuil et Bégon, 3 novembre 1715," pp. 289-90.
    15a C11A, 33, *Mémoire touchant le droit français, 12 novembre 1712*, p.
440.   *R.A.Q.*, 1947-48, "Vaudreuil à Pontchartrain, 14 novembre 1713," p.
231; "Vaudreuil à Pontchartrain, 16 septembre 1714," p. 203; "Vaudreuil au
Conseil de Marine, 14 octobre 1716," p. 330.
    16 *R.A.Q.*, 1947-48, "Vaudreuil à Pontchartrain, 16 septembre 1714," p. 264;
"Vaudreuil au duc d'Orléans, février 1716," p. 293.
    17 *Ibid.*, "Vaudreuil au Conseil de Marine, 14 octobre 1716," p. 330; "Mé-
moire du Roi à Vaudreuil et Bégon, 15 juin 1716," p. 300; "Vaudreuil à Pontchartrain, 8 septembre 1713," p. 229; "Vaudreuil à Pontchartrain, 11 septembre
1714," p. 265.
    18 *Ibid.*, "Vaudreuil au Conseil de Marine, 14 octobre 1716," pp. 327-29.
    19 C11A, 36, *Louvigny rend compte de sa campagne contre les Renards, 14
octobre 1716*, pp. 159-61.   C11A, 38, *Louvigny au Conseil de Marine, 21
septembre 1717*, pp. 171-76; *Vaudreuil, 12 octobre 1717*, pp. 91-94.
    20 *R.A.Q.*, 1947-48, "Vaudreuil au duc d'Orléans, février 1716," pp. 291-92;
"Le Ministre à Vaudreuil et Bégon, 16 juin 1716," p. 310; "Mémoire du Roi à
Vaudreuil et Bégon, 15 juin 1716," p. 300.
    21 C11A, 38, *Vaudreuil au Conseil de Marine, 17 octobre 1717*, pp. 107-10.

CHAPTER II

    1 *Edits et ordonnances royaux*, III, "Commission de Bégon, 31 mars 1712,"
p. 63.   C11A, 34, *Bégon à Pontchartrain, 12 novembre 1714*, pp. 383-98.
    2 B, 37-3, *Pontchartrain à Bégon, 13 juillet 1715*, pp. 772-74; *Pontchartrain
à Bégon, 16 juin 1716*, fol. 386.   *Documents relating to Canadian Currency,
Exchange and Finance during the French Period*, ed. by Adam Shortt (Ottawa,
1925) vol. I, n. pp. 230-32.
    3 C11A, 37, *Le Conseil de Marine, 19 janvier 1717*, p. 41; *Le Conseil de
Marine, 31 août 1717*, p. 381.
    3a B,30, *Le Ministre à Bégon, 10 janvier 1709*, fol. 180.   *Rapport de
l'archiviste de la province de Québec*, 1947-48, "Pontchartrain à Vaudreuil, et
Bégon, 8 juin 1713," p. 205; "Pontchartrain à Vaudreuil, 7 juillet 1712," p. 156.

3b Shortt, *op. cit.*, n. p. 192.   *R.A.Q.*, 1947-48, "Pontchartrain à Vaudreuil, 18 mai 1717," p. 355.   C¹¹A, 37, *Déliberations du Conseil de Marine, 7 décembre 1714*, p. 457.   C¹¹A, 124, *Sorties du Canada en 1722*, pp. 117-18.

3c C¹¹A, 36, *Nouvelle Régie des Castors, 1716*, p. 433; *Au Roi et à Nos Seigneurs de son Conseil, 1716*, p. 442.   B, 39, *Le Conseil de Marine à Vaudreuil et Bégon, 14 juillet 1717*, fol. 257.

4 C¹¹A, 36, p. 437.   F³, 7, *Ordonnance du roi au sujet des boissons, 20 juin 1707*, fol. 81.   *R.A.Q.*, 1947-48, "Mémoire du roi à Vaudreuil et Bégon, 15 juin 1716," p. 299.   C¹¹A, 29, *Rapport d'Aigremont, 14 novembre 1708*, pp. 97-98.   *R.A.Q.*, 1947-48, "Vaudreuil et Bégon au ministre, 20 septembre 1714," p. 276; "Mémoire du Sieur de la Potherie," p. 340.

4a C¹¹A, 41, *Vaudreuil et Bégon au Conseil de Marine, 26 octobre 1716*, p.5.

5 *R.A.Q.*, 1947-48, "Vaudreuil et Bégon au ministre, 20 septembre 1714," pp. 274-75; "Vaudreuil à Pontchartrain, 16 septembre 1714," p. 264.   F³, 6, *Déclaration du roi portant défense d'aller en traite, juin 1703*, fol. 335.

6 *Edits et Ord.*, I, "Edit du roi portant défense de faire le Commerce et le transport des Castors chez les Etrangers, 6 juillet 1709," p. 320.   C¹¹A, 27, *Riverin, 11 août 1707*, p. 82.   *R.A.Q.*, 1938-39, "Pontchartrain à Vaudreuil, 6 juillet 1706," p. 120.   C¹¹A, 29, *Avis de Montréal*, p. 118.   C¹¹A, 34, *Bégon à Pontchartrain, 12 novembre 1714*, pp. 381-404.   *R.A.Q.*, 1947-48, "Vaudreuil à Pontchartrain, 16 septembre 1714," p. 264; "Mémoire du roi à Vaudreuil et Bégon, 15 juin 1712," p. 143; "Vaudreuil au Conseil de la Marine, 14 octobre 1716," p. 332.

7 *R.A.Q.*, 1947-48, "Pontchartrain à Vaudreuil, 15 juin 1716," p. 306.   C¹¹A, 34, *Procès-verbal, 4 juin 1714*, p. 518.   F³, 8, *Délibération du Conseil de Marine, 18 octobre 1719*, fol. 95.

8 *R.A.Q.*, 1947-48, "Mémoire de Vaudreuil au duc d'Orléans, février 1716," pp. 293-94; "Vaudreuil et Bégon à Pontchartrain, 20 septembre 1714," p. 285.   C¹¹A, 35, *Bégon à Pontchartrain*, n.d., p. 331.   C¹¹A, 34 *Amelot, 3 octobre 1714*, p. 495.   C¹¹A, 26, *Mémoire sur les écarlatines, 1715*, fol. 182.

9 *Edits et Ord.*, I, "Ordonnance du roi accordant une amnistie, 19 mars 1714," p. 341; "Lettres patentes en forme d'Edit portant l'amnistie, mars 1716," p. 350.   C¹¹A, 22, fol. 182.

10 *R.A.Q.*, 1947-48, "Vaudreuil, 20 septembre 1714," p. 275; "Mémoire de Vaudreuil, février 1716," p. 294.   C¹¹A, 36, *Déclaration du roi, 28 avril 1716*, fol. 46.   *R.A.Q.*, 1947-48, "Mémoire du roi à Vaudreuil et Bégon, 15 juin 1716," p. 298.   C¹¹A, 38, *Requête de Collet, 5 octobre 1717*, p. 190.   *Documents relating to the Colonial History of the State of New York*, ed. by E. B. O'Callaghan (Albany, 1855-58) vol. IX, "Observations, 1er juin 1718," p. 884.

11 Shortt, *op. cit.*, I, n. pp. 406-410.   *Edits et Ord.*, I, "Lettres patentes pour l'établissement de la Compagnie d' Occident, août 1717," pp. 377-78; "Arrêt du Conseil d'Etat du Roi, 11 juillet 1718," pp. 395-99; "Arrêt du Conseil d'Etat, 4 juin 1719," pp. 401-02.   B, 42, *Le Conseil de Marine à Vaudreuil et Bégon, 24 avril 1720*, fol. 417½.

12 *Edits et Ord.*, I, "Arrêt du Conseil du roi qui ordonne l'exécution de celui du 30 mai 1721 en faveur de la Compagnie des Indes, 28 janvier 1722," pp. 441-42.   Shortt, *op. cit.*, I, n. pp. 408-10.

13 *Edits et Ord.*, I, "Arrêt au sujet des castors, 30 mars 1726," p. 504; "Ordre du roi au sujet des Marchandises étrangères, 14 mai 1726," p. 505.   C¹¹A, 48, *octobre 1726*, fol. 321.

14 *Collection de manuscrits contenant lettres, mémoires et autres documents historiques relatifs à la Nouvelle-France* (Quebec, 1883-85) III, "Mémoire du roi à Ramezay, 10 juillet 1715," pp. 13-14.   *Docts. N.Y.*, IX "Ramezay à Bégon et Pontchartrain, 13 septembre 1715," p. 931.   C¹¹A, 36, *Ramezay et Bégon à Pontchartrain, 7 novembre 1715*, pp. 3 and 25.   *R.A.Q.*, 1947-48, "Vaudreuil au Conseil de la Marine, 17 octobre 1716," p. 330.   *Docts. N.Y.*, V, "Munster to the Lords of Trade, 7 July 1718," p. 508.   C¹¹A, 43, *Vaudreuil et Bégon au Conseil de Marine, janvier 1721*, pp. 5-8.

15 *Docts. N.Y.*, IX, "Burnett à Vaudreuil, 11 juillet 1721," p. 899.   C¹¹A, 44, *Vaudreuil à Burnett, 24 août 1721*, pp. 59-67.   C¹¹A, 38, *Vaudreuil au Conseil de Marine, 24 octobre 1717*, pp. 116-17.   William Smith, *The History of New York* (Albany, 1814) p. 244.

16 *Docts. N.Y.*, IX, "Extracts of despatches written by the Governor and Intendant of Canada, October 1721, May and October 1725, September and

October 1726," pp. 961-63; "Burnett to Beauharnois, 8 August 1727," pp. 970-72. C¹¹A, 49, *Beauharnois à Burnett, 20 juillet 1727*, pp. 219-22; *Réponse au mémoire de Sa Majesté Britannique au sujet du fort de Niagara, 1727*, pp. 226-45; *Mémoire sur Niagara au cardinal Fleury, 9 mai 1727*, pp. 250-56; *Réponse au mémoire et lettres de Walpole au sujet du fort de Niagara*, pp. 264-87.

16a *R.A.Q.*, 1947-48, "Mémoire du roi à Vaudreuil et Bégon, 25 juin 1713," p. 214; "Pontchartrain à Vaudreuil, 15 juin 1716," p. 306.   Gustave Lanctot, *Situation politique de l'Eglise canadienne* (Montreal, 1942) *passim.*   *Edits et Ord.*, I, "Lettres patentes qui permettent à la supérieure de l'Hôpital Général de Québec de recevoir dix religieuses, avril 1720," p. 403; "Arrêt du Conseil d'Etat au sujet des dots des religieuses, 31 mai 1722," p. 464.   C¹¹A, 106, *Sur l'augmentation des religieuses*, 1er *février 1718*, pp. 407-10.

17 *Edits et Ord.*, I, "Arrêt du Conseil d'Etat du trois mars 1722, qui confirme le règlement pour le district des Paroisses," pp. 443-62.

18 C¹¹A, 45, *1723, pièces afférentes*, pp. 288-324.   C¹¹A, 46, *Vaudreuil et Bégon au ministre, 2 novembre 1724*, p. 17; *Longueuil et Bégon, 31 octobre 1725*, pp. 19-20.   *Edits et Ord.*, "Arrêt du Conseil d'Etat, 23 janvier 1727," pp. 509-11.

19 G¹, 461, *Recensements, 1722.*

20 *Edits et Ord.*, I, "Lit de Justice de Louis XIV, 22 février 1723," pp. 471-72.

21 B, 47, *Le Conseil de Marine à Vaudreuil et Robert, 28 mars 1724*, fol. 1082.   C¹¹A, 46, *Vaudreuil et Bégon au Ministre, 2 novembre 1724.*   B, 48, *Le Conseil de Marine à M. de Chazel, 16 janvier 1725*, fol. 9; *Le Conseil de Marine à M. de Beauharnois, 21 octobre 1725*, fol. 454; *Le Conseil de Marine à Vaudreuil et Bégon, 6 novembre 1725*, fol. 912.

22 B, 47, *Le Ministre à Bégon, 4 juin 1724*, fol. 1180.   B, 49, *Le Conseil de Marine à Bégon, 3 décembre 1726*, fol. 282.   C¹¹A, 42, *Beauharnois et Dupuy au Ministre, 20 octobre 1726*, p. 31.

23 *R.A.Q.*, 1938-39, "Vaudreuil à Pontchartrain, 4 novembre 1706," p. 167.

24 *Ibid.*, "Vaudreuil à Pontchartrain, 19 octobre 1705," p. 95; "Pontchartrain à Vaudreuil, 9 juin 1706," p. 120.   B, 27, *17 Juin 1705*, fol. 47½.

25 C¹¹A, 46, *Chaussegros de Léry, 20 octobre 1724*, p. 249.   C¹¹A, 36, *Riverin au comte de Toulouse, 9 avril 1716*, p. 381.   C¹¹G, 4, *Raudot à Pontchartrain, novembre 1709.*   C¹¹A, 30, *Raudot à Pontchartrain, 20 septembre 1709*, fol. 46.

CHAPTER III

1 C¹¹A, 47, *Longueuil au ministre, 21 octobre 1725*, p. 129.   Father Louis-Marie Le Jeune, *Dictionnaire général de biographie, histoire, littérature, agriculture, industrie, commerce et des arts, sciences, mœurs, coutumes, institutions religieuses et politiques du Canada* (Ottawa, 1931) vol. II, pp. 162-64.   B, 49, *Pontchartrain à Longueuil, 14 mai 1706*, fol. 674½.

2 *Rapport de l'archiviste de la province de Quebec*, 1938-39, "Pontchartrain à Vaudreuil, 9 juin 1706," p. 119; "Pontchartrain à Madame de Vaudreuil, 9 juin 1706," p. 123; "Vaudreuil à Pontchartrain, 4 novembre 1706," p. 166.   *R.A.Q.*, 1947-48, "Madame de Vaudreuil, Paris, 1712," p. 187; "Pontchartrain à Madame de Vaudreuil, 18 décembre 1712," p. 192; "Vaudreuil au Conseil de Marine, 7 novembre 1716," p. 336.

3 C¹¹A, 47, *Ce qu'il faut faire pour mettre le Canada en sûreté, 1725*, p. 294.

4 *Edits et ordonnances royaux*, III, "Provisions de gouverneur de M. de Beauharnois, 11 janvier 1726," p. 67; "Commission d'intendant à Dupuy, 23 novembre 1725," pp. 65-67.   Le Jeune, *op. cit.*, I, pp. 135 and 560.

5 C¹¹A, 48, *Bégon au ministre, 12 octobre 1726*, pp. 187-89; *Monseigneur de Saint-Vallier à Maurepas, 10 septembre 1726*, p. 350 *ff.*

6 B, 49, *Mémoire du roi à Beauharnois et Dupuy, 14 mai 1726*, fol. 649.

7 C¹¹A, 48, *Dupuy à Maurepas, 21 octobre 1726*, pp. 260-79; *Beauharnois à Maurepas, 29 décembre 1726*, pp. 166-67.

8 C¹¹A, 49, *Beauharnois et Dupuy à Maurepas, 20 octobre 1727*, pp. 37-39; *Dupuy à Maurepas, 20 octobre 1727*, pp. 429-30; *Extraits des comptes*, pp. 432-44.

9 *Edits et Ord.*, II, "Ordonnance, 7 juin 1727," pp. 314-21.   *Inventaire des ordonnances des intendants de la Nouvelle-France*, ed. by P. G. Roy (Beauceville 1917) "Ordonnances de Dupuy," vol. I. pp. 288-96, and vol. II, pp. 1-37.

C¹¹A, 49, *Beauharnois au ministre, 10 octobre 1727*, pp. 158-60; *Beauharnois à Forcade, 24 avril 1727*, p. 82; *Beauharnois au ministre, 15 septembre 1727*, p. 104.
C¹¹A, 50, *Beauharnois à Maurepas, 16 janvier 1728*, p. 87; *Beauharnois au ministre, 30 avril 1727*, pp. 85-86.

¹⁰ C¹¹A, 50, *Beauharnois au ministre, 6 mars 1727*, p. 61; *Beauharnois au ministre, 20 septembre 1727*, p. 94.

¹¹ C¹¹A, 50, *Dupuy à Maurepas, 20 octobre 1727*, pp. 347-54; *Dupuy à Maurepas, 27 octobre 1727*, pp. 411-13; *Dupuy à Maurepas, 21 octobre 1726*, p. 260.   B, 52, *Maurepas à Dupuy, 18 mai 1728*, fol. 519.   C¹¹A, 50, *D'Aigremont à Maurepas, 15 octobre 1728*, p. 146.

¹² B, 52, *Maurepas à Mgr de Mornay, 20 juillet 1728*, fol. 551½; *Maurepas à Beauharnois, 3 juin 1728*, fol. 554½.

¹³ *Edits et Ord.*, II, "Ordonnance de Dupuy, 4 janvier 1728," p. 322 *ff.*
Jugements et délibérations du Conseil supérieur de la Nouvelle France (Quebec, 1885-91) vol. IX, pp. 191-93.   F³, 9, *Dupuy à Faure, 28 mai 1728*, pp. 217-18.
R.A.Q., 1920-21, "Mémoire de Dupuy sur les troubles arrivés à Québec en 1727-28," pp. 78-104.

¹⁴ *Mandements, lettres pastorales et circulaires des évêques de Québec* (Quebec, 1887) vol. 1, "Mandement et Manifeste, 6 janvier 1728," pp. 522-23.

¹⁵ *Edits et Ord.*, II, "Ordonnance de Dupuy, 4 janvier 1728," p. 327.   *Inventaire des Jugements et délibérations du Conseil souverain* (Quebec, 1932-35) vol. I, "Arrêt du 5 janvier 1728," p. 340; "Arrêt du 12 janvier 1728," p. 341.

¹⁶ *Ibid.*, "Arrêt du 30 janvier 1728," p. 342; "Arrêt du 3 février 1728," p. 343; "Arrêt du 16 février 1728," pp. 343-45.   *R.A.Q.*, 1920-21, "Mémoire de Dupuy," pp. 78-104.

¹⁷ *Jug. et Dél.*, IX, pp. 291-94 and 318-19.

¹⁸ *Edits et Ord.*, II, "Ordonnance de Dupuy du 8 mars 1728," pp. 331-32.
F³, 9, *Dupuy à Faure, 28 mai 1728*, pp. 217-18.   *R.A.Q.*, 1920-21, "Mémoire de Dupuy," pp. 78-104.

¹⁹ *Edits et Ord.*, II, "Ordonnance, 8 mars 1728," p. 331.   *Inventaire des Jug. et Dél.*, I, "Arrêt du 6 avril 1728," p. 349; "Arrêt du 12 avril 1728," p. 305.   C¹¹A, 50, *Beauharnois à Maurepas, 1er octobre 1728*, pp. 101-02.   F³, 9, *Ordonnance du 29 mai 1728* (with marginal notes by Beauharnois) pp. 240-49.

²⁰ B, 52, *Maurepas à Dupuy, 1er juin 1728*, fol. 355½.   B, 53, *Maurepas à Beauharnois, 12 avril 1729*, fol. 487½.   B, 52, *Maurepas au chapitre de Québec, 3 juin 1728*, fol. 556; *Maurepas à Boullard, 3 juin 1728*, fol. 557.   *Inventaire des Jug. et Dél.*, I, "Arrêt du 17 septembre 1728," p. 21. The Abbé Marchand wrote a mock-heroic on the funeral of Mgr. de Saint-Vallier with the title: *Les Troubles de l'Eglise au Canada en 1728*.

²¹ Séminaire de Saint-Sulpice, *Cahiers de l'Abbé Faillon*.   R. P. Camille de Rochemonteix, *Les Jésuites et la Nouvelle-France au XVIIIᵉ siècle* (Paris, 1906) vol. III, pp. 313-18 and 144-50.   Abbé Auguste Gosselin, *L'Eglise au Canada depuis Mgr de Laval* (Quebec, 1911-14) vol. II, p. 449.

²² C¹¹A, 48, *Mgr de Saint-Vallier, 10 septembre 1726*, pp. 360-68.   C¹¹A, 106, *Mémoire sur l'Eglise, 1731*, pp. 228-43; *Représentations des curés missionnaires, 1730*, pp. 280-88.   C¹¹A, 53, *Dosquet à Beauharnois et Hocquart, 27 avril 1731*, pp. 13-14; *Mgr Dosquet à Maurepas, 13 octobre 1730*, p. 246.   C¹¹A, 56, *Mgr Dosquet à Maurepas, 29 septembre 1731*, pp. 96-101.   C¹¹A, 52, *Beauharnois et Hocquart à Maurepas, 10 septembre 1730*, p. 15.   *Mandements*, I, "Contre la traite de l'eau-de-vie, 20 novembre 1730," pp. 535-37.   B, 58, *Maurepas à Mgr Dosquet, 20 janvier 1733*, fol. 395.

²³ B, 70, *Maurepas à Pontbriand, 19 décembre 1740*, fol. 158.   Gosselin, *op. cit.*, III, *passim.*

²⁴ C¹¹A, 49, *Mémoire sur les Renards, 1727*, p. 584; *Beauharnois et Dupuy à Maurepas, 20 octobre 1727*, pp. 40-42.   B, 50, *Le Ministre à M. Perriers, 22 juillet 1727*, fol. 5-48.   F³, 39, *De Lignery à Beauharnois, 30 août 1728*, fol. 152.   *Voyages du R. P. Crespel dans le Canada* (Quebec, 1884) pp. 4-15.   B, 53, *Maurepas, à De Lignery, 2 mai 1729*, fol. 539; *Mémoire du roi à Beauharnois et Hocquart 19 avril 1729*, fol. 512.

²⁵ F,³ 9, *Relation de la défaite des Renards par les Français de la Louisiane et du Canada (1730)*, fol. 140.

²⁶ F³, 9, *Relation de M. de Villiers, septembre 1730*, fol. 312; *Villiers à Beauharnois, 23 septembre 1730*, fol. 314; *Défaite des Renards, 9 septembre 1730*, fol. 322.

27 C11A, 57, *Boishébert à Beauharnois, 7 décembre 1732*, pp. 181-83; *Relation de la défaite des Renards par les Hurons et Iroquois, 28 février 1732*, pp. 157-58; *Addition à la relation*, pp. 159-60; *Beauharnois à Maurepas, 15 octobre 1732*, p. 164.   C11A, 59, *Beauharnois à Maurepas, 1er juillet 1733*, pp. 13-15.

28 C11A, 61, *Beauharnois et Hocquart à Maurepas, 6 octobre 1734*, pp. 179-80; *Beauharnois et Hocquart à Maurepas, 11 novembre 1733, pp.* 139-40.

29 C11A, 61, *Beauharnois et Hocquart à Maurepas, 9 octobre 1735.*   C11A, 63, *Beauharnois à Maurepas, 9 octobre 1735*, pp. 164-76; *Entreprise de guerre contre les Renards, 9 octobre 1735*, pp. 177-95.   C11A, 65, *Beauharnois à Maurepas, 17 octobre 1735*, pp. 102-11.

CHAPTER IV

1 C11A, 67, *Hocquart à Maurepas, 1er juin 1737*, fol. 208.   B, 52, *Maurepas à d'Aigremont, 2 juin 1728*, fol. 533½.   C11A, 50, *Beauharnois à Maurepas, 2 décembre 1728*, p. 42.   B, 53, *Instructions à Hocquart, 22 mars 1729*, fol. 471.   *Edits et ordonnances royaux*, III, "Commission de Hocquart, 21 février 1731," p. 69.

2 B, 42, *Le Conseil de Marine à Beauharnois, 17 mars 1720*, p. 114.   C11A, 45, *Vaudreuil et Bégon, 14 octobre 1723*, pp. 33, 49; *A la Compagnie des Indes, 17 janvier 1727*, p. 3.

3 C11A, 50, *Beauharnois et Hocquart à Maurepas, 11 novembre 1728*, p. 81. *Edits et Ord.*, I, "Ordonnance du Roi, 2 mars 1729," p. 522.   C11A, 52, *Beauharnois et Hocquart à Maurepas, 23 octobre 1736*, p. 105.   B, 76, *Maurepas à Beauharnois et Hocquart, 8 mai 1743*, p. 312.

4 B, 58, *Maurepas à Beauharnois et Hocquart, 24 octobre 1733*, fol. 441½. C11A, 59, *Beauharnois et Hocquart à Maurepas, 1er octobre 1733*, p. 71. *Domaine d'Occident, Canada 1733*, p. 215.   B, 60, *Hocquart à Maurepas, 30 septembre 1733*, pp. 3-22.

5 B, 58, *Maurepas à Beauharnois et Hocquart, 24 avril 1733*, fol. 441½; *Maurepas à Hocquart, 24 avril, 1733*, fol. 447.

6 C11A, 59, *Beauharnois et Hocquart à Maurepas, 1er octobre 1733*, pp. 72-76. B, 61, *Maurepas à Beauharnois et Hocquart, 6 mai 1734*, fol. 551½.

7 C11A, 58, *De Léry à Maurepas, 20 octobre 1732*, p. 110.

8 C11A, 60, *Hocquart à Maurepas, 3 octobre 1733*, p. 35.

9 C11A, 61, *Beauharnois et Hocquart à Maurepas, 9 octobre 1734*, pp. 110-20. F3, 10, *Arrêt du Conseil Supérieur, 12 juin 1734*, fol. 189.   C11A, 63, *Beauharnois et Hocquart à Maurepas, 13 octobre 1735*, p. 45.

10 *Edits et Ord.*, II, "Ordonnance de Bégon, 27 janvier 1721," pp. 455-56.

11 *Edits et Ord.*, III, "Provisions en survivance de l'office de grand voyer à Pierre Robineau de Bécancourt, 24 mai 1689," p. 91.   *Inventaire des Insinuations du Conseil Souverain* (Beauceville, 1921) "Commission de grand voyer à Lanouillier de Boisclerc, 26 mars 1730," p. 187.   *Edits et Ord.*, III, "Provisions de l'office de Grand Voyer, 10 avril 1731," p. 100.

12 C11A, 60, *Hocquart à Maurepas, 14 octobre 1733*, pp. 65-68; *Boisclerc à Maurepas, 17 octobre 1733*, pp. 179-83.   C11A, 66, *Boisclerc à Maurepas, 21 octobre 1736*, p. 62.   C11A, 72, *Lanouillier à Maurepas, 29 octobre 1739*, pp. 45-61.

13 *Rapport de l'archiviste de la province de Québec*, 1938-39, "Vaudreuil et Raudot à Pontchartrain, 3 novembre 1706," p. 148.   *R.A.Q.*, 1939-40, "Le roi à Vaudreuil et Raudot, 30 juin 1707," p. 365.   B, 59, *Maurepas à Beauharnois et Hocquart, 17 mars 1732*, pp. 351-52.   B, 61, *17 mai 1734*, fol. 588.

14 C11A, 52, *Mémoire concernant l'état présent du Canada en l'an 1730*, pp. 194-233.   C11A, 57, *Paroles de Beauharnois aux chefs iroquois, 1732*, pp. 187-89.

15 C11A, 49, *Beauharnois et Dupuy à Maurepas, 20 octobre 1727*, p. 40. C11A, 52, *Mémoire de la Corne, 15 octobre 1730*, pp. 166-67.   C11A, 54, *Beauharnois et Hocquart à Maurepas, 10 octobre 1731*, p. 97.

16 B, 44, *Le Conseil de Marine à M. L'Echassier, 29 mars 1721*, fol. 505½; *Le Conseil de Marine à Vaudreuil et Bégon, 14 juin 1721*, fol. 523.   C11A, 54, *Beauharnois et Hocquart à Maurepas, 12 octobre 1731*, p. 136; C11A, 68, *De Léry à Maurepas, 28 octobre 1737*, pp. 84-86; *Petit Mémoire du Canada (1740)*, p. 58.

17 C11A, 52, *Beauharnois et Hocquart à Maurepas, 17 octobre 1730*, p. 75.

18 C11A, 61, *Beauharnois à Maurepas, octobre 1734*, p. 203.   B, 63, *Maurepas à Beauharnois, 10 mai 1735*, fol. 504; *Maurepas à Hocquart, 5 mai 1734*, fol. 499.

19 B, 39, *Mémoire du roi à Vaudreuil et Bégon, 27 juin 1717,* fol. 230.
C¹¹A, 37, *Conseil de Marine, 7 décembre 1717,* pp. 455-57.   B, 40, *Conseil de Marine à Vaudreuil et Bégon, 24 mai 1719,* fol. 541.   C¹¹A, 39, *La Noue à Vaudreuil, novembre 1719,* pp. 92-101.

20 B, 42, *Conseil de Marine à Vaudreuil et Bégon, 7 juin 1720,* fol. 451½.
C¹¹A, 16, *Mémoire du voyage du P. Charlevoix, 1723,* pp. 218-31.

21 C¹¹A, 47, *Moyens faciles pour découvrir en peu de temps la mer de l'Ouest, 1725,* p. 313 *ff.*   F³, 9, *Traité de la Compagnie des Sioux, 6 juin 1727.* fol. 69; *P. Guignas à Beauharnois, 28 mai 1728,* fol. 146.   C¹¹A, 67, *Beauharnois à Maurepas, 15 octobre 1727,* p. 136.   B, 53, *Le Conseil de Marine à Hocquart, 19 avril 1729,* fol. 509½.

22 C¹¹A, 33, *La Vérendrye à Maurepas, 15 février 1732,* pp. 578-79.   "Introduction," *Journals and Letters of Pierre Gaultier de La Vérendrye and his Sons,* ed. by Lawrence J. Burpee (Toronto, 1927) pp. 2-4, "Suite du mémoire du sieur de la Vérenderie (1730)," pp. 43-63; "Beauharnois et Hocquart à Maurepas, 15 octobre 1730," pp. 66-69.   B, 55, *Maurepas à Beauharnois, 10 avril 1731,* fol. 479½; *Beauharnois et Hocquart à Maurepas, 29 octobre,* p. 397.

23 *Journals and Letters,* "La Vérendrye à Maurepas, 1er août 1731," pp. 70-72; "Beauharnois à Maurepas, 15 octobre," pp. 91-94; "Beauharnois à Maurepas, 28 octobre 1732," pp. 102-06. See also Ernest Voorhis, *Historic Forts and Trading Posts of the French Régime and of the English Trading Companies* (Ottawa, 1930).

24 *Journals and Letters,* "Beauharnois à Maurepas (1734)" pp. 127-28 and 132-33; "Mémoire en forme de Journal (du 27 mai 1733 au 12 juillet 1734)," pp. 147-62, 177 and 182-91.   *An Historical Atlas of Canada,* edited with introd. and notes by Lawrence J. Burpee (Toronto, 1927) p. 12.

25 *Journals and Letters,* "Beauharnois à Maurepas (1734)," pp. 132-33; "La Vérendrye à Maurepas, 12 octobre 1734," p. 194; "Maurepas à Beauharnois, 12 avril 1735," pp. 196-97.

26 *Ibid.,* "Beauharnois à Maurepas, 8 octobre 1735," pp. 202-03; "Maurepas à Beauharnois, 17 avril 1736," p. 207; "Mémoire en forme de journal," pp. 170-77.

27 *Ibid.,* "Beauharnois à Maurepas, 14 octobre 1736," pp. 209-12; "Mémoire du Sieur de La Vérendrye (1736-37)," pp. 215-18; "Affaire du meurtre de 21 voyageurs, juin 1736," pp. 262-66.

28 *Ibid.*

29 *Ibid.,* "Mémoire du sieur de La Vérendrye (1736-37)," p. 219, 224, 235-37, 244-45, 260-62. On September 17, 1737 La Vérendrye sent for the bodies of his son and Father Alneau, and the heads of all the Frenchmen who had been killed by the Sioux. They were buried in the chapel at Fort St. Charles. See p. 227. "Mémoire du Sieur de La Vérendrye," p. 174.

30 *Ibid.,* "Maurepas à Beauharnois, 24 avril 1737," p. 270; "Beauharnois à Maurepas, 1er octobre 1738," pp. 278-81; "La Vérendrye à Maurepas, 1er octobre 1737," p. 268.

31 *Ibid.,* "Journal en forme de lettre (juillet 1738—mai 1739)." See also Voorhis, *op. cit.*

32 *Journals and Letters,* pp. 335-37, 353-60; "Mémoire du S. de La Vérendrye," pp. 447-48; "Mémoire en abrégé," pp. 486-87.   L. J. Burpee, *The Search for the Western Sea* (Toronto, 1908), p. 268.

33 *Journals and Letters,* "Ordonnance de Hocquart, 12 juin 1740," pp. 515-20; "Mémoire du S. de La Vérendrye (1748)," pp. 449-55; "Mémoire en abrégé (1749)," pp. 485-86; "Beauharnois à Maurepas, 14 septembre 1742," p. 381; "Beauharnois à Maurepas, 12 octobre 1742," pp. 383-89. See also Voorhis, *op. cit.*

34 *Ibid.,* "Journal du voyage fait par le Chevalier de La Vérendrye, 1742-43," pp. 406-32. The lead plate buried by the Chevalier de La Vérendrye was found on a hill near the town of Pierre on February 16, 1913. See p. 17 and note, p. 427.

35 *Ibid.,* "Maurepas à Beauharnois et Hocquart, 17 avril 1742," p. 581; "Beauharnois à Maurepas, 14 octobre 1742," p. 582.

36 *Ibid.,* "Beauharnois et Hocquart, 29 octobre 1742," pp. 396-97; "La Vérendrye à Maurepas, 1er octobre 1737," pp. 268-69; "Maurepas à Beauharnois, 20 avril 1742," p. 392; "La Vérendrye à Maurepas, 31 octobre 1744," p. 484.

37 *Ibid.,* "Beauharnois et Hocquart à Maurepas, 21 octobre 1744," pp. 400-01; "Maurepas à Beauharnois, 12 mai 1745," p. 460; "La Galissonnière à Maurepas, 23 octobre 1747," p. 468; "Rouillé à La Jonquière, 23 mai 1749," pp. 475-76.

[38] *Ibid.*, "Rouillé à La Jonquière, 4 mai 1749," pp. 473-74; "La Vérendrye à Rouillé, 17 septembre 1749," p. 477.
[39] *Ibid.*, "Le Chevalier de la Vérendrye à Rouillé, 30 septembre 1750," pp. 503-06.
[40] *Ibid.*, "La Vérendrye, fils, à Rouillé, 27 février 1750," pp. 503-07.
[41] *Ibid.*, "La Jonquière à Rouillé, 27 février 1750," pp. 480-82; "Mémoire du Journal du voyage de Jacques Repentigny Le Gardeur de Saint-Pierre, anoût 1752," *Rapport des Archives canadiennes*, 1886, pp. CLVII-CLXII. Voorhis, *op. cit.* p. 97.

CHAPTER V

[1] Frances G. Davenport, *European Treaties* (Washington, D.C., 1917-37) vol. III, pp. 208-14.   C[11]A, 47, *Moyens pour empêcher les Anglais de venir à bout de leurs vues, 1725*, pp. 280-86.   Nova Scotia State Papers, *Lords of Trade to Philipps, 21 July 1720*.   "Letters of Queen Anne, 23 June 1713," in Beamish Murdoch, *A History of Nova Scotia, or Acadia* (Halifax, 1865-67) vol. I, p. 333.

[2] N.S., *Dudley to Lords of Trade, 5 January 1711; Hartley to Lords of Trade, 20 August 1713; Stanhope to Lords of Trade, 15 May 1715*.

[3] "Mascarene to Shirley, 6 April 1748," in Murdoch, *op. cit.*, I, pp. 355-56, 371-72 and 469.   N. S., *Philipps to Lords of Trade, 28 May 1720*.

[4] C[11]B, 5, *Saint-Ovide au Conseil de Marine, 15 septembre 1721*, fol. 268. B, 49, *Maurepas à Saint-Ovide, 28 mai 1726*, fol. 705.   "Mémoire du 29 août 1749," translated in J.S. McLennan, *Louisbourg from its Foundation to its Fall, 1713-1758* (London, 1918) p. 190.   *Le Canada Français. Collection de documents inédits sur le Canada et l'Amérique* (Quebec, 1888) vol. 1, "Réponse des habitants, 10 février 1718, p. 170; "Réponse des habitants français de l'Acadie à Philipps, 26 mai 1720," p. 125.   B, 53, *Le Conseil de Marine à Saint-Ovide, 22 mai 1729*, fol. 595½.   B, 61, *Le Conseil de Marine à Saint-Ovide, 4 mai 1734*, fol. 603.

[5] *Le Canada français*, I, "Proclamation de Philipps, 10 avril 1720," p. 121; "Articles accordés par l'enseigne Wroth, 11 et 31 octobre 1727," pp. 178-79.

[6] B, 39, *Le roi aux missionaires de l'Acadie, 30 juin 1717*, fol. 298½.   *Documents inédits*, I, "Délibérations du Conseil, 23 mai 1719," pp. 193 and 196. B, 48, *Le Conseil de Marine à Saint-Ovide, 25 juillet 1725*, fol. 938.   B, 54, *Le Conseil de Marine à M. de Breslay, 27 juin 1730*, fol. 505½.

[7] *Documents inédits*, I, "Pain à Doucet, 23 mars 1718," p. 117; "Doucet à Pain, 26 mars (9 avril) 1718," p. 118; "P. Justinien Durand à Philipps, 1720," pp. 122-23.   B, 48, *Le Conseil de Marine à Saint-Ovide, 25 juillet 1725*, fol. 938; *22 mai 1729*, fol. 595½.   B, 57, *19 juin 1932*, fol. 744.   N. S., *Doucett to Philipps, 13 December 1718; Philipps to Lords of Trade, 1720*.

[8] "Warrant from the Queen," in Murdoch, *op. cit.*, I, p. 333.

[9] See "Recensement du P. Félix Pain, 1714," in Murdoch, *op. cit.*, I, p, 346. Rameau de Saint-Père, *Une Colonie Féodale en Amèrique. L'Acadie, 1604-1818* (Paris, 1889) vol. I, pp. 358 and 473.   McLennan, *op. cit.*, n.p. 18. The censuses appear to be incomplete; the figure 4,000 is taken from a "Mémoire sur les habitants de l'Acadie, 1714, in *Collection de manuscrits contenant lettres, mémoires et autres documents historiques relatifs à la Nouvelle-France*, III, p. 9,

[10] Arch. Can., Brown Collection, M 651A, *passim*.   B, 48, *Le roi à Saint-Ovide, 25 juillet 1725*, fol. 938.   Courville, "Mémoire du Canada," *Rapport de l'archiviste de la province de Québec*, 1924-25, p. 104.

[11] C[11]B, I. *Mémoire des habitants de l'Acadie, 25 août 1714*, fol. 104; *P. Dominique à Costebelle et Soubras, 7 septembre 1714*, p. 259 ff.

[12] "Père Félix Pain à Costebelle, 23 septembre 1713," in Murdoch, *op. cit.*, I, pp. 336-37.   Col. Mss., III, "Mémoire sur les habitants de l'Acadie, 1714," pp. 8-9.   B, 36, *Pontchartrain au P. Justinien, 23 mars 1714*, fol. 447.   B, 37, *Pontchartrain à Desmaretz, 20 février 1715*, fol. 261-62; *Pontchartrain à M. de Soubras, 4 juin 1715*, fol. 216.

[13] Col. Mss., III, "Mémoire sur les habitants de l'Acadie," p. 9.   B, 37, *Pontchartrain à Costebelle et Soubras, 4 juin 1715*, fol. 226. "Mémoire de Denys de La Ronde, 1717," "Déclaration des Acadiens," "Costebelle à Pontchartrain, 29 août 1714," in Emile Lauvrière, *La Tragédie d'un peuple. Histoire du peuple acadien de ses origines à nos jours* (Paris, 1922) vol. I, pp. 210-11.   B, 38, *Le*

Conseil de Marine à De Barailh, 22 avril 1716, fol. 266½.   B, 39, *Le roi à Costebelle et Soubras, 26 juin 1717,* fol. 295.

14 N. S., A, *Vetch to Lords of Trade, 24 Novembre 1714,* p. 7; *Caulfield to Board of Trade, 1 November 1715,* pp. 8-9; See also *Lords of Trade to Stanhope, 18 May 1715* and *Vetch to Lords of Trade, 9 March 1715.*

15 *Col. Mss.,* III, "Mémoire sur les habitants de l'Acadie, 1714," p. 9. N. S., A, *Caulfield to Vetch, 2 November 1715; Caulfield to Lords of Trade, 23 November 1715.*   C¹¹B, I, *Extrait pour le Conseil, 12 janvier 1715,* fol. 265. C¹¹A, 35, *Bégon à Pontchartrain, 25 septembre 1715,* fol. 106.

16 N.S., *Caulfield to Lords of Trade, 12 January 1715.*   C¹¹B, 1, *Délibérations du Conseil de Louisbourg, 7 septembre 1715,* fol. 261.

17 N.S., *Doucet to Lords of Trade, 10 February 1717,* with correspondence, pp. 15-16. See also Lauvrière, *op. cit.,* I, p. 218; *Reports by Lords of Trade, 30 May 1718.*

18 "Les Acadiens au P. Félix Pain, 23 septembre 1714," in Lauvrière, *op. cit.,* I, p. 208.   C¹¹B, 1, *Denys de La Ronde, 3 décembre 1715,* fol. 212. *Rapport de l'archiviste de la province de Québec,* 1947-48,"Vaudreuil et Bégon à Pontchartrain, 20 septembre 1714," p. 283.   N. S., *Nicholson to Lords of Trade, 16 August 1715.*

19 C¹¹B, 1, *De Costebelle, 8 octobre 1716,* fol. 404; *Le roi aux missionaires de l'Acadie, 30 juin 1717,* fol. 298½; *Le roi à Saint-Ovide, 7 juillet 1720,* fol. 476. C¹¹B, 4, *Délibérations du Conseil de Marine, 23 mai 1719,* fol. 96.

20 *Proclamation du général Philipps, 19 avril 1720,* fol. 45. The date given in *Documents inédits* is April 10. See note 5 above.

21 C¹¹D, 8, *Lettre des habitants à Saint-Ovide, 18 mai 1720,* fol. 53; *Saint-Ovide à Philipps, 27 septembre 1720,* fol. 62; *Pièce XX Lettre des Mines à Philipps, mai 1720,* fol. 55.   N. S., *Philipps to Lords of Trade, 26 May 1720* (with 17 documents), p. 26 *ff.*

22 N. S., *Philipps to Lords of Trade, Lords of Trade to Philipps, 14 (28) December 1720.*

23 N. S., *Armstrong to Secretary of State, 27 July 1726,* p. 65; *Armstrong to Secretary of State, November 1726* (with documents), pp. 66-67. *Report of the Canadian Archives,* 1902, II, "William Cotterel à Hopson, 1ᵉʳ octobre 1753," p. 114.

24 N. S., *Report by Ensign Robert Wroth, 1727; Articles granted by Wroth to the inhabitants at Mines, Pissiquit and Chignecto, 11 and 21 October 1727.* These texts are printed in *Documents inédits,* LIV, LV and LVI.

25 N. S., *Lords of Trade to Secretary of State, 16 July 1728; Commission of Philipps, 11 September 1728; Le Conseil de Marine à Bourville, 10 juillet 1731,* fol. 563.

26 N. S., *Philipps to Secretary of State, 25 November 1729 and 3 January 1730.*   Affaires Étrangères, Angleterre, *Déclaration de l'abbé de la Goudalie, 25 avril 1730.* The same text appears in Nova Scotia State Papers. The fact is confirmed in Mascarene's letter to Shirley, April 6, 1748, quoted in Murdoch, *op. cit.,* II, pp. 371-72.

CHAPTER VI

1 C¹¹B, I, *Arrêt du Conseil Royal, 1715,* fol. 3.   B, 37, *Pontchartrain à Desmaretz, 10 février 1715,* fol. 28.

2 C¹¹G, 8, *Mémoire de Raudot, 30 novembre 1706,* fol. 10.   C¹¹G, 6, *Mémoire de Raudot, 16 juillet 1708,* fol. 2; *Mémoire de Raudot, 20 août 1707,* fol. 39½.   B, 29, *Pontchartrain à Raudot fils, 30 juin 1707,* fol. 87½.

3 B, 35, *Pontchartrain à Saint-Ovide, 20 mars 1713,* fol. 11; *Pontchartrain à Costebelle, 12 avril 1713,* fol. 11; *L'Hermite à Pontchartrain, 20 août 1714,* fol. 47.

4 *Rapport de l'archiviste de la province de Québec,* 1947-48, "Vaudreuil à Pontchartrain, 14 novembre 1713," p. 233.   B, 36, *Pontchartrain à l'Hermite, 26 janvier 1714,* fol. 419.

5 F³7, *Notification par M. de Costebelle des ordres du roi* (n.d.) fol. 264. B, 36, *Pontchartrain à Costebelle, 21 mars 1714,* fol. 432½; *Instructions pour M. de Soubras, 10 avril 1714,* fol. 449 (with a commission dated April 12, 1714).

6 C¹¹B, I, *Costebelle à Pontchartrain, 29 octobre 1714,* fol. 42; *Costebelle à Pontchartrain, 2 novembre 1715,* fol. 141.   B, 37, *Pontchartrain à Costebelle,*

4 juin 1715, fol. 210½; *Pontchartrain à Costebelle et Soubras, 17 mars 1715, fol.* 207½. *Canada Census, 1871*, IV, p. 48.

7 C¹¹B, I, *Mémoire sur l'île Royale, 25 février 1715*, fol. 241; *Conseil de Marine à Costebelle et Soubras, 11 février 1716*, fol. 252½; *Conseil de Marine à Costebelle et Soubras, 22 avril 1716*, fol. 259½.   Louis Chancels de La Grange, "Voyage fait à l'Isle Royale ou du Cap Breton en Canada, 1716," *Revue d'histoire de l'Amérique française* (décembre 1959) p. 424.   J. S. McLennan, *Louisbourg, from its Foundations to its Fall, 1713-58* (London, 1918) p. 20.

8 *R.H.A.F. (décembre 1959)* pp. 425, 426, 428 and 432.   C¹¹B, 1, *L'Hermite à Pontchartrain, 1er décembre 1714*, fol. 82.   B, 38, *Etat des ouvriers pour l'île Royale, 17 mars 1716*, fol. 254½; *Le Conseil de Marine à Costebelle et Soubras, 27 mai 1716*, fol. 274½; *Le Conseil de Marine à Costebelle et Soubras, 1er mars 1717*, fol. 261½.

9 C¹¹G, 12, *Brevets de confirmation, juin 1718*, fol. 46-52; *Brevets de concession à La Boularderie, 15 février 1719; à d'Auteuil, 20 mai 1719; Lettres patentes à Saint-Pierre, avril 1719*, fols. 53, 56, 59.

10 C¹¹G, 12, *Edit du roi, juin 1717*, fol. 39.   B, 39, *Mémoire du roi à Costebelle et Soubras, 28 juin 1717*, fol. 287.

11 B, 40, *Commission de Mésy, 19 juin 1718*, fol. 534; *Mémoire du roi à Saint-Ovide, 18 juillet 1718*, fol. 539½; *Mémoire du roi, 18 juillet 1719*, fol. 592.

12 B, 39, *A. M. de Beauchesne, 7 juin 1717*, fol. 269½.   B, 41, *Le Conseil de Marine à Saint-Ovide et Mésy, 19 juillet 1719*, fol. 596½; *Mémoire du roi à Saint-Ovide et Mésy, 18 janvier 1719*, fol. 582.   B, 71, *Maurepas à Bigot, 7 mai 1740*, fol. 14.   McLennan, *op. cit.*, pp. 224, 370 and 382.

13 F²B, *Tableaux du commerce du Canada de l'Acadie de l'Ile Royale, 1732 et 1740*, vols. I and II.   McLennan, *op. cit.*, p. 382.   C¹¹G, 12, *Ordonnance du roi, 30 juin 1723*, fol. 104½; *19 août 1717*, fol. 115; *14 juin 1729*, fol. 116½.   B, 45, *Mémoire du roi à Saint-Ovide et Mésy, 12 mai 1722*, fol. 109½. B, 49, *Maurepas à Saint-Ovide et Mésy, 8 janvier 1726*, fol. 695.

14 C¹¹G, 12, *Ordre du roi, 20 juin 1720*, fol. 62; *Le Conseil de Marine à Mésy, 20 septembre 1720*, fol. 490½.   B, 46, *Le Conseil de Marine à Saint-Ovide et Mésy, 15 juillet 1722*, fol. 1153½; *Ordonnance, 26 juin 1726*, fol. 110; *Ordonannce, 30 juin 1723*, fol. 99½.   McLennan, *op. cit.*, pp. 71 and 371-79.   B, 45, *Ordonnance pour six compagnies, 12 mai 1722*, fol. 921½.   C¹¹G, 12, *Ordonnance concernant les concessions aux soldats, 26 juin 1725*, fol. 256.

15 *Collection de manuscrits contenant lettres, mémoires et autres documents historiques relatifs à la Nouvelle-France*, III, "Shute à Saint-Ovide, 24 août 1718," p. 29; "Déclaration du sieur Dominice, 28 décembre 1718," p. 39; "Le roi à Saint-Ovide et Mésy, 2 juillet 1720," p. 45.

16 C¹¹B, 5, *Procès-verbal de Pensens concernant Canseau, 11 septembre 1720*, fol. 279.   N. S., A, *Philipps to Lords of Trade, 27 September 1720.* B, 44, *Le Conseil de Marine à l'archevêque de Cambrai, 4 février 1721*, fol. 7; *Le roi à Saint-Ovide et de Mésy, 20 juin 1721*, fol. 57.

17 *Nouvelle-France, Documents historiques* (Quebec, 1893) "Instructions particulières pour M. de Vaudreuil, 1er avril 1755," p. 86.   *Calendar of State Papers, Colonial, 1720-21*, p. 135.

18 B, 71, *Le Conseil de Marine à Bigot, 13 mai 1740*, fol. 19.

19 C¹¹A, 69, *Hocquart à Maurepas, 2 octobre 1739*, fol. 243.   *Canada Census, 1871*, IV, p. 60.

20 C¹¹B, 20, *Requête des habitants pêcheurs de l'île Royale, 26 novembre 1738*, fol. 304; *Commerce que font les Anglais en cette île, 27 décembre 1738*, fol. 309.   McLennan, *op. cit.*, pp. 224 and 398.

21 B, 65, *Maurepas à Saint-Ovide et Le Normant, 17 mai 1737*, fols. 481 and 482.   McLennan, *op. cit.*, pp. 228-29 and 370.

22 B, 68, *Commission de sub-délégué à Bigot, 1er mai 1739*, fol. 8.   B, 72, *Le roi à Du Quesnel, 18 septembre 1740*, fol. 41½.   Guy Frégault, *François Bigot* (Montreal, 1948) vol. I, p. 41 *ff*. This is the essential work on Bigot. *Louisbourg in 1745:* the anonymous *Lettre d'un habitant de Louisbourg*, ed. with English translation by G. M. Wrong (Toronto, 1897).

23 McLennan, *op. cit.*, pp. 371-72 and 88-92. See also Verrier, *Veue de la Ville de Louisbourg, Port de Louisbourg vers 1734* and *Veues et Perspectives de la ville de Louisbourg.* These are all reproduced in McLennan.

24 C¹¹B, *Forant à Maurepas, 23 septembre 1749*, fol. 51.   *Louisbourg in 1745*, pp. 10 and 34-35.   C¹¹B, 26, *Du Chambon et Bigot à Maurepas, 31*

décembre 1745, fol. 55; pp. 231-34.   C¹¹B, 27, *Mémoire touchant la rente des soldats de Louisbourg, 1745*, fol. 55.   B, 52, *Le Ministre à Du Barrail, 20 août 1745*, fol. 75½.

25 *R.A.Q.*, 1947-48, "Maurepas à Vaudreuil et Bégon, 28 juin 1714," p. 219. D. G. G. Kerr, *A Historical Atlas of Canada* (Toronto, 1961) p. 22.   E. E. Rich, *The History of the Hudson's Bay Company* (London, 1958-60) vol. I, pp. 417-25.

26 Nicolas Jérémie, *Relation de la baie d'Hudson* (Amsterdam, 1720) p. 23. Rich, *op. cit.*, pp. 432, 440 and 442-43.

27 *Ibid.*, pp. 500-01, 528-31, 511-12.   B, 78, *Maurepas à Beauharnois, 30 avril 1744*, fol. 73; *Maurepas à Beauharnois et Hocquart, 30 avril 1745*, fol. 29; *Maurepas à Beauharnois, 6 mars 1747*, fol. 3.

28 Rich, *op. cit.*, I, pp. 279-99.   James F. Kenney, "The Career of Henry Kelsey," *Proceedings and Transactions of the Royal Society of Canada*, 1929.

29 Rich, *op. cit.*, I, pp. 436 and 438.

30 *Ibid.*, pp. 632-37.   L. J. Burpee, *From York Factory to the Blackfeet Country. The Journal of Anthony Hendry, 1754-55* (R. S. C., 1907) p. 307 *ff.*

31 *Ibid.*, pp. 560 and 570-71.

32 *Canada Census, 1871*, IV, pp. 48 and XX.   J. D. Rogers, *Newfoundland* (Oxford, 1911) pp. 88, 111-29.   *Cambridge History of the British Empire* (London, 1930) vol. VI, 138-43.

33 *Canada Census, 1871*, IV, pp. XXIV and XXXIV.   Rogers, *op. cit.*, pp. 137-38 and 127-28.   *Cambridge History*, VI, p. 143.   B, 114, *Choiseul à Ternay, 14 août 1762*, fol. 1.   Beamish Murdoch, *A History of Nova Scotia, or Acadia* (Halifax, 1865-67) vol. I, p. 143.

34 *Documents relating to the Constitutional History of Canada*, ed. by Adam Shortt and Arthur G. Doughty (Ottawa, 1911), "The Treaty of Paris," vol. I.

CHAPTER VII

1 *Collection de manuscrits contenant lettres, mémoires et autres documents historiques relatifs à la Nouvelle-France*, III, "Déclaration de guerre, 15 mars 1744," pp. 196-98.   C¹¹A, 61, *Beauharnois à Maurepas, octobre 1734*, p. 203. C¹¹A, 73, *Hocquart à Maurepas, 31 octobre 1740*, pp. 101-02.

2 C¹¹B, 26, *Du Quesnel et Bigot à Maurepas, 9 mai 1744*, fol. 8; *Le Conseil de Marine à Du Quesnel et Bigot, 18 mars 1744*, fol. 3.   *Col. Mss.*, III, "Capitulation de Canso," pp. 201-02.   Nova Scotia State Papers, *Mascarene to Philipps, 9 June 1744*.

3 N.S., *Mascarene to Lords of Trade, 27 July 1744; 22 September 1744*. C¹¹B, 26, *Du Quesnel et Bigot à Maurepas, 25 novembre 1744*, fol. 48; *Du Chambon à Maurepas, 18 novembre 1744*, fol. 79; *De Gannes, 28 novembre 1744*, fol. 204.   *Louisbourg in 1745:* the anonymous *Lettre d'un habitant de Louisbourg*, ed. with English translation by G. M. Wrong (Toronto, 1897) pp. 19-21.

4 C¹¹B, 26, *Du Chambon et Bigot à Maurepas, 4 novembre 1744*, fol. 32; *Bigot à Maurepas, 29 novembre 1744*, fol. 143.   *Col. Mss.*, III, "Mémoire sur la Nouvelle-Angleterre par M. Doloboratz, 19 novembre 1744," p. 212.   C¹¹A, 82, *Desauniers à Maurepas, 30 octobre 1744*, pp. 115-20.   J. S. McLennan, *Louisbourg from its Foundation to its Fall, 1713-1758* (London, 1918) pp. 119-21.

5 C¹¹A, 81, *Beauharnois à Maurepas, 30 juin 1744*, pp. 145-52; *8 octobre 1744*, pp. 174-202; *29 octobre 1744*, pp. 276-81.

6 C¹¹A, 83, *Rapport de Hocquart, 26 août 1745*, *p.* 301 *ff.*   *Col. Mss.*, III, "Extraits en forme de Journal, 1745," pp. 217-18.

7 *Louisbourg in 1745*, pp. 27-32.   C¹¹B, 26, Le Verrier, *Mémoire de ce qui reste à faire, 8 janvier 1744*, fol. 200; *Du Chambon à Maurepas, 10 novembre 1744*, fols. 60 and 70; *Du Chambon à Maurepas, 19 octobre 1744*, fol. 108.   *Col. Mss.*, III, "Extraits en forme de Journal (1745)," p. 217.

8 N.S., *Christopher Kilby to Lords of Trade, 30 August 1743*.   *Col. Mss.*, III, "Mémoire sur la Nouvelle-Angleterre par Doloboratz, 19 novembre 1744," p. 214.   C.Q. 5, *Shirley to Newcastle, 14 January 1744*.

9 McLennan, *op. cit.*, pp. 143-43.   *Col. Mss.*, III, "Bigot à Maurepas, 2 décembre 1745," p. 274.   N.S., *Registry of the Commissions in the army under the command of the Son. Wm. Pepperell*.   McLennan, *op. cit.*, pp. 133 and 126.   *Col. Mss.*, III, "Du Chambon à Maurepas, 2 septembre 1745," pp. 240-41.   *Louisbourg*

in 1745, p. 38. F. X. Garneau, *Histoire du Canada* (Paris, 1920) vol. II, p. 99. Guy Frégault, *François Bigot* (Montreal, 1948) vol. I, p. 219. Série F, Moreau de Saint-Méry, *Ordre de combat de l'escadre anglaise dans le port de Louisbourg*, fol. 417.

10 *Louisbourg in 1745*, p. 38 ff. *Col. Mss.*, III, "Du Chambon à Maurepas 2 septembre, 1745," p. 238 ff. *A letter from William Shirley with a Journal of the siege of Louisbourg*, p. 19 ff. James A. Gibson, *A Journal of the late siege* . . . p. 10 ff. F³, 50, *Bigot à Maurepas, 1er août 1745*, fol. 368; *Mémoire de M. de Drucourt, 1758*, fol. 529; *Journal du siège de Louisbourg, 1758*, fol. 539.

11 *Col. Mss.*, III, "Pepperell and Warren to Du Chambon, May 7 (18) 1745," p. 220; "Du Chambon à Warren et Pepperell, 18 mai 1745," p. 221. F³, 50, *Bigot à Maurepas, 1er août 1745*, fols. 368 and 539.

12 McLennan, *Bigot à Maurepas, 1er août 1745*, fol. 368, pp. 152-55. *Col. Mss.*, III, "Rapport de Beauharnois, 25 octobre 1745," p. 259. F³, 50, *Bigot à Maurepas, 1er août 1745*, fols. 368 and 539.

13 *Col. Mss.*, III, "Du Chambon à Maurepas, 2 september 1745," pp. 244-46 and 284-49. *Louisbourg in 1745*, pp. 44-45. F³, 50, *Bigot à Maurepas 1er août 1745*, fols. 368 and 539.

14 *Louisbourg in 1745*, pp. 46-48.

15 McLennan, *op. cit.*, pp. 177-78. (Texts of the logs of the *Mermaid* and the *Eltham*).

16 *Louisbourg in 1745*, pp. 49-51 and 56. *Col. Mss.*, III, "Du Chambon à Maurepas, 2 septembre 1745," pp. 248-52. F³, 50, *Bigot à Maurepas, 1er août 1745*, fols. 368 and 539.

17 F³, 50, *Bigot à Maurepas, 1er août 1745*, fol. 368 ff; *Journal du siège de Louisbourg*, fol. 539. *Louisbourg in 1745*, pp. 57-62. *Col. Mss.*, III, "Du Chambon à Maurepas, 2 septembre 1745," pp. 252-57; "Rapport du Conseil de guerre, 25 juin 1745," pp. 232-33; "Pepperell et Warren à Du Chambon, 16 (27) June 1745," p. 226; "A Letter from William Shirley," p. 30.

18 McLennan, *op. cit.*, pp. 167-68. *A Letter from William Shirley*, p. 30. Beamish Murdoch, *A History of Nova Scotia, or Acadia* (Halifax, 1865-57) vol. II, pp. 63-64. N.S., *Newcastle to Shirley, 10 August 1745; Pepperell to Secretary of State, 3 October 1745*.

19 *Col. Mss.*, III, "Rapport de Beauharnois, 25 octobre 1745," pp. 259-60. N.S., *Warren to Knowles, 2 June 1746; Council of War, 7 June 1746. Documents inédits*, II. "Journal de la campagne à l'Acadie et aux Mines en 1746-47," p.27.

20 *Col. Mss.*, III, "Du Chambon à Maurepas, 2 septembre 1745," pp. 254-55. *Louisbourg in 1745*, pp. 65-68.

21 B, 81, *Maurepas à Bigot, 19 juin 1745*, fol. 11; *Maurepas à Beauharnois, 19 juin 1745*, fol. 72. B, 82, *Le roi à M. de Salvert, 30 juin 1745*, fol. 115. B, 81, *Maurepas à Beauharnois et Hocquart, 1er novembre 1745*, fol. 76. *Col. Mss.*, III, "Extraits en forme de journal, 1745," p. 218.

22 Série F, Moreau de Saint-Méry, *Lettre d'un particulier des colonies anglaises, 1745*, fol. 357. N.S., *Secretary of State to Warren, 14 March 1746; Secretary of State to Shirley, 9 April 1746; Warren to Secretary of State, 9 June 1746; Knowles to Secretary of State, 10 September 1746; Pepperell to Secretary of State, 30 August 1746*.

23 B, 82, *Maurepas à Noailles, 2 août 1745*, fol. 138. *Col. Mss.*, III, "Ordonnance royale sur la révolte à Louisbourg, 1er novembre 1745," p. 262.

24 *Col. Mss.*, III, "De Léry à Maurepas, 9 novembre 1745," p. 267. C¹¹A, 83, *Beauharnois et Hocquart à Maurepas, 12 septembre 1745*, p. 3. B, 83, *Le Conseil de Marine à Beauharnois et Hocquart, 24 janvier 1746*, fol. 1. B, 84, *Mémoire du roi à d'Anville, 25 mars 1746*, fol. 47 bis; *Escadre du duc d'Anville*, fol. 100-01.

25 B, 84, *Mémoire du roi à d'Anville, 25 mars 1746*, fol. 47 bis.

26 *Documents inédits*, I, *Journal historique*, pp. 75-108. (D'Anville's expedition).

27 *Ibid.* Frégault, *Bigot*, I, pp. 258-71. Francis Parkman, *A Half-Century of Conflict* (Toronto, 1898) II, Ch. XXI.

28 B, 83, *Le Conseil de Marine à Beauharnois et Hocquart, 24 janvier 1746*, fol. 1. *Documents inédits*, II, Chevalier de La Corne, "Relation d'une expédition faite sur les Anglais dans le pays de l'Acadie, le 11 février 1747," pp. 10-16; Beaujeu. "Journal de la campagne du détachement du Canada à L'Acadie et

aux Mines en 1746-7," pp. 16-55.   B, 84, *Extraits des morts.* . . . fol. 162.

29 *Documents inédits,* II, "Journal de la campagne," pp. 58-75.   *Col. Mss.,* III, "Extrait en forme de Journal, 1747," pp. 328-30 and 343.   N.S., *Mascarene to Lords of Trade, 12 May 1747.*

CHAPTER VIII

1 C11A, 83, *Beauharnois à Maurepas, 19 juin 1745,* pp. 160-63.

2 *Collection de manuscrits contenant lettres, mémoires et autres documents historiques relatifs à la Nouvelle-France,* III, "Extrait en forme de journal, 1745," p. 219; "Hocquart à Maurepas, 30 octobre 1745," pp. 270 and 273.

3 *Ibid.,* pp. 273-313.

4 *Ibid.,* pp. 284-92 and 302.   F3, 11, *Journal de la campagne de M. Rigaud de Vaudreuil en 1746,* fol. 220 *ff.*

5 *Col. Mss.,* III, "Mémoire du Canada, 1744," p. 215; "Shirley à Beauharnois, 2 septembre 1747," p. 390; "Beauharnois à Shirley, 26 juillet 1747," p. 375. The English paid five pounds for a scalp and twenty for a prisoner.

6 *Ibid.,* "Extrait en forme de journal, 1746," p. 284.   C11A, 85, *Beauharnois et Hocquart à La Jonquière, 22 novembre 1746,* p. 250; *Rapport de M. de Repentigny, 13 octobre 1746,* p. 319; *Hocquart à Maurepas, 1746,* p. 332.

7 C11A, 85, *Beauharnois à Maurepas, 15 septembre 1746,* fol. 254-60.   *Col. Mss.,* III, "Extrait en forme de journal, 1746," pp. 275-368.

8 *Ibid.*

9 *Ibid.*

10 *Ibid.*

11 *Ibid.*

12 *Ibid.*   F3, 11, *Journal de M. Rigaud de Vaudreuil, 1747,* fol. 268 *ff.*

12a C11A, 88, *Rapport du capitaine Larréguy, 11 octobre 1747, fol. 37.*

13 *Col. Mss.,* III, "Extrait en forme de journal, 1747," pp. 348-68; "Extrait en forme de journal, 1748," pp. 401, 404, 407 and 412-13.

14 Nova Scotia State Papers, A, *Warren to Secretary of State, 2 June 1746; Secretary of State to Shirley, 30 May 1747.*   B, 85, *Maurepas à Beauharnois et Hocquart, 23 janvier 1747,* fol. 1.   *Documents inédits,* I, "Relation du combat rendu le 14 mai 1747 par l'escadre du roy commandé par M. de La Jonquière," pp. 33-36.   B, 86, *Maurepas à l'Amiral, 15 septembre 1747,* fol. 137½.

15 B, 85, *Le roi à La Galissonnière, 10 juin 1747,* fol. 35.

16 *Voyage de Kalm en Amérique* (Montreal, 1880) pp. 182-85.   P.E.G. Hennequin, *Biographies maritimes* (Paris, 1835-37) III.   *Documents relating to Canadian Currency, Exchange and Finance during the French Period,* ed. by A. Shortt (Ottawa, 1925) II, pp. 754-55.   C11A, 87-2, *La Galissonnière à Maurepas, 24 octobre 1747,* pp. 204-10.   *Col. Mss.,* III, "La Galissonnière, 6 novembre 1747," p. 399.   C11A, 96, *Mémoire sur les colonies, Silhouette et La Galissonnière, décembre 1750,* pp. 175-213.

17 C11A, 87-2, *Paroles des Iroquois, 12 août 1747,* p. 253 *ff.*   *Col. Mss.,* III, "La Galissonnière, 6 novembre 1747," p. 400; "Extrait en forme de journal, 1748," pp. 403, 405, 408, 409 and *passim.*   C11A, 91, *La Galissonnière et Bigot à Maurepas, 26 septembre et 3 novembre 1747,* pp. 20-23.

18 *Col. Mss.,* III, "Ordonnance concernant la suspension d'armes, 21 mai 1748," p. 420; "Extrait en forme de journal, 1748," p. 414.

19 For the text of the Treaty of Aix-la-Chapelle, see *A Collection of all the Treaties of Peace, Alliance and Commerce between Great Britain and other powers* . . . , ed. by the Honourable Charles Jenkinson (London, 1785) vol. II. p. 370 *ff.*   Stryenski, *Le Dix-huitième siècle* (Paris, 1913) pp. 164-65.

20 N.S., A, *La Galissonnière à Mascarene, 15 janvier 1749; Mascarene à La Galissonnière, 25 avril 1749; Mascarene to Secretary of State, 8 Septembre 1748.* C11A, 93, *La Galissonnière à Rouillé, 26 juin 1749,* p. 139.

21 C11A, 93, *Raymond à La Jonquière, 4 septembre 1749,* pp. 56-68; *La Galissonnière à Rouillé, 26 juin 1749,* pp. 141-42.   J. S. McLennan, *Louisburg from its Foundation to its Fall, 1713-58* (London, 1918) p. 183.   F3, 11, *Journal de la campagne par M. Céloron (1749),* fol. 318.

22 Father Louis-Marie Le Jeune, *Dictionnaire général* (Ottawa, 1931) vol. II, pp. 442 and 727.   C11A, 93, *La Jonquière et Bigot à Rouillé, 31 octobre 1749,* pp. 52-55.

23 *Col. Mss.,* IV, "Prise de possession de Louisburg par les Français, 1749,"

pp. 435-36.   C¹¹B, 28, *Bigot à Rouillé, 20 août 1749*, fol. 138 *ff.*   McLennan, *op. cit.*, pp. 385-86.

²⁴ C¹¹B, 28, *Prévost à Rouillé, 20 novembre 1749*, fol. 195.   C¹¹B, 29, *Des Herbiers à Rouillé, 27 juillet 1750*, fol. 14.   McLennan, *op. cit.*, Appendix V, pp. 382 and 385-86.

²⁵ *Ibid.*, p. 188 and Appendix, pp. 384 and 392-93.

²⁶ C¹¹B, 29, *Des Herbiers à Rouillé, 22 juillet 1750*, fol. 14.   C¹¹B, 33, *Mémoire sur le commerce de l'île Royale, 1ᵉʳ janvier 1753*, fol. 3.   B, 97, *Rouillé à Prévost, 17 juillet 1753*, fol. 27.   "Des Herbiers à La Jonquière, 7 avril 1751," in McLennan, *op. cit.*, pp. 403-04.

²⁷ F², B, 11, *Etat sommaire des marchandises sorties de Louisbourg pour la Nouvelle-Angleterre, 1752; Etat sommaire des marchandises venues de la Nouvelle-Angleterre à Louisbourg, 1755.*   McLennan, *op. cit.*, pp. 392-96.

²⁸ McLennan, *op. cit.*, p. 372.   C¹¹B, 30, *Prévost à Rouillé, 26 juin 1751*, fol. 198.

²⁹ B, 93, *Instruction pour le Sr. de Raymond, 24 avril 1751*, fol. 6.   C¹¹B, 32, *Prévost à Rouillé, 15 novembre 1752*, fol. 193.   C¹¹B, 33, *Raymond à Rouillé, 2 mai 1753*, fol. 53.   B, 97, *Rouillé à Prévost, 17 juillet 1753*, fol. 30.

³⁰ B, 89, *Maurepas à Bigot, 28 févier 1749*, fol. 5.   *Col. Mss.*, III, "A Short Account of what happended at Cape Breton (1760-58)," p. 484.

³¹ B, 91, *Rouillé à La Jonquière et Bigot, 19 mai 1750*, fol. 34.   B, 95, *Rouillé à Raymond, 20 mars 1752*, fol. 12.   B, 101, *Machault à Franquet, 16 février 1755*, fol. 1.   B, 105, *Maurepas à Drucourt, 24 décembre 1757*, fol. 23.   McLennan, *op. cit.*, p. 370.

CHAPTER IX

¹ *Voyage de Kalm en Amérique* (Montreal, 1880) pp. 126-27.   Le Sieur de C. (Courville), *Mémoires sur le Canada depuis 1749 jusqu'à 1760* (Quebec, 1848) p. 26.   La Jonquière, *Le Chef d'escadre, Marquis de La Jonquière* (Paris, 1895).

² C¹¹A, 92, *La Galissonnière et Bigot à Maurepas, 26 septembre, 3 novembre 1784*, p. 86; *Bigot à Maurepas, 16 septembre, 22 octobre, 25 octobre*, pp. 20, 47 and 51-52.   Guy Frégault, *François Bigot* (Montreal, 1948).

³ C¹¹A, 97, *La Jonquière à Rouillé, 1ᵉʳ mai 1751*, p. 10; *La Jonquière à Rouillé, 3 novembre 1751*, p. 216.   *Collection de manuscrits contenant lettres, mémoires et autres documents historiques relatifs à la Nouvelle-France*, III, "Extrait en forme de Journal, 1748," p. 418.   *Report of the Canadian Archives*, II, "La Corne à Rouillé, 31 mars 1750," p. 375.

⁴ C¹¹A, 96, *Bigot à Rouillé, 20 août 1750*, pp. 4-7; *La Jonquière à Rouillé, 1ᵉʳ mai 1751*, pp. 10-26.

⁵ *Documents relating to the Colonial History of the State of New York*, X, "Conference of M. de La Jonquière with the Cayugas, 15 May 1750," pp. 205-08; ". . . with the Onondagas, 11 July 1751," pp. 232-34.

⁶ C¹¹A, 95, *La Jonquière à Rouillé, 20 août 1750*, pp. 171-77.

⁷ C¹¹A, 95, *La Jonquière à Rouillé, 27 février 1750*, p. 94.   *Docts. N.Y.*, X, "Ministerial Minutes on the English Encroachments in the Ohio, 1752," p. 241.

⁸ C¹¹A, 95, *Lettres de Raymond à La Jonquière, 1749-50*, pp. 304-75; *La Jonquière à Rouillé, 24 août 1750*, pp. 178-81; *La Jonquière à Rouillé, 24 septembre 1750*, pp. 201-04.   C¹¹A, 97, *La Jonquière à Rouillé, 29 octobre 1751*, pp. 161-62.

⁹ B, 91, *Rouillé à La Jonquière, 27 mai 1750*, fol. 38½.   B, 89, *Rouillé à La Jonquière, 11 avril 1749*, fol. 11.

¹⁰ Frégault, *op. cit.*, I, pp. 364-67.   C¹¹A, 95, *La Jonquière à Rouillé, 16 septembre 1750*, pp. 185-86.   Courville, *Mémoires sur le Canada*, pp. 23-24.   *Rapport de l'archiviste de la province de Québec*, Courville, "Mémoire du Canada," p. 102.

¹¹ C¹¹A, 97, *La Jonquière à Rouillé, 19 octobre 1751*, pp. 138-42.

¹² C¹¹A, 97, *La Jonquière à Rouillé, 25 juillet 1750*, p. 97; *La Jonquière à Rouillé, 1ᵉʳ novembre 1751*, pp. 191-201.   B, 75, *Maurepas au P. Laraud, 27 avril 1742*, fol. 57½.   B, 81, *Maurepas à Beauharnois, 26 avril 1745*, fol. 37.

¹³ C¹¹A, 95, *La Jonquière à Rouillé, 25 julliet 1750*, pp. 131-44; *(Paroles des) Iroquois du Sault-Saint-Louis, 15 mai 1750*, pp. 145-47; *Ordre de La Jonquière,*

29 mai 1750, pp. 155-56.   B, 93, Rouillé à La Jonquière, 25 juin 1751, fol. 19.
14 C11A, 97, La Jonquière à Rouillé, 1er novembre 1751, fol. 191-201; Requête des demoiselles Dezaunier à Rouillé, pp. 277-81 and 282-95 (dossier).   B, 95, Rouillé à Duquesne, 16 juin 1752, fol. 31.
15 Courville, Mémoires, pp. 23-24.   La Jonquière, op. cit., p. 216.   B, 93, Rouillé à La Jonquière, 7 mai 1751, fol. 5.   C11A, 97, La Jonquière à Rouillé, 19 octobre 1751, fol. 5.   B, 95, Rouillé à La Jonquière, 28 février 1752, fol. 2. La Jonquière, op. cit., pp. 252-54.   Madame Bégon, "Correspondance," in R.A.Q., 1934-35, p. 34.
16 C11A, 98, Longueuil à Rouillé, 1er mai 1752, pp. 252-54.   Madame Bégon, "Correspondance," in R.A.Q., 1934-35, p. 73.   Courville, Mémoires, pp. 57-58.   Edits et ordonnances royaux, III, "Provisions de Gouverneur de Duquesne, 1er mars 1752," p. 77.
17 B, 95, Rouillé à Duquesne, 15 mai 1750, fol. 7.
18 C11A, 98, Du Quesne à Rouillé, 25 octobre 1752, pp. 32-33.   Docts. N.Y., X, "Longueuil à Rouillé, 21 avril 1752," p. 250; "Longueuil à Rouillé, 18 août 1752," p. 260.
19 C11A, 98, Bigot à Rouillé, 10 octobre 1752, p. 139; Duquesne à Rouillé, 3 novembre 1752, pp. 62-65; Duquesne, 26 octobre 1753, pp. 68-73.   Courville, Mémoires, p. 29.   B, 95, Récapitulation des milices, 1750, p. 268; Mémoire du Canada, p. 103.
20 C11A, 98, Bigot à Rouillé, 26 octobre 1752, pp. 175-96.   Docts. N.Y., X, "Duquesne à Rouillé, 20 août 1753," pp. 255-57.   C11A, 98, Duquesne à Rouillé, 2 novembre 1753, pp. 38-42; Duquesne à Machault, 7 octobre 1754, p. 260.
21 B, 99, Rouillé à Duquesne, 31 mai 1754, fol. 24; Rouillé à Duquesne, 29 novembre 1753, p. 53.
22 Pierre Pouchot, Mémoires sur la dernière guerre de l'Amérique Septentrionale (Yverdon, 1781) p. 11.   B, 99, Rouillé à Bigot, 1er juin 1754, fols. 26 and 27; Duquesne à Rouillé, 27 octobre 1753, pp. 33-37.
23 B, 99, Rouillé à Duquesne, 31 mai 1754, fol. 24.   Docts. N.Y., X, "Dinwiddie to St. Pierre, 31 octobre 1753," pp. 258-59.   Papiers Contrecœur et autres documents concernant le conflit anglo-français sur l'Ohio de 1745 à 1756, ed. by Fernand Grenier (Quebec, 1952) pp. 77 and 84.   Washington, "Journey to the Ohio," in P. L. Ford, Writings of George Washington, I, p. 11 ff.
24 C11A, 99, Duquesne à Machault, 12 octobre 1754, p. 285.   Papiers Contrecœur, "Sommations de Contrecœur aux Anglais, 16 avril 1754," pp. 117-18; "Duquesne à Contrecœur, 11 mai 1754," p. 125; ". . . 12 mai 1754," p. 127. Except where otherwise indicated, the documents cited in the following notes appear in to the Papiers Contrecœur.
25 "Washington's Journal, 1754," pp. 134 and 156.
26 "Sommation de Jumonville, 23 mai 1754, avec endos de Contrecœur," pp. 130-31; "Washington's Journal," p. 157.   Mémoires contenant le précis des faits avec pièces justificatives (Paris, 1756).   Col. Mss., III, "Liste du sort du parti de M. de Villiers de Jumonville, 1754," pp. 521-22.   Arch. Can., Nelson Collection, II, Rev. J. B. Boucher to Nielsen, 10 mai 1806, pp. 19-20.   Gilbert F. Leduc, Washington and "The Murder of Jumonville" (Boston, 1935). Marcel Trudel, "L'Affaire Jumonville," Revue d'histoire de l'Amérique française (décembre 1952) pp. 330-73.
27 "Washington's Journal," pp. 158-60; "Capitulation de Fort Nécéssité, 3 juillet 1754," pp. 202-05; "Duquesne à Contrecœur, 24 juin 1754," p. 192. The latest French historian to treat the question, Pierre Gaxotte, wrote in Le Siècle de Louis XV (1960 edition) pp. 252-53: "Washington, a big awkward lad, slow of mind and heavy in body and countenance, behaved, on this occasion, like a murderer."
27a B, 99, Machault à Duquesne, 19 août 1754, fol. 38.
28 "Washington's Journal," p. 161; "Duquesne à Contrecœur, 24 juin 1754," p. 192.   C11A, Varin à Bigot, 24 juillet 1754, p. 8.   F3, 12, Journal de la campagne de M. de Villiers, 6 septembre 1754, fol. 62 ff.   Leduc, op. cit., passim.
29 C11A, 99, Duquesne à Machault, 3 novembre 1754, p. 322.   C11A, 100, Vaudreuil à Machault, 21 octobre 1755, p. 115.   Paroles de Contrecœur, 16 juin 1755, p. 363.
30 C11A, 99, Bigot à Rouillé, 28 août 1753, pp. 49-53.   B, 99, Rouillé à

Duquesne, 31 mai 1754, fol. 19, fol. 21½, fol. 25; *Machault à Duquesne, 1er avril 1755,* fol. 30.   Louis Franquet, *Voyages et Mémoires sur le Canada* (Quebec, 1889) p. 146.
    ³¹ Courville, *Mémoires,* p. 58.   C¹¹A, 99, *Duquesne à Machault, 9 octobre 1754,* pp. 272-74; . . . *12 octobre 1754,* pp. 288-89; . . . *29 septembre 1754,* p. 244.

CHAPTER X

    ¹ Nova Scotia State Papers, A, *Vetch to Lords of Trade, 24 novembre 1714,* p. 7; *Caulfield to Lords of Trade, 1 November 1715,* pp. 8-9.
    ² *Le Canada Français. Collection de documents inédits,* I, "Description de l'Acadie, 1748," p. 44.   B, 78, *Maurepas à Du Quesnel et Bigot, 17 avril 1744,* fol. 6.   B, 81, *Maurepas à Mgr de Pontbriand, 12 mai 1745,* fol. 64.
    ³ "Beauharnois et Hocquart à Maurepas, 2 septembre 1745," in E. Lauvrière *La Tragédie d'un peuple* (Paris, 1922) vol. I, p. 298.   B, 81, *Maurepas à Mgr de Pontbriand, 12 mai 1745,* fol. 64.   *Documents inédits,* I, "Journal de la campagne," (Ramezay's campaign), pp. 35 and 41.   C¹¹A, 84-1, *Etat des certificats donnés aux habitants acadiens pour fournitures, 4 septembre 1746,* pp. 155-56.
    ⁴ N.S., A. *Mascarene to Lords of Trade, 7 and 9 November 1745; Representations of the state of Nova Scotia by a Committee of Council (13 May 1745); 12 May 1745; To Secretary of State, 15 June 1748.*
    ⁵ N.S., A., *Mascarene to Secretary of State, 9 December 1745* (enclosed, letter to Shirley).
    ⁶ Letters from Shirley, 15 August 1746 and 8 July 1748 in Laurière, *op. cit.,* I, pp. 304 and 309.
    ⁷ *Rapport des Archives Canadiennes,* II, "Mascarene to Newcastle, 22 January (1746) 1747," p. 103; "Newcastle to Shirley, 30 1747," p. 104; "Proclamation by Shirley (21 octobre 1747)," pp. 105-07.
    ⁸ *R.A.C.,* 1905, II, "Instructions to Cornwallis, 2 May 1749," p. 106; "Advertisements in the London Gazette, 7 March 1748 (9)."   "List of the transports, 1749," in Beamish Murdoch, *A History of Nova Scotia, or Acadia* (Halifax, 1865-67) vol. II, pp. 147-48.
    ⁹ *R.A.C.,* 1905, II, "Proclamation by Cornwallis, 14 July 1749," p. 109; "Second declaration, 1st August 1749," p. 110; "Requête des Acadiens à Cornwallis (8 septembre 1749)"; "Copie du serment de fidelité (20 octobre 1727)," pp. 361-63.
    ¹⁰ *Ibid.,* "Réponse de S. E. le Gouverneur aux députés, 5 septembre 1749," p. 364.   N. S., A, *Cornwallis to Lords of Trade, 1st September 1749; Lords of Trade to Cornwallis, 10 February 1750.*
    ¹¹ *R.A.C.,* 1905, II, "La Galissonnière à Rouillé, 25 juillet 1749," p. 367; "Requête des Acadiens au Roy de France (Octobre 1749)," pp. 361-62; "Requête des habitants de Port-Royal à M. de La Jonquière, décembre 1749," pp. 364-65.
    Selections from the Public documents of the Province of Nova Scotia, Nova Scotia Archives, ed. by T. B. Akins (Halifax, 1869) "Robinson to Lawrence, 13 August 1755."
    ¹² *R.A.C.,* 1905, II, Colonies, "Lu au Roy (1749)," p. 355; "La Galissonnière à Rouillé, 25 juillet 1749," p. 374.   B, 93, *Rouillé à La Jonquière avril 1751,* fol. 3.
    ¹³ *R.A.C.,* 1905, II, "Déclaration de guerre des Micmacs, 23 septembre 1749," p. 356; "Bigot à Rouillé, 18 octobre 1750," p. 380.   N. S., A, *Proclamation (with a letter from Shirley to Newcastle, 20 October 1747; Cornwallis to Bedford, 17 October 1749.*
    ¹³ᵃ *R.A.C.,* 1905, II, "Bigot à Rouillé, 18 octobre 1750," p. 380.   Father Louis-Marie Le Jeune, *Dictionnaire général* (Ottawa, 1931) p. 133.
    ¹⁴ *R.A.C.,* 1905, II, "Récit de la marche du détachement du Major Lawrence, 1750," pp. 383-86; "Mémoire joint à la lettre du Marquis de Puyzieulx du 15 septembre 1750," p. 396; "La Corne à Des Herbiers, 1750," pp. 386-87.
    ¹⁵ C¹¹A, 93, *Mémoire concernant l'affaire du London et du Saint-François, novembre 1750,* pp. 210-19.   C¹¹B, *Des Herbiers à Rouillé, 29 juin 1751,* fol. 118.
    ¹⁶ *R.A.C.,* 1905, II, "Journal de La Vallière, 1750-51," pp. 388-94.   C¹¹A, 96, *Bigot à Rouillé, 6 novembre 1750,* p. 100.   C¹¹B, 29, *Prévost à Rouillé, 25 octobre 1750,* fol. 124.
    ¹⁷ *Collection de manuscrits contenant lettres, mémoires et autres documents*

historiques relatifs à la Nouvelle-France, IV,"Prévost à Rouillé, 15 octobre 1750," pp. 496-98.

18 *Rapport de l'archiviste de la province de Québec*, 1905, II, p. 389. *Nova Scotia Documents*, "Shirley to Lawrence, 6 January 1755," p. 393 *ff.* C¹¹B, 29, *Prévost à Rouillé, 27 octobre 1750*, fol. 131. N. S., A, *Cornwallis to Lords of Trade, 27 November 1750. Col. Mss.*, III, "A Short Account. . . ." (1750), pp. 466-67. The most reliable account of the incident is that of La Vallière, an eye-witness.

19 B, 93, *Rouillé à La Jonquière, 23 février 1751*, fol. 1. C¹¹B, 31, *Mirepoix à de Puyzieulx, 25 mars 1751*, and *Mémoire*, fol. 253. N. S., A, 43, *Cornwallis to Lords of Trade, 3 November 1751*, pp. 135-36.

20 N. S., A, 49, *Hopson to Raymond, 10 August 1752*, p. 5; *Raymond to Hopson, 30 August 1752*, pp. 20-21.

21 N. S., A, 50, *Hopson to Lords of Trade, 10 December 1752*, pp. 43-45 and 52; *Lords of Trade to Hopson, 28 March 1753*, pp. 110-11; *Hopson to Lords of Trade, 23 July 1753*, p. 199. Courville, *Mémoires* pp. 31-33.

22 *Canada Census, 1871*, IV, p. 34. C¹¹B, 33, *Prévost à Rouillé, 16 août*, fol. 197. N. S., A, *Lawrence to Lords of Trade, 20 août 1753*, fol. 197. N. S., A, *Lawrence to Lords of Trade, 20 October 1753; Instructions to Goff, 13 January 1750*.

23 N. S., A, *Lawrence to Lords of Trade, 5 December 1753*, pp. 222-23; *Lords of Trade to Lawrence, 4 April 1754*, pp. 57-60.

24 N. S., *Shirley to Robinson, 23 May 1754*, p. 382. N. S., A, *Lawrence to Lords of Trade, 7 May 1755; Lawrence to Shirley, 5 November 1754; Lords of Trade to Robinson, 31 October 1754.*

25 *Collection des manscrits du maréchal Lévis*, ed. by the Abbé H. R. Casgrain (Montreal and Quebec, 1889-95) vol. IX. *Relations et Journaux de différentes expéditions faites durant les années 1757, 1758, 1759 and 1760* "Journal de l'attaque de Beauséjour (Jacau de Fiedmont)," pp. 7-51. Mme Bégon, *Correspondance, février 1749*, p. 364. N. S., A, *Lawrence to Board of Trade, 28 June 1755*, with terms of capitulation. *Documents inédits*, II, "Tyrell (Pichon) à Bulkeley, 26 septembre 1755," p. 129. Courville, *Mémoires*, pp. 45-51. *R.A.Q.*, 1924-25, "Mémoire du Canada," pp. 109-10. Gaston Duboscq de Beaumont, *Les Derniers jours de l'Acadie* (Paris, 1899) pp. 146-47.

26 B, 103, *Machault à Vaudreuil, 20 février 1756*, fol. 2. C¹¹A, 103, *Vaudreuil à Massiac, 12 juin 1758*, pp. 76-77. Courville, *Mémoires*, pp. 61-62. *R.A.Q.*, 1924-25, "Mémoire du Canada," pp. 131-34. B, 95, *Machault à Guillot, 23 février 1756*, fol. 38. *R.A.C.*, 1904, Appendix G, Documents concerning Bigot, Vergor and de Villeray (1755-58), pp. 5-19.

27 *R.A.C.*, 1905, II, "Extrait du Journal de Boishébert, 23 juillet 1755," p. 236. N. S., A, 58, *Lawrence to Lords of Trade, 18 July 1755*, p. 32. C¹¹B, *Boishébert à Drucourt, 10 octobre 1755*, p. 152.

28 N. S., B, *Minutes of the Council, 3 July 1755*, pp. 159-81; *14 July 1755*, pp. 182-84; *15 July 1755*, p. 197; *28 July 1755*, pp. 198-206. N. S., A, 58. cf. Guy Frégault, "La Déportation des Acadiens," *R. H. A. F.* (décembre, 1954).

29 N. S., A, *Population, 1755*, p. 47. N. S., *Lawrence to Monckton, 8 August 1755*, pp. 261-67; *Lawrence to Winslow, 11 August 1755*, pp. 271-74; *Circular letter to Governors, 11 August 1755*, pp. 55-57.

30 Nova Scotia Historical Society Collection, *Winslow's Journal*, pp. 98, 227, 277; *Diary of John Thomas*, pp. 130-31.

31 *Ibid.*, pp. 131-37; *Winslow's Journal*, pp. 100-01, 151, 185 and 228-30.

32 *Ibid.*, pp. 228, 101, 122, 137, 177 and 95; *Diary of John Thomas*, pp.134-37. *R.A.C.*, 1905, II, Boishébert, "Extrait du Journal, 30 juillet 1755," pp. 236-37. 236-37.

33 *Winslow's Journal*, pp. 272-73.

34 *Ibid.*, pp. 108-109 and 113.

35 *Ibid.*, pp. 102, 113, 171 and 187.

36 Placide Gaudet, "The Acadian Fugitives," *The New Brunswick Magazine* (January 1899) pp. 35-37. *Winslow's Journal*, pp. 122 and 185. Alexandre Dugré, "Ce qu'on a dit de l'Acadie," *Relations* (août, 1955) p. 207.

37 N. S., A, 58, *Lawrence to Lords of Trade, 18 October 1755*, pp. 84-100; *Lords of Trade to Lawrence, 23 March 1756; Order in Council, 18 December 1755*.

[38] C[11]A, 85, *Beauharnois et Hocquart à Maurepas, 8-12 novembre 1746,* p. 235.   *R. A. C.,* 1905, II, *"Requête des habitants du Port-Royal à La Jonquière,* décembre 1749," p. 365.   N. S., A, *Secretary of State to Wilmot, 11 February 1763.*

[38a] C[11]A, 101, *Vaudreuil à Machault, 7 juin 1756,* pp. 24-25.

[39] Gaudet, "The Acadian Fugitives," *supra cit., New Brunswick Magazine* (January, 1899) pp. 35-37.   *R.A.C.,* 1905, II, "Vaudreuil à Machault, 1er juin 1756," p. 240.   N. S., A, 60, *Lords of Trade to Lawrence, 8 July 1756,* p. 97.   *R.A.C.,* 1905, II, Gaudet, "Généalogie des familles acadiennes," pp. 5 and 16-18; "Loi relative à une repartition équitable des habitants français, janvier 1756," p. 217; "Vaudreuil à Machault, 5 août 1756," p. 242.

[40] C[11]A, 102, *Vaudreuil au ministre, 19 avril 1757,* fol. 30.   *R.A.C.,* 1905, p. 15; "Abbé le Guerne à Prévost, 10 mars 1756," pp. 410-11 and 415; "Vaudreuil à Machault, 6 août 1756," pp. 240-41.

[40a] *Journal des campagnes du chevalier de Lévis, 8 novembre 1757,* p. 122. C[11]A, 102, *Vaudreuil au ministre, 14 juillet 1757,* fol. 81.

[41] *R.A.C.,* 1905, II, "Vaudreuil à Machault, 1er juin 1756," p. 242; ". . . 6 août 1756," pp. 241-42.   N. S., A, *Lawrence to Board of Trade, 28 April 1756.* C[11]B, 38, *Villejoin à Massiac, 8 septembre 1758,* fol. 165.   B, 110, *Berryer à Ranché, 2 mars 1759,* fol. 75½; *Guillot, 30 avril 1759,* fol. 156.   J. S. McLennan, *Louisburg from its Foundation to its Fall, 1713-58* (London, 1918) p. 290. *R.A.C.,* 1905, II, "Séance du Conseil, 28 novembre 1761," p. 320.   N. S., A, *Belcher to Egremont, 9 January 1762; Belcher to Amherst,* 12 August 1762.

[42] B, 117, *Le Ministre à Berryer, 23 janvier 1763,* fol. 36.   B, 122, *Le Ministre à Clugny, 21 octobre 1765,* fol. 33; *Etat des personnes de l'Acadie (au Poitou), 30 octobre 1773,* fol. 179.   N. S., A, *Halifax to Wilmot, 11 February 1764.*

[43] *Canada Census, 1871,* IV, p. 35.   N. S., A, *Belcher to Lords of Trade* 14 *April 1761, and Report of Council; Belcher to Egremont, 9 January 1762.* *R.A.C.,* 1905, II, "Séance du Conseil 27 mars 1764," p. 321.

[44] *Ibid.,* "Ordre du Conseil privé, 11 juillet 1764," pp. 271-72; "Wilmot aux Lords du Commerce, 17 décembre 1764," p. 277; "Franklin à Shelburne, 28 février 1768," p. 281.   *Canada Census, 1871,* IV, p. 62.

[45] N. S., A, *Richard Cumberland to Lords of Trade, 24 March 1760; Treasury to Lords of Trade, 7 July 1761, with Baker and Saul's letter; Lords of Trade to Belcher, 3 March 1761.   Documents inédits,* I, (Letter, 1757) p. 147.

[46] N. S., A, *Lords of Trade to Lawrence, 25 March 1756; Lawrence to Board of Trade, 26 December 1758; Lords of Trade to Lawrence, 8 July 1756; Lawrence to Board of Trade, 3 Novembre 1756; . . . 16 June 1760; . . . 24 July 1760.*

[47] N. S., A, *Treaty of peace with Micmac nation, 1762, with Belcher's letter to Lords of Trade, 11 January 1762.   Canada Census,* 1871, IV, pp. 34 and 62.

CHAPTER XI

[1] *Canada Census, 1871,* IV, p. XXI.

[2] C[11]A, 34, *Mémoire de plusieurs choses, 1714,* p. 454.   *Collection de manuscrits contenant lettres, mémoires et autres documents historiques relatifs à la Nouvelle-France,* III, "Vaudreuil et Bégon au ministre, 14 octobre 1716," pp. 22-23.

[2a] F[3], 7, *Ordonnance du roi, 20 mars 1714,* fol. 280.   *Edits et ordonnances royaux,* I, "Ordonnance du Roi, 15 février 1724," pp. 485-86. (With the ordinances of November 16, 1716 and March 21, 1721.) The essential study on the subject is Marcel Trudel, *L'Esclavage au Canada* (Quebec, 1960).

[3] Gaucher, Delafosse et Debien, "Les Engagés pour le Canada au XVIIIe siècle," *R.H.A.F.* (December, 1960 and March, 1961) pp. 431-39 and 583-93. C[11]A, 93, *Bigot à Rouillé, 21 octobre 1749,* p. 327.   B, 101, *Machault à Vaudreuil et Bigot, 15 juillet 1755,* fol. 15.

[4] C[11]A, 41, *Lettre à Vaudreuil et Bégon, 23 octobre 1719,* fol. 38.   B, 44, *Ordonnance au sujet des prisonniers, 14 janvier 1721,* fol. 130.

[5] *Rapport de l'archiviste de la province de Québec, 1947-48,* "Pontchartrain à Vaudreuil, 28 juin 1712," p. 157.   C[11]A, 45, *Vaudreuil et Bégon à Pontchartrain, 14 octobre 1723,* pp. 3-4.   C[11]A, 48, *(Beauharnois) 28 septembre 1726,* fol. 155.   B, 53, *Le Conseil de Marine à Beauharnois et Hocquart, 2 mai 1729,* fol. 548½.

[6] C[11]A, 51, *Beauharnois et Hocquart, 25 octobre 1729,* fol. 22.   C[11]A, 52 . . . *15 octobre 1730,* fol. 78.   B, 49, *Le Conseil de Marine à Beauharnois et*

Dupuy, 14 mai 1726, fol. 645; . . . *à Mgr de Saint-Vallier, 14 mai 1726*, fol. 674.
B, 54, *Maurepas à Beauharnois et Hocquart, 28 mars 1730*, fol. 407.

6a Gérard Malchelosse, "Fils de Famille en Nouvelle-France," *Cahiers des Dix*, XI (Montreal, 1946) pp. 267-309.   B, 49, *Conseil de Marine à Beauharnois et Depuy, 14 mai 1726*, fol. 643½.   C[11]A, 48, *Beauharnois à Maurepas, 28 septembre 1726*, fol. 155; . . . *15 octobre 1738*.   Joseph Edmond Roy, "Des fils de famille envoyés au Canada," *Proceedings and Transactions of the Royal Society of Canada*, 1901.

6b C[11]A, 69, *Beauharnois et Hocquart à Maurepas, 15 octobre 1738*.

6c Emile Salone, *La Colonisation de la Nouvelle-France. Etude sur les origines de la nation canadienne française* (Paris, 1906) p. 350, note.   B, 49, *Conseil de Marine à Mgr de Saint-Vallier, 14 mai 1726*, fol. 674.   B, 52, *Conseil de Marine à Beauharnois et Dupuy, 15 mai 1728*, p. 238.   B, 54, *Maurepas à Beauharnois et Hocquart, 28 mars 1730*, fol. 407.

7 B, 54, *Maurepas à Beauharnois et Hocquart, 25 avril 1730*, fol. 472; *Ordre du roi pour le transport de faux-sauniers et contrebandiers, 25 avril 1730*, fol. 491.   C[11]A, *Beauharnois et Hocquart, 4 octobre 1730*, pp. 60-62.   B, 55, *Maurepas à Beauharnois et Hocquart, 27 avril 1731*, fol. 502; *Maurepas à Fagon, 31 decembre 1731*, fol. 637.

8 B, 57, *Maurepas à Beauharnois et Hocquart, 8 avril 1732*, fol. 637; *Maurepas à Mgr. Dosquet, 22 avril 1732*, fol. 650.   B, 58, *Maurepas à Beauharnois et Hocquart, 21 avril 1733*, fol. 434½.   B, 74, *11 février 1742*, fol. 1½.   C[11]A, 93, *1749*, fol. 108.   B, 55, *Maurepas à Fagon, 31 décembre 1741*, fol. 637.   B, 64, *Maurepas au gouverneur, 17 avril 1736*, fol. 427.

8a The estimates given by Malchelosse (648) and Salone (661) are necessarily inaccurate, since the numbers of deported men were not included in any official statistics. Salone also omits from his list twenty-six men deported in 1730.

8b *Edits et Ord.*, I, "Ordonnance au sujet des faux sauniers, 14 février 1742," pp. 560-61.   C[11]A, 54, *Beauharnois et Hocquart à Maurepas, 5 octobre 1741*, fol. 77.   C[11]A, 73, *Beauharnois et Hocquart à Maurepas, 14 octobre 1743*, p. 34.

9 *Ibid.*

9a *R.A.Q.*, 1930-31, "Colbert à Talon, 20 février 1668," p. 91.   *R.A.Q.*, 1947-48, "Vaudreuil à Pontchartrain, 20 septembre 1714," p. 277.

10 C[11]A, 93, *La Jonquière et Bigot à Rouillé, 4 octobre 1749*, p. 29.   C[11]A, 43, *Délibérations du Conseil de Marine, 2 décembre 1721*, fol. 320.   C[11]A, 59, *Beauharnois et Hocquart à Maurepas, 4 octobre 1733*, fol. 163.

11 C[11]A, 87, *La Galissonnière à Maurepas, 3 novembre 1747*, fol. 274.   C[11]A, 87, *La Jonquière à Rouillé, 1er novembre 1750*, p. 245.   Salone, *op. cit.*, p. 346.   *Annuaire statistique de la province de Québec*, p. 125.

12 *R.A.Q.*, 1947-48, "Vaudreuil à Pontchartrain, 14 avril 1714," pp. 252-53.   *Edits et Ord.*, I, "Lettres patentes concernant le commerce à l'étranger octobre 1727," p. 519.   B, 52, *Maurepas à Dupuy, 4 mai 1728*, fol. 480.   Charlotte Alice Baker, *True Stories of New England Captives carried to Canada during the old French and Indian Wars* (Cambridge, Mass., 1897) pp. 56, 145 and 327.

13 B, 91, *Rouillé à La Jonquière et Bigot, 31 mai 1750*, fol. 13.   C[11]A, 93, *Bigot à Rouillé, 11 octobre 1750*, p. 512.   C[11]A, 95, *La Jonquière et Bigot à Rouillé, 23 octobre 1750*, pp. 77-78.   B, 106, *Rouillé à Paulmy, 27 novembre 1759*, fol. 150.

14 *Col. Mss.*, III, "Liste du parti de Jumonville, 1754," p. 522.   *R.A.Q.*, 1918, "Ordonnance de Gage pour rendre hommes, femmes et enfants anglais prisonniers ou déserteurs, 13 mai 1761," p. 45.

14a Paul-Emile Renaud, *Les Origines économiques du Canada* (Mamers, 1928) pp. 284-85.   Salone, *op. cit.*, p. 353.

15 *Canada Census, 1871*, IV, pp. XXI, 57 and 61.   G[1], vol. 461, *Dénombrement des habitants du Détroit, 1750*.   C[11]A, 102, *Vaudreuil au ministre, 14 juillet 1757*, fol. 81.   *Journal des campagnes du chevalier de Lévis, 8 novembre 1757*, p. 122.   C[11]A, 104-1, *Montcalm à Belle-Isle, 12 avril 1759*, p. 172.   Beaumat, "Considérations sur l'état présent du Canada, octobre 1758," *Société littéraire et historique de Québec*, 1838, p. 4.   *Canada Census*, 1931, p. 141.

15a *Canada Census, 1871*, IV, "Census of 1685," p. 16; ". . . 1692," p. 28; ". . . 1698," p. 40.   C[11]A, 66, *Dénombrements des nations sauvages, 14 octobre*

1736, fol. 236 *ff.*　C¹¹A, 67, *Canada. Détail de toute la colonie* (1737).
Documents relating to the Constitutional History of Canada, ed. by Adam Shortt
and Arthur G. Doughty (Ottawa, 1911) "Colonel Burton's Report, 1762," vol. I
and "General Murray's Report, 1762," vol. I.　B, 62, *Maurepas à l'abbé
Brisacier, 8 octobre 1735*, fol. 88½.　Louis Franquet, *Voyages et Mémoires sur le
Canada* (Quebec, 1889) p. 35.　Salone, *op. cit.,* pp. 413-14.　C¹¹A, 76, *Hocquart à Maurepas, 24 octobre 1741,* p. 23.
　¹⁵ᵇ Trudel, *op. cit.,*pp. 84 and 89.　B, 63, *Mémoire du roi à Beauharnois
et Hocquart, 11 avril 1735,* fol. 462½.
　¹⁵ᶜ G1, 461, *Recensement général de la Nouvelle-France, 1739.*　*Canada
Census, 1871,* IV, pp. 60-61, 64-65.　B, 83, *Maurepas à Beauharnois et Hocquart, 7 mars 1746,* fol. 16.　*Edits et Ord.,* II, "Ordonnance, 20 avril 1749,"
pp. 399-400.

CHAPTER XII

　¹ *Edits et ordonnances royaux,* I, "Arrêt du sujet des concessions, 6 juillet
1711," pp. 324-425; "Arrêt au sujet des terres, 11 juillet 1711," p. 326.　*Rapport de l'archiviste de la province de Québec, 1947-48,* "Le Conseil de Marine à
Vaudreuil et Bégon, 15 juin 1716," p. 304.
　¹ᵃ *Pièces et documents relatifs à la tenure seigneuriale* (Quebec, 1852). 4
vols.　C¹¹A, 85, *Hocquart à Maurepas, 24 octobre 1746,* fol. 345.　Ivanhoé
Caron, *La Colonisation du Canada sous la domination française* (Quebec, 1916)
vol. II, pp. 61-63.　Emile Salone, *La Colonisation de la Nouvelle-France* (Paris,
1906) pp. 363-68.
　¹ᵇ *Canada Census, 1871,* IV, p. 53.　G1, vol. 461, *Recensement général de
la Nouvelle-France, 1739; Recensement de 1732.*　B, 54, *Maurepas à Hocquart,
21 mars 1730,* fol. 400.　B, 83, *Maurepas à Hocquart, 7 mars 1746,* fol. 11.
C¹¹A, 93, *Bigot à Rouillé, 25 septembre 1749,* pp. 350-52.
　¹ᶜ G1, 461, *Recensements, année 1739.*　*Canada Census, 1871,* IV, p. 65.
　¹ᵈ C¹¹A, *Vaudreuil et Bégon au Conseil, 4 novembre 1721; Beauharnois et
Hocquart à Maurepas, 1ᵉʳ septembre 1736.*　B, 97, *Le ministre à La Jonquière
et Bigot, 30 avril 1750,* fol. 28; *La Jonquière et Bigot à Maurepas, 2 janvier 1750,*
fol. 8.　G1, 461, *Recensements du Détroit, 1750.*
　¹ᵉ G1, 461, *Recensements de 1721, 1739, 1746.*
　¹ᶠ "Considérations sur l'état présent du Canada," in Courville, *Mémoires sur
le Canada,* pp. 14-15 and 26-28.　Louis Franquet, *Voyages et Mémoires sur le
Canada* (Quebec, 1889) pp. 177-78.　B, 96, *Le ministre à Montavan, 3 août 1752,*
fol. 125.　*Inventaire des Ordonnances,* III, "21 août 1752," p. 173.　C¹¹A, 98,
Mémoire de Toché, 1732, fol. 460.
　¹ᵍ *Edits et Ord.,* II, "Règlements généraux du Conseil Supérieur, 11 mai
1676," p. 67.　*Canada Census, 1871,* IV, pp. 53 and 57.　C¹¹A, *Ferme de
Tadoussac, 1728,* fol. 409.　G1, 461, *Recensement général, 1739.*　B, 76,
Maurepas à Hocquart, 13 juin 1743, fol. 3; *Hocquart au Ministre, 27 octobre
1744,* fol. 446.
　² C¹¹A, 46, *Prat à Maurepas, octobre 1723,* pp. 240-42.　B, 53, *Le Conseil
de Marine à Hocquart, 19 avril 1729,* fol. 504½.　B, 55, *Mémoire du roi à
Beauharnois et Hocquart, 8 mai 1731,* fol. 521.　B, 58, *12 mai 1733,* fol. 470½.
　C¹¹A, 60, *Liste des vaisseaux construits en 1732 et 1733,* fol. 487-88.　B, 68,
Mémoire du roi à Beauharnois et Hocquart, 1ᵉʳ mai 1739, fol. 34.　B, 76-1,
Maurepas à Levasseur, 11 avril 1743, fol. 19.
　²ᵃ B, 81, *Maurepas à Beauharnois et Hocquart, 1ᵉʳ mai 1745,* fol. 54.　C¹¹A,
95, *Beauharnois et Hocquart à Maurepas, 19 septembre 1746,* p. 8.　B, 110,
Machault à Vaudreuil, 15 juillet 1755, fol. 16.　Guy Frégault, *François Bigot*
(Montreal, 1948) vol. I, p. 420.　C¹¹A, 103-2, *Levasseur au ministre, 30 octobre
1758,* pp. 505-07.　Pierre Georges Roy, "La Construction Royale de Québec,"
Cahiers des Dix, XI, 1946, pp. 142-46 and 151-84.　B, 99, *Le ministre à Bigot,
14 juin 1754,* fol. 37; *Le ministre à Levasseur, 30 juin 1753,* fol. 53.
　³ B, 54, *Mémoire du roi à Beauharnois et Hocquart, 16 avril 1730,* fol. 132½.
　C¹¹A, 57, *Beauharnois et Hocquart à Maurepas, 15 octobre 1732,* fol. 200.
B, 58, *Maurepas à Francheville, 30 avril 1732,* fol. 437½.　B, 61, *Maurepas à
Beauharnois et Hocquart, 13 avril 1734,* and fol. 313.
　⁴ B, 65, *Arrêt du 22 avril 1737,* fol. 436½; *Maurepas à Orry, 25 mars 1737,* fol.
39.　B, 76, *Maurepas à Beauharnois et Hocquart, 30 avril 1743,* fol. 48; *Arrêt*

du roi, 1er mai 1743, fol. 51.   B, 86, Maurepas à Bigot,11 décembre 1747, fol. 178.   C11A, 88, Etat du produit des forges, 1er janvier 1757, fol. 178.   C11A, 96, Mémoire de l'état du Canada (Payet), 1705, fol. 298.

5 B, 61, Maurepas à Beauharnois et Hocquart, 20 avril 1734, fol. 520½.   B, 58, 6 mai 1733, fol. 499½; Mémoire du roi à Beauharnois et Hocquart, 20 avril 1734, fol. 537½.   B, 78, 24 mars 1744, fol. 33.

6 Noël Fauteux, Essai sur l'industrie au Canada sous le régime français (Quebec, 1927) vol. II, p. 316.   C11A, 60, Chevigny à Maurepas, 14 octobre 1739, p. 215.   C11A, 84, Hocquart à Maurepas, 18 octobre 1745, fol. 270.   B, 94, Rouillé à Beauharnois, 20 avril 1742, fol. 68.

7 C11A, 46, Etat des pêches à Marsouins en 1724, fol. 269.   C11A, 48, Mémoire sur la pêche aux Marsouins, 1728, fol. 448.   C11A, 50, Etat des pêches de Marsouins, 1728, fol. 155.   Fauteux, op. cit., pp. 536-37.

8 R.A.Q., 1947-48, "Vaudreuil et Bégon à Pontchartrain, 12 novembre 1712," p. 173; "Mémoire du roi, 15 juin 1716," p. 303.   C11A, 83, Etat des huiles de loup-marin, 1744, p. 353.   Charles de La Morandière, Les Français au Labrador au XVIIIe siècle (Académie de Marine) vol. II, pp. 246-57.

9 Fauteux, op. cit., II, pp. 468-73.   F3, 6, Lettres patentes pour établir des manufactures à l'hôpital général, 20 mai 1698, fol. 109.   B, 87, Maurepas à La Galissonnière et Hocquart, 6 mars 1748, fol. 48.   C11A, 91, La Galissonnière et Bigot à Maurepas, 26 septembre 1748, Bigot à Maurepas, 1er octobre 1748, p. 39.

10 Jugements et délibérations du Conseil souverain, VI, 1714, p. 841.   C11A, 36, Vaudreuil et Bégon au Conseil, 14 novembre 1716, pp. 24-28.   C11A, 43, Bégon au Conseil, 2 novembre 1721, fol. 354.   C11A, 48, Dupuy à Pontchartrain, 14 octobre 1726, fol. 261; Mémoire de la veuve de Ramezay, 1726, fol. 243.

11 C11A, 49, Dupuy à Maurepas, 20 octobre 1727, fol. 329.   B, 52, Maurepas à Beauharnois et Dupuy, 14 mai 1728, fol. 490.   B,57, Mémoire du roi à Beauharnois et Hocquart, 22 avril 1732, fol. 562½.   B, 58, Maurepas à Hocquart, 6 mai 1733, fol. 455.   B,63, Maurepas à Beauharnois, 19 avril 1735, fol. 487.   Inventaire des ordonnances, III, "Ordonnance, 30 juin 1756," p. 198.

12 B, 62, Maurepas à Salvy, 27 décembre 1735, fol. 110.   B, 64, Mémoire du roi à Beauharnois et Hocquart, 15 mai 1736, pp. 609-11.   Fauteux, op. cit., II, pp. 488-90.   B, 88, Maurepas à La Galissonnière et Hocquart, 6 mars 1748, fol. 48.   Caron, op. cit., p. XIII.

13 Edits et Ord., I, "Lettres patentes de la Compagnie d' Occident, août 1717," pp. 377-78; "Arrêt du Conseil au sujet du castor, 4 juin 1719," p. 410.   B, 109, Berryer à Bigot, 8 janvier 1759, fol. 6.

14 F3, 7, Déclaration du roi rétablissant les 25 congés, 28 avril 1716, fol. 356.   C11A, 40, Vaudreuil et Bégon au ministre, 2 octobre 1719, fol. 50.   C11A, 50, Etat de la distribution des congés rétablis par Sa Majesté, 1728, fol. 151.   B, 52, Maurepas à Dupuy, 14 mars 1728, fol. 497.   C11A, 79, Etat de distribution des congés en 1743, pp. 259-62.   Caron, op. cit., p. 76.

15 Querdisien-Tremais, "Considérations sur l'état présent du Canada," in R.A.Q., 1959-60, p. 10.   B, 48, Le Conseil à Chazel, 11 août 1725, fol. 891.   B, 52, Maurepas à Dupuy, 14 mai 1728, fol. 497.   B, 74, Mémoire du roi à Beauharnois et Hocquart, 30 avril 1743, fol. 100-01.   C11A, 47, Bégon à Maurepas, 31 octobre 1725, fol. 258.   C11A, 83, Beauharnois et Hocquart à Maurepas, 23 octobre 1745, fol. 42.

16 Querdisien-Tremais, "Considérations," supra. cit.   (Hocquart), "Mémoire sur le Canada," (Societe littéraire et historique de Quebec, 1840) pp. 6-7 and 10.   C11A, 44, Vaudreuil et Bégon au Consiel, 8 october 1721, fol. 29   C11A, 67, Mémoire sur la colonie, 1747, fol. 97.   C11A, 60, Mgr Dosquet à Maurepas, 3 novembre, 1733, fol. 332   B, 66, Maurepas à Mgr. Dosquet, 14 avril 1738, fol. 12.

17 C11A, 48, Dupuy à Maurepas, 30 octobre 1726, p. 291 ff.   C11A, 53, Hocquart à Maurepas, 10 octobre 1730, p. 150.   C11A, 68, Hocquart à Maurepas, 14 octobre 1737, p. 27.   C11A, 96, Mémoire sur l'état du Canada, 1760, p. 221.   Documents relating to the Constitutional History of Canada, ed. by Adam Shortt and Arthur G. Doughty (Ottawa, 1911), "General Murray's Report, June 5th, 1762," vol. I, p. 57.   Emile Garnault, Les Rochelois et le Canada, pp. 14-16. It must be remembered that Garnault does not distinguish between imports from Canada and those from the other colonies.

18 R.A.Q., 1929-30, 1930-31, 1931-32, "Répertoire des engagements pour

l'Ouest."

[19] *Edits et Ord.*, I. "Arrêt du 11 mai 1717," pp. 269-70.

[20] C11A, 46, *Prat à Maurepas, octobre 1724*, pp. 219-20. F2 B, I, *Liste des bâtiments venus à Québec en 1734.* C11A, 76, *Mémoire sur le commerce du Canada (1741)*, p. 142 *ff.* C11A, 96, *Mémoire sur l'Etat du Canada, (1760)*, p. 221. F2 B, I, *Etat des marchandises, vivres, denrées et effets du Canada, 1732.*

[21] Jean Lunn, *Economic Development in New France*, Unpublished Ph.D. thesis, McGill University, 1942, pp. 477-78. C11A, 58, *Hocquart à Maurepas, 27 octobre 1732*, pp. 71-72; . . . *27 octobre 1704*, pp. 95-97. Querdisien-Tremais, "Considérations," *supra cit.*, p. 7. Allana G. Reid, "General Trade between Quebec and France during the French Regime," *Canadian Historical Review* (March, 1953) p. 23. C11A, 79, *Hocquart à Maurepas, 8 octobre 1743*, p. 375 *ff.* Jean Hamelin, *Economie et société en Nouvelle-France* (Quebec, 1960). B, 101, *Machault à Vaudreuil et Bigot, 15 juillet 1755*, fol. 15.

[22] C11A, 60, *Bordereau des recettes et dépenses, 1731*, fol. 381. C11A, 119, *Mémoire sur les dépenses du Canada*, fol. 470. Shortt and Doughty, *op. cit.*, vol. I, "General Murray's Report, 1762," pp. 42-49.

[23] C11A, 78, *Hocquart à Maurepas, 30 octobre 1742*, fol. 97. Salone, *op. cit.*, p. 419.

[24] *Documents relating to Canadian Currency, Exchange and Finance during the French Period*, ed. by Adam Shortt (Ottawa, 1925) pp. 48-49. *Affaires étrangères. Mémoires et Documents: Amérique*, V, p. 121. Guy Frégault, "Essai sur les finances canadiennes," *R.H.A.F.*, vol. XII and XIII.

[25] C11A, 60, *Bordereau des recettes et dépenses, 1731*, fol. 381. Shortt, *op. cit.*, II, pp. 419-25.

[26] C11A, 59, *Hocquart, Mémoire sur le régime du Domaine d'Occident (1719-1732)*, fol. 319-32. Salone, *op. cit.*, pp. 419-25. C11A, 92, *Bigot à Maurepas, 3 novembre 1748*, p. 87 *ff.*

[27] B, 58, *Maurepas à Beauharnois et Hocquart, 24 avril 1733*, fol. 44½. C11A, 80, *Droits royaux, mars 1743*, fol. 379. C11A, 99, *Capitulation du Canada*, pp. 489-91.

[28] B, 35, *Mémoire du roi à Vaudreuil et Bégon, 25 juin 1713*, fol. 50. B, 58, *Maurepas à Beauharnois et Hocquart, 24 avril 1733*, fol. 44½. C11A, 80, *Droits royaux, mars 1743*, fol. 379.

[29] *Edits et Ord.*, I, "Arrêt du Conseil, 23 janvier 1747," p. 590. *Edits du roi 1748*, p. 591.

CHAPTER XIII

[1] Gustave Lanctot, *L'Administration de la Nouvelle-France* (Paris, 1929) pp. 143-46.

[1a] *Collection de manuscrits contenant lettres, mémoires et autres documents historiques relatifs à la Nouvelle-France*, IV, "Suite de la campagne en Canada, 1760," pp. 304-06. *Journal du Marquis de Montcalm* (Quebec, 1894) p. 516.

[2] *Edits et ordonnances royaux*, I, "Déclaration du roi, 16 juin 1703," pp. 299-300. *Insinuations du Conseil souverain*, II, "Arrêt du 10 mars 1685," p. 303. *Jugements et délibérations du Conseil souverain*, "1er juillet 1714," pp. 794-99; "30 juillet 1714," pp. 804-05. B, 49-2, *Mémoire du Roy, 14 mai 1726*, p. 286. *Registres du Conseil Supérieur, 26 novembre 1728*, pp. 151-52; *16 mai 1729*, p. 235.

[3] C11A, *Capitation, 1754*, fol. 529 *ff.* *Documents relating to the Constitutional History of Canada*, ed. by Adam Shortt and Arthur G. Doughty (Ottawa, 1911), "General Murray's Report, 5 June 1762," vol. I, pp. 45-47. Nicolas Gaspard Boucault, "Etat présent du Canada," in *Rapport de l'archiviste de la province de Québec*, 1920-21, pp. 37, 43 and 46.

[3a] *Edits et Ord.*, II, "Ordonnance de Dupuy, 27 mars 1728," p. 335. *Documents relating to Canadian Currency, Exchange and Finance during the French Period*, ed. by Adam Shortt (Ottawa, 1925), "Adresse des citoyens de Montréal (février 1762)," vol. II, p. 970. A translation of the address is appended to this volume. See p.

[4] "Mémoire de l'abbé de l'Isle-Dieu, 8 janvier 1756," in Emile Salone, *La Colonisation de la Nouvelle-France* (Paris 1906) p. 407. Honorius Prévost, "Le Système des cures au Canada français," *Rapport de la Société Canadienne de l'histoire de l'Eglise, 1947-48*, p. 19 *ff.* Salone, *op. cit.*, pp. 314-16.

5 Shortt and Dought, *op. cit.*, I, "General Murray's Report, 5 June 1762," I, p. 59; "Le Chanoine de Lorme à son père, 1er juillet 1737," *Bulletin des Recherches historiques,* fol. 14, p. 39.   C¹¹A, 51, *Mgr Dosquet à Maurepas, 15 octobre 1729,* p. 552.   C¹¹A, 54, *Maurepas à Mgr Dosquet, 10 avril 1730,* fol. 446. C¹¹A, 106, *Mémoire sur l'Eglise, 1731,* p. 228.

6 Gustave Lanctot, "Servitude de l'Eglise sous le régime français," *Une Nouvelle France inconnue* (Montreal, 1952) pp. 131-71.   *Edits et Ord.,* I, "Ordonnance, 19 février 1732," pp. 528-29.   B, 99, *Le Ministre à Duquesne et Bigot, 30 mai 1754,* fol. 5,   B, 101, *Le ministre à Vaudreuil et Bigot, 15 juillet 1755,* fol. 15.

7 F³, 10, *Arrêt du Conseil supérieur, 22 avril 1722,* fol. 14.   Canadian Archives, Quebec, vol. V, *Etat général de la noblesse canadienne, novembre 1761,* p. 269 *ff.*   D², 48, *Liste de 1760,* p. 69.   Haldimand Papers, B, 3, *Murray to Shelburne, 20 August 1766,* p. 1 *ff.*   Shortt and Doughty, *op. cit.,* I, "General Murray's Report, 5 June 1762," p. 69.

8 B, 36, *Le Ministre à Bégon, 24 mai 1714,* fol. 502½.   F³, 8, *Arrêt de mai 1714,* fol. 16.   Salone, *op. cit.,* pp. 360-61.

9 F³, 11, *Procès verbal d'une assemblée, 26-30 juillet 1753,* fol. 222.   Canadian Archives, Quebec, vol. I, *Adresse des citoyens de Montreal, février 1762,* pp. 67 *ff.*   *Edits et Ord.,* I, "Règlement au sujet des honneurs dans les Eglises, 27 avril 1716," p. 354; "Arrêt du Conseil d'Etat, 1er juin 1753," p. 620.

10 Gustave Lanctot, *Histoire du Canada* (Toronto, 1964) vol. II, pp. 285-89. Raynal, *Histoire philosophique et politique des établissements et du Commerce des Européens dans les deux Indes* (La Haye, 1774) vol. VI, pp. 180-81. Francis Parkman, "Introduction," *The Pioneers of France in the New World* (Boston, 1897).   Alexis de Toqueville, *L'Ancien Régime et la Révolution* (Paris, 1887 ed.) p. 373.

11 *Edits et Ord.,* I, "Arrêt du 11 mai 1717," pp. 369-70.   *Edits et Ord.,* III, "Provisions de Gouverneur pour Vaudreuil de Cavagnal, 1er janvier 1755," p. 79.

12 Abbé Amédée Gosselin, *L'Instruction au Canada sous le régime français* (Quebec, 1911).   Antoine Roy, *Les Lettres, les sciences et les arts sous le régime français* (Paris, 1930).   Abbé Olivier Maurault, *Le Petit Séminaire de Montréal* (Montreal, 1918) pp. 8-10.   Louis Franquet, *Voyages et Mémoires sur le Canada,* pp. 7, 8, and 31.   B, 78, *Le ministre à Beauharnois et Hocquart, 24 mars 1744,* fol. 25.   *Voyage de Kalm en Amérique* (Montreal, 1880) p. 149.

13 Shortt and Doughty, *op. cit.,* I, "General Murray's Report, 5 June 1762," p. 44.   C¹¹A, 68, *Hocquart à Maurepas, 12 mai 1738,* fol. 191.   B, 91, *Le ministre à Bigot, 19 mai 1750,* fol. 32.   Salone, *op. cit.,* p. 417.

14 B, 105, *Ordonnances, 25 février 1757,* fol. 2½; *15 mars 1757,* fol. 6.   C, 5, *Amherst to Pitt, 4 October 1760,* p. 153.   Franquet, *op. cit.,* p. 156.   Lanctot, *Une Nouvelle France inconnue,* p. 78.

CHAPTER XIV

1 C¹¹A, 104, (Potot de Montbeillard) *Journal tenu à l'armée que commandait feu M. de Montcalm,* pp. 276-77.   Courville, *Mémoires,* p. 58.   Father Louis-Marie Le Jeune, *Dictionnaire général* (Ottawa, 1931) vol. II, p. 964.   Guy Frégault, *Le Grand Marquis* (Montreal, 1952).   B, 76, *Maurepas à Beauharnois, 30 avril 1743,* fol. 58½.   *Collection de manuscrits contenant lettres, mémoires et autres documents historiques relatifs à la Nouvelle-France,* IV, "Montcalm à d'Argenson, 12 juin 1756," p. 25; ". . . 19 juin 1756," p. 45.

2 *Rapport de l'archiviste de la province de Québec,* 1923-24, Bougainville, "Mémoire sur l'état de la Nouvelle-France," p. 54.

3 Bibliothèque Nationale, Nouvelles Acquisitions, Liasse 1761; *Articles convenus.*   Courville, *Mémoires,* pp. 62-69.   *R.A.Q.,* 1924-25, "Mémoire du Canada," pp. 116-19.   B, 99, *Le ministre à Bigot, 1er juin 1754,* fol. 27. Charles Nicolas Gabriel, *Le Maréchal de camp Désandrouins* (Verdun, 1887). Mme Bégon, "Correspondance," in *R.A.Q.,* 1934-35, p. 134.   Guy Frégault, *François Bigot* (Montreal, 1948).

4 B, 93, *Rouillé à Bigot, 7 mai 1751,* fol. 5½.   B, 99, *Rouillé à Bigot, 1er juin 1754,* fol. 27.

4a Frégault, *Bigot,* II, pp. 92-97.   *R.A.Q.,* 1936-37, "L'Isle Dieu à Pontbriand, 25 mars 1755," p. 401; "Pichon à Surlaville, 12 novembre 1754," in Beaumont, *Les Derniers jours de l'Acadie* (Paris, 1899) p. 132.   *Col. Mss.*, IV, "A Short Account, 1758," p. 484.   Mme Bégon, "Correspondance," in *R. A. Q.*, 1934-35, p. 134.   P. G. Roy, *Bigot et sa bande et l'affaire du Canada* (Lévis, 1950) p. 20.

    [5] Courville, *Mémoires* p. 62.   Affaires Etrangères, Mémoires et Documents. Amérique. *Tableau des dépenses en Canada, 1750-1760*, p. 121.   B, 101, *Machault à Vaudreuil et Bigot, 15 juillet 1755*, quoted in Frégault, *La Guerre de la Conquête* (Montreal, 1952) p. 99.

    [6] C11A, 100, *Vaudreuil à Machault, 28 octobre 1755*, pp. 113-14.   *R.A.Q.*, 1924-25, "Mémoire du Canada," p. 196.   Gabriel, *op. cit.*, pp. 126-27.

    [7] and [7a] *Mémoire des Commissaires du Roi et de ceux de Sa Majesté Britannique* (Paris, 1755-57). 4 vols.   C11A, 95, *Limites de l'Acadie, 1755*, fol. 31.

    [8] *Extraits des Archives des Ministères de la Marine et de la Guerre* (Quebec, 1860) pp. 278-79.   J. R. Seely, *The Expansion of England* (London, 1900). Pierre Gaxotte, *Le Siècle de Louis XV* (Paris, 1958). Ch. VII.

    [9] Clarence V. Alvord, *The Illinois Country, 1673-1818* (Chicago, 1922) pp. 186-87.   Lawrence Henry Gipson, *Zones of International Friction, The Great Lakes Frontier, Canada, etc.*, pp. 113-16.   *Col. Mss.*, III, "Mémoire sur les limites de l'Acadie, 1755," pp. 527-28.

    [10] B,101, *Machault à Duquesne, 17 février 1755*, fol. 21.   *Documents relating to the Colonial History of the State of New York*, X, "Dieskau à Doreil, 16 août 1755," p. 312; "Lotbinière à d'Argenson, 24 octobre 1755," p. 366. F3, 12, *Vaudreuil à Machault, 10 octobre 1755*, fol. 199. For Braddock's instructions, see *Docts. N. Y.*, VI.

    [11] B,101, *Machault à Duquesne, 17 février 1755*, fol. 21; *Instructions au Sr Doreil, 25 mars 1755*, fol. 65.   C11A, 100, *Etat de l'embarquement des troupes à Brest*, p. 349.   Julian S. Corbett, *England in the Seven Years' War* (London, 1907) vol. I, p. 67.

    [12] *Col. Mss.*, III, "Relation du combat de *l'Alcide*, 8 juin 1755," pp. 540-42.   C11A, 100, *Vaudreuil à Machault, 30 octobre 1755*, p. 164; *Machault à Vaudreuil, 15 septembre 1755*, p. 78.   *Extraits des Archives*, "Joint à la lettre de M. Chastenye, 19 septembre 1755," p. 57-58; "L'Isle-Dieu à Machault, 30 juillet 1755," p. 210.

    [13] and [14] "Précis de l'affaire qui s'est donnée en Canada, le 9 juillet 1756," in Beaumont, *op. cit.*, pp. 150-55.   *R. A. Q.*, 1932-33, "Mémoires du chevalier de La Pause," pp. 307-08.   F3, 12, *Contrecœur à Vaudreuil, 14 juillet 1755*, fol. 119; *Liste des officiers, cadets, soldats, miliciens et Sauvages, 6 août 1755*. p. 118.   C11A, 101, *Dumas à Machault, 24 juillet 1756*, pp. 391-407.   Winthrop Sargent, *The History of an Expedition against Fort Duquesne in 1755*.   Stanley Pargellis, "Braddock's Defeat," *American Historical Review*, XXI, pp. 253-59.

    [15] F3, 12, *Liste des officiers, miliciens, etc. tués ou blessés*, fol. 117; *Etat de l'artillerie, munitions de guerre et autres effets appartenant aux Anglais*, fol. 116.   Sargent, *op. cit.*, p. 238.   *Derniers jours de l'Acadie*, pp. 154-55. F3, 12, *Vaudreuil à Machault, 10 octobre 1755*, fol. 199. According to an unauthenticated rumour, Braddock's mistress was captured, raped, and later eaten by the Indians.   *R.A.Q.*, 1928-29, "Journal de Pascau du Plessis, 1756," pp. 233-34.

    [16] C11A, 100, *Vaudreuil à Machault, 24 juillet 1755*, pp. 64-67.   *Col. Mss.*, III, "Instructions de Vaudreuil au baron Dieskau, 1755," pp. 548-51.

    [17] *Col. Mss.*, III, "Lettre de Montreuil, 1er août 1755," p. 547; "Vaudreuil à Machault, 25 septembre 1755," pp. 555-65; "Détail de la marche de Dieskau par Montreuil, août 1755," pp. 1-4.

    [18] *Col. Mss.*, III, "Dieskau à Vaudreuil, 19 novembre 1755," p. 5 ;"Montreuil à d'Abadie, 18 septembre 1755," pp. 6-7; ". . . 10 octobre 1755," pp. 9-10. F3, 12, *Relation du Combat du lac Saint-Sacrement, 4 octobre 1755*, fol. 205; *Journal d'un officier anglais, 19 août 1755*, fol. 247.

    [19] *Col. Mss.*, III, "Vaudreuil à Machault, 25 septembre 1755," pp. 561, 564-65.   *Col. Mss.*, IV, "Lettre de Montreuil, 2 novembre 1755," p. 13.   F3, 12, *Liste des officiers, tués ou blessé au las Saint-Sacrement, 30 octobre 1755*, fol. 205; *Journal d'un officier anglais, 19 août 1755*, fol. 247.

    [20] *Nouvelle-France. Documents Historiques* (Quebec 1893), "Instructions au sieur de Vaudreuil, 14 juin 1755," p. 91.   C11A, 100, *Vaudreuil à Machault, 31 octobre 1755*, pp. 115-20; *20 octobre 1755*, pp. 101-03.   F3, 12, *Vaudreuil à*

Machault, 25 septembre 1755," fol. 148 *ff.*   *Docts. N. Y.,* X. "Lotbinière à d'Argenson, 24 octobre 1755," p. 367.
    21 Gaxotte, *op. cit.,* p. 256.   *Docts. N. Y.,* X, "Louis XV à George II, 24 décembre 1755," pp. 378-79; "Remarks of the British Ministry, January 1756," pp. 387-91.
    22 *Col. Mss.,* IV, "Commission du marquis de Montcalm, 17 mars 1750," p. 19; "Citation de Montcalm," p. XII.   Thomas Chapais, *Le Marquis de Montcalm* (Quebec, 1911) pp. 5-22.   B, 103, *Mémoire du roi pour servir d'instructions au Marquis de Montcalm, 14 mars 1756,* fol. 7.   Courville, *Mémoires, pp.* 166-67.   *R. A .Q.,* 1924-25, "Mémoire du Canada," pp. 172 and 176.
    23 *Col. Mss.,* IV, "Lettre de Monsieur de Gragnard, 1756," pp. 33 and 37; "Montcalm à Machault, 26 septembre 1756," p. 73; "Journal de l'expédition de M. de Villiers, 1756."   *Relations et Journaux de différentes expéditions faites durant les années 1755 à 1760,* "Journal de la campagne de M. de Léry, 1756," (Quebec, 1855) pp. 63-64 and 65-67.

CHAPTER XV

    C[11]A, 101, *Vaudreuil à Machault, juillet 1756,* pp. 506-18.   Pierre Gaxotte, *Le siècle de Louis XV* (Paris, 1958) pp. 258-59 and 265.   *Collection de manuscrits contenant lettres, mémoires et autres documents historiques relatifs à la Nouvelle-France,* IV, "Déclaration de guerre (16 juin 1756)," pp. 15-18.
    2 Gaxotte, *op. cit.,* p. 270.   H. L. Gipson, *Zones of International Friction* (New York, 1954), vol. VI, p. 401.   Nova Scotia State Papers, A, *Census of Colonies, August 1755,* p. 62.
    3 *Col. Mss.,* IV, "Montcalm à d'Argenson, 12 juin 1756," pp. 24-25 and 27; "19 juin 1756," p. 45.   C[11]A, 101, *Vaudreuil à Machault, 8 juin 1756,* p. 38. Gipson, *op. cit.,* pp. 188-95 and 205-08.
    4 F[3], 12, *Instruction de Vaudreuil à Montcalm, 12 août 1756,* fol. 287. *Documents relating to the Colonial History of the State of New York,* X, "Journal du siège de Chouagen," p. 441.   *Col. Mss.,* IV, "Relation de la prise des forts de Chouagen, 1756," pp. 48-50.   Gipson, *op. cit.,* p. 199.   *Col. Mss.,* IV, "State of facts relating to the loss of Oswego," p. 59.
    5 *Col. Mss.,* IV, "Relation de la prise," p. 52-55; "State of facts," pp. 61-65.   C[11]A, 101, *Journal de la victoire au siège de Chouagen,* pp. 467-78.   *Rapport de l'archiviste de la province de Québec,* 1923-24, Bougainville, "Campagne de 1756," p. 217.
    6 *Col. Mss.,* IV, "Montcalm à d'Argenson, 28 août 1756," p. 68.   "Mémoires du sieur de La Pause," quoted in Thomas Chapais, *Le Marquis de Montcalm* (Quebec, 1811) p. 138, note.
    7 These figures, which are not all in agreement, are taken from various sources: *Col. Mss.,* IV, "'Relation de la prise," p. 55.   *R.A.Q.,* 1923-24, "Journal de l'expédition et du siège de Chouagen, 22 août 1756," p. 222.   F[3], 14, *Recensement des vivres: Liste des batîments, Inventaire de l'artillerie,* fol. 324-27.
    8 Montcalm, *Journal du marquis de Montcalm* (Quebec, 1894) p. 169. B, 103, *Machault à Vaudreuil et Bigot, 7 novembre 1756,* fol. 28.
    9 *Col. Mss.,* IV, "Lettre de Montreuil, 12 juin 1756," p. 31; "Montcalm à d'Argenson, 28 août 1756," p. 67.   F[3], 12 *Vaudreuil à Machault, 1er septembre 1756,* fol. 297; *Articles de capitulation, 14 août 1756,* fol 307.   *Docts. N. Y.,* X, "Vaudreuil à d'Argenson, 20 août 1756," p. 473; "Paulmy à Montcalm, 20 mars 1757," p. 536.   Chapais, *op. cit.,* p. 439.
    10 Gipson, *op. cit.,* p. 208.   *Col. Mss.,* IV, "Lettre de Montcalm, 26 septembre 1756," p. 74.
    11 *Docts. N. Y.,* X, "Conférence entre Vaudreuil et les Indiens, décembre 1756," pp. 499-517.   *Col. Mss.,* IV, "Montcalm à d'Argenson, 24 avril 1757," p. 90.
    12 C[11]A, 101, *Vaudreuil à Machault, 6 novembre 1756,* p. 154.
    12a C[11]A, 101, *Vaudreuil à Machault, 13 novembre 1756,* pp. 184-85. *R. A. Q.,* 1922-23, "Le Procès de Robert Stobo," pp. 299-347.   *Memoirs of Major Robert Stobo* (Pittsburgh, 1854).
    13 *R.A.Q.,* 1924-25, "Mémoire du Canada," p. 112.   C[11]A, 101, *Vaudreuil à Machault, 6 novembre 1756,* pp. 154-64.   *Col. Mss.,* IV, "Montcalm à d'Argenson, 24 avril," p. 106.   B, 103, *Machault à Vaudreuil, 12 avril 1756,* fol. 24. C[11]A, 99, *Duquesne à Machault, 31 octobre 1754,* fol. 114.

13a F³, 14, *Relation de la campagne sur le lac Saint-Sacrement, 1757*, fol. 106-07.   "Expédition de M. de Rigaud, 1757," in *Relations et Journaux de différentes expéditions faites durant les années 1755 à 1760*, pp. 71-86.
14 C¹¹A, 102, *Lettre de Brest, 1757*, pp. 166-68.   J. S. McLennan, *Louisbourg from its Foundation to its Fall, 1713-1758* (London, 1918) pp. 202-03. C¹¹A, 102, *Vaudreuil à Machault, 1er juin 1757*, p. 64 ff.   Col. Mss., IV, "Instructions à Montcalm, 9 juillet 1757," pp. 100-08.   R.A.Q., 1923-24, Bougainville, "Journal de l'expédition d'Amérique," pp. 290-96.   C. N. Gabriel, *Le Maréchal de camp Désandrouins* (Verdun, 1887) p. 87.   F³, 14, *Précis des événements de la campagne de 1757, 20 août 1757*, fol. 69.   Docts. N. Y., X, "Journal de l'expedition contre le fort William-Henry du 12 juillet au 16 août 1757," pp. 598-605; "Relation de la prise du Fort George," pp. 645-51. "Relation de la campagne du Canada, 1757," in *Relation et Journaux.*
15 R.A.Q., 1923-24, pp. 296-301 and 305-06.   F³, 13, *Précis des événements*, fol. 69; *Articles de la capitulation, 9 août 1757*, fol. 37; *Estat de la garnison du Fort George, 14 août 1757*, fol. 56. This roster shows a garrison of 2,372 men, of whom 108 were killed or died of wounds.
16 R.A.Q., 1923-24, pp. 301-04 and 306.   F³, 15, *Vaudreuil à Moras, 15 septembre 1757*, fol. 73.   Col. Mss., IV, "Extract of a letter, Albany, 17 August 1757," p.121; "Montcalm à Loudoun, 14 août 1757," pp. 112-13.   Gabriel, *op. cit.*, pp. 109-11.   R. A. Q., 1924-25, "Mémoire du Canada," p. 131.   *Lettres édifiantes et curieuses écrites des missions*, "Lettre du P. Bouchard, octobre 1757," (Paris, 1781) vol. VI, p. 302.   Chapais, *op. cit.*, pp. 278-90.
16a R.A.Q., 1924-25, p. 135.
17 Col. Mss., IV, "Extract of a letter, 15 August 1757," pp. 120-21.   Frye, *Journal of the attack of Fort William Henry.*   Jonathan Carver, *Travels through the Interior Parts of North America* (Dublin, 1779).
18 R.A.Q., 1923-24, pp. 302-03.   "Affidavit of Miles Whitworth, 17 October 1757," in Francis Parkman, *Montcalm and Wolfe* (Boston, 1884) pp. 278-79. Col. Mss., IV, "Extract of a letter from Albany, 17 August 1757," p. 121. Bigot states that twenty of those who resisted were killed.   F³, 15, *Bigot à Moras, 24 août 1757*, fol. 58.
19 R.A.Q., 1923-24, pp. 302-03.   F³, 15, *Précis des événements*, fol. 69; *Instructions à Montcalm, 7 juillet 1757*, p. 103.
20 *Lettres du chevalier de Lévis*, p. 136.   C¹¹A, 102, *Vaudreuil à Moras, 8 août 1757*, pp 384-85.   B, 107, *Moras à Vaudreuil, 14 février 1758*, pp. 129-30.
21 C¹¹A, 102, *Montcalm à Paulmy*, 11 juillet 1757, pp. 308-20.
21a Col. Mss., IV, "Montcalm à Moras, 18 avril 1758," p. 157.
22 B, 105, *Circulaire, 10 février 1757*, fol. 2; *Circulaire,10 juin 1758*, fol. 39; 7 septembre 1758, fol. 54½.   *Documents relating to Canadian Currency, Exchange, and Finance during the French Period*, ed. by Adam Shortt, II, pp. 860-61 and 864-65.   Arnoux Laffrey, *Siècle de Louis XV* (Paris, 1796) vol. II, p. 193. Gaxotte, *op. cit.*, pp. 266-68.
23 R.A.Q., 1923-24, Bougainville, "Journal, octobre 1757," pp. 312-13. C¹¹A, 102, *Lettre anglaise de Pennsylvanie, 1er novembre*, pp. 396-99, *Vaudreuil à Moras, 9 septembre 1757*, p. 184.   *Journal des campagnes du chevalier de Lévis en Canada de 1756-1760*, ed. by Abbé H. R. Casgrain (Quebec, 1889) pp. 113-19.
24 R.A.Q., 1923-24, pp. 310-12 and 315.   Courville, *Mémoires*, pp. 62-69, 84-88 and 123.   Guy Frégault, *François Bigot* (Montreal, 1952) vol. II, pp. 184-86.   Col. Mss., IV, p. 242.   R. A. Q., 1959-60, Querdisien-Tremais, "Mémoire," p. 12.   Montcalm, *Lettres du marquis de Montcalm* (Quebec, 1894) pp. 89 and 92-93.
25 C¹¹A, 103-2, *Daine au ministre, 19 mai 1758*, pp. 486-87.   Montcalm, *Journal*, "13 mai 1758," p. 353.   C¹¹E, 10, *Exposition des prix des denrées en Canada, 1759*, fol. 231.
26 Montcalm, *Journal*, "22 janvier 1758," pp. 121-22; "3 février 1758," p. 125. Mme Bégon "Correspondance, 26 janvier 1749," in *R. A. Q.*, 1934-35, pp. 31 and 48.
26a Montcalm, *Lettres*, "16 juin 1757," p. 168.   R. A. Q., 1934-35, p. 36.
27 Ministère de la Guerre, *Lettre de Bernier, 19 avril 1759.*   C¹¹A, 103-2, *Levasseur au ministre, 30 octobre 1758*, pp. 505-07.

CHAPTER XVI

1 C¹¹A, 103-1, *Vaudreuil à Massiac, 4 août 1758*, p. 158.   C. N. Gabriel,

Le Maréchal de camp Désandrouins (Verdun, 1887) pp. 126-27. Courville, *Mémoires*, p. 105.

2 C11A, 103-1, *Montcalm à Vaudreuil, 2 août 1758*, pp. 118-22.   C11A, 103-2, *Bigot à Massiac, 13 août 1758*, pp. 458-61; *Projet de mémoire, 28 décembre 1758*, pp. 576-80.

3 *Collection de manuscrits contenant lettres, mémoires et autres documents historiques relatifs à la Nouvelle-France*, IV, "Lettre de Belle-Isle, 13 janvier 1757," pp. 84-85.   J. S. McLennan, *Louisbourg from its Foundation to its Fall, 1713-1758* (London, 1918). See pp. 261-62 for lists of the English fleet and land forces, 1758.

4 John Knox, *An Historical Journal of the Campaigns in North America for the years 1757, 1758, 1759 and 1760* (Champlain Society, 1914-16) vol. I, p. 267. McLennan, *op. cit.*, p. 248.

5 "Relation de la descente des Anglais dans l'île Royale," *Relations et Journaux de différentes expéditions faites durant les années 1755 à 1760*, pp. 142-47.   C11B, *Journal ou relation de Drucourt, 1758*, fol. 57 ff; *Prévost à Massiac, 7 juillet 1756*, fol. 36.   *Col. Mss.*, III, "The short account of what passed at Cape Breton, 1758," pp. 477-85.   *Col. Mss.*, IV, "La Houlière au ministre, 9 août 1758," pp. 176-86.   F3, 50, *Mémoire de M. Drucourt, 10 novembre 1758*, fol. 539.   *Journal du siège de Louisbourg, 1758*, fol. 539.   John Knox, *An Historical Journal*, I, pp. 218-60.

6 C11B, 38, *Représentations de M. Prévost, 26 juillet 1758*, fol. 38; *29 juillet 1758*, fol. 43.   McLennan, *op. cit.*, p. 285.

7 Knox, *An Historical Journal*, I, pp. 254-58.   McLennan, *op. cit.*, pp. 290-91.

8 *Documents relating to the Colonial History of the State of New York*, X, "Abercromby to Pitt, 12 July 1758," p. 725; "Montcalm à Belle-Isle, 12 juillet 1758," pp. 732-33.   *R.A.Q.*, 1923-24, Bougainville, "Journal," pp. 336-37.

9 *Rapport de l'archiviste de la province de Québec*, 1923-24, pp. 335-37. F3, 15, *Lévis à Belle-Isle, 13 juillet 1758*, fol. 106.   "Journal de la victoire remportée par les Anglais, le 8 juillet," in *Relations et Journaux*, pp. 149-55.

10 *R.A.Q.*, 1923-24, pp. 335-37.   *Doct. N. Y.*, X, "Abercromby to Pitt, 12 July 1758," p. 726-27; "Another Account of the Operations at Ticonderoga, 14 July 1758," p. 736; "An account of the Victory gained at Carillon, 1758," p. 737-41; "Journal of Occurrences in Canada, 1757, 1758," pp. 846-47; "Journal de la victoire," pp. 151-63.   *Col. Mss.*, IV, "Montcalm à Vaudreuil, 9 juillet 1758," pp. 168-72; "Journal de l'affaire du Canada, passée le 8 juillet 1758," pp. 219-21.

11 *R.A.Q.*, 1923-24, p. 338.   Montcalm, *Lettres du marquis de Montcalm* (Quebec, 1894). Letter to his mother, July 21, 1758.

12 F3, 15 *Vaudreuil à Massiac, 28 juillet 1758*, fol. 102.   Arch. Nat., K, 1013, no. 218, *Relation, 1 octobre 1758*.

13 H. L. Gipson, *Zones of International Friction* (New York, 1954), vol. VII p. 240.   *R.A.Q.*, 1923-24, pp. 363-64.   Courville, *Mémoires*, pp. 113-17.   *Col. Mss.*, IV, "Vaudreuil à Massiac, 2 septembre 1758," pp. 189-90.   *Docts. N.Y.*, X, "Conditions (of surrender of Fort Frontenac), 27 August 1758," p. 825-26.   *R.A.Q.*, 1924-25, "*Mémoire du Canada*," pp. 142-45.   Knox, *op. cit.*, I, *An Impartial Account of Co. Bradstreet's Expeditions*. By a volunteer in the expedition (London, 1859).

14 F3, 15, Vaudreuil à Massiac, 1er novembre 1758, fol. 211; *Ligneris à Vaudreuil, 18-23 octobre 1758*, fol. 225.   Gipson, *op. cit.*, VII, pp. 268-69. Montcalm, *Journal*, pp. 473-75.   *Docts. N.Y.*, X, "Montreuil, Campagne de 1758," p. 922.   C11A, 104, *Vaudreuil à Massiac, 20 janvier 1759*, p. 12; *Letters of General John Forbes relating to the Expedition against Fort Duquesne*, ed. by Irene Stewart (Pittsburgh, 1927) pp. 59 and 67.

15 F3, 15, *Montcalm à Vaudreuil, 27 février 1759*, fol. 255.   Gipson, *op. cit.*, VII, p. 278 and 281.   C11A, 104-1, *Vaudreuil à Massiac, 15 février 1759*, p. 22.

16 *Col. Mss.*, IV, "Lettre de Montreuil, 12 juin 1756," p. 31.   *R.A.Q.*, 1923-24, pp. 340-44.

17 C11A, 103-1, *Montcalm à Vaudreuil, 2 août 1758*, pp. 118-32; *Vaudreuil à Massiac, 4 août 1758*, pp. 127-40.   *Col. Mss.*, IV, "Montcalm à Belle-Isle, 9 septembre 1758," p. 199.   *R.A.Q.*, 1923-24, p. 354.

18 C11A, 103-2, *Bigot à Massiac, 13 août 1758*, pp. 458-61.

19 C11A, 103-2, *Projet de mémoire, 28 décembre 1758*, pp. 576-80.

20 B, 99, *Le Ministre à Bigot, 1er juin 1754, fol. 26.*   C11A, 103-2, *Causes des dépenses énormes du Canada, décembre 1758,* p. 685.   *Col. Mss.,* IV, "Montcalm à Belle-Isle, 12 avril 1759," p. 226.   "Effets de l'augmentation du papier-monnaie sur les prix, joint à la lettre de M. de Bernier, 19 avril 1759," Shortt, *Documents relating to Canadian Currency,* II, p. 908.   B, 109, *Berryer à Vaudreuil, 19 janvier 1759,* fol. 10; *Berryer à Bigot, 19 janvier 1759,* fol. 12.   *R.A.Q.,* 1923-24, p. 191.

21 Gabriel, *op. cit.,* pp. 133-35.   Mme Begon, "Correspondance," in *R.A.Q.,* 1934-35, p. 134.   *R.A.Q.,* 1924-25, "Mémoire du Canada," pp. 135-36, 176 and 191.

22 B, 109, *Berryer à Bigot, 19 août 1759,* fol. 61; *Berryer à Vaudreuil, 9 février 1759,* fol. 44.   C11A, 103-1, *Vaudreuil à Massiac, 4 août 1758,* p. 158. C11A, 104-1, *Vaudreuil à Berryer, 15 octobre 1759,* pp. 104-05.   Courville, *Mémoires,* pp. 87 and 107.

22a *R.A.Q.,* 1924-25, "Mémoire du Canada," pp. 194-95.

23 C11A, 104-1, *Montcalm à Le Normand, 12 avril 1759,* pp. 73-186; Montcalm, *Journal,* pp. 493 and 503-04.

24 C11A, 103-2, *Mémoire d'après une lettre de Vaudreuil, 28 décembre 1758,* p. 568; *Vaudreuil à Massiac, 5 novembre 1758,* pp. 296-310.   *Col. Mss.,* IV, "Montcalm à Belle-Isle, 21 octobre 1758," p. 202.   *R.A.Q.,* 1923-24, p. 378. Montcalm, *Journal,* p. 492.

CHAPTER XVII

1 *Documents relating to the Colonial History of the State of New York,* X, "Colonel Montrésor's Plan of the Campaign in 1759," pp. 907-12.

2 *Rapport de l'archiviste de la province de Québec,* 1923-24, "Mémoire sur la position des Anglais et des Français dans l'Amérique Septentrionale, janvier 1759," p. 312.   B, 109, *Berryer à Vaudreuil, 16 février 1759,* fol. 45.   *R.A.Q.,* 1923-24, p. 390.   Arnoux Laffrey, *Le Siècle de Louis XV,* II, p. 205.

3 Ministère de la Guerre, 3540, *Belle-Isle à Montcalm, 19 février 1759,* pièce 16.

4 B, 109, *Berryer à Vaudreuil et Bigot, 3 février 1759,* (two letters) fols. 63 and 66½.   Pierre Gaxotte, *Siècle de Louis XV* (Paris, 1958) p. 275.   *The History of the Life of William Pitt* (London, 1783) pp. 86-87.

5 *R.A.Q.,* 1923-24, pp. 390-92.   Courville, *Mémoires,* pp. 126-27.   *Docts. N.Y.,* X, "Minute providing for the office of Governor General, 28 January 1759," pp. 939-40.   B, 109, *Berryer à Vaudreuil et Bigot, 3 février 1759,* fol. 66.

6 *R.A.Q.,* 1924-25, "Mémoire du Canada," p. 149.   C11A, 104-1, *Vaudreuil, Précis du plan des opérations générales de la campagne de 1759, 1er avril 1759,* pp. 63-76.   Montcalm, *Le Journal du marquis de Montcalm* (Quebec, 1894) pp. 521-23.   Courville, *Mémoires,* pp. 125-26.

7 Montcalm, *Journal,* pp. 323-24 and 327-28.   Courville, *Mémoires,* pp. 127-29.   Foligné, "Journal," in Doughty and Parmalee, *The Siege of Quebec and the Battle of the Plains of Abraham* (Quebec, 1901) vol. IV, pp. 163-5, 170.

8 C11A, 104-1, *Montbeillard, Journal tenu à l'armée,* pp. 188-91.   Montcalm, *Journal,* p. 551.   *Mandements, lettres pastorales et circulaires des Evêques de Québec* (Quebec, 1887) vol. II, p. 130.

9 *Docts. N.Y.,* X, "Narrative of the Siege of Quebec," p. 995.   Montcalm, *Journal,* pp. 544 and 558.   Foligné, "Journal," in *The Siege of Quebec,* IV, p. 170.

10 William Wood, *The Fight for Canada* (London, 1905) pp. 166-79 and 183.   Thomas Mante, *An Impartial History of the late Glorious War from its Commencement to its Conclusion* (London, 1769) p. 210. Wood gives a total of 27,000 for the English force: 13,000 members of the Royal Navy, 5000 sailors in the merchant marine and 9000 soldiers.   Beckles Wilson, ed., *The Life and Letters of James Wolfe* (London, 1909) p. 415.

11 C11A, 104-1, *Manifeste du général Wolfe, 28 juin 1759,* pp. 426-31.

12 Montcalm, *Journal,* p. 387.   John Knox, *An Historical Journal of the Campaigns in North America for the years 1757, 1758, 1759 and 1760,* ed. by A. G. Doughty (Champlain Society, 1914-16) vol. I, pp. 381-83.

13 *R.A.Q.,* 1923-24, Bougainville, "Journal," p. 387.   Knox, *Journal,* I, p. 386; pp. 392 and 395, notes.   Montcalm, *Journal,* pp. 562 and 574-75.

Abbé Récher, "Journal du Siège de Québec, 1759," *Vie Française*, XIII, pp. 287-94.   Foligné, "Journal," p. 197.
    14 Knox, *Journal*, I, pp. 409 and 448-56.   Foligné, "Journal," pp. 177, 184 and 188-90.   *R.A.Q.*, 1923-24, Bougainville, "Journal," p. 388.   Hippolyte de Maurès, comte de Malartic, *Journal des campagnes en Canada de 1755 à 1760* (Paris, 1890) pp. 260-62.   C11A, 104-1, *Relation de ce qui c'est passé au Canada, 1759*, p. 432.   Récher, *Journal*, p. 324.   "Journal du siège de Québec, 1759," in *Relations et Journaux de différentes expéditions faites durant les années 1755 à 1760*, pp. 200-04.
    15 "Relation de la campagne du chevalier de La Corne à Chouaguen, 1759," in *Relations et Journaux*, pp. 215-18.   Knox, *Journal*, III, p. 38 and pp. 495 and 501-11.   Pierre Pouchot, *Mémoires sur la dernière guerre de l'Amérique Septentrionale, entre la France et l'Angleterre* (Yverdon, 1781) vol. II, pp. 45 *ff* and 165 *ff*.   F3, 15, *Bourlamaque à Belle-Isle, 1er novembre 1759*, fol. 354.
    16 Montcalm, *Journal*, p. 589.
    17 Récher, *Journal*, pp. 326-40.   René de Kerallain, *Les Français au Canada. La Jeunesse de Bougainville et la guerre de Sept Ans* (Nogent-sur-Rotrou, 1896) p. 138; "Journal of John Montrésor," in Doughty and Parmalee, *op. cit.*, p. 330.
    18 Knox, *Journal*, I, p. 386 and p. 410, note.
    19 Montcalm, *Journal*, p. 575.   *R.A.Q.*, 1923-24, Bougainville, "Journal," p. 388-89.
    20 Montcalm, *Journal*, p. 587.
    21 "Wolfe to his mother, 31 August 1759," in Wood, *The Fight for Canada*, p. 203.   Knox, *Journal*, II, pp. 84-86.   Courville, *Mémoires*, p. 164.
    22 The story of the battle is based upon contemporary diaries and memoirs too numerous to be listed here. References are limited to essential or controversial points.   Knox, *Journal*, II, pp. 94-102.   Récher, *Journal*, p. 343.   Montcalm, *Journal*, pp. 610-14.   Foligné, *Journal*, pp. 203-06.   "Extracts from Journal of particular Transactions during the Siege of Quebec," in Doughty and Parmalee, *op. cit.*, V, pp. 187-89.   *Collection de manuscrits contenant lettres, mémoires et autres documents historiques relatifs à la Nouvelle-France*, IV, "Strength of British Army, 13 September 1759," pp. 229-300.
    22a Aegidius Fauteux ed., *Journal du Siège de Québec* (Quebec, 1922) p. 65.   "Letter of Admiral Holmes, 18 September 1759," in Doughty and Parmalee, *op. cit.*, p. 297.
    23 *Docts. N.Y.*, X, "Montreuil à Belle-Isle, 22 septembre 1759," pp. 1013-14.   Pouchot, *op. cit.*, pp. 142-44.   Malartic, *Journal des campagnes au Canada*, pp. 283-86.   "Journal du siège de Québec," in *Relations et Journaux*, pp. 208-11.
    24 *Col. Mss.*, X, "Caractère de Monsieur de Montcalm," pp. 270-77; Johnston, "The Campaign in Canada," p. 232.   Colonel Beatson, "Notes on the Plains of Abraham," in Thomas Chapais, *Le Marquis de Montcalm* (Quebec, 1911), p. 666.
    24a Fauteux, *op. cit.*, p. 66.   Knox, *Journal*, pp. 102 and 117-18.   Bougainville, in *R.A.Q.*, 1923-24, p. 389.   *Journal du Siège de Québec*, p. 212.
    24b A letter from Montcalm, September 1759, in the Archives Museum, Ottawa.
    24c "Doreil à Paulmy, 31 juillet 1758," in Roy, "Les Lettres du commissaire des guerres Doreil," *Cahiers des Dix*, IX, 1944, p. 151.
    25 F3, 15, *Vaudreuil à Montcalm, 13 septembre 1759*, fol. 318.   Arch. Can., M.G. 3, Series 8, vol. 4, *Vaudreuil au Ministre, 30 octobre 1759*, pp. 309-17.
    26 *Ibid.*
    27 Foligné, "*Journal*," p. 207.   Fauteux, *op. cit.*, p. 67.

CHAPTER XVIII

    1 F3, 15, *Copie du Conseil de guerre, 13 septembre 1759*, fol. 324.   C11A, 103-2, *Vaudreuil au ministre, 3 mars 1758*, p. 570; *Mémoire pour servir d'instruction à M. de Ramezay, 13 septembre 1759*, fol. 326.   *Collection de manuscrits contenant lettres, mémoires et autres documents historiques relatifs à la Nouvelle-France*, IV, "The Campaign in Canada," pp. 234-35.
    2 C11A, 104-2, Mgr de Pontbriand, *Description imparfaite de la misère du Canada, 5 novembre 1759*, fol. 551.   *Documents relating to the Colonial History of the State of New York*, X, "Minute of the Council of War, 15 September

sm294 A HISTORY OF CANADA

1759," pp. 1007-09. John Knox, *An Historical Journal of the Campaigns in North America for the years 1757, 1758, 1759 and 1760*, ed. by A. G. Doughty (Champlain Society, 1914-16) vol. II, pp. 177-78 and 124-25. F³, 15, *Rochebeaucourt à Vaudreuil, 18 septembre 1759*, fol. 316; *Articles de capitulation de Québec, 18 septembre 1759*, fol. 296. Foligné, "Journal" in A. G. Doughty and C. W. Parmalee, *The Siege of Quebec and the Battle of the Plains of Abraham* (Quebec, 1901) vol. IV, p. 209.

3 F³, 15, *Lévis à Belle-Isle, 10 novembre 1759*, fol. 270; *Bigot à Berryer, 15 octobre 1759*, fol. 334; *Ramezay à Vaudreuil, 18 septembre 1759*, fol. 312; *Vaudreuil à Ramezay, 19 septembre 1759*, fol. 311. C¹¹A, 104-2, *Mémoire du sieur de Ramesay, 1759*, pp. 453-57. B⁴, 91, *Campagne 1759, 10 décembre 1759.* Thomas Marie Charland, *Histoire de Saint-François-du-lac* (Ottawa, 1942) pp. 110-17.

4 Knox, *Journal, passim.* F³, 15, *Vaudreuil à Berryer, 15 avril 1760*, fols. 12 and 20. Hippolyte de Maurepas, comte de Malartic, *Journal des Campagnes en Canada, de 1755 à 1760* (Paris, 1890) p. 307, note. C¹¹A, 104-2, *Description de la misère, 5 novembre 1759*, p. 551. "Relation de l'expédition sous M. de Lévis, 1760," in *Relations et Journaux de différentes expéditions faites durant les années 1755 à 1760*, pp. 219-23.

5 Knox, *Journal*, II, p. 333. C¹¹A, 10, *Exposition des prix des denrées, janvier 1759*, fol. 231. F³, 16, *Vaudreuil à Berryer, 23 avril 1760*, fol. 26. *Inventaire des Ordonnances des Intendants*, III, pp. 206 and 210. *Col. Mss.*, IV, "The Campaign in Canada, 1759," p. 242. Courville, *Mémoires*, p. 180.

6 F³, 16, *Vaudreuil à Berryer, 23 avril 1760*, fol. 26. *Col. Mss.*, IV, p. 242. Courville, *Mémoires*, pp. 178-83. *Col. Mss.*, IV, "Bigot à Berryer, 1er juin 1760," p. 267. *Docts. N.Y.*, X, Ordinance of the Governor General, 16 April 1760," p. 1074. C¹¹A, 105-1, *Circulaire de Vaudreuil, 16 avril 1760*, pp. 9-15. *Relations et Journaux*, pp. 221-23.

7 Knox, *Journal*, II, pp. 379 and 382-83. Malartic, *Journal*, p. 314. *Relations et Journaux*, pp. 224-25.

8 Knox, *op. cit.*, pp. 390-95 and 397. *Col. Mss.*, IV, "The Campaign in Canada," pp. 252-54; "Campagne de 1760 en Canada," pp. 293-98. (Also in C¹¹A, 105-1, pp. 66-76); "Relation de l'expédition de Québec, 3 mai 1760," pp. 29-57. Malartic, *Journal*, pp. 315-18. *Journal des campagnes du chevalier de Lévis*, pp. 263-68. *Relations et Journaux*, pp. 230-35.

9 *Journal des campagnes de Lévis*, pp. 257 and 259. Knox, *Journal*, pp. 397, 405, 415, 419 and 425. Malartic, *Journal*, pp. 325-26. *Col. Mss.*, IV, "The Campaign," p. 255; "Campagne de 1760 en Canada," p. 294. *Relations et Journaux*, pp. 240-42.

10 "Journal de Vauquelin," in *Journal des campagnes du chevalier de Lévis*, pp. 263-71. *Col. Mss.*, IV, "The Campaign in Canada," p. 255.

11 *Journal des campagnes de Lévis*, p. 282. *Col. Mss.*, IV, "Suite de la campagne du Canada, 1760," p. 298. *Rapport de l'archiviste de la province de Québec*, 1923-34, Bougainville, "Journal," p. 391.

12 B, 112, *Instructions sur la campagne du 2e de la Giraudais, 15 février 1760*, fol. 47. Knox, *Journal*, II, p. 435. B⁴, 98, *Campagne d'Amérique, 1760.* Gustave Lanctot, "Le Dernier effort de la France au Canada," M.S.R.C., 1918. *Annual Register for the year 1760*, p. 137.

13 Knox, *Journal*, III, pp. 306-08. (Murray's Journal). Courville, *Mémoires*, pp. 186-88. Courville gives June 22 as the date of the first bombardment.

14 and 14a Knox, *Journal*, III, pp. 308, 324 and 333. (Murray's Journal). Malartic, *Journal*, p. 337. *R.A.Q.*, 1924-25, p. 179.

15 *Col. Mss.*, IV, "The Campaign in Canada," pp. 256-60; "Suite de la campagne en Canada," pp. 301-02. H. L. Gipson, *Zones of International Friction* (New York, 1954) vol. VII, p. 449, note. Knox, *Journal*, II, p. 515. *R.A.Q.*, 1924-25, p. 179.

16 Gipson, *loc. cit.* Pierre Pouchot, *Mémoires sur la dernière guerre de l'Amérique Septentrionale, entre la France et l'Angleterre* (Yverdon, 1781). *Col. Mss.*, IV, "Suite de la campagne en Canada, 1760," pp. 303-04. Courville, *Mémoires*, p. 204.

17 *Col. Mss.*, IV, pp. 303-05. Knox, *Journal*, III, p. 330. *Lettres de Bourlamaque à Lévis, 30 août 1760*, p. 119; *2 septembre 1760*, p. 126. Knox, *Journal*, II, p. 516. F³, 16, *Vaudreuil à Berryer, 10 septembre 1760*, fol. 121. C¹¹A, 105-2, *Bernier à Accaron, 25 septembre 1760*, p. 295.

18 F3, 16, *Procès verbal d'un conseil de guerre, 6 septembre 1760*, fol. 127. *R.A.Q.*, 1924-25, Bougainville, "Journal," p. 392.   Knox, *Journal*, II, p. 561. C11A, 105-1, *Amherst à Vaudreuil, 7 septembre 1760*, p. 323.   *Col. Mss.*, IV, "Lévis à Vaudreuil, 8 septembre 1760," pp. 278-79; "Suite de la campagne," pp. 305-06.   Malartic, *Journal*, pp. 351-52.   *Journal du chevalier de Lévis*, ed. by H. R. Casgrain (Montreal and Quebec, 1889-95) p. 308.

19. C11A, 105-2, *Articles de la capitulation de Montréal, 8 septembre 1760*, pp. 324-51. A translation is appended to this volume.

20 C11A, 105-2, *Lévis à Belle-Isle, 27 novembre 1760*, pp. 367-71; *Bernier à Accaron, 25 septembre 1760*, pp. 393-95.   *Journal des campagnes de Lévis* (Quebec, 1894) p. 315.   Courville, *op. cit.*, p. 81.

21 L.F.G. Baby, *L'Exode des classes dirigeantes à la cession du Canada* (Montreal, 1899).   Gustave Lanctot, *Faussaires et Faussetés en histoire canadienne*, pp. 33-35.   *Documents relating to the Constitutional History of Canada*, ed. by Adam Shortt and Arthur G. Doughty (Ottawa, 1911), "General Gage's Report, March 20, 1762" "Burton's Report, April 1762," vol. I.

22 *Rapport des Archives Canadiennes*, 1918, "(Placard) Amherst, 22 September 1760," pp. 21-23.   *Documents relating to Canadian Currency, Exchange and Finance during the French Period*, ed. by A. Shortt (Ottawa, 1925) "Vaudreuil et Bigot aux capitaines de milice, 15 juin 1760," vol. II, p. 940.

23 *R.A.Q.*, 1924-25, "Mémoire du Canada," pp. 196-97.   Courville, *Mémoires.*   *Col. Mss.*, IV, "The Campaign in Canada," pp. 233-35.   C11A, 104-2, *Pontbriand à Berryer, 9 novembre 1759*, pp. 539-50.   *Bulletin des Recherches historiques*, vol. XXVII, p. 31. *Malheurs*, which appears in the text, is probably an erroneous reading for *maldeuils*.   Knox, *Journal*, II, pp. 246-47.   Mme Bégon, "Correspondance," *R.A.Q.*, 1934-35, p. 43.

24 *Docts. N.Y.*, X, Dumas, "Mémoire sur les frontières du Canada," pp. 434-38; Bourlamaque, "Mémoire sur le Canada," pp. 1139-55.   Emile Salone, *Colonisation de la Nouvelle-France* (Paris, 1906) pp. 428-30.   Schone, *La Politique coloniale sous Louis XV et Louis XVI* (Paris, 1907) p. 49.   Pierre Gaxotte, *Siècle de Louis XV* (Paris, 1958) pp. 228-41.   Gailly de Taurines, *La Nation canadienne* (Paris, 1894) p. 316.   Voltaire, *Correspondance*, ed. by Besterman, vol. L, p. 11. The original letter, addressed to Choiseul, is in the Canadian Archives.

25 *R.A.Q.*, 1924-25, Letters from the Chambers of Commerce of Saint-Malo, Aunis, Marseilles, Nantes, Havre, Dunkirk, Bayonne, Guyenne and Montpellier, pp. 201-28.   B, 112, *Berryer à Vaudreuil, 5 décembre 1760*, fol. 280.   *Chroniques de la Régence et du règne de Louis XV. Journal de Barbier* (Paris, 1886) vol. VII, p. 304.

26 Arch. Can., *Affaire du Canada, Arrêt, 12 décembre 1761*.   F3, 16, *Jugement rendu souverainement et en dernier ressort dans l'affaire du Canada, 10 décembre 1763*, fols. 165 and 171 *ff*.   *R.A.Q.*, 1924-25, "Mémoire du Canada," pp. 196-98. For details of the trial, see Frégault, *François Bigot* (Montreal, 1948) vol. II, Ch. 17. See also "Canada's Millionaires," appended to this volume.

27 F3, 16, *Jugement . . . dans l'affaire du Canada*, fols. 167 and 171.   B, 125, *Le ministre à Mme Pénissault, 28 février 1766*, fol. 63½.   Pierre Georges Roy, *Bigot et sa bande et l'affaire du Canada* (Lévis 1950) pp. 103-04, 120-21 and 123.   *Ibid.*, pp. 323-67, (Journal de Moreau).   J. E. Labignette, "Recherches en Suisse sur François Bigot," in *R.A.Q.*, vol. XLI, pp. 205-07.

28 C11A, 105-3, *Précis concernant la dette du Canada*, pp. 887-93; *Résumé, 29 juin 1764*, pp. 896-98; *Résumé de la liquidation de la dette du Roi pour le Canada, 1764*, pp. 909-19.   "Arrêt du Conseil d'Etat du Roi, 29 juin 1764," *Documents relating to Canadian Currency*, II, pp. 1012-18.   "Lévis à Berryer, 25 juin 1760," in *Collection des Manuscrits du maréchal de Lévis*, II, p. 362.

29 Alfred Barbier, *Un Munitionnaire du Roi à la Nouvelle-France, Joseph Cadet* (Poitiers, 1900).   *Documents relating to Canadian Currency*, II, pp. 912-20, notes.   Richard Waddington, *La Guerre de Sept Ans* (Paris, 1899-1919) vol. IV.

CHAPTER XIX

1 On the period of military administration, see the study by A. L. Burt, in the *Cambridge History of the British Empire*, vol. VI, *Canada*, pp. 146 *ff*.

1a *A scheme to drive the French out of all the continent of North America* (London, 1755).

1b Rapport des Archives Canadiennes, 1918, *Ordonnances et Proclamations du Régime Militaire*, "Proclamation de Monckton, 22 septembre 1759," p. 1; "Proclamation de Murray, 15 novembre 1759," p. 2; "Murray's Manifesto, 25th February 1760," p. 7; "Proclamation de Murray, 13 juillet 1760," p. 13.

2 *Ibid.*, "Ordonnance du Général Amherst, 22 sept. 1760," pp. 21-23; "Egremont to Amherst, 12 December 1761," pp. 119-20.

3 *Ibid.*, "Ordre de remettre les armes et de prêter serment, 21 septembre 1760," p. 84; ". . . 22 septembre 1760," p. 85; "Commissions de capitaine de milice, 1760," p. 12; "Ordonnance de Gage, 26 octobre 1760," pp. 32-33; "Ordonnance de Burton, 1er octobre 1760," p. 88; "Ordonnance de Gage, 4 octobre 1760," p. 33; ". . . 13 octobre 1760," p. 48.   "Ordonnance de Murray, 21 octobre 1760."   *Documents relating to the Constitutional History of Canada*, ed. by Adam Shortt and Arthur G. Doughty (Ottawa, 1911), "Ordonnance de Murray, 31 octobre 1760."

4 *R.A.C.*, 1918, "Commissions de notaires," pp. 23-30; "Ordonnances au sujet des seigneuries," pp. 37, 62, 65, 66 and 67; "Ordonnance, 20 février 1761," p. 41; "Ordonnance, 31 juillet 1762," pp. 58-59.   G. M. Wrong, *A Canadian Manor and its Seigneurs* (Toronto, 1908) pp. 271-72.

5 Public Record Office. C.O.5, vol. 59, *Amherst to Colonial Governors, 13 Sept. 1760*, pp. 174-75; *Bernard to Amherst, 27 Sept. 1760*, p. 361; *Amherst to Pitt, 8 Dec. 1760*, p. 3.   *R.A.C.*, 1918, "Ordonnance sur la traite, 1er avril 1761," p. 43.

6 *R.A.C.*, 1918, "Ordonnance, 20 février 1761," pp. 39-41.   Shortt and Doughty, *op. cit.*, I, "General Murray's Report, 6 June 1762."   Burt, *op. cit.*, p. 150.

7 *R.A.C.*, 1918, "Egremont to Amherst, 12 December 1761," p. 10.

8 *R.A.C.*, 1918, "Ordre pour le deuil, 26 janvier 1761," p. 38; "Proclamation, 7 février 1761," p. 38; "Annonce, 1er novembre 1761," p. 114; ". . . 4 février 1762," p. 118.

9 Shortt and Doughty, *op. cit.*, I, "General Murray's Report, 6 June 1762." "Burton's Report, April 1762," p. 118. Haldimand Papers, B, I, *Haldimand to Amherst, 26 December* 1762, p. 216.

9a *R.A.C.*, 1918, "Regulation of coin, 23 November 1759," pp. 3-4; "Pour le Commerce, 1er avril 1761," p. 43.

10 Shortt and Doughty, *op. cit.*, I, "Placard du général Amherst, 22 sept. 1761," "Address of French Citizens, 1764."

11 *R.A.C.*, 1918, "Proclamation du Roi, 7 février 1761," p. 38; ". . . 19 février 1761," p. 100; "Bruyère à Louis Gouin, 25 juin 1761," p. 106.   Shortt and Doughty, *op. cit.*, I, "General Murray's Report, 6 June 1762."   Marcel Trudel, *L'Eglise canadienne sous le régime militaire* (Montreal, 1957) pp. 152-55 and 170-73.

12 *Mandements, lettres pastorales et circulaires des Evêques de Québec*, II, "Mandement de Montgolfier, 1er février 1762," pp. 157-58; "Mandement de Perrault, 3 février 1762," pp. 159-60; "Mandement de Briand, 14 février 1760," pp. 160-62.

13 Shortt and Doughty, *op. cit.*, I, "General Gage's Report, 20 March 1762." *Mandements*, II, "Mandement de Perrault, 22 mai 1763," pp. 167-68.

14 *R.A.C.*, 1918, "Proclamation de Gage, 7 février 1761," p. 38.   Shortt and Doughty, *op. cit.*, II, "General Murray's Report, 4 June 1762."   *Documents relating to Canadian Currency*, ed. by A. Shortt, II, "Address of the Citizens of the town of Montreal (1763)" pp. 969-71.

14a *Mémoire historique sur la négotiation de la France et de L'Angleterre depuis le 26 mars 1761 jusqu'au 20 septembre de la même année* (Paris, 1761) p. 24.

15 Pierre Gaxotte, *Siècle de Louis XV* (Paris, 1958) pp. 274-76.

15a B, 114, *Le ministre à Ternay, 14 août 1762*, fol. 1.   Daniel Woodley Prowse, *A History of Newfoundland* (London, 1895) pp. 112-16.

16 Shortt and Doughty, *op. cit.*, I, "Treaty of Paris, 10 February 1763," p. 73.

16a *Reasons for keeping Guadaloupe at a Peace, preferable to Canada, explained in five letters from a Gentleman in Guadaloupe to his friend in London* (London, 1761).

W. L. Grant, "Canada versus Guadeloupe," *American Historical Review* (July, 1912) p. 735 *ff.*   G. L. Beer, *British Colonial Policy* (New York, 1909.).   C11A, *Jenkins to Amherst, 21 January 1763*, p. 402.
   17 Shortt and Doughty, *op. cit.*, I, "Treaty of Paris, 10 February 1763," p. 73. A translation of the articles relevant to Canada is appended to this volume.
   18 *R.A.C.*, 1918, "Proclamation de Gage, 17 mai 1763," pp. 71-72; "Proclamation de Burton, 21 mai 1763," pp. 140-41.

CHAPTER XX

   a Gustave Lanctot, "Nouvelle-France ou Canada," *Revue d'Histoire de l'Amérique Française* (septembre 1960) pp. 71-72.
   1 *Edits et ordonnances royaux*, I, "Acte pour l'établissement de la Compagnie des Cent Associés, 29 avril 1627," p. 5.
   2 *Ibid.*, "Acceptation du Roi de la démission de la Compagnie de la Nouvelle-France, mars 1663," pp. 31-32.
   3 Shortt and Doughty, I, "Articles of Capitulation, Montréal, 1760,"   *Ibid.*, "Treaty of Paris, 1763," p. 73.
   4 *Relations des Jésuites* (Quebec, 1858), "Année 1641," p. 38; "Année 1642," p. 49; "Année 1647," pp. 18-36; "Année 1649," pp. 13-15.
   5 "Les Papiers de La Pause," in *Rapport de l'archiviste de la province de Québec*, 1933-34.   Abbé Arthaud, "Relation d'un Voyage de France au Canada en 1731," *R.H.A.F.*, I, p. 109.   Joannès Tramond, *Manuel d'histoire maritime* (Paris, 1915) pp. 366-67.   C11A, 103, *Mémoire de Beaucas, 1758*, fol. 508.
   6 *Reasons for keeping Guadaloupe at a Peace, preferable to Canada, explained in five letters from a Gentleman in Guadaloupe to his friend in London* (London, 1761).
   7 *Nova Scotia State Papers*, A, 58, *Census of Colonies, 29 August 1755*, p. 62.   *Canada Census, 1871*, IV, p. 61.   *State of the British and French Colonies in North America with respect to Number of People* . . . (London, 1755).
   8 *A Scheme to Drive the French out of all the Continent of America* (London, 1754).   *Proposals for Uniting the English Colonies on the Continent of America so as to enable them to act with Force and Vigour against their Enemies* (London, 1757).
   9 De Longchamps, *Histoire impartiale de la dernière guerre* (Paris, 1888).
   10 In his prize poem *Le Commerce* (1755).
   11 Baby, *L'Exode des classes dirigeantes à la cession du Canada* (Montreal, 1899).   Lanctot, *Faussaires et faussetés en histoire canadienne*, pp. 33-35.

CHAPTER XXI

   1 F3, 14, *Vaudreuil à Berryer, 10 septembre 1760*, fol. 121 *ff.*   Public Record Office, C.O.5, vol. LIX, *Amherst to Pitt, 5 October 1760*, p. 163.   *Canada Census, 1871*, IV, "Census of 1755," pp. 60-65.
   1a *Relation par lettres de l'Amérique Septentrionale*, ed. by Camille de Rochemonteix (Paris, 1904) p. 6.   *Aventures militaires au XVIIIe siècle, d'après les mémoires de Jean Baptiste d'Aleyrac* (Paris, 1935) pp. 29, 30 and 53.   *Rapport des Archives Canadiennes*, 1886, "Mémoire de Hocquart, 30 octobre 1737," p. XXXLV.   Jean-Carmine Bonnefons, *Voyage au Canada dans le Nord de l'Amérique Septentrionale fait depuis l'an 1751 à 1761 par J.C.B.* (Quebec, 1887) p. 49.   *Aventures du Sr. C. Le Beau ou Voyage curieux et nouveau parmi les Sauvages de l'Amérique Septentrionale* (Amsterdam, 1758) p. 65.   *Voyage de Kalm en Amérique* (Montreal, 1880) pp. 146-93.   Lucien Campeau, "Le Jansénisme en Nouvelle-France." *Analecta Gregoriana*, vol. LXXI, pp. 308-10. Abbé Auguste Gosselin, *L'Eglise au Canada depuis Mgr de Laval* (Quebec, 1911-14) vol. I, pp. 321-35.   *Inventaire des Ordonnances des Intendants*, III, "14 août, 1731," p. 13; "21 janvier 1748," p. 102; "4 juin 1751," p. 160.   Louis Franquet, *Voyages et Mémoires sur le Canada* (Quebec, 1889) pp. 134-35.
   2 *Rapport de l'archiviste de la province de Québec*, 1923-24, Bougainville, "Mémoire sur l'état de la Nouvelle-France, 1757," p. 58.   *Aventures militaires au XVIIIe siècle*, pp. 30-31.   Franquet, *op. cit.*, pp. 5 and 56 *ff.*   *Voyage de Kalm*, pp. 42-44, 54, 142, 146 and 193-94.   Ministère de la guerre, 3417, *Relation de M. Leduchat* (1756) p. 364.   Abbé Arthaud, "Relation d'un voyage de France au Canada en 1731," *R.H.A.F.*, I, p. 109.   Montcalm, *Journal du*

marquis de Montcalm, (Quebec, 1894) "5 janvier 1757," p. 145.   Courville, *Mémoires*, p. 205.

2a *R.A.Q.*, 1924-25, Bougainville, "Mémoire sur l'état de la Nouvelle-France," p. 64.   Bonnefons, *op. cit.*, p. 36.   *Voyage de Kalm*, pp. 39, 120 and 157. Franquet, *op. cit.*, pp. 197-200 and 26-27.   Montcalm, *Journal*, p. 63.

3 *Aventures militaires au XVIIIᵉ siècle*, p. 30.   *Memoirs of Major General Riedesel*, I, pp. 279-80.   *Voyage de Kalm*, pp. 102-03 and 193-94.   *La Grande Encyclopédie*, "costume." See also the contemporary engravings of Richard Short and the illustrations of the present volume.

4 L.F.G. Baby, *L'Exode des classes dirigeantes à la cession du Canada* (Quebec, 1899).   André Vachon, *Histoire du notariat canadien* (Quebec, 1962) p. 35.   Arch. Can., Series Q., vol. V, "Eat général de la noblesse, 1767," p. 269.   *Edits et ordonnances royaux*, I, "Ordonnance, avril 1667," p. 107.

5 F3, 11, *Procès-verbal d'une assemblée, 30 juillet 1746*, fol. 225.   F3, 9, *Très humbles remontrances faites à Sa Majesté, 4 mars 1730*, fol. 257.

6 B, 35, *Mémoire du roi, 25 juin 1713*, fol. 54.   C11A, 50, *Hocquart à Maurepas, 30 octobre 1732*, fol. 121.   *Edits et Ord.*, I, "Arrêt du Conseil, 26 juin 1747," p. 589.   Bonnefons, *op. cit.*, p. 36.   Franquet, *op. cit.*, pp. 56 and 115.   Montcalm, *Journal*, p. 338.   Courville, *Mémoires*.   *R.A.Q.*, 1923-24, Bougainville, "Mémoire," p. 54.

7 Can. Arch., Series Q, vol. IXL, *List of Proprietors of fiefs, 1790*, p. 183 *ff*. Series B, Haldimand Papers, vol. VIII, *Murray to Shelburne, 20 August 1766*, p. 1*ff*.   Montcalm, *Journal*, p. 52.   Abbé H. R. Casgrain, *Une Paroisse canadienne au XVIIIᵉ siècle* (Quebec, 1880).   Philippe Aubert de Gaspé, *Les Anciens Canadiens* (Quebec, 1863).

8, 8a and 8b *Voyage de Kalm*, pp. 52 and 54-55.   Bonnefons, *op. cit.*, pp. 4, 31-35, 46 and 48.   Nicolas Gaspard Boucault, "Etat présent du Canada" (1754) in *R.A.Q*, 1920-21, pp. 35, 43 and 45.

9 *R.A.Q.*, 1923-24, Bougainville, "Mémoire," pp. 63-64.   Bonnefons, *op. cit.*, p. 169.

10 Gustave Lanctot, *Montréal au temps de la Nouvelle-France* (Montreal, 1942) p. 22.

10a Mme Bégon, "Correspondance," in *R.A.Q.*, 1934-35, pp. 17-18, 21, 23, 29 and 37-38.

11 *Voyage de Kalm*, pp. 5, 126-27 and 401.   *R.A.Q.*, 1923-24, Bougainville, "Mémoire," pp. 23-24 and 57.   E. Z. Massicotte, "Contributions à la petite histoire," *Cahiers des Dix*, IX, 1944.   *Edits et Ord.*, II, "21 décembre 1748," p. 398.   C11A, 52, *Réjouissance à l'occasion de la naissance du Dauphin, 1730*, pp. 37-46.

12 Bonnefons, *op. cit.*, p. 35.   *R.A.Q.*, 1923-24, Bougainville, "Mémoire," p. 61.   Franquet, *op. cit.*, p. 56.

13 Abbé Amédée Gosselin, *L'Instruction au Canada sous le régime français* (Quebec, 1911).   Antoine Roy, *Les Lettres, les sciences et les arts au Canada sous le régime français* (Paris, 1930).   Allana G. Reid, "The Nature of Quebec Society during the French Regime," *Canadian Historical Association Report*, 1951.   Mme Bégon, "Correspondance," in *R.A.Q.*, 1934-35, février 1749, p. 37. *Voyage de Kalm*, pp. 4-6.   *Bulletin des Recherches historiques*, vol. XXVII, p. 31.   Bibliothèque Nationale, Fonds français, 12506.

14 Franquet, *op. cit.*, p. 57.   Bonnefons, *op. cit.*, pp. 35-36.   *Voyage de Kalm*, pp. 214-17.   Bertrand de La Tour, *Mémoires sur la vie de Mgr de Laval* (Cologne, 1761).

15 Montcalm, *Journal*, "5 janvier 1757," p. 145.

16 *R.A.Q.*, 1931-32, "Relation de M. Poularès," p. 66.   *Aventures militaires au XVIIIᵉ siècle*, pp. 29-31.   "Relation d'un voyage," *R.H.A.F.*, p. 109. Ministrère de la guerre, 3417, *Relations de M. Leduchat, 1756*, p. 364. *R.A.Q.*, 1924-25, "Mémoire du Canada," p. 115.

17 *Documents relating to Canadian Currency, Exchange and Finance during the French Period*, ed. by A. Shortt, "Addresse des citoyens de la ville de Montréal, février 1763," I, pp. 968-70.   Abbé Auguste Gosselin, *L'Eglise du Canada après la conquête*, I, p. 86.

INDEX

Abenaki Indians, 70, 108, 147
Abercromby, 155, 156
Acadia, 3, 41-8, 195, 199
   administration, 42
Acadians,
   clergy, 43
   deportation, 97-100
   emigration, 93
   Indian hostility, 42
   neutrality, 90
   oath of allegiance, 44-8, 80, 92, 96
   population, 43, 91
   Treaty of Utrecht, 41
Amherst, Lord Jeffry, 59, 99, 154, 181, 182, 183, 188
Annapolis, N.S., 42, 47, 68, 97
Anne, Queen, 43, 46
Anse-au-Foulon, 169
Anson, 73
Anville, Duc d', 67
Aréthuse, the, 154
Armstrong, Lawrence, 47
Assiniboine Indians, 37, 38
Assiniboine River, 38
Atalante, the, 179
Aulac, 97
Aulneau, Father, 37
Aussonville, Comte d', 59
Auteuil, d', 19
Auteuil, Ruette d', 51

Baie des Esquimaux, 115
Baie St.-Paul, 17
Bâtard, Etienne, 93
Batiscan, 17
Beaubassin, 42, 43, 68, 91, 93
Beaubassin, Mme. de, 152
Beaucours, Mme., 151
Beauharnois, Charles de, 5, 22, 104
   administration, 25-6, 67, 68, 70, 74, 105, 110, 111
   aggression v. English, 70
   Compagnie des Sioux, 36
   fortification of colony, 35, 62, 70
   Indian relations, 28, 71-3
Beaujeu, Liénart de, 137
Bécancour, Pierre de, 33
Bégon, Michel, 11, 33, 122
   card money, 5
   illicit practices, 11-12, 14, 18, 101
   land grants, 111
   recall, 19
Bégon, Mme., 151, 208
Belcher, 99
Belle-Isle, 99
Belle-Isle, Comte de, 61

Benoist, Dr., 32
Berg-op-Zoom, 74
Berry, Duc de, 4
Berryer, Nicholas René, 149, 163, 165, 184
Berthier, Dr., 32
Bigot, Fançois, 54, 80, 95, 113, 122, 159, 165, 196
   fraudulent practices, 78, 81, 86, 88, 96, 132-4, 147, 150-1, 160-2, 183, 186
Black Hills, Dak., 39
Boisclerc, Lanouillier de, 33-4
Boishébert, Louis, 75, 80, 97, 186
Bonnécamps, Father, 151
Boscawen, Admiral, 136, 154, 155, 164
Boston, 62, 63, 64, 65, 71, 72, 147
Bouat, Judge, 14
Boucherville, 10
Bougainville, Comte de, 140, 146, 163, 165, 169, 179, 182
Boularderie, Sieur de, 51
Boullard, Canon Etienne, 24-5
Bourbon, Duc de, 18
Bourlamarque, Chevalier de, 156, 180
Braddock, General Edward, 135, 198
Bradstreet, Colonel John, 158
Bréard, Michel, 81, 132
Breslay, Abbé, 34
Briand, Father, 190
Burnett, Governor William, 16
Burton, Colonel, 189, 192
Byron, Commodore, 179

Cadet, Joseph, 132, 147, 150, 161, 165, 177, 182, 186
Callières, Louis-Hector de, 122
Canada, Company, 12, 101
Canada, the, 113
Canadians, 201-2, 207-11
Canso, 42
Cape Breton Island, (*See* Ile Royale)
Cape Ortégal, 73
Cape Sable, 99
Carillon, battle of, 155-7
Carolina, 99
Carrot River, 58
Cartier, Jacques, 195
Caulfield, 43, 44
Cayenne, 99
Cayuga Indians, 80
Céloron de Blainville, 76, 80
Chameau, the, 19
Champigny, 4-5, 122
Champlain, Samuel de, 195
Charles VI, 61
Charlevoix, Father, 36

Châteauguay, 72
Châteauguay, Le Moyne de, 17, 62
Chaudière, River, 111
Chauvin, 195
Chazelles, Guillaume de, 19
Chepody, 97
Chevreux, Father, 91
Chebucto, 67, 92
Chignecto, 80, 93, 97, 99
Chinese, 112
Choiseul, Duc de, 164, 186, 193
Chouaguen, 80, 143
Churchill, the, 58
Clavery, Mme., 151
Clergy, 18, 126-7, 209
  and parishes, 17, 126
Colbert, 7, 196
Collet, Mathieu, 17
Colonization, 101-9, 197
Colville, Lord, 59, 179
Commerce Act, 134
Commissaire-ordonnateur, 122
Compagnie du Canada, (*See* Canada
  Company)
Compagnie d'Occident, 15, 117
Compagnie des Sioux, 36
Company of New France, 196
Congés, 15, 117
Connecticut, 98
Contrecœur, 87, 88, 137
Corlaër, 156
Cornwallis, Charles, 80
Cornwallis, Colonel Edward, 91
Corvées, 10, 33
Costebelle, Governor, 50, 52
Coureurs de bois, 13, 14, 117, 118
Courtemanche, Augustine de, 115
Cree Indians, 37, 38
Cristinaux Indians, 35
Crozat, 12
Cuba, 193
Culloden, battle of, 66
Cumberland, Duke, of 72, 135

Dauphin Royal, the, 136
Demi-Roi, Chief, 86
Désandrouins, 160
Desauniers, Misses, 81-3
Deschenaux, Brassard, 132
Desenclaves, Father, 91
Dieskau, Baron, 138-9
Diana, the, 179
Dinwiddie, Robert, 86
Dobbs, Arthur, 58
Doreil, 163
Dosquet, Mgr., 27-8, 105
  on alchohol, 27-8, 117
Doucette, John, 45
Drucourt Governor, 154-5
Drucourt, Mme., 154
Dubois, Cardinal, 7, 18
Dubois de la Mothe, 136
Du Chambon, 62, 64-5
Dumas, Captain, 137
Dunkirk, the, 136

Duplessis, Mother Andrée, 208
Dupuy, Charles Thomas, 22, 23-4, 25,
  116, 122
Duquesne de Menneville, Marquis de,
  84, 88, 123
  defence policy, 85
Du Quesnel, Governor, 54, 56, 62, 63
Du Vivier, Captain, 59, 62

Economy, 11-15, 112-21, 129, 152, 162,
  196, 197
Eléphant, the, 30
Engagés, 102, 107, 111, 196
Estournelles, d', 68
England,
  and Acadia, 41-8, 68, 75, 90-100, 134
  administration of Canada, 188-91
  Canadian aggression, 70-3, 142
  conquest of Canada, 66, 154-9, 163,
    165-82, 183, 194, 198-9
  and fur trade, 15-16
  hostility to France, 62, 73, 139, 142
  and Ile Royale, 53, 154-5
  and Iroquois, 8, 73, 80
  North American colonies, 9, 34, 71-3,
    86, 98, 135, 198-9

Family Pact, 193
Fiedmont, Jacau de, 95
Fils de famille, 103-4, 107
Finance,
  budget, 120, 160
  card money, 4-6, 31
  defrauds, 132-4, 150-1, 160-2, 185,
    186-7
  problems, 4, 31-3, 183
  royal debt, 186
  taxes, 31-2, 100
Fisheries, 115
Fleury, Cardinal, 16, 18, 35, 45, 61
Fontainebleau, 194
Fontenoy, 66
Forbes, General, 158
Fort-aux-Boeufs, 85, 87
Fort Beauharnois, 36
Fort Beauséjour, 95
Fort Bourbon, 39
Fort Chouaguen, 143
Fort Carillon, 139, 155-7
Fort Dauphin, 39
Fort Duquesne, 86, 135, 136, 138
Fort Frontenac, 12, 76, 158
Fort George, 143
Fort La Jonquière, 40
Fort La Présentation, 76
Fort La Reine, 38, 39
Fort Lawrence, 93
Fort Machault, 165
Fort Massachusetts, 71
Fort Maurepas, 37, 38
Fort Miami, 28, 85
Fort Necessity, 87, 135, 136, 138
Fort Niagara, 16, 76
Fort Ontario, 143
Fort Paskoyac, 40, 58

Fort Presqu'île, 85
Fort Rouillé, 80
Fort St. Charles, 36
Fort St. Frédéric, 35, 70, 71-4 *passim*,
     138, 143, 154, 155-7, 168
Fort St. John, 99
Fort St. Joseph, 28
Fort St. Pierre, 36
Fort Sarastau, 72
Fort Sault Ste. Marie, 81
Fort William Henry, 145-8
Fort York, 58
Fox Indians, 9, 28-9, 36
France, (*See* Versailles)
Francheville, Mme. de, 32
Fraser, Captain, 170
Frederick II, 142, 149
Frontenac, Louis de Buade, Comte de,
     122
Fur trade, 12-15, 117-18, 152, 198
     English competition, 15-16, 57
     illicit, 14, 81

Gage, General, 188, 192
George I, 44
George II, 53, 61, 139, 190, 193
George III, 190, 192, 193, 194
Ginseng, 112
Gorham, Colonel, 75
Grande-Société, the, 116, 132, 150, 160-
     2, 177, 202
Grand-Pré, 97
Graut, Major, 158
Guadeloupe, 194, 197
Guignas, Father, 28

Haldimand, Sir Frederick, 168, 182, 191
Halifax, 92, 100
Handfield, 97
Havana, 193
Haviland, Colonel William, 181
Havre-à-l'Anglais, 50
Hawke, Admiral, 164
Hayes River, 58
Hébécourt, 168
Hendry, Anthony, 58
Henry IV, 195
Herbiers, Charles des, 76
Heron, Patrick, 62
Hocquart, Captain, 136
Hocquart, Gilles,
     character, 30, 80, 122, 129, 196
     development of colony, 33, 34, 105,
     110-11, 113, 129, 204
Holbourne, Vice-Admiral, 145
Hôpital-Général (Montreal), 115
Hôpital-Général (Paris), 103
Hôpital-Général (Quebec), 24, 25
Hopson, Governor, 93, 94
Hospitals, 129
Hospital Sisters, 126
Howe, Captain, 93, 136
Hudson Bay, 3, 199
Hudson's Bay Company, 56-7
     explorations, 57-9

Hunter, Governor, 16
Huron Indians, 9, 73

Iberville, Pierre le Moyne d', 12
Ile-aux-Noix, 168, 179, 181
Ile Lévis, 179, 181
Ile Royale, 199
     administration, 50-2
     conquest, 154-5
     economy, 11, 49, 51, 52-4, 76-7
     foundation and colonization, 49-56
Ile St. Jean, 45, 65, 93, 99, 155
Ile Perrot, 72
Illinois Indians, 9, 28
India, 193
Indians,
     alcohol, 13
     hostility to English, 72, 94, 140, 150
     in the West, 80, 85, 86
Iron, 114, 196
Iroquois Indians,
     domiciled, 108
     hostility to French, 168, 196
     neutrality, 8, 71, 80, 145
     trade, 76

Jansenism, 202
Jesuits, 18, 36, 108, 126, 182
Johnson, Colonel, 138, 165
Joncaire, 16, 62
Jumonville, Ensign, 87

Kalm, Per, 208
Kaministiquia, 35, 36
Kamouraska, 17
Kanon, 164
Kelsey, Henry, 57-8

Lachine Canal, 34
La Canadière, 166
La Clue, 164
La Corne, Chevalier de, 80, 93
La Demoiselle, Chief, 85
Lafitau, Father, 112
La Giraudais, Captain, 179
La Galissonnière, Marquis de, 74, 79,
     106, 111, 134
     and Acadia, 75
     character, 74
     clashes in Ohio, 76
     Indian relations, 74, 80
     and La Vérendrye, 39
La Jonquière, Marquis de, 40, 67, 68, 73,
     79, 83-4, 106
     administration, 80-4
     fur trade, 81-3
     illicit practices, 80, 81, 123, 132
     Indians, 80, 81
Lake Knee, 58
Lake of Two Mountains, 14, 108
Lake Nipigon, 57
Lally-Tollendal, 193
La Mothe-Cadillac, Governor, 12, 19
Langlade, 85
Lanoue, Robert de, 35

La Porte, Sieur de, 133
La Roche, 195
La Rochebeaucour, 175
La Salle, Robert Cavelier de, 16, 35
La Tour, Father, 208
Lauberivière, Mgr., 28
La Vérendrye, Jean-Baptiste de, 37
La Vérendrye, Louis-Joseph de, 38
La Vérendrye, Pierre Gaultier de, 36,
    57
  explorations, 36-9, 40
Law, John, 15
Lawrence, Colonel, 93-100 passim
Le Gardeur, Captain, 86
Le Loutre, Abbé, 62, 90-6 passim
Le Mercier, 86
Le Moyne, Charles, 84
Lepage, Abbé, 116
Levasseur, 113
Le Verrier, 161
Lévis, Chevalier de,
  battle of Ste. Foy, 178
  battle of the Plains of Abraham,
    156-7, 167
  capitulation of Montreal, 182
  character, 140, 151, 165
  Fort William Henry, 147
Ligneris, M. de, 28, 158
Littlehales, Colonel, 144
London, (See England)
Longueuil, 10
Longueuil, Charles le Moyne de, 21,
    73, 85
Lotbinière, Archdeacon, 24, 126
Loudoun, 145
Louis XIV, 4, 6, 199, 204
Louis XV, 7, 18, 59, 126, 200
Louisbourg, 50, 52, 62, 118
  defences, 63, 78, 199
  mutiny, 56
  population, 54
  sieges, 64-5, 154-5, 199
Louisiana, 12
Louvigny, Louis la Porte de, 9, 19
Lowestoffe, the, 178
Lys, the, 136

Machault, 133, 149
Machault, the, 179
Maestricht, 75
Maintenon, Mme. de, 3
Maisonfort, M. de la, 64
Maria-Theresa, Queen, 61
Marin, Captain Paul, 70, 81, 85, 86
Marine Council, 5, 7, 12, 14, 18
Martel de Brouage, 115
Martin, Paul, 63
Martinique, 193, 194, 197
Maryland, 98
Mascarene, Major, 68, 75, 91
Mascoutin Indians, 9, 28
Maskinongé, 17
Massachusetts, 98
Massiac, Admiral, 149
Maurepas, Comte de, 18, 19, 66, 79, 83

Lachine Canal, 34
La Vérendrye, 39
  taxes, 32
Maurin, 186
Melin, Mme., 151
Méloises, M. des, 186
Mercer, Colonel James, 143, 144
Meulles, Chevalier Jacques de, 4
Miami Indians, 73
Michillimackinac, 9, 73, 81
Micmac Indians, 50, 62, 92, 100
Middleton, Christopher, 59
Mildmay, William, 134
Minago River, 58
Minas, 47, 97
Miniac, Father, 91
Minorca, 142, 149
Mohawk Indians, 71, 72, 138, 145, 150
Monceau, 87
Monckton, Robert, 95, 97, 188
Monongahela, battle of, 137-8
Monsoni Indians, 37
Montagnais Indians, 115
Montbrun, Boucher de, 36
Montcalm, Louis Joseph Marquis de,
    140, 143, 146, 165, 208
  defence of Carillon, 156-7
  Quebec and the battle of the Plains
    of Abraham, 165-73
  and Vaudreuil, 144-5, 148, 153, 159
Montespan, Mme. de, 7
Montesquieu, 184
Montgolfier, Father, 191
Montmorency, battle of, 167-8
Montreal, 10, 35, 176, 205
  capitulation, 181-2, 196
  population, 109
Montreal Exchange, 118, 128
Monts, de, 195
Moody, Colonel, 50
Moose Lake, 58
Moose River, 57
Moras, 149
Mornay Mgr. de, 27
Morville, Comte de, 18
Munro, Colonel, 146
Murray, General, 97, 176, 177-8, 180-1,
    188, 189-91, 202
Musquash, the, 58

Negroes, 109
Néret, 12, 14, 15
New Beauce, 111
Newfoundland, 3, 59, 199
New York, 16, 98
Nicholson, Colonel, 41, 44
Nicolas, Chief, 73
Niverville, Chevalier de, 40, 72
Noailles, 61
Nobility, 127, 204
Noble, Colonel, 68, 69
Norton, Richard, 58
Nova Scotia, (See Acadia)
Noyan, Commander de, 158
Noyelles, Nicholas Joseph de, 28, 29, 39

Ohio region, 76, 80, 84, 94, 134, 198
Onondagua Indians, 8, 80
Orange, 14
Orléans, Phillippe Duc d', 7, 18
Oswego (Chouaguen), 16, 62, 138, 168
Ottawa Indians, 9, 71, 78

Parishes, 17
Péan, Hughes, 81, 132
Péan, Mme. Angélique, 132, 151, 186
Pénissault, 151, 186
Pénissault, Mme., 182, 186
Peoples' deputy, 128
Pepperell, William, 64-5
Perrault, Abbé, 191
Philipps, Richard, 42, 43, 45-8, 90
Philippines, 193
Phipps, William, 197
Piquet, François, 76
Pitt, William, 145, 153, 193, 198, 200
Pittsburg, 158
Piziquid, 97
Placentia, 59
Plains of Abraham, 165-73
Pointe-à-la-Chevelure, 35
Pointe-aux-Trembles, 170, 177
Pointe-Lévis, 166, 188
Poitou, 99
Pompadour, Mme. de, 79, 140, 163
Pondichéry, 193
Pontbriand, Mgr. de, 28, 79, 127, 151
Pontchartrain, 4, 5, 12
Population, 33, 101, 106-9, 110, 129,
    182-3, 196, 198, 200, 201, 203-4
Portage-la-Prairie, 38
Portneuf, Father, 169
Port Royal, 41, 198
Potawatomi Indians, 73
Pouchot, 168, 179, 181
Poulariès, 178
Prévost, 76, 78
Prideaux, 168
Prie, Marquise de, 18
Prussia, 193

Quebec, 113, 119, 205
    fortification, 10, 35
    population, 109
    sieges, 166-75, 177
Quebec Exchange, 118, 128
Quebec Seminary, 126

Rainy Lake, 174
Ramezay, Claude de, 4, 14, 19, 116
Ramezay, Roch de, 68
Raudot, Jacques, 5, 122, 204
Raymond, Comte de, 77, 93
Récollets, 18, 126, 182
Red Deer River, 58
Red River, 38
Relations, Jesuit, 197
Richelieu, Cardinal, 196
Robert, Edmé-Nicolas, 19
Roberval, Jean François de la Rocque,
    Sieur de, 195

Robinson, Minister, 94
Rogers, Major Robert, 176
Roquemaure, Captain de, 151, 174
Rouillé, 79, 81, 83, 133

Saint-Ange, 28
St. Clair, General, 66
Saint-François, the, 93
St. François-du-Lac, 176
St. John's, Nfld., 59, 193
Saint-Luc, M. de, 72
Saint-Ovide de Brouillan, 46, 50, 52
Saint-Pierre, Comte de, 51
Saint-Pierre, le Gardeur de, 40, 81
Saint Pierre and Miquelon, 60, 194
Saint-Sauveur, Grasset de, 81, 134
Saint-Vallier, Mgr., de, 17, 24, 27, 103,
    126
Ste. Anne-de-la-Pérade, 17
Ste. Foy, 177, 178, 211
Ste. Lucie, 193
Saki Indians, 29
Salt- smugglers, 104, 107, 196
Salvert, Périer de, 66
Sarastau, 70
Sarrazin, 31, 114
Saskatchewan River, 38, 58
Sault-à-la-Chaudière, 111
Sault-au-Récollet, 14
Saulteux Indians, 73
Sault St. Louis, 14, 72, 108
Saunders, Vice-Admiral, 166, 169, 176
Seal-hunting, 115
Seigneurs, 204-5
Seigniories, 110-11, 196
Seneca Indians, 8, 16
Senezergues, 174
Seven Years' War, 142
Shipbuilding, 112-13, 152, 196
Shirley, Governor William, 63, 65, 66,
    91, 94-5, 134, 143
Silesia, 193
Silhouette, 134
Sioux Indians, 35, 37
Smart, Captain, 53
Social conditions, 123-9, 202-10
Soubras, 50
Stobo, Captain Robert, 88, 136, 138,
    145
Stuart, Charles Edward (The Pretend-
    er), 66, 75
Sulpicians, 18, 108, 126

Tobacco, 112
Taché, Jean, 208
Tadoussac, 12, 195
Talon, 196, 199
Taxes, 31-2
Ternay, Chevalier de, 59, 193
Thibault, Claude, 33
Third Estate, 127-8
Three Rivers, 12, 17
Toulouse, Comte de, 7
Tournois, Father, 81-3
Townshend, General, 175

Transport, 33-4, 206
Treaty of Aix-la-Chapelle, 75, 79, 134
Treaty of Nymwegen, 7
Treaty of Paris, 60, 192, 194
Treaty of Utrecht, 3, 7, 41, 49, 56, 59, 90, 196

Ursulines, 126

Valérian, Father, 151
Van Bram, Captain, 88
Vanguard, the, 179
Vaudreuil, Philippe de Rigaud de, 3-10 *passim*, 19-20, 21, 22, 122
    colonists, 101, 106, 111
    defence, 16, 35
    illicit trade, 13, 14, 19, 123
    Indians, 9, 19-20
Vaudreuil, Mme. Philippe de, 3
Vaudreuil, Pierre de Cavagnal de, 88, 129, 131, 153, 165, 172, 182, 183-4
    and English, 143, 145, 156, 158, 159, 165
    fall of Montreal, 181, 182
    fall of Quebec, 172, 174, 175
    illegal practices, 133, 150, 161, 185-6
    Indians, 139, 140, 147
    Montcalm, 144-5, 148, 153, 157, 172-3
Vaudreuil, Rigaud de, 71, 72, 144, 145
Vauquelin, Captain, 154, 164
Venango, 85
Vergor, Du Chambon de, 95, 96
Vergors, 170
Varrazano, 195
Versailles, 5, 61, 142
    Acadia, 42, 67, 92, 98, 99, 134
    Canada's finances, 4-6, 120-1

Canadian exploration, 35
colonial policy, 12, 22, 23, 30, 73, 84, 87, 102, 115, 116, 128, 164, 184, 197, 199
and English colonies, 9-10, 35, 87, 134
fur trade, 14, 88
Ile Royale, 49-56 *passim*, 66-8, 76, 77-8
Indian policy, 23, 84-5
military aid to Canada, 130, 135, 164, 179, 199
Placentia, 59-60, 67
religious policy, 17, 126
seigniories, 110
trial of the "forty millionaires," 185
Vetch, Colonel, 41, 44
Vezins, Olivier de, 114
Vigilant, the, 64
Villeray, 95
Villiers, Antoine Coulon de, 28, 29
Villiers, Antoine Coulon de (son), 68
Villiers, Louis Coulon de, 87-8
Virginia, 75, 86, 99, 135
Voltaire, 184
Voyageurs, (*See coureurs de bois*)

Walpole, Sir Robert, 35
War of the Austrian Succession, 59, 61
Warren, 63, 64, 65, 73
Washington, George, 86-8
Weaving, 115
West India Company, 12, 15, 31, 73, 119
Western Sea, route to, 35-6
Winslow, 97
Wolfe, General James, 154, 166-72, 180
Wroth, Ensign, 47